D1593804

BALLOT
How Would You Vote?

Major Isaac Lynde was not granted a hearing after surrendering his troops at San Augustine Springs. This book is an attempt provide him with that hearing.

If you were a member of a court of enquiry or court-martial board judging Major Isaac Lynde's conduct at Fort Millard Fillmore and San Augustine Springs, how would you cast a theoretical vote on the following issues: Major Isaac Lynde was:

_____ totally at fault for surrendering his command and guilty of cowardly behavior, incompetence and/or conduct unbecoming an officer.

_____ totally at fault for surrendering his command but not guilty of cowardly behavior, incompetence and/or conduct unbecoming an officer.

_____ partially at fault due to the surrender, but with mitigating circumstances in his favor due to the actions of others in the chain of command, both above and below.

Choose one or both of the below if you view Lynde as not guilty.

_____ Not guilty, due to conditions brought about by superiors which were beyond his control.

_____ Not guilty, due to conditions brought about by his subordinates which were beyond his control.

Detach this ballot and return to:
 Richard Wadsworth
 139 N. Riverside Drive
 Truth or Consequences, New Mexico 87901

The results will be available at the above address when fully tabulated. It is expected that a magazine article will be submitted upon final review.

Cut along this line

Also by Richard Wadsworth

Forgotten Fortress: Fort Millard Fillmore
and Antebellum New Mexico, 1851-1862

INCIDENT AT
SAN AUGUSTINE SPRINGS
A Hearing for Major Isaac Lynde

Richard Wadsworth

Yucca Tree Press

First cloth printing - October 2002

Wadwsorth, Richard

    INCIDENT AT SAN AUGUSTINE SPRINGS: A Hearing for Major Isaac Lynde
          1. Southwest United States - History.   2. New Mexico - Frontier History.   3. New Mexico - Indian Wars.   4. Indian Wars - New Mexico.   5. U.S. Civil War, 1861-1865 - New Mexico. 6. Fort Fillmore, New Mexico.
          I. Richard Wadsworth.   II. Title.

Library of Congress Control Number: 2002102681
ISBN: 1-881325-56-3

Printed in Canada

CONTENTS

Illustrations   vi

Acknowledgments   vii

Introduction   1

Chapter 1   The Arrival   9

Chapter 2   A Disaster in Texas   41

Chapter 3   Like Lemmings Marching to the Sea   65

Chapter 4   The Bascom Affair   85

Chapter 5   Isaac Lynde Takes Command   103

Chapter 6   A Response to Texas Belligerence   125

Chapter 7   The Enemy Within   145

Chapter 8   Special Order Number 134   159

Chapter 9   Lynde Arrives at Fort Fillmore   187

Chapter 10 The Texans   213

Chapter 11 The Battle of Mesilla   225

Chapter 12 A Day to Make Decisions   255

Chapter 13 A July New Mexico Sun   281

Chapter 14 Surrender at San Augustine Springs   305

Chapter 15 The Aftermath   333

Chapter 16 Isaac Lynde after San Augustine   349

Bibliography   366

Index   368

ILLUSTRATIONS

Fort Fillmore, painting   30

First Lieutenant William B. Lane   88

Assistant Surgeon Charles Henry Alden   194

Lieutenant Colonel John Baylor   214

Twelve-pound brass mountain howitzer   230

Fort Fillmore Cemetery   246

Proposed line of march   254

Proposed route of Lynde's march   260

Brevet-Captain Alfred Gibbs   288

First Lieutenant Francis Crilly   296

Ash tree at San Augustine Springs   316

Captain Joseph Haydn Potter   326

ACKNOWLEDGMENTS

I would like to thank the members of the Doña Ana County Historical Society for supporting this study with advice and direction and the Museum of New Mexico for allowing me to view their collection of Fort Fillmore artifacts. Many people have contributed information and/or access to artifacts which came from Fort Fillmore. Special among these are Dr. Edward Staski, New Mexico State University, who provided all available information on the 1986-87 NMSU Excavation at Fort Fillmore. Special help along the way was provided by Tom Leachman, Karl Laumbach, Paul Russell, Terry Humble, William Kupke, James Kuethe, F. William Kuethe Jr, David O'Bannon, Paul and Mary Taylor, Sally Meeks, Dr. Glenna Dean, Rose Apodaca, Carolina Carbajal, Nermina Paz, Bob Hart, and Ken Davis. Special thanks to Karl Laumbach, John Smith, Leroy Grizzel, Steven Grizzel, Russell Schneider and John Saige of the Friends of Fort Selden Group for a very special day in October 2000 at the Fort Fillmore Cemetery. I don't think any of us will forget what we saw.

John Salopek and Charlotte Priestley, landowners on whose property Fort Fillmore and the Fort Fillmore Cemetery lie, are to be thanked for allowing the author access to the historic sites and for allowing members of special groups to wander the grounds and create some special days in the memory of the author. Special thanks to John Salopek for preserving the Fort Fillmore area for the future. Also, special thanks to Charlotte Priestley for going above and beyond the call for historic preservation and allowing the author so much special access in order to prove that an occupied Fort Fillmore Cemetery actually existed.

The Geronimo Springs Museum in Truth or Consequences, New Mexico, must be singled out for special appreciation, for providing a home for the Tom Leachman Collection of Fort Fillmore reconstructed china, as well as for the military artifacts being gathered from many different collections in order to save that part of the New Mexico's past for the future. Several of those artifacts are directly attributable to Major Isaac Lynde's 7th Infantry Regiment.

Finally, I want to give special thanks to Anthony Romero of Santa Clara, New Mexico, who, with the author, spent some time at San Augustine Springs trying to find clues to the surrender site. Thanks to Rob and Murnie Cox, the owners of the San Augustine Ranch, for allowing us to make that search and to discover what we did.

INTRODUCTION

James Cooper McKee was appointed an assistant surgeon in the Medical Corps of the Army of the United States on October 2, 1858. At that time he aided Lieutenant Colonel Dixon Stansbury Miles and his troops in conducting the Navajo Campaign of that year. McKee is an important character in this story, for his words, right or wrong, set the tone for much of what is remembered as the Incident at San Augustine Springs.

The core of the Incident can be found in historical fact. On July 27, 1861, seven companies of the 7th Infantry Regiment, augmented by portions of four companies of the Regiment of Mounted Rifles (R.M.R.), marched east out of Fort Millard Fillmore, the southern-most post in Federal hands in New Mexico Territory, to an unchallenged fate. After marching almost twenty-five miles, the column of troops was surrendered, by their commander, to an inferior force of Texas Confederate volunteers commanded by Lieutenant Colonel John Baylor. The surrender was achieved without fighting.

There were other first-hand accounts, but Assistant Surgeon McKee's account provides much of the color and most of the historical memory related to the Incident at San Augustine Springs. His version of the affair has never been effectively challenged, and continues to this day as the source most often quoted when the subject of the surrender is discussed.

McKee hated the commanding officer of the 7th Infantry Regiment, Major Isaac Lynde, the man whose name is still today equated with cowardly behavior, mediocrity, and military incompetence. Like Inspector Javert pursuing Jean Valjean in *Les Miserables,* McKee pursued the reputation of Isaac Lynde through life, without mercy. Although Assistant Surgeon McKee was only one of those who contributed to the vilification, his words are the more memorable by virtue of the degree of hatred they convey, and because of the way in which historians have taken them to heart.

It is true Major Isaac Lynde surrendered his force to John Baylor, and did so without a fight. He stands guilty of that charge. It is also true that Lynde was never given an opportunity to explain his reasons for doing so. His insistent pleadings for a hearing were cut short by a United States Congress so involved in a great civil war it had little time for the trivia of that war, and by President Abraham Lincoln, who closed his mind and heart to Lynde's plea for fairness. Without court-martial or hearing, Lincoln ordered Lynde's name stricken from the rolls of an Army he had served honorably for thirty-four years.

What Abraham Lincoln would not give, this work will now attempt to provide—a hearing for Major Isaac Lynde. There will be no attempt to vilify anyone or distort the obvious. Major Lynde's conduct and decision-making process will be challenged, as will the motives and words of his detractors. The historical context in which the surrender of the forces was effected will be examined for the first time in detail. There is much that has not been brought forth in any previous account, especially relating to the conditions both national and local, within the context of which Isaac Lynde's decisions were made. Was Major Lynde a coward? Was he a traitor? Was he simply a doddering old fool who, because of the lack of a suitable Army retirement policy in that day, was in command long after his decision-making faculties were gone? Lynde was accused of being all of these and more. There are few military-negative phrases which have not been used against him in the intervening years. Even today, the former major remains the only West Point cadet to have an unconditionally negative remark in the brief biography outlining his career in the Academy Register of Graduates.

Major Isaac Lynde's meeting with such a terrible destiny began in the summer of 1860 when the separate companies of the 7th Infantry Regiment were ordered to leave Utah Territory, where they had been part of the force sent to face down the Mormon leader Brigham Young. The entire 7th Infantry, all ten companies, were transferred to New Mexico Territory, to replace the companies of the 3d Infantry Regiment—the latter ordered to Texas following ten years service on the frontier in New Mexico.

In the context of that move the 3d Infantry left an old fort in southern New Mexico which was once the former headquarters of the regiment. In September 1851, Lieutenant Colonel Dixon Stansbury Miles, then commanding the 3d Infantry, brought two companies from the region of modern-day El Paso, Texas, to a desert landscape tent city forty miles north, then housing one company of mounted dragoons. This was to be the site of Fort Millard Fillmore, named for the presiding President of the United States. 3d Infantry troops built the fort, with the assistance of native Mexican labor, out of the adobe bricks so commonly used in the region. From 1851 to 1856 the post was the regimental headquarters of the 3rd Infantry, and a major United States Army enclave of its day. It usually housed two or more companies of infantry and one company of mounted troops, from the 1st or 2d Dragoon Regiments, or, after 1856, the Regiment of Mounted Riflemen.

Several Mexican farming communities were in the area of the fort. Doña Ana and Las Cruces lay on the American side of the border several miles to the north. The Mexican border in 1851 was across the river a mile to the west. Over there the tiny communities of Santo Tomás and La Mesilla conducted their daily farming-oriented business. Mesilla later became an American town of some importance, the result of the Gadsden Purchase agreement of 1854.

The fort's basic mission was to protect the Mesilla Valley communities from depredations committed by Apache Indians— the territories of two major branches, Mescalero and Chiricahua, joined at the Rio Grande River. In fact, Fort Fillmore's theoretical extended authority once stretched from the Texas border on the east to the California border on the west, and from the Mexican town of Paso del Norte (modern Juárez) to the south, up to the end of the virtually waterless desert region known today, as then, as the *Jornada del Muerto*, the Journey of Death.

This huge portion of land was impossible to negotiate easily, let alone control. In the early days the mission of protecting the Mesilla Valley was difficult enough, given the fact that mounted Apaches could easily leave behind pursuing infantry. Other problems often rendered the resident mounted dragoon company unable to perform its mission. The best thing the Fort Fillmore troops did was protect themselves. Not once in the entire period of its existence was the fort in any way threatened by the Apaches. The garrison was simply too strong for the small Apache raiding bands to challenge.

By the time of the 7th Infantry's arrival in New Mexico Territory in 1860, Fort Fillmore's best days were over. The 3[d] Infantry headquarters had been pulled out and sent to Albuquerque by 1856 and, with the establishment of Fort Stanton in the Mescalero country and Fort Bliss only forty miles to the south across from Paso del Norte, the need for Fort Fillmore was greatly reduced. Had it not been for the protests of the citizens of the booming town of La Mesilla, the fort would probably have been closed in 1858, three years before Lynde's arrival.

Two other posts, Fort Buchanan and Fort Breckinridge,[*] were established to the west of Fort Fillmore, along what later became the Arizona-New Mexico border. These two posts removed Fort Fillmore's claim to a modest responsibility for protecting that region which was becoming more important as mining and ranching interests pushed into what is today the State of Arizona. By 1860, the Army was being pressured by mining interests in the Santa Rita and Pinos Altos regions near the Gila and Mimbres Rivers to establish another fort to protect against Apache depredations there. Previous posts in that region had long been abandoned. This

---

[*] Often spelled Breckenridge.

demand for protection led to the founding of Fort McLane, the post Major Isaac Lynde was originally assigned to command.

Fort Fillmore was reduced to an area post, and hence to the point in 1860 when there was usually only one infantry or mounted company on duty. The wind blew through many abandoned adobe buildings and former officers' quarters on what had once been one of the nation's largest garrison posts.

The 7th Infantry Regiment gradually infiltrated into New Mexico Territory from Utah in that summer of 1860. Initially no companies were sent to garrison either Fort Bliss or Fort Fillmore; these posts were then garrisoned by elements of the 8th Infantry Regiment. The headquarters of the 8th Infantry was at San Antonio, Texas, but the four companies serving in New Mexico Territory were on detached service to the Department of New Mexico, by order of the General-in-Chief of the United States Army, Lieutenant General Winfield Scott.

Three companies of the 7th Infantry were sent to Forts Buchanan and Breckinridge in Arizona, under the command of Lieutenant Colonel Pitcairn Morrison, the acting regimental commander. Major Isaac Lynde, with two companies, was to establish his new fort in the mining region in land claimed by Mangas Coloradas, a well-known Apache leader. The rest of the 7th Infantry filtered into the northern posts such as Fort Defiance, Albuquerque, and Santa Fe.

Isaac Lynde and his battalion of two companies, some one hundred and fifty strong, settled in at a well-known watering site south of present-day Silver City, New Mexico, just off what is now the main highway to Deming, New Mexico. The spring was called Apache Teju, or Tejo. Major Lynde first named the post Fort Daniel Webster, a name given to two other U.S. Army posts which had been in the same general area. The Department of New Mexico commander at that time, a future Confederate general officer, Thomas Turner Fauntleroy, ordered Lynde to rename the post Fort Floyd, in honor of the current Secretary of War. Ironically, Lynde's post changed names a third time when Floyd defected to the Confederacy. In the last instance the post took the name Fort McLane, a safe title, as the officer whose name was used had recently been killed by the Navajos.

This narrative begins with the arrival of Major Isaac Lynde at Apache Tejo and will attempt to shed light the darkness surrounding the events leading to the surrender of Lynde's entire force to an inferior force of Texas Confederates at San Augustine Springs on July 27, 1861. To tell that story, the scope will widen greatly from that of simply examining the few days at Fort Fillmore and at the springs when the two forces were in actual contention.

Nothing happens in a vacuum. Decisions made over two thousand miles away impacted critically upon the nature of the struggle in southern New Mexico. For example, Major Isaac Lynde never had a hearing in which to point out how the indecisiveness of the Federal Government in the months when the Union of States was self-destructing impacted his decision-making capability. He never had a chance to point to the many precedents established during the debacle surrounding the secession of the state of Texas, in which several United States Army regiments were surrendered, with their arms and munitions, without a single shot being fired in anger. Lynde had no opportunity to note for the record that, at the time of the Incident at San Augustine Springs, he was not aware of a declared war between the United States and the Confederacy, save a war of words.

Isaac Lynde did not know that the Northern and Southern forces had engaged in the first great battle of that war, at Bull Run, Virginia, seven days before his travail at San Augustine Springs. The Army command in New Mexico knew little of the swift flow of events in the East. For all Major Lynde knew, if he fought the Texans at San Augustine Springs, he could start the very civil war Abraham Lincoln was still making efforts to avoid.

When Major Lynde slowly made his way east, after the humiliation of surrendering his command at San Augustine Springs, the American Civil War was fully underway. Everyone had forgotten the days of indecision while the conflict developed; nobody wanted to be reminded that Isaac Lynde was a creature of those days of doubt, ineptitude, and inaction. The Congress and President Lincoln never bothered to examine the time line of events taking place elsewhere against the reality on the ground at Fort Fillmore and San Augustine Springs. To them, Major Isaac Lynde, thirty-four-year veteran of the Army on the frontier, was nothing but a coward, a possible traitor, and certainly a man who deserved only their contempt. And they treated him with contempt, as they did no one else in the entire history of the American Civil War.

The above are only a few among the many factors that will be brought forth in this hearing. None, by themselves, will ever override the fact that a surrender occurred, nor do they mask the complicity of Major Isaac Lynde in a very shoddy military drama. At the end of this book Major Lynde will still stand guilty as charged for surrendering seven companies of the 7th Infantry Regiment and parts of four companies of the Regiment of Mounted Rifles to an inferior enemy force. Lynde will not be exonerated in these pages; the brutal light of history will always surround him with a negative aura.

In the end, it is hoped that both the man and his time of travail will be better understood, and some of the worst accusations put to rest. Even that is doubtful, the events having occurred so very long ago. Isaac Lynde was a most convenient scapegoat, so convenient that a host of his peers, in New Mexico and throughout the nation, were able to wash themselves clean in the muddied waters Lynde helped create. This is a sad tale—no matter the outcome of the debate—for Major Isaac Lynde, for the 7th Infantry Regiment, for the United States Army, and for New Mexico, then and now.

Future Confederate general officers and other high-ranking officers who held a New Mexico command during Isaac Lynde's tenure, impacting events at Fort Fillmore up until July 1861.

Lieutenant Colonel George Bibb Crittenden - commanding, Regt. of Mounted Rifles (RMR), the only mounted unit in New Mexico in 1861 - major general, CSA, 1861.

Colonel Thomas Turner Fauntleroy - commanding, Dept. of NM, 1860-part of 1861 - brigadier general, CSA, May 1861.

Captain Robert R. Garland - 7th Infantry, commanding Ft. Fillmore before Isaac Lynde's arrival - colonel, 6th Texas Volunteer Infantry, CSA, 1861.

Brigadier General Albert Sydney Johnston - Dept. of California commander in 1861 - in Ft. Fillmore area at time of surrender - senior general office, CSA, 1861 - killed at Shiloh in 1861.

Paymaster-Major James Longstreet - Dept. of NM paymaster, 1861 - lieutenant general, CSA, 1862 - Robert E. Lee's most trusted infantry commander.

Colonel William Wing Loring - commanding, Dept. of NM, until June 1861 - major general, CSA, 1862.

1st Lieutenant Henry McNeill - R. M. R., Ft. Fillmore, 1860 - colonel 5th Texas Cavalry, 1862 - fought against his old company at Valverde Mesa, 1862.

2d Lieutenant John Marmaduke - served under Isaac Lynde at Ft. McLane - final Civil War rank was major general, CSA, 1865.

Captain Dabney Maury - assistant adjutant general in Santa Fe, controlling all major correspondence in the Dept. of NM - former professor of infantry tactics at West Point - discharged for treasonous talk, May 1861 - probably at Ft. Fillmore in June - brigadier general, CSA, 1862.

Major Henry Hopkins sibley - 2d Dragoons, 1861, commanding at Taos and Ft. Union, the principle supply base in New Mexico in 1861 - appointed brigadier general, CSA, 1861 - invaded New Mexico with Confederate force in 1862.

Paymaster Thomas Grimke Rhett - Ft. Fillmore 1860-1861 - Major CSA, 1861 - absconded with funds for Ft. Fillmore garrison, 1861.

Donald C. Stith - 5th Infantry. Surrendered to Texans in Mexico, 1861 - colonel, CSA, 1861.

Joseph Wheeler - R.M.R., Ft. Fillmore 1861 - highest grade, lieutenant general, CSA, 1865, brigadier general US Volunteers, brigadier general, USA 1900.

Cadmus Wilcox - 7th Infantry, commanding a company at Ft. Fillmore in June 1861 - major general, CSA, 1863.

1

THE ARRIVAL

The initial report following the arrival of the first units of the 7th Infantry Regiment in New Mexico was sent to the commander of the Department of New Mexico, Colonel Thomas Turner Fauntleroy, near the end of August 1860. Brevet-Lieutenant Colonel Pitcairn Morrison, acting commander of the 7th Infantry, addressed Colonel Fauntleroy on the trivialities of command while on the march from Camp Number 80 (somewhere in Arizona), en route from Camp Floyd, Utah Territory, to Fort Buchanan, New Mexico Territory. Morrison wrote:

> Headquarters 7th Infantry
> Camp No 80, enroute from
> Camp Floyd U.T. to Ft. Buchanan
>
> Arizona, August 31, 1860

Sir,

    I have the honor very respectfully to request that, upon the arrival of the recruits for the 7th Infantry at the Dept. Head Quarters, they may be drawn for by lot and assigned to companies according to the subjoined schedule. Should the number of recruits fall short of that expressed in this calculation, you will oblige me by adhering to the same ratio, with the exception of the five musicians, en route for the Band. In case field musicians should accompany the detachment, please have our documents forwarded to Head Quarters for Company 'H' and one fifer to the same post for

Company 'C' after this distribution. Please send one fifer to Company 'K,' a drummer and fifer to Company 'D,' a drummer and fifer to Company 'G' and a drummer to Company 'B.' And should there not be a sufficient number to supply this demand, please send them in the order mentioned as far as they will go. I should greatly prefer that some officer at Department Head Quarters be appointed to draw for the different Companies, and that the recruits should be assigned to them at that place and by your order. Should there be two clerks in the detachment, you will oblige me by sending one to Company 'C' and one to Company 'H.'[1]

I am, Sir
Very Respectfully,
Your Obt. Servt
P. Morrison
Lieut Colonel
Comdg. 7 Inf.[*]

The recruits coming over the Santa Fe Trail from Jefferson Barracks near St. Louis, or elsewhere, were to be parceled out to the varied companies of the 7th Infantry mentioned by Brevet-Lieutenant Colonel Morrison. In one respect those mentioned as being destined for Companies 'H' and 'C' could be considered out of luck in the short run. Because of where these recruits were sent, the scorching desert region near the modern Arizona/New Mexico border, they might be considered unlucky by their mates, from the fact that day-time temperatures often registered far over 100 degrees for days at a time. The boys destined for the other three mentioned companies, 'G,' 'B,' and 'K' may have rejoiced at their good luck. At least two, 'G' and 'B,' were headed for the cooler climes of the region around modern-day Silver City, New Mexico, which may have seemed the better place to be, especially in the summer and early fall.

---

[*] Note - The author used the entire structure of Colonel Pitcairn Morrison's letter in order to show the elaborate and formal nature of correspondence as was carried on between commands during the antebellum period in New Mexico. Hereafter, the opening and closing embellishments will not be included whenever a letter is referenced. 'Your Obedient Servant,' was a common closing phrase in this period.

Unfortunately, those destined for the 7th Infantry Regimental Band were attached to the 7th Infantry headquarters staff. The band was co-located with the regimental commander, and he was initially at Fort Buchanan, in the heat. Their luck appeared to change for the better, when toward the end of the year the regimental headquarters shifted to the post occupied by Companies 'B' and 'G' in the grasslands just south of the modern Gila National Forest. There, the newly appointed regimental commander, Major Isaac Lynde, was located. The bandsmen may have been cooler and more comfortable for a while, but the move sealed their fate for future events.

In fact, in less than a year the luck factor changed for both groups. The boys of Companies 'G,' 'B,' 'K,' and the 7th Infantry Band, along with others of their regiment, felt the sting of humiliation and heard the name coward, and even worse, directed at them for being part of an action which disgraced their regiment, its colors, and the United States Army. Because of being sent to the eastern Arizona furnaces, the boys of Companies 'C' and 'H' avoided the disgrace which was heaped upon their fellows at a place called San Augustine Springs in July 1861.

On September 12 a large detachment of recruits destined for New Mexico and Arizona camped at Camp 38, fifty-five miles east from Fort Union in northern New Mexico. The command included some 523 soldiers, of which 108 were destined for the Regiment of Mounted Rifles, 24 for the 1st Dragoons, 120 for the 5th Infantry, 192 for the 7th Infantry, and 79 for the 8th Infantry.[2]

The name infantry will be familiar to most readers, but the title dragoons and the Regiment of Mounted Riflemen (R.M.R.) may not be. Both were horse-mounted formations, numbering some ten companies and approximately seven hundred men per regiment. The name 'dragoon' was used from 1832 to 1861 for two mounted formations. The name was dropped in 1861 and all mounted formations in the United States Army became 'cavalry.' The 1st and 2[d] Dragoon Regiments became the 1st and 2[d] Cavalry Regiments.

Two buttons excavated at Fort Fillmore in the early 1970s. *l:* Infantry
officer's frock coat, circa 1851-1861. *r:* Regiment of Mounted Rifles
officer's frock coat button, circa 1851-61.
Courtesy: Author's collection

The Regiment of Mounted Riflemen was, in the 1850s and
early 1860s, the only regiment of its kind in the United States Army.
They were mounted infantry, designed to ride to battle, then to
dismount and fight on foot. The R.M.R. was disbanded at the same
time as the two dragoon regiments in late 1861, becoming the 3[d]
Cavalry Regiment. But in 1860, the R.M.R. was the premier
mounted regiment in that part of New Mexico Territory now
encompassing the state of New Mexico. They garrisoned the
principal forts there and were the rapid reaction force when an
Indian attack occurred anywhere in their region of control. R.M.R.
companies were often stationed at Fort Bliss, Fort Fillmore, Fort
Craig, Los Lunas, Fort Defiance, Fort Union, Fort Stanton, Cantonment Burgwin, and sometimes at Santa Fe or Albuquerque.

The R.M.R. arrived in New Mexico Territory in 1856. They
displaced several companies of the two dragoon regiments; a few
dragoons remained on duty at posts located in what would later
become the Territory of Arizona—Forts Buchanan and Breckinridge. The remaining dragoon companies were still on duty when
the first of the 7th Infantry companies arrived. The rest of the
regiment had been sent elsewhere, including the Washington
Territory, where they remained until called East for duty in the
American Civil War.

That same September 12, an important historical decision with respect to New Mexico Territory and the coming civil conflict was made by the commanding general of the Army, General-in-Chief Winfield Scott, in a letter addressed to Colonel Fauntleroy from the Headquarters of the Army, then in New York City. One should remember when reading this letter that Abraham Lincoln was favored to win the Presidency, a sure signal for at least some Southern States that secession would follow. Texas was one of those hotbeds of secessionism. Scott, through his aide, Colonel George Thomas, ordered:

> The attention of the General-in-Chief having been directed to the dispersed condition of the four Companies of the 8th Regiment of Infantry in the Department of New Mexico, he desires, when it can properly be done, that these Companies be concentrated as far as possible and stationed at posts most contiguous to the major part of the Regiment serving in the Department of Texas.
>
> In this view, Fort Bliss would be the most proper post, to the extent of its garrison, and especially so, as this post— transferred from the Department of Texas for a specific purpose which is supposed no longer to exist—may soon be put back in that Department.
>
> Of course, it is not intended, by these suggestions, to interfere with any of your field operations, but after they have ceased, in your future distribution of Companies, you make the arrangement referred to.[3]

This author sees the hand of treason in this letter, given what later happened in Texas. If not treason, then fate was truly acting against the Union of the United States. Fort Bliss, only forty miles south of Fort Fillmore, was to be handed over to the Department of Texas at the most interesting, and crucial, of times. The soldiers of the 8th Infantry, then stationed at Fort Fillmore and Fort Bliss to the south, were sent deep into Texas, with their brand new arms. They were soon to become prisoners of war of that Confederate State. This letter shows, in the best of a bad light, the unpreparedness and naivete of General-in-Chief Winfield Scott in the face of a growing national crisis. The ardent words of Southern secessionists must have been blaring loudly in his ears, even two months before Lincoln's election.

Not only did General Scott allow himself to be convinced to send the 8th Infantry Regiment deep into Texas during a coming period of turbulence, he was swayed to break Fort Bliss loose from the Department of New Mexico at the same crucial time. Fort Bliss had been under the control of the Department of New Mexico since its founding in 1854. Both decisions had disastrous impacts on the Department of New Mexico, on Major Isaac Lynde, and on the 7th Infantry Regiment, not to mention what happened to the 8th Infantry. Giving up control of Fort Bliss by the Department of New Mexico allowed the Texas Confederates to take that post, its cannon and public property without a fight. Those cannon and supplies became an immediate threat to Lynde's command at Fort Fillmore and were later used in the invasion of New Mexico Territory by General Sibley.

Protocol of the Army in New Mexico was so rigid that the Department commander would not allow troops stationed at Fort Fillmore to go to Fort Bliss in May/June 1861, before Isaac Lynde's arrival, and re-take Fort Bliss and its Federal equipment after Texas seceded. At this time no Texas troops were yet at the fort. Troops from Fort Fillmore could have walked into that post without opposition, but did not do so because Fort Bliss had been transferred, by Scott, to the Department of Texas in September 1860. The United States Army in New Mexico was not permitted to interfere in the affairs of another Department, no matter what was happening there. Such an act might have been misconstrued as an inexcusable interference with the prerogatives of the commander of the Department of Texas, a Department which in fact no longer existed.

The state of Texas was a Confederate state by May/June 1861, yet the Department of New Mexico received no instructions on how to respond to that State's secession from Abraham Lincoln's government. As late as the end of June 1861, one month before the Incident at San Augustine Springs, Lincoln and his government still vacillated over how to treat the seceded states.

This is getting ahead of the story, but it is so very important to the coming travail of Major Isaac Lynde and the 7th Infantry Regiment that early emphasis is necessary. Eleven months before San Augustine Springs the seeds of that defeat were already sown. General-in-Chief Winfield Scott was not a traitor, but he should have foreseen that what he was being goaded into doing was not the right thing to do, given the political climate. His immediate superior, Secretary of War John Floyd, believed in secession. He was soon to be a high ranking Confederate leader. The adjutant-general of the Army at the time, Samuel Cooper, was a Northerner, although sympathetic to the South, and became the Confederate States' Army's senior general officer, outranking even Robert E. Lee. Both were in a position to pressure Scott to make these changes at this time. The only question is whether they were at that point secession-minded enough and foresighted enough to have helped in making the decision to shift Fort Bliss and the 8th Infantry to the Department of Texas with strategic intelligence. Were they already thinking as Confederates?

The Department of New Mexico, in September 1860, was also commanded by a future secessionist, and remained in hands sympathetic to the South up to the time of Lynde's arrival at Fort Fillmore in July 1861. Colonel Thomas Turner Fauntleroy, commanding in September when the decision to transfer Fort Bliss to Texas was made, did not object to Scott's order, even though the order reduced his power to complete his military mission. He was a Southerner, and left his command of the 1st Dragoon Regiment as soon as his state seceded. Fauntleroy actively aided the transfer of the 8th Infantry *and* Fort Bliss into the hands of Texas authorities, when he might easily have turned that decision around.

Colonel William Wing Loring, commanding the Regiment of Mounted Rifles, and the second-ranking officer in the Department of New Mexico, didn't care either. He was a Southerner and soon resigned his Federal commission. If there were no traitors in the Federal Government ranks that pushed for this very odd transfer at this exact moment, there were at least none who thought through the process in political terms and attempted to stop this monumental mistake.

above: Major Isaac Lynde late in his life.
below: Mrs. Isaac (Margaret Wight) Lynde.
Courtesy: Museum of New Mexico, Neg. No. 10250

General David Twiggs, commanding the Department of Texas, from San Antonio, was delighted to have the rest of the 8th Infantry freed from New Mexico control. He was probably ecstatic to finally take Fort Bliss under his wing—his goal since that post was founded in 1854. The geographic borders of the state of Texas were now fully under his control. General Twiggs was a Southerner and also resigned his commission, but not before he surrendered the Department of Texas and all its men and equipment to the mercies of a secessionist Texas government, the 8th Infantry and Fort Bliss included. Floyd, Cooper, Fauntleroy, Loring, Twiggs, et al, had loyalties in open opposition to the government they were sworn to support.

M.L. Crimmons, writing in the *New Mexico Historical Review* in 1931, commented on the potential for treason by both Floyd and Cooper:

> The disgraceful surrender at San Augustine Pass probably was part of the plan of our treacherous secretary of war, John Floyd, and of our equally treacherous adjutant general, Samuel Mason Cooper, who had taken care to place confederate sympathizers in posts of importance in New Mexico.[4]

The person whose name has become synonymous with Fort Fillmore and San Augustine Springs was in the Department of New Mexico by September 16, 1860. Major Isaac Lynde had orders to establish a battalion-size post somewhere in the region of Pinos Altos and the Santa Rita Copper Mines.[5]

Lynde was certainly far from being a raw recruit, unlike most of his soldiers, when he arrived in New Mexico Territory. He was an officer of the United States Army with thirty-four years service, all of it honorable. He once commanded Fort Laramie, Wyoming Territory, one of the most critical posts on the far-flung American frontier, and did his duty without official complaint. An 1827 graduate of West Point, the Vermonter Lynde was fifty-seven years old in September 1860. As a young man just out of the Point he was commissioned a brevet-2[d] lieutenant and a 2[d] lieutenant of the 5th Infantry Regiment on July 1, 1827. The double commission indicates Lynde found a slot in a regiment without having to wait until one opened, a very rare occurrence within the Army of that time. Normally one cooled his heels for many months as a brevet-2^d lieutenant before finding such a permanent slot. Lynde stayed with the 5th Infantry for many years, being promoted to 1st lieutenant on February 18, 1836, and captain on January 1, 1839. During this period there is no sign in the record that he served in action, although he may have.[6]

The next part of his career is unusual. Lynde served during the Mexican War but did not receive a brevet for bravery against the enemy. Brevets were handed out in Mexico like candy. Virtually every officer in New Mexico Territory who was in the war had a brevet awarded. All one seemed to have to do was appear on a battlefield. It should be pointed out that lack of a brevet did not indicate cowardice or failure to do one's duty. William Tecumsah Sherman, the famous Civil War general, also served through the Mexican War without a brevet. Such things happened, but failure to achieve one was rare if any combat was experienced.

Between 1820 and 1850 there was a tradition of granting a brevet to any officer who went ten years in grade without receiving a promotion. Lynde was a captain from January 1839 until he was promoted to major in the 7th Infantry Regiment on October 18, 1855, a period of almost sixteen years. Why the courtesy of an honorary time-in-grade brevet was not provided to Isaac Lynde is not known. Perhaps such brevets only applied through non-field grades up to captain. No clarification was found in Army regulations. During that period there were two major-grade positions with the 5th Infantry, a standard before the Civil War. Six appointments were made to the grade of major while Lynde remained a captain.[7]

Isaac Lynde served in Utah as a major in the 7th Infantry, essentially on occupation duty to quell the potential for a Mormon uprising, immediately before coming to New Mexico. His regimental headquarters was at Fort Buchanan during September; his commanding officer was Lieutenant Colonel Pitcairn Morrison, a forty-year veteran of the Army. Morrison, whose actions during the first days of the American Civil War will be discussed in some detail since they gravely impacted Isaac Lynde's situation at that time, was commanding the regiment in the name of Colonel Henry Wilson. Wilson, an even older and longer-serving gentleman than Morrison and Lynde, held the title to command the 7th Infantry but did not take the field command. Regimental colonels before the American Civil War were usually too old for field command, that duty falling to the regiment's lieutenant colonel.

Isaac Lynde was not even the senior major of the 7th Infantry Regiment. That honor went to Major J.R. Smith, whose rank dated to June 11, 1851. Smith, however, was ill. As a result, the command of the future Fort Floyd fell on Lynde. What this indicates is that when the call to honor and combat came for the 7th Infantry Regiment the next year, the fourth-ranking officer in the regiment, the most junior in field-grade rank, and hence the one least experienced in commanding a regiment-size unit, found himself in complete command. This is an important fact, and the reader can begin to understand the events that occurred at Fort Fillmore in July 1861. One must understand Isaac Lynde, his world, and the surrounding circumstances which may have impacted his decisions, for good or bad.

The total number of Indians in the region where Lynde was about to establish the new fort was not as high as Eastern expectations conceived. During October 1860 and into November, Michael Steck, Indian Agent for the Apaches on both sides of the Rio Grande, sought an agreement with the Mescaleros and the Mimbres (Chiricahua) region bands to establish a reservation for both tribes at Santa Lucia Springs in Mangas Coloradas's country in southwestern New Mexico, not far from where Fort Floyd (McLane) would be located. Steck counted the total Indians in Lynde's battalion area of control as numbering three hundred men and sixteen hundred women and children, hardly a threat to Lynde or to the large numbers of non-Indians entering the mining region. Steck's supposedly tame Mescaleros, outside Lynde's control on the east side of the Rio Grande, numbered only one hundred warriors and six hundred women and children living in the area of

Fort Stanton. These numbers seem incredibly small, considering how Hollywood movies portray great numbers of Apaches swarming around a wagon train, disdainful of casualties as they circled the riflemen, who picked them off easily. The numbers Steck provided would scarcely allow the taking of casualties on a level such as the movies produced. Of course, the Apaches living near Apache Pass were not counted in Steck's survey, nor were untamed Mescaleros, although both branches were greater in number and the nearest to open hostility. Lieutenant Colonel Pitcairn Morrison, at Fort Buchanan, and nearer to some of these hostile Indians, especially those belonging to the band of Cochise, recommended that the Apaches in his area either be fed or exterminated.[8]

Major Isaac Lynde established his new post on the banks of a small stream flowing out of Apache Tejo Spring on October 9, 1860. Lynde described the arrival of his two-company battalion at Apache Tejo in a letter to the Department of New Mexico on the day of the founding. Lynde may have dictated this letter, but he certainly did not write it. Lynde's adjutant probably took direction from him or even wrote the missive himself for Lynde's signature. The letter is written in a beautiful hand but signed with Isaac Lynde's characteristic, almost illegible, shaky scrawl. All letters attributed to Isaac Lynde, while he was in New Mexico, exhibit this same characteristic, save for a letter written after the debacle at San Augustine Springs, which was composed without assistance. Lynde stated:

> I have the honor to report that I arrived on the Mimbres River on the 16th of September 1860 and from that time till the 9th of October I was engaged in examining the country for a suitable military post, and have selected this point as the most eligible point that I could find. This place is about fifteen miles south of the Santa Rita Coppermines, twenty miles South-East of the Gold-mines and about twelve miles west of the point where the road travelled by the Overland Mail crosses the Mimbres River.
>
> No point nearer the Mines could be found where a post could be sustained. There is at this point a sufficient supply of good water, wood & timber within reach, and plenty of the finest grazing for stock.

I encamped at this place today and shall proceed to build huts for my command which will be all I can do till Spring.

I have recommended that the post be called "Fort Webster." There is a great objection to calling the Post "Fort Floyd," as was suggested by the Commanding Officer of the Department, in the fact that the Post in Utah is called "Camp Floyd," and letters addressed to this Post would inevitably be mis-sent in many cases.

The nearest Post Office is Mesilla N.M.[9]

Major Lynde's surrogate wrote, and Isaac Lynde signed, a second letter on October 10. Lynde notified those living in the surrounding communities that he was establishing a new Post at Apache Tejo:

NOTICE

Is hereby given, that the land included in the following named limits, is declared a military reservation, subject to the approval of the War Department.

Beginning at a point now occupied by the tent of the Commanding Officer of the Battalion of the 7th Infantry, composed of "B" and "G" Companies, running on a line through said point north and south, five miles north and five miles south of said point, and extending five miles each side of said line east and west.

No claims or settlements will be permitted within said limits, before the decision of the War Department is known.[10]

On October 23 Lynde more closely defined the new camp, but he did not give an exact location of the post center. He intended to include the Apache Tejo Spring and its running course, some two and a half miles in extent before it faded underground, in his military reservation so that bars and houses of ill repute could not spring up closer than six to seven miles, the next source of water. The military commanders' hatred of the enticements to their soldiers never waned. When the bars and 'hog ranches' came, trouble with discipline soon followed, as did desertions.

Such enticements were close enough in any case, and ready to serve the growing population a fort in the vicinity usually brought.

The *Mesilla Times* issue of October 25 noted that trade was increasing between the county of Doña Ana, the county in which Major Lynde's fort was situated, and the state of Missouri. In that issue the results of a census taken for 'Eastern Arizona' was provided for readers. It must be remembered there was no official Eastern Arizona, except in the minds of those men, mostly from Mesilla, who illegally established that entity without the approval either of Congress or the New Mexico Territorial Legislature. According to the earliest version of a Mesilla newspaper, the *Mesilla Miner*, the population of the towns in the federally recognized Territory of New Mexico were: Mesilla and surrounding ranches - 3,000; Doña Ana - 780; Las Cruces - 820; Mesa - 700; Amoles - 90; Pinos Altos Mines - 500; Santa Rita Copper Mines - 160 and Hanover Copper Mines - 240. The total population was said to be 6,309, including small towns not mentioned. Mesilla's totals may have included Santo Tomás. No mention was made as to how, or if, the Federal post at Fort Fillmore was included in the numbers.[11]

The American presence was indeed growing in 1860. There was even a stagecoach express serving communities north of Lynde's new post. The Catlett Express, a mail and passenger service, linked Mesilla with the growing mining community at Pinos Altos. Catlett's was a private concern and their postal and shipping rates are not known. The first trip on the Catlett route brought out fifty-five letters and it took twenty-two hours to make the one-hundred-twenty mile trip from Pinos Altos to Mesilla, where the United States Post Office received the mail.[12]

On November 6, 1860, Abraham Lincoln was elected President of the United States, an act sure to bring a negative response from the Southern States, including Texas. No mention was found concerning when the people of Fort Floyd (McLane), Fort Fillmore, Fort Bliss, Mesilla, Las Cruces, Doña Ana, La Mesa and the mining region received the word that Lincoln had won. The first reports coming out of El Paso were that John Breckinridge, the Democratic Party candidate, was totally victorious over Abraham Lincoln. Out of 1,052 votes recorded in El Paso County only eleven were cast for Lincoln.

Life went on as usual, at least temporarily. On November 11, Colonel Fauntleroy, through the pen of Brevet-Captain and 1st Lieutenant Dabney Maury, his adjutant, notified Major Isaac Lynde at Apache Tejo that he was to construct a post there, and also that his request to name the post Fort Webster was denied.[13]

With Abraham Lincoln elected, and the possibility of secession looming, problems with the Indians in the Department of New Mexico continued, increasing day by day as the year 1860 ended. A November 13 military circular brought the news from Brevet-Lieutenant Colonel George Bibb Crittenden, of the Mounted Rifles, that Captain George McLane had been killed in battle against the Navajo Indians. Captain McLane was one of the original appointees to the Regiment of Mounted Rifles at the time of the Mexican War. He was twice breveted for gallantry in battle during the war with Mexico, and lost his life while leading a charge of his company against the Navajos. McLane's last words were, "Follow me men." As a mark of respect the officers of the Regiment of Mounted Rifles wore black crepe on the left arm, and on the hilt of the sabre, for thirty days.[14]

Not yet notified of the Department commander's curt denial to name the new site Fort Webster, 2d Lieutenant John Sappington Marmaduke, soon to pass through Mesilla and Fort Fillmore, on his way to a career as a Confederate general officer, wrote the Department of New Mexico on November 14, using the Fort Webster designation one last time.

> I have the honor to request that Private John Brennan of Company "G" 7th Infantry, reported as a deserter in the July and August Muster Rolls for 1860, be restored to duty without trial for the following reasons.
> Private Brennan was Hospital Cook on the 28th of August 1860, the day on which the Company left Albuquerque, and was present with the Command. He got enebriated [sic] on the road and dropped behind the Command. When he arrived at Los Lunas, which was on the 19th of August, he reported to Bvt. Major Paul, 7th Infantry—who told him to remain there until an opportunity would occur to send him to

join his Company—He accordingly joined with the recruits when they arrived on the 28th of October 1860.[15]

John Marmaduke never came back to Fort Webster/Floyd/ McLane as the new post was variously called. His was the first secessionist defection from Major Isaac Lynde's 7th Infantry command. There were soon to be a flood of such defections—many of the best and brightest officers choosing to see the United States dismembered for the sake of states rights. The many defections and officers leaving on orders ensured that when the 7th Infantry companies most needed trained and familiar officers they would not be there. By the time of the Incident at San Augustine Springs, Major Isaac Lynde could provide no more than one of the three officers needed per company; several companies were commanded by detached service officers who had no knowledge of the men under their command.

The death of Captain George McLane led to a meeting at Fort Defiance on November 17 involving the officers responsible for carrying out the Navajo Campaign of 1860. Among these gentlemen were Brevet-Major Henry Hopkins Sibley, soon to command Confederate forces against his former Department; Captain Lafayette McLaws, a future prominent Confederate general officer in the East; Captain Henry Selden, for whom Fort Selden, New Mexico was eventually named, and who fought Sibley's troops at Valverde Mesa in 1862. More junior officers included Captain Alfred Gibbs, who surrendered his small detachment of Mounted Rifles at San Augustine Pass in 1861, only to rise to the rank of major general in the Civil War in the East, and lastly Assistant Surgeon James Cooper McKee, soon to appear at Fort Fillmore and to be a dominant figure in the final history of that post and in the life of Major Isaac Lynde. This group of officers formed a committee which resolved to honor Captain George McLane following his death. They had already named the spot of his death McLane's Peak, a point near the head of Canyon de Chelly, in Navajo country. Of course, one further outcome of Captain McLane's death was the imminent change from Fort Floyd to Fort McLane.[16]

Abraham Lincoln may have won the office of President of the United States but Judge Ned McGowan was elected over Indian Agent Michael Steck in the November 9 election as the delegate from the 'Arizona Territory' to the United States Congress. McGowan beat Steck handily but refused to acknowledge Lincoln's election. According to the *Mesilla Times* newspaper of November 22, McGowan was not willing to represent Arizona under a 'black' Republican administration. The *Times* said if the South should separate McGowan would attend the Southern Convention and pledge Arizona to the Confederacy. The *Mesilla Times* continued, that of the total of one thousand American, or 'white' population in Arizona, nine-tenths were for a disruption of the Union of States. The *Mesilla Times* editor expressed surprise that California had gone for Lincoln.[17]

After losing the election, Agent Steck reported from Las Cruces on November 26, 1860, that he had completed the distribution of the annual presents to the Apaches. He left Apache Agency near what is now modern-day Hatch, New Mexico, on October 12, 1860, headed for Santa Lucia Springs, just northeast of Lynde's camp at Apache Tejo. There, the Agent distributed gifts to the Mimbres and Mogollon Apaches. He then headed west to the 'Chilicagua' (Chiricahua) Mountains and made a distribution to the Apaches at Apache Pass. Following that, Steck moved on farther west to distribute presents in the Coyotero country near the Gila River, southwest of Fort Floyd. At the end of 1860 the Apache peoples and the Americans were still at peace.[18]

Secessionist forces in Mesilla reached a first-level peak in their anti-Union rhetoric in the November 29, 1860, issue of the *Mesilla Times*. The *Times* printed an editorial which was nothing short of treasonous, given that there was no Confederacy as yet, Texas had not seceded, and Abraham Lincoln was not yet inaugurated. The Mesilla Americans were among the most vocally ardent secessionists in the country, with little reason for being so. New Mexico Territory was not a state in the Union, and slavery and states rights were not a problem in that territory. The editor, Mr. Robert Kelley, used words of sedition so strong that military authorities might have arrested him for treason, if the commander at Fort Fillmore had available the abrogation of habeas corpus which Colonel Canby would only promulgate after Isaac Lynde surrendered his command at San Augustine Springs. Kelley editorialized:

> Arise! Let the Tocsin sound! Hang out your banner on the outer wall! Let a living bulwark of fiery valor guard your rights and your bodies! Go not beyond them. Let your boundary eastward be the brink of fate where the hell of northern fanaticism yearns beneath! Where the upas [sic] of abolition, as it poisons liberty, erases her charter and blackens the holiest memories of the past! Men of the South, look up! There is a star beaming in your glorious Southern sky, with a fixed light. It is the star of destiny. Smiling on hope as she points to a regenerated race, a renovated government, and the highest and noblest form of freedom.
>
> Remember that eternal vigilance is the price of liberty. Every son of the South is now a sentinel on the watchtower. Stand to your posts, and never surrender while there is a sod beneath your feet, or a thread on your banner! Awake! [19]

Over at Fort Floyd, Isaac Lynde may or may not have seen a copy of this seditious editorial. If he did, he did not report news of it to Santa Fe. Why would he? The First Amendment to the Constitution permitted free speech then as now, unless the President declared an end to that privilege due to an emergency.

On December 3, President Buchanan, about to give his fourth and final annual message, was on his way out as President and Abraham Lincoln was about to be sworn in, an event for which Buchanan had morbid feelings. He asked that the south be allowed to answer to God in their own way for the issue of slavery, and that they be allowed to go about their business in their own way as well. Then, in a reference to Lincoln without mentioning his name, James Buchanan said, "... and this brings me to observe that the election of any one of our fellow-citizens to the office of President does not of itself afford just cause for dissolving the Union ... ." In order to justify a resort to revolutionary resistance, Buchanan warned, the federal Government must be guilty of a "... deliberate, palpable, and dangerous exercise of powers not granted by the Constitution. The late Presidential election, however, has been held in strict conformity with its express provisions. How, then, can the result justify a revolution to destroy this very Constitution?"

Colonel Thomas Fauntleroy, at Santa Fe, notified the Adjutant General's Office in Washington on December 4 that Fort Floyd, 'Arizona,' was established and occupied by U.S. troops on September 16, 1860. Of course, Fort Floyd was still in New Mexico Territory at the time, the only 'Arizona' in existence being in the minds of the many secessionists yearning for that entity. Since the United States Congress had not sanctioned an Arizona Territory as yet this slip of Fauntleroy's pen may have been an early indication of his change in loyalty.[20]

Most of the Regular Army officers who opted for the Confederate cause waited until their state seceded before taking that action, no matter how much they sympathized with the South. Colonel Fauntleroy's state, Virginia, did not secede from the Union until April 17, 1861; Fauntleroy's resignation was tendered on May 13, no doubt close in time to when he received word of Virginia's move. Colonel Fauntleroy's mind set in the period between Lincoln's election and the secession of Virginia is very important to events that were to transpire in New Mexico Territory. Who can doubt Colonel Fauntleroy's future intentions should Virginia secede? Who can doubt that he made some decisions with Southern good at heart? The entire known correspondence of the Department of New Mexico in this period requires a thorough examination for signs of treason by Colonel Fauntleroy, Secretary of War Floyd, Adjutant General Cooper (in Washington), Colonel William Wing Loring, Colonel Henry Hopkins Sibley, Captain Lafayette McLaws, 1st Lt. John Marmaduke, Brevet-Captain Dabney Maury, the Department of New Mexico adjutant, Paymaster-Major Thomas Grimke Rhett, the paymaster for troops in southern New Mexico, and Paymaster-Major James Longstreet, the paymaster for troops in northern New Mexico, to name but a few Confederates-to-be.

Other officers, those loyal to the Union, made their plans as well. The more conspiratorial among them must have realized that when civil war came, he who reached the banks of the Potomac first might find a general's commission waiting. On December 4, Lieutenant Colonel Pitcairn Morrison, commanding the 7th Infantry Regiment, requested permission to take a leave of absence, for the sake of the health of his wife and that of himself. This move by Morrison may or may not have been designed with a view to returning East to see what kind of position he could gain in the coming conflict. His wife's health had been bad for many years; he had not seen her for three years in that period. It was an awkward time to use her illness to make such a request. Because he made the decision to take leave, command of the 7th Infantry devolved on the fourth ranking officer in the regiment, Major Isaac Lynde, at exactly the moment when the most experienced officer should have been at the helm.[21]

If thoughts of rising rank were in Colonel Morrison's mind, he succeeded, in part, in bringing them to fruition. Such may have been coincidence, but, on returning East he was able to obtain a Colonel's commission in the 8th Infantry as of June 6, 1861. Morrison had over forty years service at the time. Older officers were asked to step aside for the relatively young. His age probably kept him from an immediate general's commission. Morrison resigned from the Army in 1863 but received a brevet to brigadier general on March 13, 1865, for long and faithful service. There is no way to know his intentions. Whatever his thoughts, he had time between the request to leave, and the leaving, to set the United States on a twenty-year war course with the Apaches and to place Major Isaac Lynde in the most untenable of positions a military commander could have. Why Morrison asked for and received his leave pales when considering what happened as a result of his actions while commander at Fort Buchanan.[22]

No state had yet seceded by December 13, 1860, regardless of the harsh and violent rhetoric which filled the air and newspaper accounts following Abraham Lincoln's election. In Texas, where the 3ᵈ Infantry had only recently been transferred, and where the 8ᵗʰ Infantry had orders to go, General David E. Twiggs raised the question of southern secession with General Winfield Scott at Army Headquarters in New York. Twiggs asked for guidance on what to do with the public property should Texas secede. Should he oppose that secession? The question was beyond Scott's ability to answer. Only the President of the United States could answer that question. Twiggs, an ardent man of the South, from the state of Georgia, predicted:

> I think there can be no doubt that many of the Southern States will secede from the Union. The State of Texas will be among the number, and, from all appearances at present, it will be at an early day, certainly before the 4th of March next. What is to be done with public property in charge of the Army? The arsenal at this place has some ordnance and other munitions of war. I do not expect an order for the present for the disposition of them, but I would be pleased to receive your views and suggestions. My course as respects myself will be to remain at my post and protect this frontier as long as I can, and then, when turned adrift, make my way home, if I have one. I would be pleased to hear from you at your earliest convenience.[23]

A disaster was about to happen while the Federal Government and the Army sat on their hands that December of 1860. Events were allowed to simply take their course. Rather than urgently responding to General Twiggs's request for guidance, Scott chose not to reply. Adjutant General Cooper did not reply. President Buchanan did not reply. General Twiggs was forced to act on his own sympathies which, being a Southerner, he did.

David Twiggs was commissioned a captain in the 8ᵗʰ Infantry in 1812, at a time when America was fighting its second war against the British; other career changes followed until he was appointed a brigadier general at the beginning of the War with Mexico. Twiggs was recognized for heroism during the battles in and around Monterrey. For his overall efforts during the Mexican War General Twiggs was awarded a Sword of Honor by the Congress of the United States. He was then sent to manage the

Painting of Fort Millard Fillmore and the Organ Mountains by A.J. Fountain, Jr.
Courtesy: Museum of New Mexico, Neg. No. 1687.

military forces in the 8th Department in Texas, perhaps the most prestigious posting on the frontier.[24]

Twiggs had been in command when Brevet-Colonel Edwin Vose Sumner came to New Mexico Territory in 1851. Sumner shook up the 9th Military Department, as the military authority in New Mexico was then titled. He moved the troops out of the towns, placing them in forts at key locations selected by himself. Forts Fillmore, Conrad (later moved and renamed Fort Craig), Union, Defiance, Massachusetts, and Webster were begun in the fall of 1851, with others to follow. One of the main reasons Fort Fillmore was located forty miles north of El Paso was that Brevet-Colonel Sumner wanted to be sure the post fell under his New Mexico command. In 1854, when Fort Bliss was established, that post's proximity to Fort Fillmore kept it from being handed over to David Twiggs and his Department of Texas command.

David Twiggs never walked the sandy grounds at Fort Fillmore, yet his decisions, made over the next several months, severely impacted that fort's final days as a United States Army post. Twiggs's decisions also impacted the career of Major Isaac Lynde and the 7th Infantry Regiment more than those of any other man, save perhaps President Lincoln. Twiggs cleared the path of invasion that put Fort Fillmore in the forefront of military activity in the earliest days of the coming civil conflict, before first blood had truly been shed between North and South. He also provided Major Isaac Lynde with an unfortunate precedent on how to act in the presence of a perceived threat from those who were formerly fellow countrymen. Twiggs did not shed blood, did not fight those who were once brothers in nationhood. Twiggs also provided Major Lynde with a precedent for handling public property in the face of demands from a local populace which was claiming sovereignty over that property, as the Southern-sympathizing 'Territorial Government of Arizona' was even then beginning to do across the Rio Grande from Fort Fillmore. General Twiggs taught lessons that Major Lynde could not help learning. Twiggs provided them to a man who was desperate for advice on what to do and how to handle a situation never before encountered by any American Army officer.

In early December 1860, all this was in the future; no state from the South had yet crossed the line and left the Union. On December 15, the main duty for Major Isaac Lynde was keeping peace with the Apaches. Lynde's command was, in fact, surrounded by forces which could, at any time, become hostile. A meeting was held on the 11th of December between Captain Mathew Rider Stevenson of Company 'B' and Mangas Coloradas, the famous Apache Chief. Stevenson was one of the two company commanders serving in Major Lynde's battalion at Fort Floyd. He reported:

> In compliance with Special Order No. "3" dated Hd Quarters Fort Floyd N.M. December 10th 1860, I left this post with my Company, "B" 7th Infantry, on the morning of the 11th Inst. And arrived at the point on the Mimbres river known as Fort Webster on the evening of the same day.
>
> The day after my arrival, Mangas Colorado, the principal Apache Chief, came to my camp. To him I reiterated what Lt. Marmaduke, the officer who preceded me to the Mimbres, had told Chaboncito, a sub Apache Chief, and which Lt. Marmaduke has communicated to the major commanding; also that I required him and Chaboncito to come to see me the following day—they came—I informed them that I required them to deliver at Fort Floyd all the stock and arms which the Apaches had stolen from the whites during the past months & with Jose, Victorio & Pinon to meet at that post Dr. Steck & Major Lynde, to the former of whom Major Lynde had written: that they must cease their stealing, keep peaceable with whites and to ensure their keeping faith, I should retain & take with me to Fort Floyd the prisoners whom I had received from Lt. Marmaduke. To which they assured—tho they denied having any stolen stock in their possession. Mangas Colorado said their Agent Dr. Steck had [kept] not his promise to them, that the reason of Elias' band being on the Mimbres was to meet Dr. Steck who had promised to meet him at Fort Floyd, or rather Apache Tiju [sic] and the Dr. instead of keeping his promise, failed. I also informed them that the Commanding Officer would notify them of the arrival at this post of their agent.
>
> Being satisfied that no depredations would be committed on the settlers on the Mimbres River I broke up my camp on the 13th Inst. and arrived at this post on the 15th Inst.[25]

While the situation with the Apaches promised peace that December, the coming turmoil in the eastern States promised anything but peace. There was little mention in Colonel Fauntleroy's correspondence concerning events happening as a result of Lincoln's election. He never once said anything to Major Lynde at Fort Floyd/McLane concerning what to do given Texas' secession. Fauntleroy kept Lynde's nose to the Indian grindstone, so to speak. Yet events already happening that December were impacting the efficiency of the Department, especially as related to the crucial delivery of mail. On December 16 Colonel Fauntleroy, concerned by the fact that the mails from Independence to Santa Fe were disrupted, wrote the Postmaster General of the United States about the problem:

> I have the honor respectfully to call your attention to the subject of the great irregularity of the Mails between Independence & this place.
>
> No mail has arrived here, "on time," since the 25th ultimo. The mail due on the 2nd Inst. was behind time—part of it did not reach here, before the 5th instant. And no mail has arrived here from the states since.
>
> The Overland Mail Company will not bring us any mail matter and we are thus cut off entirely from such intercourse with the States.
>
> The official as well as the private correspondence appertaining to this military Department is very large and important & I therefore feel it my duty to call your attention to the matter & to request, that you will either make such arrangements as will enable us to receive our mails via the Southern, or Overland route—or as will ensure their punctual and certain delivery via Independence.[26]

A breakdown of the mails would cut the Department off from its higher commands if allowed to continue, particularly at a time when the political situation was beginning to deteriorate rapidly. This early cutoff of information from the East may have been the result of the rising tumult over secession in the state of Missouri, which spent the American Civil War trying to determine whether it would be for the North or the South.

Although the slowdown in mail service ensured a delay in Colonel Fauntleroy getting the word, on December 20, 1860, a convention favoring secession met at Charleston, South Carolina, and proclaimed the state of South Carolina an independent commonwealth. The Union was dissolved, at least according to the delegates of the people of South Carolina. In Washington, representatives of the 'Territory of Arizona' were getting nowhere in having their new Territory recognized by the United States Government. South Carolina's declaration of secession some months later led to the only official recognition the self-declared 'Territory of Arizona' ever received, and that from the Confederate side of the issue.[27]

Would civil war come to America with South Carolina's secession? At that time none knew. In fact, nothing happened quickly. Months passed before any event transpired that indicated force of arms might be the final result.

Having received no answer, or advice, from his first missive of December 13, Brevet-Major General David Twiggs tried again on December 27, two weeks later, to get the Army high command to advise him on matters in Texas. This second letter was not received at Army headquarters in New York City until January 12, 1861. Twiggs must have known of South Carolina's secession by the latter date. He urged Assistant Adjutant General Lorenzo Thomas to hasten getting the Adjutant General Samuel Cooper to provide him with advice with the concurrence of General-in-Chief Winfield Scott. Important time was being wasted. Twiggs explained:

> As there can be no doubt that many of the Southern States, and Texas among the number, will cease to be members of the Union, I respectfully ask instructions, or some intimation, as to the disposition of the United States property, such as arms, ammunition, and transportation. It appears to me some steps should be taken very soon. I shall remain here until my services can no longer be available.[28]

General Winfield Scott, having rushed to Washington from New York in the face of the South Carolina secession, at last wrote General Twiggs on December 28, 1860. Scott gave no specifics as to what Twiggs should do, pleading illness. Instead of giving specific instructions to either fight, flee, or surrender the arms and equipment, Scott simply waffled and said nothing. He passed the buck to Twiggs, who had warned Scott where his sympathies would lie—with the South. Had Scott advised Twiggs to get his troops out or fight any attempts to confiscate the arms and other public properties in the Department of Texas, General Twiggs would probably have attempted to do so. He was a long-time Army officer; his words speak of the turmoil under which he was then laboring. At worst David Twiggs might have resigned and turned the public property over to an officer who would be staying loyal to the Union. By saying nothing, Scott must be accounted culpable for what eventually happened. It should also be remembered that General Scott's nominal superior, John Floyd, was a Southerner. What Scott could not decide, Floyd would not. Only President Buchanan could have decided and his term in office was, in effect, over. Scott's Adjutant, George W. Lay, addressed General Twiggs in the commander's name:

> The General-in-Chief, himself laboring for the time under an attack of sickness, desires me to acknowledge and thank you for your letter of the 13th instant, the spirit of which he highly approves. He says you will understand its reminding him vividly of the interview he had with you in Augusta in 1832.
>
> In cases of political disturbance, involving local conflict with the authority of the General Government, the General-in-Chief considers that the military questions, such as you suggest, contain a political element, with due regard to which, and in due deference to the chief executive authority, no extraordinary instructions concerning them must be issued without the consent of such authority.
>
> He has labored hard in suggesting and urging proper measures to vindicate the laws and protect the property of the United States without waging war or acting offensively against any State or community. All such suggestions, though long since made in good time to have been peaceably and efficiently carried out, have failed to secure the favorable attention of the Government.

The President has listened to him with due friendliness and respect, but the War Department has been little communicative. Up to this time he has not been shown the written instructions of Major Anderson, nor been informed of the purpose of those more recently conveyed to Fort Moultrie by Major Buell.

Probably the policy of the Government in regard to the forts and depots within the limits of seceding States will have been clearly indicated before events can have caused a practical issue to be made up in Texas.

The General does not see at this moment that he can tender you any special advice, but leaves the administration of your command in your own hands, with the laws and regulations to guide, in the full confidence that your discretion, firmness, and patriotism will effect all of good that the sad states of the times may permit.[29]

In effect, David Twiggs was cast adrift, to make the best deal he could. Buchanan, Scott, Cooper and Floyd passed the buck. That Twiggs went ahead and did what he did can hardly be faulted in the face of such confusion and dissembling within the ranks of the highest leadership in the nation. If confusion at the highest levels could lead to a disaster in an important department like Texas, what more might be expected at a much lower level involving a single regiment then scattered over the New Mexico countryside.

Toward the end of December, Major Isaac Lynde was notified by Colonel Thomas Fauntleroy, that he personally approved of Lynde's actions in the matter of an attack by Santa Rita area miners upon the Apaches living along the Mimbres, an attack which led to the death of the Apache sub-Chief Elias. Lynde was ordered to dissuade and prevent the miners from "inflicting unnecessary outrage upon the Indians." At the same time Major Lynde was to prevent the Indians from becoming hostile or aggressive. Very soon the relations between Lynde and those miners degraded into a condition very near armed conflict. Unfair actions taken against the Apaches would not be the cause; the turmoil of secession would be.[30]

On the last full year of operation as United States Army garrisons, and on the last day of that year, Fort Fillmore, Fort Bliss, and Fort McLane, the three southern New Mexico posts, were at peace. The small garrison remaining at Fort Fillmore, Company 'E,' 8th Infantry, commanded by 2[d] Lieutenant Royal Thaxter Frank, had only one officer and forty-six enlisted men, a force barely able to protect the four cannon and other public property the post retained. The wind blew through a number of virtually abandoned officers quarters and barracks. Given that Frank was unmarried, or at least didn't have his wife with him at this time, the long row of six houses for officers and their families, which Lieutenant Colonel Dixon Miles of the 3[d] Infantry Regiment constructed after 1851, were mostly empty. Only one of four of the enlisted barracks was occupied, provided the men did not spread out to give themselves more room. The same was true with the lone infantry company at Fort Bliss and the infantry battalion at Fort Floyd/McLane.

Infantry rarely served well in the field against the Apaches. They simply could not catch them. Hence, throughout the history of New Mexico Territory there had always been a horse-mounted unit, either of dragoons or Mounted Rifles, at each post in the south. In December 1860, there were no mounted troops assigned there. Colonel Fauntleroy, for his own reasons, had pulled them all into northern New Mexico, leaving the Texas border region without cavalry protection. Although no documentation exists explaining exactly why this was done—it may have had to do with the Navajos or other problems out on the Red River—the absence of sufficient cavalry when Texas seceded early the next year ensured that the intelligence gathering capability of the military forces in the south was reduced. Worse, the transfer of the 8th Infantry during the same period, to an uncertain fate in Texas, was an abominable decision. Fort Bliss was literally abandoned, whereas Fort Fillmore was reduced to chaos and ineffectiveness. Were at least some of these decisions deliberate, made with the good of the Southern cause in mind? That is very difficult to prove, although the outcome of the decisions certainly aided the cause of the secessionists in Mesilla, El Paso and in the mining regions around Santa Rita and Pinos Altos.

NOTES - Chapter 1

1. Morrison to Assistant Adjutant General, Santa Fe, August 31, 1860, *National Archives Microfilm: Register of Letters Received and Letters Received by Headquarters Department of New Mexico, 1854-1865, Record Group M1120, Rolls 11/12.* (Hereafter cited as M1120, Roll(s) #.)

2. Crittenden to Assistant Adjutant General, Santa Fe, September 12, 1860, M1120, Rolls 11/12.

3. Thomas to Fauntleroy, September 12, 1860, M1120, Rolls 11/12.

4. M.L. Crimmons, "Fort Fillmore," *New Mexico Historical Review,* Vol. 6, No. 4, 1931, p. 327.

5. Maury to Lynde, September 30, 1860, *National Archives Microfilm: Letters Sent by 9th Military District, Department of New Mexico, Group M1012, Roll 2.* (Hereafter cited as M1012. Roll#.)

6. Francis B. Heitman, *Historical Register and Dictionary of the United States Army, From Its Organization, September 29, 1789, to March 2, 1903.* (Hereafter cited as Heitman, U.S. Army officer's name). Washington: Genealogical Publishing Co., Inc., 1994.

7. Ibid.

8. Edwin Sweeney, *Cochise.* Norman and London: University of Oklahoma Press, 1991, p. 140.

9. Lynde to Assistant Adjutant General, Santa Fe, October 9, 1860, M1120, Rolls 11/12.

10. Lynde to Assistant Adjutant General, Santa Fe, October 9, 1860, M1120, Rolls 11/12.

11. *La Posta,* Volume II, #6, November-December 1970, p. 3.

12. Ibid., p. 8.

13. Maury to Lynde, November 11, 1860, M1012, Roll 2.

14. Jackson circular, November 13, 1860, M1102, Rolls 11/12.

15. Marmaduke to Fauntleroy, November 14, 1860, M1120, Roll 11/12.

16. Death Notice for Captain George McLane, November 18, 1860, M1012, Roll 2.

17. *The San Francisco Herald,* Volume 11, #158, December 4, 1860, reporting on an article in the *Mesilla Times,* November 22, 1860.

18. Steck to Collins, November 26, 1860, *U.S. Interior Department Microcopy No. T21: Indian Affairs Bureau Records of the New Mexico Superintendency, 1849-1860, Roll 2.* (Hereafter cited as Indian Bureau. Roll #.)

19. *The San Francisco Herald,* Volume 11, #158, December 4, 1860, reporting on an article in the *Mesilla Times,* November 22, 1860.

20. Fauntleroy to Thomas, December 4, 1860, M1012, Roll 2.

21. Morrison to Assistant Adjutant General, Santa Fe, December 4, 1860, M1120, Rolls 11/12.

22. Heitman, Pitcairn Morrison.

23. Heitman, Twiggs. Brevet Major General David Twiggs openly admitted he was loyal to Southern principles and would act as a man of the South in the matter of Texas, should that state secede. He was guilty of no duplicity, in that he never hid who he was.

24. Ibid.

25. Stevenson to Lynde, December 15, 1860, M1120, Rolls 11/12.

26. Fauntleroy to Postmaster General, December 16, 1860, M1120, Rolls 11/12.

27. *La Posta*, Volume II, #6, November-December 1970, p. 3.

28. Twiggs to Adjutant General Cooper, Washington City D.C., December 23, 1860, M1120, Rolls 11/12.

29. Lay to Twiggs, December 28, 1860, M1120, Rolls 11/12. It is interesting that when direct personal contact was needed between Scott and Twiggs on the matter of Texas secession General Scott, claiming illness, allowed an aide, George W. Lay, to make the statements that no junior officer should have been making at such a critical time.

30. Fauntleroy to Lynde, December 30, 1860, M1120, Rolls 11/12.

2

A DISASTER IN TEXAS

The fate of the Department of Texas in 1861 is inextricably linked to that of those United States military forces stationed farther west in the Department of New Mexico. The Department of Texas Headquarters, at San Antonio, was usually presided over by a commander of brigadier general rank, whereas the Department of New Mexico was commanded by a colonel. 'General' John Garland, when he commanded in New Mexico, was a brevet-brigadier general, actually a colonel, though he made full use of that brevet star in negotiations and on social occasions. Bigger was better, rank-wise, and Texas was a large and populated state, compared to the vast unpopulated areas of New Mexico Territory. To patrol the critical regions of Texas required more troops, hence a higher-ranking commander.

In the first months of 1861 the Department of Texas, considered part of the frontier defense forces, generally supported three missions. These were to protect the border with Mexico, control the Comanches in the northwest and the Apaches in the west, and control the routes through to California, up to the Department of New Mexico border, which in early 1861 was where it is now, just west of the city of El Paso, Texas.

In order to accomplish these missions there were twenty-five forts and camps located at strategic points. New Mexico Territory at that time had thirteen forts and camps. In the southeast and eastern parts of Texas there was Fort Sam Houston (1845), Point

Brazos Santiago (1849), Fort Ringgold (1848), Fort Brown (1846), Fort McIntosh (1849), Camp Austin (1845), Camp Wood (1857) and Camp Ives (1859). Protecting trade routes in the north and central portions, including the Butterfield Overland Mail route coming south to join the San Antonio-El Paso road, were Fort Belknap (1851), Camp Cooper (1856), Fort Griffin (1857), Fort Phantom Hill (1847), Camp Colorado (1857), Fort Chadbourne (1852), Fort Mason (1851), Fort McKavitt (1852), and Fort Martin Scott (1848). Protecting the military road from San Antonio to Fort Fillmore, New Mexico Territory, where the road divided for California or Santa Fe, were Camp Verde (1856), Fort Inge (1849), Fort Clark (1852), Fort Lancaster (1855), Fort Stockton (1858), Fort Davis (1854), Fort Quitman (1858) and Fort Bliss (1854). Of course, until late in 1860, Fort Bliss belonged to the Department of New Mexico and did not count on Texas strength totals.

Save for a few engineer and artillery units, mostly situated along the coast, there were three infantry regiments, one cavalry regiment, and part of a third infantry regiment spread among the twenty-five posts. Present in January 1861 were the 3^d Infantry Regiment, only recently transferred from New Mexico Territory, the 1st Infantry Regiment, a long-serving unit in the Department of Texas, and the 2^d Cavalry Regiment. The latter was considered an experimental and elite unit of the United States Army in this period. The colonel commanding the 2^d Cavalry in January 1861 was Colonel Edwin Vose Sumner, the former commanding officer of the Department of New Mexico, and the man who established Fort Fillmore in September 1851.

As an aside, in March 1861 the 2^d Cavalry Regiment was commanded briefly by Robert E. Lee, before he left to seek his Southern destiny. Later in 1861, as part of the change that eliminated the use of the terms dragoon and Regiment of Mounted Rifles, the 1st and 2^d Dragoon Regiments became the 1st and 2^d Cavalry Regiments; the Regiment of Mounted Rifles became the 3^d Cavalry Regiment; while the 2^d Cavalry Regiment became the 5th Cavalry Regiment by protocol. After the Civil War the 5th Cavalry returned to serve in Texas.

The other infantry regiment assigned in Texas, the 8th Infantry, had nine companies available, rather than the normal ten. Four of these companies were in New Mexico Territory in January 1861, one at Fort Fillmore, one at Fort Bliss, and two at other posts farther north. The five companies then serving within the actual state of Texas boundary were in western Texas, at Fort Quitman, Fort Davis, and points south along the San Antonio road. In total there were thirty-four companies in the Department of Texas composed of 102 officers and 2,328 enlisted men serving with the regiments, normally in one-company posts spread among the twenty-five locations, excluding the four companies still in New Mexico that January.

In January 1861 Texas was still a state in the United States, a condition that was soon to end by means of a tragic and sad parting, a parting which brought dishonor to the United States military and created a premonition of doom within the troops of the Department of New Mexico as well. What happened at Fort Fillmore in late July 1861 cannot be separated from what happened in Texas in January through May. The Texas debacle is an ingredient in the general mix of events which terminated for this particular research in the surrender of the 7th Infantry Regiment, and Fort Fillmore, to a smaller force of Confederate soldiers from Texas. To what degree the Texas debacle, as viewed from the United States military point of view, impacted the thought processes of Major Isaac Lynde can only be conjectured. That there were impacts can hardly be doubted. Precedents were set in Texas which must have been known and considered when Colonel Canby, in Santa Fe, and Major Lynde, at Fort Fillmore, were making decisions on how to respond and react to a threat which up until that time could hardly have been imagined. Americans fighting Americans in civil conflict was a new experience, an experience which took a great deal of time to bring to bloodshed, even though there had long been a condition of turbulence over the issues of slavery and states's rights.

In San Antonio, Texas, on January 15, Brevet-Major General David Twiggs put his forty-year military career on the line in a heartfelt letter to General-in-Chief Winfield Scott. Scott had done nothing to help Twiggs in the matter of the troops and public property then in Texas. Given the consequences, such lack of assistance seems at this date unconscionable. Twiggs pleaded for help in making his decision, even offering to resign. He warned:

> Yours, through Colonel Lay, of the 29th (28th) December received. I am placed in a most embarrassing situation. I am a Southern man, and all these states will secede. What is left will not be the "United States," and I know not what is to become of the troops now in this Department.
>
> Louisiana, Alabama, Mississippi, and Georgia will certainly secede. As for coercion, that I consider impossible to keep them in the Union. A guard would have to be put at every house in the country, and that would not keep them in the Union. The feeling is universal, and the people are determined to secede. Coercion might have done at first; now it cannot. As soon as I know Georgia has separated from the Union I must, of course, follow her.
>
> I most respectfully ask to be relieved in the command of this department on or before the 4th of March next. All I have is in the South, and as my health will not allow me to take an active part in the scenes that will probably be enacted, I must be a looker-on.[1]

General-in-Chief Scott acted on David Twiggs's request as soon as he received the letter. Scott asked the new Secretary of War to relieve General Twiggs in Texas, and replace him with Colonel Carlos Waite. Scott's request was approved, but only at a time when the situation in Texas was no longer in doubt. The debacle had already begun.

On January 18 David Twiggs reported that the legislature of the state of Texas was to meet on January 21 and the Convention one week after. Twiggs felt Texas would secede by the end of January. He was angry about comments demanding the use of United States troops against the people of the South. Twiggs said he would "never fire on American citizens."[2]

On January 20 Texas Governor Sam Houston clearly indicated a deal was about to be made between himself and Brevet-Major

General Twiggs to turn over all the federal property to the state of Texas, if Texas seceded. Houston noted:

> The present pressure of important events necessarily induces prompt action on the part of all public functionaries. In this view of the matter I send to you General J.M. Smith, of this State, on a confidential mission, to know what, in the present crisis, you consider it your duty to do as maintaining in behalf of the Federal Government or passing over to the State the possession of the forts, arsenals, and public property within this State, and also if a demand for the possession of the same is made by the executive, you are authorized, or if it would be conformable to your sense of duty, to place in possession of the authorities of the State the forts, arms, munitions, and property of the Federal Government, on the order of the executive, to an officer of the State empowered to receive and receipt for the same.
>
> This course is suggested by the fact that information has reached the executive that an effort will be made by an unauthorized mob to take forcibly and appropriate the public stores and property to uses of their own, assuming to act on behalf of the State.
>
> Any arrangements made with you by General Smith will be sanctioned and approved by me; and should you require any assistance to aid you in resisting the contemplated and unauthorized attack upon the public property, etc., and to place the same in possession of the State authorities, you are authorized to call on the mayor and citizens of San Antonio for such assistance as you may deem necessary.
>
> I will hope to hear from you, general, through my confidential agent, General Smith, so soon as he can have the honor of a conference with you on matters embraced in the present epoch of our national affair.[3]

Two days later Twiggs issued Special Order No. 10, ordering two six-pounder cannon armed with fixed ammunition, and readied for immediate service, to the San Antonio garrison. The commander at Camp Verde was ordered to send an infantry company for support. The commanding officer at Fort Clark was to send two companies of infantry. Was General Twiggs, at this moment, contemplating armed resistance, even though he once stated he would never fire? He was at least taking precautions, though perhaps only to protect his troops and headquarters from unwarranted assault.[4]

Although he ordered troops closer to San Antonio as a precaution, General David Twiggs sat at his desk that same January 22 and wrote to Adjutant-General Samuel Cooper in Washington warn-ing that, if Texas seceded, he intended to turn over all public property to the state of Texas forces. The die was finally cast. Cooper was probably not overly concerned. He would have done the same thing. The Adjutant-General was himself preparing to clean out his desk, getting ready to head South to take up his new duties with the Confederacy, in the same position he then occupied as an officer of the United States Army. Twiggs informed:

> Inclosed [sic]I transmit a letter from the governor of Texas and my answer. As I do not think anyone in authority desires me to carry on a civil war against Texas, I shall, after secession, if the governor repeats his demand, direct the other arms and property to be turned over to his agents, keeping in the hands of the troops the arms they now have. I have asked for instructions as to what I was to do after secession four times, viz, on the 27th ultimo, the 2d, 7th, and 18th instants, and have received no answer. The troops in this department occupy a line of some twelve hundred miles, and some time will be required to remove them to any place. *I again ask, what disposition is to be made of them?*[5]

Although David Twiggs did not know it, Washington was finally acting on his earlier missives. Special Order No. 22, issued on January 28, in Washington, stripped Twiggs of his command and replaced him with Colonel Carlos A. Waite. This action, done earlier, might have saved the Army regiments in Texas from their sad fate. The action may also have led to bloodshed. Communications being slow, word of the replacement did not reach Texas in time to stop what was coming.[6]

On that same January 28, unaware he was about to be relieved, Brevet-Major General Twiggs countermanded his own Order No. 10, directing two companies of infantry from Fort Clark to San

Antonio to protect the 8th Department Headquarters. The troops were to stay where they were, pending further orders. Twiggs was no longer intending to resist and wanted no possibility of antagonism.[7]

Although too late for Texas, the rusty wheels of the military machine in Washington were moving once Waite was placed in command. On January 30, 1861, Assistant Adjutant General Lorenzo Thomas ordered Colonel H.L. Scott, Headquarters of the Army in New York City, to charter a steamer destined for Key West and the coast of Texas to take ordnance there and bring back troops. The decision was made to evacuate Texas, removing all the troops and equipment then in service there.

In New Mexico Territory, on January 30, Colonel Fauntleroy set the four 8th Infantry companies then in New Mexico out on the road toward Texas, as per previous orders from Washington. Fauntleroy made no move to fight this incredible decision, although how much he knew of the political situation in Texas is conjectural. From the modern perspective, sending the 8th into Texas at this time appears treason. But, the Army being the Army, communications being slow once an order was sent out, Fauntleroy may have been unable to change the situation no matter his political views.

As of January 31, in a case of too little too late, Assistant Adjutant-General Lorenzo Thomas ordered the costly artillery reserves in Texas to be evacuated. The matter of the saving of the infantry was of secondary importance to the saving of these crucial weapons. The order was addressed to the commander of the Department of Texas, on January 31, as follows:

> The General-in-Chief directs that you take immediate measures for replacing the five companies of artillery on the Rio Grande and put them in march for Brazos Santiago, to which place a steamer will be sent to bring them out of Texas. The light companies will take their guns and equipments, but will leave their horses.[8]

The final decision to evacuate the Texas public property was made in Washington while 8th Infantry troops still garrisoned Fort Fillmore and other posts. A simple order to send the other five companies of the 8th Regiment, then stationed in western Texas, to southern New Mexico at the same time the artillery was to be evacuated could have changed future events significantly. The presence of the 7th and 8th Infantry Regiments in southern New Mexico, with all their high-powered weaponry and cannon, would have made invasion most difficult. Of course, no such orders were issued.

On February 1, a resolution of secession was voted on and passed by a Secession Convention Governor Sam Houston was forced to convene. The vote to leave the Union was 168-8. Texas was out of the Union, although a vote of the people was required to be taken, for or against, on February 23. The outcome of that vote was not considered to be in doubt by the secessionists.

A few days after the secession vote, on February 4, Colonel Thomas, at the behest of General-in-Chief Scott, directed that Brevet-Colonel Carlos Waite should use his brevet rank upon taking command. He was reminded of instructions to remove the artillery to Brazos Santiago for embarkation. Instructions as to the disposition of the troops were to follow. No mention was made of the 8th Infantry. Of course, by the time Colonel Waite received these instructions and could take up the reins of command, General Twiggs had already surrendered all of the public property in Texas.[9]

That fateful action was finalized on February 17, 1861, following days of haggling over terms, in the form of a letter from General Twiggs to the commissioners working on behalf of the people of Texas—Messrs. Thomas J. Devine, S.A. Maverick, and P.N. Luckett. Twiggs stated, when the question of surrender was put to him:

> In reply to your communication of this date, I have to say that you are already aware of my views in regard to the delivery of the public property of this department, and I now repeat that I will direct the positions held by the Federal troops to be turned over to the authorized agents of the State of Texas, provided the troops retain their arms and clothing, camp and garrison equipage, quartermaster's stores, subsistence, medical, hospital stores, and such means of transportation of every kind as may be necessary for an efficient and orderly movement of the troops from Texas, prepared for attack or defense against aggression from any source.[10]

The Texas commissioners responded with pleasure to this by now expected turn of events. How pleased they must have been to gain all without a fight or even a struggle. The Federal Army in Texas would simply march away, leaving behind much of their equipment and arms, save for what they could carry on their persons or in the small number of allotted wagons. After Fort Sumter, not even these amenities would be allowed. There would be no fighting. The Texas commissioners noted:

> In reply to your communication of this date, we have to say that we accept your terms therein set forth, with the conditions stated in our note of the 14th instant, viz, that the troops shall leave Texas by the way of the coast, and, upon arriving at the point or points of embarkation, will deliver up to the authorized agents, appointed for that purpose, all means of transportation of every kind used by them, as likewise the artillery, if any be taken.[11]

On February 18, while the Texas commissioners were still finalizing their deal with General Twiggs, the first of the confrontations between the United States military and the state of Texas authorities took place, at Camp Cooper. Texas militia units reacted swiftly to the secession decision. The Texans appeared willing, even before any declaration of war, to shed blood. It would be a long time before the Federal Army would agree to do so. The commander of Camp Cooper, Captain S.D. Carpenter, 1st Infantry, was the first to face Texas troops under threatening conditions. Finding a Texas secessionist military force outside his gates, Carpenter demanded that their intentions be made known. Camp Cooper was situated in the Comanche country in north-central Texas, north of the current town of Albany. Rumors were rife within the garrison that the Texas militia intended to attack the camp.[12]

Aide-de-camp to Governor Houston and colonel commanding the Texas militia forces outside Camp Cooper, W.C. Dalrymple, answered the besieged Captain Carpenter's query by saying,

> In reply to your communication of this day I have to say that the assembly of soldiery here has for its object the reduction

of Camp Cooper. The State of Texas having, by the action of a convention of the people, virtually renounced her allegiance to the Government of the United States, and being here in command of the State troops, and also in command of the citizen soldiery encamped in this vicinity, I shall, in the name of the sovereign State of Texas, demand within twenty-four hours a surrender of the garrison under your command, with all arms, munitions, and property of every description heretofore belonging to the United States.[13]

Reducing this message to its simplest form, Colonel Dalrymple was ordering Captain Carpenter to surrender or fight.

Captain Carpenter chose to surrender, without a fight, to an inferior and probably untrained force on February 18, 1861. He made no attempt to get instructions from any higher command before doing so. Carpenter's justification was no better than Isaac Lynde's several months later. True, there was as yet no civil war. Carpenter possibly had General Twiggs's orders to evacuate as a justification, as later Isaac Lynde would have a similar order signed by the Department of New Mexico commander. Ironically, Captain Carpenter's name did not go down in history as a coward as did Major Lynde's. Carpenter replied to Dalrymple's demand by saying:

Until the reception of your first note I was satisfied, from all the information I could obtain, that I was threatened with an attack by an unauthorized force, and accordingly took such measures as were necessary for my defense. My reply to your demand, notwithstanding it is made in the name of Texas, and by an officer holding a commission from its governor, as commanding officer of the Federal troops stationed at this camp, could be no other than an unqualified refusal; but in the present agitated political condition of our country I feel compelled to regard, in connection with this demand and its refusal, the perilous consequences that must result to the whole nation. The policy of the administration and the wisest statesman of the land is to avert, if possible, the shedding of blood ... .[14]

In other words, Captain Carpenter did not feel justified in fighting, in shedding Texan blood, before there was a clear order from the government of Abraham Lincoln to do so. In July 1861 the very same situation faced Major Isaac Lynde, under very similar circumstances, as we shall see. Lynde, trying to defend Fort Fillmore, had no more legal justification to take on Colonel Baylor than did Captain Carpenter in fighting Colonel Dalrymple at Camp Cooper. Lynde may have known of the bloodless surrender of Fort Sumter and the attack at Fort Pickens, yet no declaration of war was formalized through those events. In fact, until blood began to flow at First Bull Run, the issue was in doubt as to whether the South would, or would not, be allowed to leave the Union peaceably.

Had Captain Carpenter been unable to "avert the shedding of blood" he might have started the American Civil War right there at Camp Cooper. He chose not to do so and, given his orders and understanding of the political situation, he made the right decision.

February 23, 1861, brought popular acclaim and backing for a seceded, temporarily restored, Republic of Texas. The vote of the people of Texas was 46,129 for secession and 14,697 against. From this point on the Commissioners acting in the name of the Republic, soon to be the Confederate State of Texas, had a popular mandate to go about their work of confiscating Federal property.

The Texans took over the artillery park at Brazos Santiago on the day of the vote and began pressuring other United States troops in the area to surrender. Captain B.H. Hill, commanding at Fort Brown, was addressed by E.B. Nichols, commissioner of the state of Texas, and by H.B. Waller, his secretary, on the subject of Hill making any attempt to attack the Texas troops at Brazos Island. Hill was warned that a civil war could be the result; no doubt Captain Hill understand the need to avoid such a shedding of blood. Commissioner Nichols also warned Captain Hill:

> Texas is virtually out of the Union already, it being now about 4 o'clock in the evening, and the destiny of this State has been fixed by the people in their sovereign capacity at the ballot box, and no one who knows anything of the sentiment of this people can doubt for a moment that this is now a sovereign and independent republic. As such the United States

troops placed here for our protection are not needed by us—are upon foreign soil. They, therefore, have no further duty to perform here; therefore I presume they will soon be removed.[15]

Captain Hill declared that it would be impossible for him to accede to the request to turn over all public property to the state of Texas, without authority from the government of the United States. There was a temporary standoff, at least at far as the public property at Fort Brown was concerned. While Captain Hill and Texas Commissioner Nichols stared at each other over the edge of a bayonet, Brevet-Captain Dabney Maury in Santa Fe seemed totally ignorant of the situation in Texas. On that same February 23, Maury notified the Adjutant General of the Department of Texas in San Antonio on the mundane issue of charges to be brought against certain enlisted men in Companies 'E' and 'I,' 8th Infantry Regiment, recently part of the troops being transferred to the Department of Texas. Had word of the perfidy of Brevet-Major General Twiggs not yet reached the New Mexico Department? Such a situation must be considered doubtful.[16]

Captain E. Kirby Smith, of the 2d Cavalry, soon to be appointed a general in the Confederate Army, evacuated the Camp Colorado post without a fight. Smith said, when confronted by a large force of Texas militia demanding his public property:

> These demands met with an unqualified refusal, and in my interview with Colonel McCulloch on the 22d, my reply was that I could never, under any circumstances, give up my arms and horses, or negotiate upon terms that would dishonor the troops under my command, and that, were such a demand persisted in, I would mount my command, and endeavor to cut my way through any force opposed to me.

Strong words, but Smith didn't fight. Instead, he agreeed to give up the public property and the post, although he did march out of Camp Colorado with his horses and arms. Smith explained his hasty evacuation was necessary "as the presence of the undisciplined troops of the Convention [Texas], with the irritable feelings of our men under their unceremonious removal, might soon have occasioned a collision." In other words, the troops wanted to fight, but their leaders didn't believe this was the best course to take given the situation. The Federal officers simply did not know how to react to the belligerency of those who had until recently been fellow countrymen.[17]

Brevet-Lieutenant Colonel David T. Chandler, formerly commanding 3^d United States Infantry troops stationed at Fort Craig, New Mexico Territory, was in San Antonio in late February 1861. Chandler was to be sent on a special mission to New Orleans with dispatches for Washington. He was to meet with the governor of Louisiana to determine if that state would give the troops from Texas safe passage through Louisiana on their way north. After delivering his dispatches and messages, Chandler was to return to Texas. He never completed this mission, later joining the Confederate cause, although waiting until 1862 to do so officially.[18]

Captain S.D. Carpenter, the officer who surrendered Camp Cooper without a fight, arrived at Fort Chadbourne with Company 'H,' 1st Infantry Regiment, along with Companies 'D' and 'H,' 2^d Cavalry. While at Fort Chadbourne, his troops were under the watchful eye of Texas militia Colonel H.E. McCulloch, who commanded Texas troops on the northwest Frontier. McCulloch stated that he had, while "feeling empowered by my commission and instructions to negotiate with them," offered Carpenter's command the opportunity to join in service to the state of Texas. The offer was refused. McCulloch then set about assisting them to leave Texas for the East, via San Antonio.[19]

Fort Chadbourne was next on the list for surrender. Lieutenant-Colonel Gouveneur Morris, formerly the commander at Fort Fillmore and at Fort Daniel Webster in New Mexico back in the early 1850s, was then the commanding officer of the 1st Infantry Regiment, his headquarters at Fort Chadbourne. Morris could have beaten the Confederate forces arrayed around him, but instead followed Brevet-Major General Twiggs's orders to give up his post and leave. Morris even entered into agreement with his enemies. Lieutenant Colonel Morris informed Colonel Waite, who had by then replaced Twiggs, of his decision to surrender. He said:

> I have the honor to report to you, that in compliance with General Orders no. 5, dated Headquarters Department of Texas, February 18, 1861, I have this day entered into a written agreement with Col. H.E. McCulloch (commissioner on the part of Texas for this district), to deliver to him the public property at this post, when and as soon as transportation can be sent here to remove this command to the coast. I therefore earnestly request that you will cause to be dispatched for this purpose twelve wagons, if the supplies have to be transported the whole way; but if drawn at San Antonio, or other points on the route, ten wagons in addition to the three now at the post will answer. Even this may be considered an unusual allowance of transportation; but if it is considered that there are to be moved one Lieutenant-colonel, one captain, one assistant surgeon with the rank of captain, one second lieutenant, one chaplain, and their servants, consisting of one man, four women, and three children (slaves), Company G, First Infantry, laundresses and children belonging to it, together with a detachment of Company I, First Infantry, with laundresses of the same company, and the hospital matron and stores, as also the records of the post, the requisition cannot be deemed extravagant, or more than is required to move the command as stipulated by treaty. The treaty in question does not state which party shall furnish the necessary transportation to enable the troops to vacate Texas, and I therefore make this requisition on the commander of the department, and the commissioner has agreed with me to make the same requisition to the commissioners on the part of Texas at San Antonio.[20]

Lieutenant Colonel Morris was most concerned, not with the public property of his regiment, but for the personal property of himself and his staff, to include personal black slaves, who were worth a great deal of money. Later, at San Augustine Springs, Major Isaac Lynde signed a similar surrender document, but only after he had been assured that his and his officers' private property would be safe. Morris probably got his personal property out of Texas, but his infantry regiment surrendered much of its arms and other public property. Lieutenant Colonel Morris did not fight in the

Civil War thereafter, resigning from the Army in September 1861 at the age of sixty. He was never tried or reprimanded for any actions he took in Texas. No stain of cowardice was attached to his name, nor did acrimonious accusations follow him wherever he went thereafter.

On March 16, 1861, the word "surrender" was used in relation to the final abandonment of Fort Brown. The public property and the post were to be turned over to Texas commissioners as soon as possible. Major C. C. Sibley, 3^d Infantry, was expected at Fort Brown by March 16, 1861. Sibley traveled some two hundred and thirty miles from Fort McIntosh to join up with the other companies of his regiment. Colonel Bonneville, who still commanded the 3^d Infantry, was out of the Department of Texas during this most critical of times; Lieutenant Colonel Electus Backus, second in command, was absent on temporary sick leave.[21]

Before going on sick leave, Backus abandoned Fort Brown without a fight. The public property was turned over to Mr. H.B. Waller, agent and attorney for E.B. Nichols, the commissioner for the state of Texas. Captain Andrew Bowman handled the ceremony which saw the lowering of the United States flag. Backus and Bowman were long-serving officers at Fort Fillmore in New Mexico. Fort Brown was then turned over to Brownsville police, no Confederate militia having yet arrived. The term "surrender" was appropriate, as with the public property went some of the arms of the 3^d Infantry Regiment. The fate of the men was in doubt—permission not having been received for their orderly evacuation. How many of the new weapons recently issued to the 3^d Infantry in New Mexico fell into Confederate hands is not clear, although many must have.[22]

On March 22, Texas Commissioner P.N. Luckett, wrote to Colonel C.A. Waite that the Texas Convention endorsed the seizure of funds that were to pay Federal troops in Texas. One of the paymasters whose funds were to be seized was Major Thomas Grimke Rhett. Rhett was the paymaster at Forts Quitman, Bliss, and Fillmore, and also an ardent supporter of the secessionist cause. The troops at Fort Fillmore and other posts in New Mexico were going through a period in which they would not be paid for their services as a result of Rhett's perfidy in willingly turning over the money.[23]

By March 27, Colonel Carlos Waite found himself surrounded with his few troops in San Antonio. Waite warned the Assistant Adjutant-General in Washington that an attempt might be made to make prisoners of war of his soldiers, who were laying down their arms without fighting. He wrote:

> In case the difficulty between the General Government and the seceding States should result in hostilities, there is reason to apprehend that an attempt may be made to prevent the embarkation of the troops and to detain them as prisoners of war. This can only be effected by their seizing and removing all lighters, preventing transports of light draught entering the bay at Indianola, and by cutting off our supplies of provisions, etc. To avoid an attempt of that kind, and to be prepared to meet it if made, I am concentrating the troops at the camp near Green Lake as rapidly as possible. The camp is full twenty miles from Indianola and is the nearest place to the coast where fresh water can be obtained. The difficulty, amounting almost to impossibility, of supplying the troops with water at Indianola, prevents my moving them down to that place. Not a line has been received at these headquarters from the headquarters of the Army, or from the War Department, since I entered upon duty as the department commander, except unimportant matters, and I am inclined to believe from inspection of the envelopes that they have been opened, and that all important communications have been withheld.[24]

Of course, there was as yet no declared war and any attempt to make the men prisoners would have violated established conventions, as well as abrogating the agreement between the former Department of Texas commander, David Twiggs, and the Texas authorities. On that same day, March 27, Colonel Waite, in a separate letter, reported that three companies of the 1st Infantry, four companies of the 3d Infantry, two companies of the 8th Infantry, and six companies of the 2d Cavalry had passed through San Antonio on their way to Green Lake, twenty miles from the disembarkation point at Indianola. Four additional companies were expected before the end of March.[25]

The Texas authorities did not challenge the departure of the first Federal troops to disembark at Indianola. Brevet-Colonel Waite reported that the first transport left safely for New York, loaded with nearly six hundred soldiers. Another transport with an equal number of troops was scheduled to leave soon after. Waite intended to keep his headquarters at San Antonio until the troops from the interior arrived. No attempt had been made to make them prisoners of war, although his soldiers were considered paroled as if captured in battle.[26]

The first of the disembarked infantry units which left Texas arrived off the Florida coast in mid-April, just in time to become embroiled in one of the first major conflicts of the American Civil War. The state of Florida seceded on January 10, 1861. When it did so there was a small garrison of Federal troops stationed at Fort Pickens off the Florida coast, and at two other posts nearby on land. The federal garrison burned the shore posts and retreated to Fort Pickens when confronted by Florida militia. Fort Pickens was never taken by the Confederacy during the war.

Three additional companies of the 3ᵈ Infantry arrived at Indianola on April 13, preparatory to embarking for New York. These troops were under the command of Lieutenant Colonel Electus Backus. They were to embark on the steamer *Star of the West*. Problems arose with the transport and they were sent to New York on the *Mystic*, while the ship *Horace* and the schooner *Urbana* later carried the men of the 1ˢᵗ Infantry and the two companies of the 8ᵗʰ Infantry which were able to escape the closing Confederate trap.

On April 14, 1861, South Carolina militia fired on Fort Sumter. By April 17, the situation in the East worsened as the result of the fall of Fort Sumter and the calling for volunteers by Abraham Lincoln. When Lincoln made that call, an act which was not yet a declaration of war, other states in the South began their secession process. Soon after, delegates to a Richmond convention passed a resolution wherein Virginia agreed to secede from the Union and join the Confederacy.

News of the Fort Sumter surrender reached San Antonio by April 17. After that the situation relative to the still departing Federal garrisons changed. Texas militia units quickly gathered at San Antonio with the full intention of arresting the Department of Texas commander. Colonel Waite wrote the Adjutant General's Office in Washington, as to the change in the political situation, reporting:

> I have the honor to inform you that a force of Texas State troops is now assembled in this city, and I have this evening learned that the officers, etc., here stationed will be arrested tomorrow, and held as prisoners of war. Two transports have sailed with troops, and it is hoped and expected that the third, Star of the West, will sail in a day or two with the whole force now in camp at Green Lake. There will then remain seven companies of the Eighth Infantry, numbering, say, 370, the headquarters of that regiment, and the headquarters of the department. The Eighth Infantry will not reach Indianola before the 10th of May, if permitted to proceed to the coast. This, of course, requires that a fourth transport should be sent out for the embarkation of these troops.[27]

On April 20 Colonel Waite and the military staff in San Antonio surrendered to Texas State militia. The Department of Texas leadership were unofficially held as prisoners of war based upon Lincoln's call for volunteers, rather than a formal declaration of war. Waite and his staff were paroled, but could not leave the vicinity of San Antonio.

Major C.C. Sibley, commanding the remains of the 3[d] Infantry Regiment, in the absence of the actual commanders, was near the point of transport for his troops by April 16, 1861. Sibley had traveled some two-hundred and thirty miles from Fort McIntosh, picking up Federal troops on the way. His force joined with other units waiting to evacuate. On April 25 Major Sibley, confronted by a Confederate ultimatum, surrendered his mixed and very strong force, consisting of two companies of the 1st Infantry, with the adjutant and non-commissioned staff and band, along with three companies of the 3[d] Infantry and two companies of the 8th Infantry. Nine officers surrendered with this force to the state militia commanded by Colonel Earl van Dorn, Confederate States Army.

Sibley earlier made attempts to disembark some of his force, troops which had boarded the *Star of the West* before that vessel was itself captured. On April 24 three steamers full of Confederate troops arrived at the disembarkation point and, rather than defend his rights under the Twiggs agreement, Major Sibley surrendered under the most favorable terms he could obtain. No shots were fired by either side.[28]

The surrender of Major Sibley's force had a written document associated with it. There were few differences between the document Major Lynde signed at San Augustine Springs and that signed by Major Sibley. The latter received no approbation of cowardice for signing these terms, as Lynde did. The agreement stated:

> Articles of agreement this day entered into between Maj. C. C. Sibley, of the U.S. Army, on the one part, and Col. Earl Van Dorn, of the C.S. Army, on the other part, viz:
>
> It is stipulated and agreed to that the United States troops, officers, and men, shall become prisoners of war, with the privilege of giving their paroles of honor if officers, and their oaths if soldiers, not to bear arms or exercise any of the function of their office, under their commissions or enlistments, against the Confederate States of America, unless an exchange of prisoners shall be made, or until released by the authority of the President of the Confederate States. The arms and equipments of the men, and all the public property in the possession of the company commanders, to be given up to an agent, appointed for the purpose, on board the transport which shall be employed to convey those who may desire it to the United States; private property to be unmolested.
>
> It is further stipulated and agreed to, that all the officers and men who shall give their paroles and oaths, as above stated, shall be allowed to pass unmolested through the Confederate States of America, by the way of Galveston and up the Mississippi River to any point they may see fit to go within the limits of the United States of America, or by any other route they may see fit to take.[29]

Sibley's troops disembarked, with families, children, and personal, as well as public, property. They were not lined up in the field, ready to do battle with an enemy when ordered to do so. Sibley's troops were not a fighting force. They were an abandoning force, with all the baggage that term implies.

The words 'prisoners of war' is misleading. There was no declaration of war by either side following the firing on Fort Sumter. That action did not take place officially until July, although many men on both sides assumed the war to be on following the cannonading. In New Mexico Territory, no war order is known to have been issued. During the interval between Fort Sumter in April and Bull Run in July, both sides began building and training their respective armies. The confusion of the status of the conflict not only led to the sad surrender of all forces in Texas but carried over into the situation in New Mexico Territory.

Even the Texans, the more warlike of the two sides at this point, were reluctant to shoot. They preferred to see the Federal forces lay down their arms. Not a single member of the Texas militia is recorded as having fired his weapon in anger. Had there been war this certainly would not have been the case.

Two former long-time Fort Fillmore officers, Captain Andrew Bowman and Captain William Whipple, were the subject of a letter written aboard the schooner *Urbana* on their way to New York after being paroled. Bowman and Whipple were among the 3rd Infantrymen who hoped to escape the Confederate trap at Indianola. Finding they were too late in doing so Bowman, the senior officer, surrendered the arms and men aboard the ships to Confederate authorities. The officers and men were disarmed, and immediately paroled. 1st Lieutenant James B. Greene, 1st Infantry, described the entire incident to C.C. Sibley, 3d Infantry, in a letter dated May 1, 1861:

> In compliance with verbal directions from you, I left the command on the 24th of April, then on two schooners anchored just within the bar of Passo Caballo, and with a party of two non-commissioned officers and twenty-three privates, under the command of Capt. A.W. Bowman, of the Third Infantry, proceeded to the wharf at Powderhorn. We left in the morning in the steamer Fashion, and arrived in the afternoon at the

wharf at Powderhorn. Captain Bowman told me nothing as to what his orders were, but shortly after arriving at Powderhorn he directed me to proceed, in company with Lieutenant Whipple, to Lavaca, and endeavor to secure the brig Mystic, which brig had already been hired for the transportation of the command by Lieutenant Whipple, but for some cause had been kept back.

Lavaca is distant from Powderhorn sixteen miles. We left at about 6 in the evening, and returned at about 12 the same night, without being able to effect anything definite, and I learned afterwards that the brig had been seized by a band of armed men, although at the time I knew it not.

On my return to the Fashion at about 12 the same night, I was informed of the existence of a rumor that our command was to be taken prisoners. I could not find the origin of the rumor satisfactorily, and on consideration of the compact between the State of Texas and General Twiggs concerning the exit of the United States troops from the State, I thought the rumor an idle one. Nevertheless, willing to err on the safe side, if at all, I determined to get up steam on the Fashion and return down the bay to the schooners. On examination I discovered that the fireman and all the hands of the steamer, as well as the engineer, had left the boat. Early the next morning I discovered a steam propeller coming down the bay, and when it came nearer I discovered that it was filled with men, surrounded by a barricade of cotton bales. I immediately informed Captain Bowman of this fact. The steam propeller came down to the pier-head below where we were fastened, and made fast. Shortly after, a party of men, consisting of one hundred or more, came to the shore end of the pier. Captain Bowman left the steamer and went on shore. After remaining on shore about two hours or more, he returned with a paper containing a written agreement, by which the troops on the steamer were to deliver up their arms and surrender themselves, "prisoners of war," to be at liberty to go where they chose, after swearing not to bear arms against the "Confederate States of America," during the now existing war between the Confederate States and the United States, unless exchanged or released. I immediately had the arms stacked, and read the agreement to the men of the command; told them they were at liberty to leave the vessel and go where they chose, as far as I was concerned, and left the ship myself.[30]

Save for seven companies of the 8th Infantry Regiment, then still making their slow progress down the military road toward San Antonio, the sad story of the Federal surrender in Texas was at an end.

NOTES - Chapter 2

1. Twiggs to Scott, January 15, 1861. The Honorable Elihu Root, Secretary of War, et al, *The War of the Rebellion: A Compilation of the Official Records of the Union and Confederate Armies, 128 Volumes.* Harrisburg PA: The National Historical Society, 1985. (Hereafter cited as (specific letter referenced), *Civil War Letters.*)

2. Twiggs to Assistant Adjutant General, January 18, 1861, *Civil War Letters.*

3. Houston to Twiggs, January 20, 1861, *Civil War Letters.*

4. Twiggs, Special Orders Number 10, January 22, 1861, *Civil War Letters.*

5. Twiggs to Cooper, January 23, 1861, *Civil War Letters.*

6. Special Order Number 22, January 28, 1861, Adjutant General's Department, Washington D. C. *Civil War Letters.*

7. Special Orders Number 13, January 28, 1861, *Civil War Letters.*

8. Thomas to Twiggs, January 31, 1861, *Civil War Letters.*

9. Thomas to Waite, February 4, 1861, *Civil War Letters.*

10. Twiggs to Messrs Devine, Maverick and Luckett, February 17, 1861, *Civil War Letters.*

11. Devine, Maverick and Luckett, Texas commissioners, to D.E. Twiggs, February 17, 1861, *Civil War Letters.*

12. Carpenter to Commanding Officer, State Troops of Texas, February 18, 1861, *Civil War Letters.*

13. Dalrymple to Carpenter, February 18, 1861, *Civil War Letters.*

14. Carpenter to Dalrymple, February 18, 1861, *Civil War Letters.*

15. Nichols to Hill, and reply, February 22, 1861, *Civil War Letters.*

16. Maury to Assistant Adjutant General, Department of Texas, February 23, 1861, M1102, Rolls 12/13.

17. Smith to Assistant Adjutant General, Department of Texas, March 1, 1861, *Civil War Letters.*

18. Nichols to Headquarters Department of Texas, February 26, 1861, *Civil War Letters.*

19. McCulloch to Carpenter, February 28, 1861, *Civil War Letters.*

20. Morris to Waite, February 28, 1861, *Civil War Letters.*

21. Waite to Thomas, March 16, 1861, *Civil War Letters*.

22. Backus to Cooper, March 30, 1861, *Civil War Letters*.

23. Luckett to Waite, March 22, 1861, *Civil War Letters*.

24. Waite to Assistant Adjutant-General, Washington D.C., March 26, 1861, *Civil War Letters*.

25. Waite to Assistant Adjutant-General, Washington D.C., March 27, 1861, *Civil War Letters*.

26. Waite to Assistant Adjutant-General, April 1, 1861, M1102, *Civil War Letters*.

27. Waite to Assistant Adjutant-General, Washington, D.C., April 19, 1861, *Civil War Letters*.

28. Sibley to Assistant Adjutant-General, Washington D.C., April 25, 1861, *Civil War Letters*.

29. Sibley Surrender Document, April 25, 1861, *Civil War Letters*.

30. Greene to Sibley, May 1, 1861, *Civil War Letters*.

3

LIKE LEMMINGS MARCHING TO THE SEA

Brevet-Major and Infantry Captain P.T. Sprague, 8th Infantry, then on leave at Albany, New York, was notified by the Headquarters of the Army in New York City that he was to delay his departure for Fort Fillmore in New Mexico Territory until February 20, 1861. Brevet-Major Sprague was the commanding officer of Company 'E,' then commanded at Fort Fillmore by young 2[d] Lieutenant Royal Thaxter Frank. Sprague never arrived at Fort Fillmore. The American Civil War got in the way. Had he reported, he would have found his company gone.[1]

On January 31, Colonel Thomas Fauntleroy completed his task of issuing orders for the four 8th Infantry companies to leave his command for their new posting. Fauntleroy cannot possibly have been unaware of the situation that was developing in Texas. Fauntleroy's four companies were safely out of any debacle that might threaten to engulf the other regiments then serving in that Department. It is true the headquarters of the 8th was in San Antonio, but that situation never bothered anyone before in the case of companies that were on detached service. In effect, those in New Mexico in late January operated completely independent from their headquarters, and were not even in communications with the parent unit. Fauntleroy could have ordered them to stay put and await events. He did not.

By February 1 the Texas legislature had passed a resolution of secession. On that day Royal Frank's Company 'E' was still safe at Fort Fillmore. They were waiting for the other three companies under the command of Brevet-Lieutenant Colonel Reeve to arrive from Fort Craig. It is not known when the soldiers of Company 'E' learned of the Texas secession, but one would assume they knew before they left for Fort Bliss on February 18.

The War Department in Washington, knowing of the hazardous situation being faced by their troops in Texas, and realizing the tragedy resulting from Brevet-Major General Twiggs's actions, made no attempt to countermand the order setting the 8th Infantry Regiment on the road, and hence to its doom. Orders could easily have been sent to Fauntleroy in New Mexico or Waite in Texas. There was plenty of time to turn the 8th Infantry around. The fate of one regiment was probably at too low a level for decision makers at a time when they had bigger fish to fry.

On February 22 as the Texas militia began receiving the surrender of all Federal forces and equipment in Texas, the last company of the 8th Infantry, now commanded by Brevet-Lieutenant Colonel Reeve, arrived at Fort Bliss. Reeve was to take overall command of the seven 8th Infantry companies headed for San Antonio, those formerly stationed in New Mexico and at Forts Bliss, Quitman, and Davis.

As the 8th Infantry troops prepared to march south a Lieutenant Jones of that regiment, returning from New Orleans with $30,000 to pay the troops, was arrested and his funds were confiscated by representatives of the state of Texas. Brevet-Colonel Carlos Waite complained to the Texas authorities about the confiscation, but made no other attempts to recover the funds. A letter was sent on March 12 from Waite to Lieutenant Colonel Lorenzo Thomas in Washington, telling of the departure of the 8th Infantry companies from Fort Bliss as of February 21st. Waite said:

> I have the honor to inform you that a communication, under date of 25th ultimo, was received on the 8th instant from Brevet-Colonel Reeve, Captain, Eighth Infantry, advising me of the arrival at that post [Fort Bliss] of the "four

companies of the Eighth Infantry recently stationed in the Department of New Mexico—the last one, Company B, arriving on the 21st instant."

Brevet Major Sprague's company ['E,' 8th Infantry] left Fort Bliss the 25th ult. for Fort Davis, under Lieutenant Frank, Eighth Infantry.[2]

What appears as near treasonous conduct to a historian today, because of the apparent collusion of higher authority to ensure the humiliation and defeat of the 8th Infantry, must in actuality be attributed to the fact that there was no 'official' civil war yet in progress. There was no apparent strategic planning as to what would happen if war came. Waite showed absolutely no understanding, as of February 21, that the 8th Infantry, or indeed any of the Federal forces then in New Mexico, were under any threat from the seceded state of Texas. Since neither Colonel Thomas nor Colonel Waite joined the Confederacy, one can only believe that they could not conceive of the civil conflict that was nearing. They were only intent in withdrawing all troops under their command from Texas, not with any strategic planning revolving around what might happen to New Mexico, or California, if they were to continue following their current orders.

One might point the finger of blame at the Southern sympathies of Brevet-Captain Maury, the Department adjutant, or Colonel Fauntleroy for the fate of the 8th Infantry. However, it seems nothing that happened to the troops can be laid strictly at that Confederate duo's doorstep. The Army high command in Washington authorized the transfer of the 8th Infantry, motives unknown, and was aware and involved in the issue the entire time.

By March 13, 1861, three companies of the 8th Infantry were still at Fort Bliss, and an additional four companies, including Company 'E,' under 2d Lieutenant Royal Thaxter Frank were along the military road at Fort Quitman. The companies were staggered on their march through the western desert country, since the availability of water necessitated their marching separately so as to not abuse limited water resources were all the troops to arrive at a spring at once. They linked up later at Fort Clark. The troops marched all the way to Green Lake, near Indianola, Texas, on the Gulf Coast, where they boarded transports for the East. Brevet-Colonel Waite intended by April 10 to have sufficient transport ready to take forty-five officers and thirteen hundred men.[3]

As of March 27, Colonel Waite reported that three companies of the 1st Infantry, four companies of the 3d Infantry, two companies of the 8th Infantry, and six companies of the 2d cavalry had passed through San Antonio on their way to Green Lake. The remainder of the 8th Infantry companies were expected to reach Green Lake after April 15 or 20, a truly unfortunate arrival date, given the events at Fort Sumter as of April 12-14.[4]

All seemed to be going according to Twiggs' agreement plan through the first weeks of April. On the fateful April 17, with two 8th Infantry companies transiting toward Indianola with C.C. Sibley's force and the other seven companies of the regiment marching on the road between Fort Davis and Fort Clark, news of the surrender of Fort Sumter in South Carolina reached Texas. Lincoln's subsequent call for volunteers brought with it an immediate change in the goals and attitude of the seceded Texas government. The Texas agreement with General Twiggs was considered no longer operative. Rumors spread in San Antonio that all Federal forces were to be considered prisoners of war. Colonel Waite immediately reported the change in the Twiggs agreement and in his status as commander of the Department of Texas in a letter to the Adjutant General in Washington, saying:

> I have the honor to inform you that a force of Texas State troops is now assembled in this city, and I have this evening learned that the officers, etc., here stationed will be arrested to morrow, and held as prisoners of war. Two transports have sailed with troops, and it is hoped and expected that the third, Star of the West, will sail in a day or two with the whole force now in camp at Green Lake. There will then remain seven companies of the Eighth Infantry, numbering, say 370, the headquarters of that regiment, and the headquarters of the department. The Eighth Infantry will not reach Indianola before the 10th of May, if permitted to proceed to the coast. This, of

course, requires that a fourth transport should be sent out for the embarkation of these troops.[5]

It was not until April 23 that Colonel Waite and his Department of Texas staff were forced to surrender. On that same day the troops under the command of Major C.C. Sibley, nearing Indianola, and with some soldiers already in the process of disembarking, were surrendered by their commander, as was earlier related.

By April 23 all of the troops, save the outlying 8th Infantry formations, were either surrendered and in captivity or had departed the state before Fort Sumter. A trap was set for the remaining 8th Infantry companies by Texas authorities at a point near San Antonio. On May 9 Brevet-Lieutenant Colonel L.V.D. Reeve surrendered his seven companies, without a shot being fired, near San Lucas Spring, Texas. Marching with Reeve into a prison camp near San Antonio were 1st Lieutenant Henry Lazelle and 2[d] Lieutenant Royal Thaxter Frank, both of whom had only recently commanded the post at Fort Fillmore. Another Fort Fillmore post commander, Captain Henry Freedley, 3[d] Infantry Regiment, happened to be with the column of 8th Infantry and was captured as well. Such was the finality of the disgraceful order sending this regiment from safety and need in New Mexico to prison camps in Texas.

How Reeve's surrender came about is important to what happened only two months later in New Mexico at San Augustine Springs. The two forces, that commanded by Reeve and that commanded by Isaac Lynde, were roughly comparable, although Reeve had no mounted contingent. Both forces were composed of seven companies of an infantry regiment; both surrenders happened after the fall of Fort Sumter and before the receiving of notification that hostilities had begun between the United States of America and the Confederate States.

Should the 8th Infantry Regiment have fought it out, before surrendering? Out of context one would think they should have. After all, they were fully armed soldiers, under an officer's orders. But, as with Major C.C. Sibley's larger contingent, the seven companies of the 8ᵗʰ Infantry serving with Reeve were not truly a fighting formation. They were a band of soldiers saddled with wives, children, private and public property. They were not a free-wheeling regiment in the field seeking a fight with an enemy. They were, in fact, obeying an order to leave Texas as per an agreement between General Twiggs and the state authorities. The fact that Confederate demands for their surrender rendered that agreement invalid, did not change the situation in which they found themselves. One simply did not put women and children in front of the guns, not in 1861.

Were Major Sibley and Brevet-Lieutenant Colonel Reeve cowards for surrendering without a fight? They were not accused of being cowards, their reputations remaining unsullied by these actions. No one viciously challenged their behavior as disgraceful. No one came forward to defame their reputations forever. West Point did not put an asterisk by their names, with the title coward implied. They flamed not a single cap from a single musket, yet they escaped all approbation.

Brevet-Lieutenant Colonel Reeve reported on the surrender of his command at San Lucas Spring, Texas, in a brief letter to the Adjutant General's Office in Washington on May 12, 1861:

> I take the earliest opportunity possible to inform you that the six companies of the Eighth Infantry under my command, while marching for the coast under an agreement made between General Twiggs (late of the U.S. Army) and the State of Texas, to the effect that the troops should leave the State, were met by a force under command of Col. Earl Van Dorn, of the Southern Confederacy, and made prisoners of war. This occurred on the 9th Instant, at San Lucas Spring, fifteen miles west of San Antonio. The force under my command, comprising the garrisons of Forts Bliss, Quitman and Davis, amounted to an aggregate, when leaving the latter post, of 320. This embraces ten officers, two hospital stewards and twelve musicians. Colonel Bomfors, Sixth Infantry, was also with the command. On the day of surrender my command numbered 270 bayonets, being thus reduced by sickness, desertions and stragglers (some of whom have since joined) who remained at Castroville from drunkenness and other causes. The force

opposed to me numbered, as (then variously estimated at from 1500 to 1700 men) since ascertained to be, was 1370 aggregate, the total being 848 cavalry, 361 infantry, and 95 artillery, with six field pieces.

When the demand for a surrender was made, I was told that the force opposed to me was "overwhelming." I had halted in a good position for defense, and could have been overpowered only by a greatly superior force; and as none was before me, I declined to surrender without the presentation of such force. It was on the march, and soon came in sight, but I was not satisfied of its strength until an officer of my command was permitted to examine and report to me the character and probable number of the forces. Upon his report I deemed resistance utterly hopeless, and therefore surrendered. My command is now encamped near the head of the San Antonio River, awaiting the orders of President Davis, to whom a messenger has been dispatched by Colonel Van Dorn. The officers on duty with the command were Captain Blake, Lieutenants Bliss, Lazelle, Peck, Frank, Van Horn and W.G. Jones, Eighth Infantry; Lieutenant Freedley, Third Infantry, and Assistant Surgeon Peters, Medical Department. A more detailed report will be made as soon as practicable.[6]

Colonel Earl Van Dorn was the opposing Confederate leader at the time of the Reeves surrender. Van Dorn reported on the fate of the prisoners of war he was then holding, stating:

... proclamation of the President of the United States declaring certain persons 'pirates' under the laws of the United States for seizures of vessels or goods by persons acting by authority of the Confederate States, I have determined to hold these prisoners of war until I receive further instructions from you. If the officers prefer it I shall allow them to proceed to Montgomery on parole, to report to you for your decision."

Van Dorn was addressing Brigadier General Samuel Cooper, Inspector General of the Confederate Army in Montgomery, Alabama, the town which was still the Confederate capital in May. Samuel Cooper was also the former adjutant general of the United States Army when the now surrendered 8th Infantry was first ordered to march into Texas. No doubt he was pleased by the end product of his handiwork, whether he set up the action deliberately or not.[7]

Brevet-Lieutenant Colonel Reeve later wrote a more detailed report on the activities of the 8th Infantry units after they left New Mexico. From this letter we know he had ample opportunity to save his command by returning to New Mexico, but chose not to do so for reasons he clearly stated:

> In connection with the report which I have this day forwarded, relating to the surrender of the battalion of the Eight Infantry under my command to the forces of the Confederate States of America, near this place, I also present the following details of the latter part of the march, and the circumstances which determined that surrender.
>
> This report was not transmitted with the other, as it is extremely uncertain whether any reports of an official character are permitted to pass through the post office here or those elsewhere in the South.
>
> On leaving Fort Bliss sufficient transportation could be procured to carry subsistence for only forty days, in which time it was expected the command would reach San Antonio, making some little allowance for detentions by the way.
>
> At Forts Quitman and Davis, stores were taken to last the commands from those posts to San Antonio, not being able to carry more with the transportation at hand. From Camp Hudson to Fort Clark, persons were occasionally seen on the road which appeared to be watching our movements, but they said they belonged to rangers who had been on a scout.
>
> At Fort Clark, where I arrived on the 2d of May, I learned that the mails had been detained for several days to prevent me from receiving information. It was reported by a stage passenger that the officers at San Antonio had been made prisoners of war. On all these subjects there were contradictory reports, and no information could be obtained which would warrant any hostile act on my part. Such supplies as were called for were readily furnished, and offers of services were proffered by the commanding officer. This did not look much like hostility nor did I really suspect any. The garrison had been reinforced (being about 200 men), the post fortified to some extent, guns loaded and matches lighted on our approach; yet there did not appear any hostile intent towards us, as the explanation for all this was, that they "had heard that I had orders to attack and take Fort Clark."

From this point rumors daily reached me, but so indefinite and contradictory as to afford no sure ground for hostile action on my part; and by taking such I could not know but I should be the first to break the treaty under which we were marching.

On reaching Uvalde on the 5th, I felt more apprehension of hostility, though rumors were still very contradictory. To attempt, from this point, to return to New Mexico for the purpose of saving the command, would have been impracticable, for I had but five days' rations, and our transportation was too much broken down to make the march without corn (which could not be had), even if everything but subsistence had been abandoned. Behind us was the mounted force at Fort Clark, and a large mounted force said to be at San Antonio, reported to be from 700 to 2000. At this time the only other method of escape left was to cross the Rio Grande, this being easy of accomplishment, but of very doubtful propriety, particularly as it was yet uncertain whether we should not only break the treaty with Texas, but also compromise the United States with Mexico by crossing troops into her soil.

On the 6th, while continuing our march, we heard that those companies at the coast had been disarmed, and that in all probability we would be also on our arrival there; that there would be a force of from 2000 to 6000 men against us. We then had no course open to us but to proceed, and, unless overpowered by numbers, to endeavor to fight our way to the coast, with the hope that some way of escape would be opened to us. On the 7th we heard that there were not more than 700 men in San Antonio, and such a force I knew would not be able to overpower us; and still with strong hope that we might be able to advance successfully, I purchased (on the 8th) at Castroville a small additional supply of subsistence stores (all I could), enough for two days, which included the 12th instant, but could have been made to last several days, had I a reasonable prospect of seizing more in San Antonio. Before reaching Castroville I learned that there were troops encamped on the west side of the Leon, several miles from San Antonio; that there were cavalry, infantry, and artillery, with four guns. I encamped on the 8th on the east side of the Medina, opposite to Castroville. Late that evening I heard that the enemy would march to surround us in our camp, and I had before heard that a section of artillery was on the way down from Fort Clark, following on our rear; and there was further report that it would pass us that night on the way to San Antonio. To avoid surprise and be in possession of plenty of water, I marched that night at 12 o'clock to reach the Lioncito [sic], six miles east of the Medina, and on my arrival there, finding no signs of the advance of the enemy, I marched on three miles further to a point suggested and brought to my memory by Lieut. Z.R. Bliss, Eighth Infantry, called San Lucas Spring. There is quite a high hill a few hundred yards from the spring, having some houses, corrals, etc. which, together with the command-ing position and a well of water in the yard, rendered this point a very strong one for a small command. This place is known as Allen's Hill. It is eight miles from where the enemy was encamped, and there I made a halt to await his advance, and parked the wagon train for defense; all of which preparations were made a little after sunrise on the 9th.

About 9 o'clock two officers approached, bearing a white flag and a message from Colonel Van Dorn, demanding an unconditional surrender of the United States troops under my command, stating that he had an "overwhelming force." I declined to surrender without the presentation of such a force or a report of an officer, whom I would select from my command, of its character and capacity of compelling a surrender. The advance of the enemy came in sight over a rise of ground about a mile distant, and as the whole force soon came in sight and continued in march down the long slope, Colonel Van Dorn's messenger returned to me with directions to say that, "if that display of force was not sufficient I could send an officer to examine it." I replied that it was "not sufficient." I directed Lieutenant Bliss to proceed, conducted by the same messenger, to make a careful examination of the enemy. He was taken to a point so distant that nothing satisfactory could be ascertained, and he informed his conductors that he would, "make no report upon such an examination." This being reported to Colonel Van Dorn, he permitted as close an examination as Lieutenant Bliss desired. The enemy had formed line on the low ground some half-mile in front of my position, perpendicular to and crossing the road, and neither force could be plainly seen by the other in consequence of the high bushes which intervened. Lieutenant Bliss rode the whole length of the enemy's line within thirty yards, estimating the numbers and examining the character of his armament. He reported to me that the cavalry were armed with rifles and revolvers; the infantry with muskets (some rifle) and revolvers; that there were four pieces of artillery, with from ten to twelve men each; that he ascertained the force at 1200 at least, and there might be 1,500 (since ascertained to be 1,400). With this force before me, and odds of about five to one, being short of provisions, having no hope of re-inforcements, no means of leaving the coast, even should any portion of the command succeed in reaching it, and with every probability of utter annihilation in making the attempt, without any prospect of good to be attained, I deemed that stubborn resistance and consequent bloodshed and sacrifice of life would be inexcusable and criminal, and I therefore surrendered.

Colonel Van Dorn immediately withdrew his force, and permitted us to march to San Antonio with our arms and at our leisure. We arrived there on the 10th, and on the 11th an officer was sent to our camp to receive our arms and other public property, all of which was surrendered.

I will state here that we have been treated, in the circumstances of our capture, with generosity and delicacy, and harrowed and wounded as our feelings are, we have not had to bear personal contumely and insult.[8]

Reeve sent forth an officer to check the opposing command and make an estimate of its strength before surrendering. The officers who surrendered their forces in Texas used estimates of enemy strength as reason for their not fighting. There seems to have been an unwritten custom that if you could count one more enemy than yourself you could somehow surrender with honor. If there was one less enemy in the opposing force the surrendering officer might be open to a charge of cowardice; hence the effort to justify an inferior position, true or not. Waite, Sibley and Reeve all made the same claims of inferiority as being why they did not engage the enemy forces. Isaac Lynde tried the same tack, but he was not believed, whereas the others were not even questioned.

The whole situation appears rather laughable, if not somewhat deadly. If enemy troop strength estimates were a valid reason for not fighting there would never be any war. One group would simply mass a bunch of people, point to some perceived advantage in numbers, and demand surrender of the opposition, who would immediately acquiesce by laying down their arms. Yet in the earliest days of the American Civil War such actions were not unknown. After Bull Run the inferior force fought, as it should.

Major Isaac Lynde paid the supreme price for performing the same head count as Reeve did, using it as a means to surrender with honor, then found himself proven in the final bargain to have miscounted. Did he miscount? That is a matter of conjecture that will be interpreted later. The numbers game allowed an officer to escape negative reaction to their decisions, if the review board afterwards 'believed' the count. Reeve certainly got away with questionable conduct in not even firing one volley from his troops, who were all standing to arms. Major C.C. Sibley did the same before Reeve when he surrendered without a fight. Neither Reeve or Sibley mentioned the presence of women, children, private property and large quantities of public property, then with their columns. Using these as an excuse for not fighting would have been unacceptable, even though they may have been the most important factor in the surrender.

Reeve's comments on not returning to the safety of New Mexico when he had ample opportunity to do so appear less satisfying at this distance in history, especially when he didn't even try. He believed he was marching into the path of superior Texas forces. He knew they were unfriendly, if not hostile. No doubt the move into Texas had long been a subject of inflamed conversation among the officers and men of the 8th Infantry Regiment. By May 6, when he arrived at Uvalde, Reeve was well aware that at least the Texans thought they were at war. As such, his claims of being unable to return to New Mexico because of sustenance needs, and the broken-down condition of deteriorated wagons, seems the poorest of excuses. It was his right, in enemy territory, to confiscate whatever he needed to save his command. Vouchers could have been provided assuring of future reimbursement, if he was not clear on his rights. Reeve should have taken what he needed and returned up the road to hold Fort Davis, Fort Quitman, and Fort Bliss for the Union.

This is not an attempt to demean the reputation of Brevet-Lieutenant Colonel Reeve. He found himself in a very tenuous set of circumstances beyond his control, and did what he thought was right. Had the date been May 1862 instead of May 1861 he may have reacted differently. Reeve could not even be sure that if he fought he might be bringing on the civil war nobody wanted. Indeed, Fort Sumter had fallen and Lincoln had called for volunteers but, in effect, nothing else had happened. Southern troops had not yet fired on Northern troops in a set piece battle. There were no precedents upon which Brevet-Lieutenant Colonel Reeve could draw for making decisions. He took the safe way out, saving his troops, the wives, children, and servants traveling with his command, as well as the private property.

The colors of the 8th Infantry Regiment were in mortal danger of being captured by Texas military forces that May. They were saved by a soldier of the 8th, Corporal John C. Hesse. Hesse described his act in an appeal to receive the Medal of Honor on September 6, 1864:

> Report of Corporal John C. Hesse, Company A, Eighth U.S. Infantry, of the rescue of the colors of his regiment, at San Antonio, Tex.
>
> Believing that I am entitled to receive a "medal of honor," as provided by the resolution of Congress under date of July 12, 1862, to provide for the presentation of medals of honor to enlisted men of the Army and volunteer forces who have distinguished or may distinguish themselves in battle during the present war, I have the honor to make the following statement:
>
> At the outbreak of the rebellion the headquarters of the Eighth U.S. Infantry were stationed at San Antonio, Tex. I was a corporal of Company A of that regiment, and detailed as a clerk at its headquarters. On the 23rd of April, 1861, the officers and a few enlisted men at that time present at San Antonio were taken prisoners by the rebel troops under the command of Colonel Van Dorn. All the officers, with the exception of Lieut. Edward L. Hartz, adjutant Eighth Infantry, left a few days afterwards for the States. A few days subsequent, upon going to the former office of the regimental headquarters, the building being then in possession and under control of the rebels, I met there Lieutenant Hartz and Serg. Maj. Joseph K. Wilson, Eighth Infantry (now second lieutenant Eighth Infantry). Our regimental colors being in the

office, Lieutenant Hartz proposed to us to take the colors from the staffs, conceal them beneath our clothing, and try to carry them off. We did so. I took the torn color which the regiment had carried through the Mexican War, put it around my body under my shirt and blouse, and passed out of the building, which was strongly guarded by the rebels. Fortunately the rebels did not suspect what a precious load we carried concealed with us, for if they had our lives would not have been worth much. We put the colors in one of Hartz's trunks, and next day left San Antonio for the North. On the route we guarded the colors with our lives, always fearing that the rebels might find out what we had taken away and come after us; but they did not, and we arrived safe with our colors on the 26th of May, 1861, in Washington City, and turned them over to the regiment.

Under these circumstances I think that I am entitled to the honor of receiving a medal, as I believe that Congress intended to award them to enlisted men who have done acts similar to mine. I therefore very respectfully request that I may receive one, believing that I have performed one of the highest duties of a soldier, having saved the colors of my regiment, and it will always be a happy day for me if I can see my regiment marching with their colors flying, and can say, "That color I have carried on my body, and have rescued it from the hands of the rebels." [9]

Captain Edward L. Hartz, formerly 8th Infantry, held the statement as true. On September 10, 1864, a Medal of Honor was engraved and presented to Corporal John C. Hesse, for saving the 8th Infantry Regiment colors. The Secretary of War so directed.

Hesse's award of the Medal of Honor is important to the rest of this story from one standpoint. At San Augustine Springs the colors of the 7th Infantry were open to capture by Texans as well. What happened to those colors would not bring their savior a Medal of Honor. Instead, his name would go down in history as being the base lackey of a coward and a man worthy of the contempt of an entire nation. As with everything about the surrender at San Augustine Springs, a totally different standard was applied than that used in Texas.

With the surrender of the 8th Infantry Regiment the sad story of the United States Army forces in Texas came to an end. Following the surrenders there was an immediate concern among the Confederate leaders over the defense of the western Texas borders. The Texans established two lines of defense, the second line being the more important to the situation at Fort Fillmore. The second line embraced the former military posts of Fort Bliss, Fort Quitman, Fort Davis, Camp Stockton, Fort Lancaster, Fort Clark, Fort Inge, and Camp Wood. This line, which in actuality was nothing but the old U.S. line of forts from San Antonio to Fort Bliss, was to be garrisoned by the 2[d] Regiment, Texas Mounted Rifles, Teel's Company of Artillery, McCallister's Company of Infantry, and another battery of artillery. The whole was to be commanded by a Colonel Ford. This force was certainly not large for that region of coverage. The force to be stationed at Fort Bliss was named as being two companies of cavalry, Teel's Company of Artillery, and McCallister's Company of Infantry. One cavalry company each was to be stationed at Fort Davis, Camp Stockton and Fort Lancaster. Two companies of cavalry were to be placed at Fort Clark, one company of cavalry and a battery of light artillery at Fort Inge, one company of cavalry at Camp Wood, and one company of cavalry at Fort McIntosh. Thus, the larger number of troops were to be stationed at Fort Bliss, closest to the Union forces.

There was no intent in the original orders that they form an assault force to attack New Mexico Territory. That this was a purely defensive maneuver can be found in a paragraph of Texas General Order No. 8 (1861) which states that "The commanders of these lines will be held responsible for their defense against the enemies of the Confederate States, as far as it is in their power." The key word was "defense." Lieutenant-Colonel John Baylor was to give the necessary orders for these assignments, serving as second in command to Colonel Ford when the latter arrived to take command.[10]

*   *   *

Although Major Isaac Lynde demonstrated little knowledge of Eastern events he must have had more information than his letters in this period indicate. Certainly, events such as the surrender of sizable units in Texas could not have escaped his interest, although his knowledge of the true situation there was probably limited to rumor and gossip passed on by travelers who came by.

On May 27, an interesting letter related to the future situation at Fort Fillmore was sent from Colonel Earl Van Dorn to Colonel Ford, commanding the 2^d Regiment, Texas Mounted Rifles. The letter shows there was already a plan to invade New Mexico, or at least to capture the garrison at Fort Fillmore. Van Dorn wrote:

> Copies of your communications to the governor and your letter to me were duly received. I am very much pleased with all you have done on your line. I herewith enclose you a copy of General Orders, No. 8, from these headquarters, wherein you will see the disposition of your regiment and your assignment to command. You will perceive that your regiment extends from Fort Bliss to Fort Inge, and, until the regiment of infantry is completely organized, as far as Brazos Santiago. The battery of artillery will be sent to Fort Inge as soon as it can be got in readiness. You had better send the artillery horses with you to Inge, as they are better adapted to that service than any of those I could have selected here from the cavalry horses. Please order all the cavalry horses and equipments turned over by the United States troops on the Rio Grande to San Antonio. Please also designate some officer of experience and discretion to receipt for all the property turned over by the State to the Confederate States at Fort Brown and Brazos Santiago, and direct him to make a complete return of the same to the chief of the staff, Major Maclin, C.S. Army. Please do the same at each one of the posts of your command.
>
> Within a short distance of El Paso or Fort Bliss there are several hundred United States troops. I have, therefore, ordered four companies there. There are five or six pieces of artillery at Forts Davis, Quitman, and Bliss, which I have ordered to Fort Bliss. It may be found practicable to capture the United States troops. You will perceive that you are authorized to concentrate the troops on your line of defense. If the United

States troops could be surprised, they could be easily taken. If they heard of your designs they could get out of your reach by falling back into New Mexico too far to be pursued. It is possible for them to retake Fort Bliss and all the public property before our troops can reach there.

I was very much pleased to know that you were cultivating friendly feelings with our neighbors over the river. I think it is our policy to do so, especially at this time. In regard to Cortinas, you will have a force soon that will enable you to crush him and his followers without trouble. I do not feel much apprehension from such a source when we have so many young men now in arms and eager for a fight.

I hardly anticipate any trouble at Brazos Santiago now. It is too near the yellow-fever season for our enemies of the North to venture any move in that quarter. You will not do so until fall. You will not discourage your command, of course, by giving expression to the opinion. You will select your point for headquarters. I suggest Fort Clark as the most central point on your line and most convenient to these headquarters.

You will perceive that I have ordered no company to Fort Quitman, although it is mentioned as one of the posts on your line. When everything is settled at Fort Bliss you can direct one of the companies there to garrison it; Forts Clark, Inge, and McIntosh, and Camp Wood are so near Fort Duncan that it is hardly necessary to garrison that post. It is completely enveloped. I would be pleased if you will inspect your line of defense at once, and make such suggestions as may be necessary. Before leaving Fort Brown please muster into the service of the Confederate States the infantry companies at Fort Brown, and put the senior officer in command, with letter of instructions for his guidance.

Having the highest opinion of your ability and discretion, I turn over the command of the Rio Grande line to you with perfect confidence that section of our frontier will be well guarded.[11]

Van Dorn appeared to be planning his own version of a twentieth century Pearl Harbor-type attack on southern New Mexico, if he could truly gain the element of surprise. The United States Army was not at war with the Texans, not yet, no declaration of war having been handed down, but the Texans certainly felt they were at war with the United States Army. Had there been a declaration of war United States troops most certainly would have taken Fort Bliss and perhaps Fort Quitman as well if they received orders from Washington to do so. The truly horrendous news is that the 8th Infantry command had abandoned several pieces of artillery in usable condition, at Fort Davis, Fort Quitman, and at Fort Bliss. This artillery played a small but key role in the Fort Fillmore drama later in July.

The United States troops in New Mexico did not yet know, as the Confederate leaders in Texas apparently did, that an order was about to be issued removing all Federal troops from the Department of New Mexico. On May 28, Colonel Van Dorn informed Colonel McCulloch, who was in charge of defending the State of Texas borders in the north, that United States troops were falling back toward Fort Leavenworth. This was not yet true, but Van Dorn's information must have come from a source close to the events which were about to transpire. One can only wonder at the source.[12]

The paroled troops of the 1st, 3d and 8th Infantry, who had managed to escape before the cannon balls falling on Fort Sumter led to the rest being made prisoners of war, arrived in New York Harbor in June. They had departed Matagorda Bay in Texas on April 25.

On June 18, at San Antonio, prisoner of war Brevet-Lieutenant Colonel Reeve was paroled and sent home upon receiving news of the death of his oldest daughter. Colonel Van Dorn allowed his departure as a matter of honor. Within a year most of the officers had been paroled. The enlisted troops of the seven 8th Infantry companies Reeve surrendered were first maintained in former U.S. Army barracks in San Antonio. Even with an effort to bring them over to the Confederate side, only a few enlisted men joined the Southern cause. The men were later moved to a camp where they would come under the more careful watch of Confederate authorities. These former 8th Infantrymen were never paroled. They were held for the duration of the war and later sent to garrison some of the same posts they once abandoned, this time without pay. What happened to them is not known. It is assumed they were eventually discharged, or simply walked away as the Confederate cause folded its tent.[13]

The question as to why none joined the Confederate cause is partially answerable. Most of the soldiers of the 8th Infantry in 1861 were either Irish or German immigrants. They had little reason to abandon the government which gave them their first opportunities in the new land. As to the non-immigrants, virtually all of them were from the North. This was because most of the recruitment was carried out in the North, and on the docks in New York City. Southern boys, long held to be military-minded, more often served in state militia units than in the Regulars, at least before the American Civil War.

NOTES - Chapter 3

1. Scott to Sprague, January 5, 1861, M1102, Rolls 13/14.
2. Waite to Thomas, March 12, 1861, *Civil War Letters.*
3. Waite to Thomas, March 13, 1861, *Civil War Letters.*
4. Waite to Assistant Adjutant General, Washington D.C., March 27, 1861, *Civil War Letters.*
5. Waite to Assistant Adjutant General, April 17, 1861, C*ivil War Letters.*
6. Reeve to Thomas, May 12,1861, *Civil War Letters.*
7. Van Dorn to Cooper, May 10, 1861, *Civil War Letters.*
8. Reeve to Thomas, May 12, 1861, *Civil War Letters.*
9. Hartz to Townsend, September 6, 1864, *Civil War Letters.*
10. General Orders Number 8, W.T. Mechling, May 24, 1861, *Civil War Letters.*
11. Van Dorn to Ford, May 27, 1861, *Civil War Letters.*
12. Earl Van Dorn to Col. H.E. McCulloch, May 28, 1861, *Civil War Letters.*
13. Reeve to Thomas, June 18, 1861, *Civil War Letters.*

4

THE BASCOM AFFAIR

O n January 9, 1861, the State of Mississippi seceded from the Union of States called the United States. The leaders and people of Mississippi believed they had a constitutional right to leave that Union. They may have, although President Abraham Lincoln's eventual determination was that they did not. On January 10, Florida seceded, followed by Alabama on January 11. Such events were remarkable, and precedent setting. On the frontier in New Mexico Territory the Army high command went on with their normal daily business in the face of such cataclysmic events, sometimes appearing impervious to the fact that the nation they served was disintegrating.

On January 2, 1861, Brevet-Lieutenant Colonel Edwin R.S. Canby, of the 10th Infantry, was newly arrived in New Mexico from the Utah Campaign. Canby commanded the recently established Fort Thomas Turner Fauntleroy, named for the current Department of New Mexico commander, as a replacement for Fort Defiance. The Department adjutant, Brevet-Captain Dabney Maury, informed Canby that two companies of the 7th Infantry were being held at Albuquerque to assist in field operations. As part of his new duties Edwin Canby was preparing to conduct a new campaign against the Navajos, even though the latter were pleading for peace after almost two years of war. Canby warned the Navajos that the ending of depredations would be the test of their sincere desire for peace. Colonel Fauntleroy agreed to allow Canby to hold a conference with the Navajo chiefs to gain time, though not necessarily to gain a peace.[1]

On that same January 2, Maury notified Brevet-Major Gabriel Rene Paul, 7th Infantry, then at Albuquerque commanding a two-company battalion, to stand in readiness to take his companies into the field if Canby needed assistance. Army terminology used in the nineteenth century in reference to 'brevet' ranks becomes important at this point. Major Isaac Lynde and Brevet-Major Gabriel Paul served together in the 7th Infantry Regiment. While Paul was on detached service at Albuquerque with his two company battalions he was acting in the rank of major, this because Paul received a brevet to that grade resulting from acts of bravery during the Mexican War. In fact, his actual Army rank was captain, a rank normally associated with command of a single company. Isaac Lynde was an actual Army major and outranked Gabriel Paul whenever the two were stationed in the same place. Thus it was that Isaac Lynde and Gabriel Paul both commanded battalions (two companies), but should the battalions be merged Lynde would have the overall command, as happened months later at Fort Fillmore.[2]

Save for the Navajo turmoil in the north, which was simmering rather than being at the point of heated conflict, there was peace in most of the Department as of January 10. That was the day Colonel Fauntleroy urged Lieutenant Colonel Pitcairn Morrison at Fort Buchanan to use the plans "for the position of buildings at Fort Buchanan, New Mexico" in constructing the post there. This peaceful message to continue building activity is an indicator that the Department of New Mexico was in no way unsettled in that period over conditions in the eastern part of the country. The United States was splitting apart and yet there was no sign in official correspondence that any disturbance was on the horizon, as far as the New Mexico command was concerned.[3]

A train of public animals and goods from Fort Buchanan destined for Fort Floyd/McLane was attacked at Burro Canyon about thirty-five miles west of the fort on January 11. Twelve public mules and four private animals were driven off. The wagon train had no escort; the teamsters were not even armed, apparently expecting no trouble because the Apaches and the Americans were at peace. Almost immediately after the express carrying this news was dispatched Major Lynde learned that another man was attacked by Indians within three miles of his post and badly wounded. The man was robbed of two mules and other property.[4]

During this same period Lynde was ordered to change the name of his post. Secretary of War John Floyd had defected to the secessionist cause on December 19, and his name was now in disfavor. The change was handled diplomatically by the Department of New Mexico. Rather than name Floyd a traitor, the resulting Department order simply changed the name without comment. Fort Floyd was to be renamed Fort McLane in honor of Captain George McLane who had recently been killed by the Navajos. The date of the official change is often given as January 15, but this date seems somewhat early, as the name Fort Floyd continued to be used in correspondence well into February.[5]

At Fort Craig, Fort Fillmore's future most famous female resident, who would help besmirch the reputation of Isaac Lynde, was in the process of packing her personal belongings. The order to move to Fort Fillmore was given her husband's company on January 20. A company was needed to replace the company of the 8th Infantry which was departing for Texas. Her name was Lydia Lane and her husband was 1st Lieutenant William Lane, Company 'A,' Regiment of Mounted Riflemen. Lydia Lane became famous because she later wrote, *I Married A Soldier*, an account of her life at various military posts in the Southwest from the 1850s to the 1880s. Some of her reminiscences are a little off in time and she had an overly protective attitude toward her husband's career and reputation, but her insights into military life in the 1850s and early 1860s are valuable.

Lydia Lane's account of the difficulty in attaining mail, which applied to all the American women who came to New Mexico in the 1850s, will serve as an introduction to a character of some importance to this study. She wrote:

First Lieutenant William B. Lane - McKee's "Fightin' man
who had to be got rid of," commanded Company 'A,' R.M.R.
Courtesy: U.S. Army Military History Institute.

The greatest drawback to my happiness, while at home, was the time required for letters to come from and go to New Mexico,—a whole month between mails, which were carried on a stage, running from Independence Missouri, and Santa Fe, New Mexico. The mail stations on the plains were few and far apart, where there were only enough hardy, determined men to look after the mules required for the stage. These stations were almost fortresses on a small scale, built of stone, with a high wall around them to protect the stock from Indians. The stage drivers were experienced frontiersmen, who knew well the risks they ran, and those who travelled with them have told me there was no time lost between stations, going at a full gallop most of the way. Often wild and unbroken animals were harnessed to the stage, and at the first crack of the whip they were off with a bound, and kept at a run or gallop, never slowing up until the house was in sight.[6]

Lydia was hardy in her opinions and rarely held back in her writings from giving them, whether to praise or condemn. She was headed for a Fort Fillmore which was in the middle stages of falling apart. Reduced to a one-company post, the days of importance for that particular adobe fortress had come and gone, or so it must have appeared to her soon after her arrival there. Forty miles to the south, in Texas, forces were gathering that would make Fort Fillmore the focus of attention, at least for one more brief moment in history.

Texas had not seceded from the Union when Lydia Lane and her husband received orders to go to Fort Fillmore, although the will to secede was everywhere apparent. At Fort Fillmore, and still out of harms way as of January 23, 1861, Company 'E,' 8th Infantry, prepared for the arrival at the post of Lane's R.M.R. company. Once 1st Lieutenant Lane arrived, 2[d] Lieutenant Royal Thaxter Frank began final preparations for marching his company to Texas as per orders.

On January 19, the State of Georgia seceded, followed on January 26 by Louisiana, the fifth and sixth states to leave the Union. Rumors must have been rife in Santa Fe that Texas might soon follow. It was at this point that an additional factor other than secession impinged on the consciousness of every officer, soldier, farmer, miner, and tradesman in the Territory of New Mexico. Out in what was later to be Arizona, a band of Pinal Indians took captive an eleven-year-old white boy named Felix, the adopted son of a squatter named John Ward. After receiving word of the boy's kidnaping, Lieutenant Colonel Pitcairn Morrison at Fort Buchanan decided to adopt a hostile posture toward the local Apaches, choosing to honor a Santa Fe directive which stated that in case Indian depredations occurred, the hostiles were to be chased and chastised.

Chase and Chastise! Those were the orders Morrison gave to young 2$^\text{d}$ Lieutenant George Nicholas Bascom as he left Fort Buchanan in an effort to find the kidnappers. Bascom was fresh from West Point, and certainly eager to obey. On January 29, 1861, he led his troops eastward toward an encounter which would forever change the relationship between the American government and the Apaches, and between the Americans and all Indians west of the Mississippi River. American soldiers fighting the Apache people over the next twenty years owed a portion of their fate to young Bascom. After leaving Fort Buchanan, he headed for the Butterfield Overland Company stage station at Apache Pass, intending to use the station as a base from which to meet or confront the Apache leader Cochise, whom Lieutenant Bascom wanted to talk to concerning the kidnaping of the boy Felix.[7]

Bascom had fifty 7$^\text{th}$ Infantry soldiers with him when he arrived at Apache Pass station. A meeting with Cochise was quickly arranged, the famous Chiricahua leader appearing at the station under a white flag of truce. During the following negotiations the Lieutenant blamed Cochise and his people for the abduction of the boy, as well as the theft of a number of cattle. He demanded Cochise bring the boy and the cattle to Fort Buchanan. When Cochise appeared both offended and indignant, the result of being wrongfully accused, Bascom ordered the peace talks tent surrounded by soldiers. Cochise drew a knife, slit the tent side open and moved to escape. Firing erupted inside and outside the tent. A bullet struck Cochise in the arm, wounding him; six Apaches of Cochise's band were taken prisoner. Heavy return fire came from nearby trees as the Apaches counterattacked. The fighting went on until nightfall. Several soldiers were wounded though none were killed. A Mr. Wallace, the stage station leader who had backed the talks, warned Bascom to leave quickly, but he did not. A short time after this terrible incident the Overland Mail stage arrived from the East and was attacked, one horse killed, the driver wounded, and a passenger also shot. The period in American history called the Indian Wars had begun.[8]

There were Indian troubles elsewhere in the Territory that January and yet four 8th Infantry companies, an armed force which was almost desperately needed in New Mexico, were being transferred. On January 31, that transfer and general Indian problems were the subject of a letter from Colonel Fauntleroy to Assistant Adjutant General Lorenzo Thomas in Washington. Fauntleroy stated:

> I have the honor to report for the information of the General-in-Chief, that I have taken proper measures for the immediate transfer of the four Companies of the 8th Infantry, serving in this Department to the Department of Texas.
>
> The occasion is a suitable one for me to acknowledge the excellent services rendered by these Companies since they have been under my command.
>
> I transmit herewith a report of Captain E.B. Holloway Commanding Company 'K,' 8th Infantry of his surprise of a party of Comanches on the 3rd October last.
>
> When the disabled condition of Captain Holloway is remembered, and the fact, that his attacking force on this occasion consisted chiefly of raw recruits never before under fire great praise seems due to him for planning & executing his attack. My absence from Hd. Qrs. at the time of its occurrence accounts for my not having sooner reported it.
>
> Colonel Canby reports that on the 19th of November 1st Lieut. Brooks, 7th Infantry, with 50 men had a sharp action with a force of 50 Navajos killing three, capturing four prisoners & seven horses with equipment and destroying a large amount of property.
>
> On December 14th. Lt. Stith 5th Infantry surprised a Camp on the Puerco, taking three prisoners and all the property & stores.
>
> December 24th the same officer surprised another small Indian force inflicting a loss of one warrior and one horse.

December 29. 30. 31. & January 3. Captain Wingate was engaged with Indians in the Chusco Mountains inflicting the loss of four warriors, nine horses and 120 sheep, besides stores. In his skirmish of January 3. Private Donohue of Company 'K', 5th Infy. was killed.

January 9. Lt. Lewis, 5th Infantry, surprised a Navajo Camp killing two Indians and capturing 17 prisoners, 8 horses and mules, and destroying property.

These affairs, although each in itself unimportant, indicates the great activity of the troops under Colonel Canby's command notwithstanding the snows have been deep—& the thermometer [was] 17 degrees below zero, his officers and men without example or hesitation continued to carry on field operations in one of the most inhospitable regions of the continent, with such success as justifies the belief that a proper peace will be concluded with the whole Nation in the conference which is to be held by Colonel Canby with the Chiefs on the 5th proximo.

Colonel Canby makes my cordial acknowledgment in his report of Captain McLaws, 7th Infantry, his second in command. He also reports very favorably of the valuable assistance he has received from Major Myer, Signal Officer, U.S. Army, and the Signal Corps he has authorized.

Reports received from the Comanches themselves state that thirty five of them were killed in the attack made upon them by Colonel Crittenden on the 2nd Instant.[9]

Fauntleroy did not yet know of 2^d Lieutenant Bascom's problem at Apache Pass, nor the conflict that would arise because of it. One of the soldiers, 1st Lieutenant Edward J. Brooks, 7th Infantry, was commended for bravery during an action against the Navajos. Brooks became an important figure in the events that transpired at Fort Fillmore in July. The same was true of another of those mentioned, 1st Lieutenant Donald C. Stith. Both men had an impact on the mind set of Major Isaac Lynde.

The fighting between Bascom's 7th Infantrymen and the Chiricahua Apaches continued into the month of February. On February 1, 1861, Cochise's warriors attacked a small wagon train at the western end of Apache Pass. Most of those in the train were killed. 2^d Lieutenant Bascom was still trapped at the stage station with

Wallace, surrounded by hostiles. Cochise asked for a truce with the surrounded soldiers and found agreement. While George Bascom prepared to meet with Cochise some of the men noticed Indians creeping toward the meeting place through the brush. The fighting started again. Bascomb was wounded slightly in the ensuing fight. Wallace and a couple of his stage station employees, believing they were long-time friends of Cochise and safe from his wrath, attempted to make peace on their own. Wallace and two others were captured and led away as a result. For the next two days Bascom and his remaining command waited for another assault. Their horses fell into Apache hands. A number of soldiers were wounded in minor skirmishing. For seven days thereafter the siege continued before Cochise offered to exchange Wallace and the others for six warriors that Cochise knew had been captured earlier by the soldiers.[10]

About the time this exchange of prisoners was being discussed a messenger reached Fort Buchanan, telling of the events at Apache Pass. A rescue party led by Post Assistant-Surgeon, B.J.D. Irwin started to the rescue with only fifteen men, all the post allowed. Cochise made no effort to prevent the reinforcements from arriving. Twenty-four hours later the Apaches had given up the siege, but not the war. Before the fighting stopped, Cochise had killed Wallace and the other white men. Their bodies were found by the retreating soldiers. In retaliation, Assistant-Surgeon Irwin, commanding the relief force, ordered the execution of the six Apache prisoners. They were hung at the stage station before the troops departed. Later, it was learned that three of the six Chiricahuas hung were close relatives of Cochise. From that sad day, and for many years to follow, no traveler was safe on the former Butterfield Overland Trail.

Following the Bascom fight, Indian troubles throughout the Territory and all along the route from Santa Fe to Missouri increased significantly, more than at any time since the American Army first arrived in New Mexico. The Bascom Incident became a convenient marker to which historians could point and say the Indian Wars period started there. Those wars would not end for another thirty years with the total subjugation of the tribes in all regions of the country. No doubt the disintegration of the nation into civil war had far more to do with the problems with all the tribes than the Bascomb incident did, although the latter did fit a future pattern. The subjugation of the tribes was going to happen anyway. The reservation system and the movement of the bands had been discussed much earlier in the 1850s. Movement trends among the American population, the coming of the railroads, mining interests, farming, etc., all ensured that a final conflict would have to take place in some fashion.

At this point in the growing atmosphere of conflict, the mail from the East was of primary importance. That mail had to get through, slow and out of date though it was. On February 4, Lieutenant Colonel Crittenden of the R.M.R., then at Fort Union, was given orders to escort the mail all the way from Fort Union to Independence, Missouri and return, whenever he felt this was necessary and troops were available. On that same day Brevet-Captain Maury directed Fort Fillmore and Fort Craig to provide similar escorts for the Santa Fe-El Paso mail.[11]

The Lanes and Company 'A,' Regiment of Mounted Rifles, departed Fort Craig for Fort Fillmore in early February. Lydia Lane noted she was glad to be going to Fort Fillmore because of the presence of a couple of small settlements nearby, unlike being buried at Fort Craig with little opportunity to acquire the goods she needed. She remarked that Captain Washington Elliot, the Company 'A' commander, was off on leave in the East. Second Lieutenant Joseph Wheeler was present with her and her family on the trip to Fort Fillmore over the Jornada del Muerto. She seemed to like Joe Wheeler, remarking,

> Wheeler messed with us. I remember well one breakfast on the road. He had not then travelled enough with troops to know the necessity of an early start in the morning, and of eating rapidly, that things might be cleared away and packed in good time, with as little delay as possible. We ate our break-fast by candle-light. Lieutenant Wheeler and I were disposed to dawdle, politely handing each other the delicacies on the table. Lieutenant Lane finished his meal in frantic haste, and left the

tent, hoping to expedite matters which were going on so leisurely within. But Wheeler did not notice husband's impatience, and it became necessary, at last, to warn us we must not waste time, that we had a long and dangerous drive before us that day, and it was getting late. That noble and polite gentleman understood later on the necessity of haste when a march of many miles was to be made, better than he did when about to cross the Jornada del Muerto ... .[12]

Joe Wheeler might have been thinking of his future as he crossed the Jornada with the Lanes. He must have known of the South Carolina secession at least, but could not have known yet that his home state of Georgia had also seceded, on January 19. As soon as Wheeler learned of that event, nothing could prevent his leaving for the East at once.

Legend says that Mangas Coloradas's group and those of Francisco, another Apache leader, joined Cochise in the battle against the 7th Infantry soldiers surrounded at the Apache Pass Stage station. Even Geronimo, a young and unknown warrior at the time, was said to be involved. After the siege was over the Indians broke off the engagement and disappeared into their respective mountain retreats. Mangas and Francisco went back to the Gila and Cochise took the remainder of his people to Sonora.[13]

On February 10, in Santa Fe, orders were sent to Major Isaac Lynde to punish any Apaches in the vicinity of Fort McLane who were causing trouble. Major Lynde did not know of Bascom's problems as yet; the two messages informing him of the battle and charging him to do his duty against the Indians no doubt arrived at about the same time.

William Lane's column of horsemen, dressed in their blue uniforms with emerald green trim on the collar, front and cuffs of their short cavalry jackets, and on the face of the headgear of those who wore the regulation shako, arrived at the Fort Fillmore reservation on February 9. Fifty-nine men and fifty-one cavalry horses provided the strongest military force Fort Fillmore had housed in some time. The men without horses in the wagons of the train followed just behind the mounted column. The small Army wagon train carried company public property, personal goods and subsistence, as well as the wife of 1ˢᵗ Lieutenant Lane. Other company property was still on the road when the Lanes arrived. After settling in his troops and his family, 1ˢᵗ Lieutenant Lane sat down the next day and gave word of his arrival to the Department command. He wrote:

> I have the honor to state that I arrived here yesterday, in obedience to order No. 5 from the Hd. Quarters of the Department, dated January 20, 1861. I enclose herewith post orders No. 29 for your information—A part of my Company property (four wagons with oxen) is on the road for this place, and should arrive in a few days; with these wagons, and one mule now at the post, I will send Company 'E' 8th Infantry to Fort Bliss, Texas. The wagons (four) that transported my Company to this place, I have today sent back to Fort Craig, with directions to the escort to give protection to the Santa Fe mail as far as Fort Craig.
>
> I would also state for your information that on my arrival here I found Dr. E.N. Covey, U.S.A. on leave from Fort Floyd, and as the small pox was raging near this post, I made a written request for him to remain a few days beyond his leave, for the purpose of vaccinating the men of my Company, and to take any other measures to prevent the small pox reaching the garrison. He has agreed to delay his departure for a few days. I would while on this subject, respectfully request permission to call on Dr. Covey for medical attendance for this post when it is necessary. The Dr. will cheerfully comply with such instructions from Department Hd. Quarters.
>
> Since my arrival here I have heard of a great many instances in this vicinity of Indian depredations, supposed to be Apaches and Navajos. A few days before my arrival here, some six or eight thousand sheep were driven off from within four miles of Mesilla, and some two or three persons killed and as many more taken prisoners. I learn that twenty miles below this, about a week ago, six horses were taken from a station of the Overland Mail Company, and about the same time, about twenty eight head of beef cattle were taken a short distance below this station. These depredations were supposed to have been

committed by the Apaches. Many other instances have been reported, but I am not certain of the truth of the reports. I of course will do my utmost to put a stop to these troubles.

I have neglected to state that a train of wagons from Fort Stanton with lumber was attacked about thirty five miles from this post—one man killed and several other wounded—Some mules taken—These Indians were supposed to be Navajos, but in my opinion they were Apaches.[14]

Lydia Lane, appearing somewhat depressed at what she saw, commented differently from her husband concerning their arrival at the run-down post. Her view of Fort Fillmore was more home oriented, less filled with talk of local Indian depredations, stolen animals and small pox raging just outside the gates. Lydia's eyes and thoughts were on the appearance of the home she was going to have to make there in the desert, and a very sharp eye and alert mind were hers to use. She noted:

> Most dreary and uninviting did Fort Fillmore look to us as we approached it. It was a cold, gray day, with a high wind which blew the loose sand and dust in clouds all around us. The stiff line of shabby adobe quarters on three sides of a perfectly bare parade-ground suggested neither beauty nor comfort, and for once I felt discouraged when we went into the forlorn house we were to occupy.
>
> It was filthy, too, and the room we chose for a bedroom must have been used as a kitchen. The great open fireplace had at least a foot of dirt in it, which had to be dug out with a spade before a fire could be lighted. It took time to make the quarters comfortable; but by hard scrubbing and sweeping they at last looked clean and habitable. The woodwork was rough and unpainted; the modern method of oiling pine was not known in army quarters then.
>
> I was the only lady at the post except for the wife of the post sutler. Lieutenant Lane and Lieutenant Wheeler, and possibly one other officer, attended to all duties of the garrison. Lieutenant Lane was in command.[15]

Given the time between the events and Lydia Lane's memory of them she did a remarkable job of recalling her first day at Fort

Fillmore. The other woman mentioned was probably Ellen Hayward, the twenty-two year old wife of Post Sutler George Hayward. One has to wonder, however, if Lydia Lane, by custom, refused to view the wives of the soldiers, or laundresses, etc. as ladies. Usually, there were several such women traveling with each company. What she may have meant was only one woman on her social level was at the fort, the United States Army being extremely class conscious at the time. Of course, she also did not count her servants, who may have been Negro slaves, as women either. The officer whose name she couldn't remember was 2^d Lieutenant Royal Thaxter Frank, who was at the post making preparations to leave for Texas.

About the middle of February as the Lanes settled in at Fort Fillmore, the Apache Chiefs Victorio, Pinon, and Chaboncito approached Fort McLane to talk with Major Isaac Lynde. Lynde persuaded these Apache bands to keep peace with the whites, at least for a time. This peace held through April, in spite of Bascom, mostly due to the fact that the Apaches were provided with rations on February 18, March 8, March 28 and April 18.[16]

Not all Apaches were at peace and not all among the Mexican and American communities were satisfied with a few bands being rationed, certainly not after what had been happening recently. On February 13, the citizens of Mesilla petitioned Colonel Fauntleroy for additional troops at Fort Fillmore because of the recent surge in depredations in the area. Present and signing this petition were such notable figures in Mesilla history as Anson Mills, George Lucas, Robert Kelley, James Oury, Samuel Bean, William McGrorty and Thomas Masten. Rumors of the fight at Apache Pass were no doubt filtering in. The well meaning-citizens pleaded:

> The undersigned citizens of Dona Ana County respectfully represent that they have heard with pain and regret that the order sending additional troops to Fort Fillmore has been countermanded, and submit the following to show the necessity of more troops in this section of country. Within the last thirty days not less than ten persons have been killed & some children taken prisoners; and sheep mules & other animals to the number of at least six thousand have been stolen by

Indians (Navajos & Apaches) The mails of the United States have been attacked. Trains bearing rations for the troops of the Army have been assaulted & delayed, private trains and teams have been stopped on the highway & robbed of their animals, and a general feeling of insecurity is felt by all residents in this part of the Department under your command. The number of troops within this portion of the Territory notwithstanding their desire to stay the hands of our ruthless enemies, is insufficient to protect us. We therefore respectfully request that not only will the troops now at that post be permitted to remain, but that others may be ordered there, that we may be protected against the incursions of those murderous bands of savages devastating our otherwise flourishing and rapidly increasing communities.[17]

On one hand some of the citizens, the bulk of the American population of Mesilla, were demanding a separate, and secessionist, Territory of Arizona, with its capital at Mesilla, and on the other hand, some were asking that Company 'A,' the loyal United States Army garrison at Fort Fillmore, be reinforced due to the Indian problems that made the garrison at the post absolutely essential for Mesilla's safety. Soon there was more hell to pay. On February 15, a letter was addressed to 1st Lieutenant Lane at Fort Fillmore by William Buckley, of the Butterfield Overland Mail Company. Buckley was in Mesilla, awaiting more bad news from his stations further west in the Apache country. Stage traffic west was about to be curtailed for the near future. Buckley warned:

The Indians in the vicinity of Apache Pass on the Overland Mail route between Mesilla & Tucson have committed serious depredations within the past two weeks. They attacked the station at Apache Pass, fired about fifteen shots wounded the driver severely. They attacked a train of five wagons near the Apache Pass & killed eight men and burnt them to the wagons. They stole from the Apache Pass forty two mules belonging to Government and seventeen belonging to the Overland Mail Co. They also stole three hundred head of sheep six mules and three oxen from the San Crimoni [?] Station. As there are many bad passes in the Mountains between Stein's Peak and Dragoon Springs, I do not consider it safe for the stage to travel without an escort. The stations also are in danger of being attacked by Indians. If you can possibly send troops to escort our mails through the bad passes I would like very much to have you do so, as I am fearful the Indians will attack the stage if we do not have an escort.[18]

Confirmation of the Bascom incident was provided in a letter from 1st Lieutenant William Lane at Fort Fillmore to Brevet-Captain Dabney Maury in Santa Fe, along with other details of recent events which Lane viewed at that time as of equal significance. Lane reported:

> I have the honor to enclose herewith for the information of the Dpt. Commander, a letter from the Superintendent of the Overland Mail Company, and my reply to the same. I learned from Lt. Cook [Cooke] 8th Infantry, who passed here in the stage the other night, in substance the same, as given in the enclosed letter. He also told me that Lieut Bascom of the 7th Infty, with a Company of Infantry had had some skirmishing with these Indians, and that some soldiers had been wounded. I also learned from passengers by the next stage, that Lieut. Lord with a Company of Dragoons was in the vicinity of Apache Pass, and that troops from Fort Floyd were scouting in the same direction.[19]

Not only was Bascom mentioned, but troops from Fort Floyd and Isaac Lynde's command were mentioned as well. Lane was unfamiliar with the name change from Fort Floyd to Fort McLane as late as this date. The officer, Cook, mentioned in this dispatch as being a passenger on an incoming Butterfield Overland stagecoach, can only have been 2d Lieutenant John Rogers Cooke, of the 8th Infantry, earlier at Fort Fillmore, and now returning to his regiment in Texas following leave or detached service. Cooke was another Confederate-to-be.

Lane enclosed his response to Mr. Buckley's request for military assistance in the mail to Santa Fe, stating that he had too few troops at Fort Fillmore. His reply is interesting, if unhelpful to Buckley's situation. Lane said:

I have your note of February 16th, giving a detailed account of the Indian depredations on the Overland Mail line between this and Fort Buchanan, and asking for an escort for the mails through the bad passes, etc. etc.—I am unable to comply with your request for the following reasons—There being only one Compy. at this post, and the scene of the Indian depredations is so distant comparatively, it would be impossible to give the escort asked for.—If I was to divide my command and send a part of it to the passes spoken of, it would leave the settlements on the river, in the vicinity of the post almost unprotected, and I might by these means, defeat the object of the Dpt. Commander in sending my Company to this post—But I will enclose to the Dpt. Hd. Quarters, your letter, in order that any steps deemed necessary in the matter may be taken.[20]

As was usual of the fort commanders in New Mexico Territory before the American Civil War, independent action could not be taken without an order of approval from the Department of New Mexico. Had Lane done so on his own volition he might have been court-martialed. No matter that Americans were being killed along the Butterfield route, or threatened by secessionists in Texas. Without a direct order to do so Lane would not move an inch to save them. Such was the antebellum Army, at least as it existed in New Mexico Territory. At Fort McLane, Major Isaac Lynde was given carte blanche on responding to any Indian provocation. Had Lane been given such an order he might have responded differently, even sending troops out that far to engage hostiles.

This was a tragic time for southern New Mexico. Indian troubles were on the rise; the incredible decision to send the 8th Infantry companies into Texas was about to lead to the abandonment of Fort Bliss and the loss of an important military force; Texas officially seceded from the Union on February 1 with unforeseeable consequences; the Butterfield Overland Mail route was shutting down due to Indian problems and the results of the Texas secession. With only one mounted company at Fort Fillmore, southern New Mexico was now woefully underprotected. Reinforcements were a necessity and the only troops available were the remaining companies of the 7th Infantry Regiment stationed at Albuquerque under Brevet-Major Rene Paul.

NOTES - Chapter 4

1. Maury to Canby, January 2, 1861, M1012, Roll 2.

2. Maury to Paul, January 2, 1861, M1012, Roll 2.

3. Maury to Morrison, January 10, 1861, M1012, Roll 2.

4. Lynde to Assistant Adjutant General, Santa Fe, January 15, 1861, M1120 Rolls 13/14.

5. Dale F. Giese, *Forts of New Mexico - Echoes of the Bugle.* Silver City: Privately Printed, p. 18.

6. Lydia Spencer Lane, *I Married A Soldier.* Albuquerque: Horn & Wallace, 1964, pp. 58, 59.

7. John Upton Terrell, *Apache Chronicles.* New York: World Publishing, Times Mirror, 1971, pp. 219, 220.

8. Ibid.

9. Fauntleroy to Thomas, January 31, 1861, M1012, Roll 2.

10. John Upton Terrell, *Apache Chronicles,* pp. 220-222.

11. Maury to commanding officers, February 4, 1861, M1012, Roll 2.

12. Lydia Spencer Lane, *I Married A Soldier,* pp. 97,98.

13. Edwin Sweeney, *Cochise*, pp. 161,162.

14. Lane to Maury, February 10, 1861, M1120, Rolls 13/14.

15. Lydia Spencer Lane, *I Married A Soldier*, pp. 97,98.

16. Edwin Sweeney, *Cochise*, p. 179.

17. Mesilla Petition to Fauntleroy, February 13, 1861, M1120, Rolls 13/14.

18. Buckley to Lane, February 15, 1861, M1012, Rolls 13/14.

19. Lane to Maury, February 17, 1861, M1120, Rolls 13/14.

20. Lane to Buckley, February 17, 1861, M1120, Rolls 13/14.

5

ISAAC LYNDE TAKES COMMAND

The tight control exerted by the Department of New Mexico over its scattered forces was apparent in the fact that Company 'E,' 8th Infantry, made final preparations to depart Fort Fillmore on February 17, 1861, as per orders. This, regardless of the fact that it had to be known at all levels of the New Mexico command that Texas had seceded. Common sense would have demanded that all troops in New Mexico stand firm where they were in the face of the changing political situation in Texas. They didn't. So it was that a few days after 1st Lieutenant Lane arrived at Fort Fillmore with Company 'A' the last of the 8th Infantry troops departed the post.

On February 18, while Company 'E,' 8th Infantry, was just arriving at Fort Bliss, an Indian War was on in earnest to the west, as if in accompaniment to the secession in Texas. American citizens and the Army were just beginning to understand the seriousness of the situation which followed the Bascom Incident. At Fort McLane there were stories of other attacks in the region. Major Lynde wrote:

> I have the honor to report that a public Ox train from Albuquerque bound to Fort Buchanan, was attacked at Cook's Springs by Indians (supposed to be Navajos) and some forty head of oxen driven off. This train had no escort with it. I have sent oxen from this post to bring in the train and an escort to protect it.

The Apache Indians west of this point have attacked the Overland Stage and some trains; killing a number of men and driving off much stock. No train is safe in travelling between Fort Craig and Fort Buchanan without an escort at this time, as the Navajos infest the road between Fort Craig and Cook's Springs, and the Apaches between this place and Fort Buchanan. I have sent a party of men to Steen's Peak, 75 miles west of this place, to protect the road in that vicinity, and I learn that a command from Fort Buchanan is guarding the road west of that point.

A few day's since, three sub-Chiefs of the Apaches (Chabnocito [sic], Pinion [sic] & Victorio) came here and professed to be friendly to the whites and promised to do all in their power to keep peace and prevent any depredations by the men of their bands, and I think they are sincere. I delivered up to them the captives taken by the men from the mines, who have been in confinement here since that time. Chabnocito [sic] promised to send for Mangas Colorado, the Head Chief of the Apaches, and thought he could induce him to come in and make peace. The three sub-Chiefs mentioned above are of the Bands residing on the Mimbres and vicinity.[1]

The mention of Steen's Peak, named in honor of Major Enoch Steen, provides interesting proof that what is now called Stein's Peak near the settlement of Stein on the Arizona border somehow had its name changed over the years. Victorio, the famous Apache Chief who kept the United States Army busy into the 1880s, is mentioned here for the first time as part of Lynde's documentation.

On the day Captain Carpenter surrendered the first Federal troops at Camp Cooper in Texas (February 19), an equally ignoble act was taking place in New Mexico Territory, at Apache Pass. This was the day Cochise's relatives were hung for the deaths of the Butterfield Stage Line employees. The Indians sang their death songs. They were then hung from the branches of four oak trees under which the bodies of the slain whites were buried. All the hanged were men. The women and children captives were set free.[2]

First Lieutenant Lane, now fully in command at Fort Fillmore, was directed to protect the local settlements in his surrounding area from the depredations of the risen Apache bands. He received word that additional troops were going to be sent to Fort McLane and Fort Fillmore in the near future. These troops, said to be set in motion already, were in fact still awaiting orders. An assistant surgeon, Dr. James Cooper McKee, was to be sent to Fort Fillmore as well, to re-staff the hospital.[3]

Second Lieutenant Joseph Wheeler was denied leave in that same letter. Colonel Fauntleroy must have known why Joe Wheeler wanted that leave. By February 24, Wheeler was probably aware that his home state of Georgia had seceded. News was slow but after almost a month word would have arrived. Fauntleroy and his able assistant adjutant-general, Dabney Maury, were Virginians. In February there was still major doubt that Virginia would leave the Union. In fact that state did not secede until April, among the last to do so. Until Virginia seceded these two men could remain neutral, no matter to which side they were pulled politically. After that date they, like Joe Wheeler, had to make a decision.

Other infantry forces were entering New Mexico just as the last of the 8th Infantry companies were departing. Most of these forces were concentrated in the northern part of the Territory. Brevet-Captain Maury indicated how New Mexico troops were to be reorganized in a February 24 letter to Brevet-Lieutenant Colonel Canby at Fort Defiance:

> In consequence of the very gratifying result of your operations and of the hostile attitude of the Mescaleros and other bands of Apaches, the Colonel Commanding directs the following dispositions to be made of the troops under your Command, at the earliest practicable moment viz:
>
> Three Companies of the 7th Infantry will proceed to Fort Fillmore, and the other two to Fort McLane.
>
> Two Companies of the 5th Infantry, will proceed to Hatch's Ranch, and another to Albuquerque.
>
> 'A' Company of the 10th Infantry, will return to its station at Fort Garland. Through the Navajo Country if practicable.
>
> Six Companies of the 5th Infantry will occupy Forts Defiance & Fauntleroy until the stores at Fort Defiance can be transferred to Fort Fauntleroy and the Post abandoned. It is

desired, that this should be accomplished as quickly as possible, and that the Subsistence & Ordnance stores should be removed first. The temporary garrison of Fort Defiance will take Post at Fort Fauntleroy as soon as the transfer of property enables it to abandon Fort Defiance.

Major Albert J. Myer, Signal Officer U.S. Army will resume his proper station at Department Hd. Qrs.

Lieut. L.L. Rich 5th Infantry will proceed to rejoin his Company at Fort Stanton

Asst. Surgeon J. Cooper McKee will resume his station at Fort Fillmore.

Asst. Surgeon J.C. Bailey will proceed to Fort Garland, where he will relieve Asst. Surgeon Alden as medical officer of the Post.

After giving the necessary orders for the carrying out of these instructions the Department Commander desires that you will report in person to these Head Quarters.

P.S. It is desired that the Companies of the 7th Infantry shall take with them sufficient subsistence stores to last until they reach their destinations, if they can do so without too much diminishing the supplies of Fort Fauntleroy.[4]

Dabney Maury did not say whether the 7th Infantry forces being concentrated in the south at Fort Fillmore and Fort McLane were the result of the increasing war with the Apaches, or because of the situation in Texas. One has to believe the former was the primary consideration. The Butterfield Overland Company stage line was virtually shut down by Apache raids, although limping along as best it could.

In the south at Mesilla, James Lucas, a fervent backer of secession, yet one of the signers of the petition to have more Federal troops sent to Fort Fillmore, was notified by Maury on February 25 that Colonel Fauntleroy had agreed to the petition's request for troops. Both Forts Fillmore and McLane were to be reinforced. Major Lynde was alerted that same day that he might soon be conducting a major campaign against the Apaches. Maury stated:

The Department Commander intends making a Campaign against the hostile Apaches, west of the Rio Grande, which he wishes you to conduct.

Two additional Companies of the 7th Infantry have been ordered to Fort McLane, which, with the present garrisons of Forts McLane, Buchanon and Beckenridge [sic], it is hopeful will be sufficient to enable you to sustain vigorous operations. The state of Lt. Colo. Morrison's health has become so bad as to compel him to apply for a leave of absence. It has been granted to him & the Head Quarters of the 7th Infy. has been consequently ordered to your post.

Fort Breckinridge will be immediately added to your command.

It is presumed that Col. Morrison will at once avail himself of his leave of absence. As soon as he does so, Fort Buchanan will be added to your Command, and in the meantime, the Commanding Officer of that Post, will be instructed to cooperate with you in every way possible for the object herein contemplated, and to afford you every aid in his power, you may call upon him for.

The whole resources of Forts Buchanan, Breckinridge and McLane will be subject to your wishes & orders. And should they be insufficient, the Dept. Quartermaster & Commissary at Albuquerque, will be instructed to fill all of your requisitions on them, as promptly as possible. And to prevent delay, you will please send any requisitions you may make for Qr. Master's or Subsistence Stores direct to those offices.

You may employ guides & packers for your troops not to exceed one guide for column, and two packers for each Company, while in the field. They will furnish their own animals and Arms—you will supply them with Ammunition when necessary.

The Department Commander hopes, that it may not be necessary for you to suspend the construction of Fort McLane on account of these operations. But in this, as in all else, he desires to entrust the largest discretion to you.

You will organize your troops where and how you think best; and conduct your operations according to the best information you can procure.

I am directed to inform you that active operations will be commenced at once against the Apaches, east of the Rio Grande.

It is not likely that the Companies of the 7th Infantry ordered to reinforce you can reach Fort McLane at a very early day as they were in the Navajo country when ordered.[5]

Maury made no mention to Isaac Lynde of 7th Infantry troops being sent to Fort Fillmore, or that a second campaign was anticipated against the Mescalero. Obviously, until civil war became the over-riding issue, a major field campaign, conducted against the recalcitrant Apaches in the region Major Lynde controlled, would be a Department priority. Americans had been killed by Apaches. In the past that had always led to a violent and overwhelming response. It was at this point that Lieutenant Colonel Morrison, the man who permitted 2^d Lieutenant Bascom to create the severe breakdown in American-Apache relations, was allowed to escape responsibility and to leave for the East. Isaac Lynde was now in full command of all of the regiment's assets.

What, in effect, did these orders ask Major Lynde to do? He was to build Fort McLane and at the same time lead a major expedition against the Apaches in the west, even though communication with Forts Buchanan and Breckinridge were at best difficult. In the midst of doing this he was to take over command at both Arizona forts for the duration of the action. Lynde was to prepare to accept two additional companies at Fort McLane, although the date of their arrival was not provided. Ordered to attack immediately with force, there was no way Major Lynde could possibly have carried out these orders in less than several month's time. A base of operations was needed, supplies had to be gathered, troops prepared. Were Fauntleroy and Maury simply tying the troops down by issuing impossible orders to their commander? In 1857, it took six months to set up a campaign of the size envisioned for Lynde's command.

Lynde's campaign was to occur at the same time a second major campaign was to be launched east of the Rio Grande against the Mescalero. Supplying a dual mission of this type was unprecedented in New Mexico Territory history. Both expeditions would strain to the utmost the inadequate transportation system in the Department, not to speak of the added requirement for munitions and subsistence. Canby's campaign against the Navajos was ongoing as well. Add to this the fact that Colonel Fauntleroy had, without objection and against all logic, despatched the 8th Infantry companies to their doom in Texas, reducing the strength of his Department at the most critical of moments.

No mounted units were offered for Lynde's support during the campaign against the Apaches. Only 2ᵈ Lieutenant Lord's dragoon company, then at Fort Buchanan, was available. Trudging infantry marching alone against mounted Apaches was a formula doomed to failure from the start. Colonel Fauntleroy made no effort to send mounted forces into an area where cavalry was absolutely necessary, whether the troops were to fight Apaches or Texans. Nine companies of the Regiment of Mounted Rifles were held north of the Jornada del Muerto, north of the Texas border, where Texas cavalry were soon to make an appearance at the now abandoned Fort Bliss. Was this collusion a thought-out act, or simply fate determined by the convergence of events? We will probably never know.

A peculiar letter was dispatched to Colonel Pitcairn Morrison at Fort Buchanan, even as Major Lynde was being ordered to undertake his near impossible mission at Fort McLane. In effect, Brevet-Captain Dabney Maury, at the behest of Colonel Fauntleroy, warned Morrison to get out while he could, and hand the entire situation over to Major Lynde. Maury said:

> The Department Commander has decided on making a Campaign against the Apaches, west of the Rio Grande, and to place Major Isaac Lynde in charge of it.
> You will therefore please cause a prompt compliance to be made with any wishes Major Lynde may communicate to you respecting aid of troops or supplies from Fort Buchanan.
> Please immediately on receipt of this inform Major Lynde of the effective strength of your garrison, and of all resources for field service, stating the number of mules, packsaddles & equipments, the supply of subsistence and ordnance stores. The disposition, the strength and the haunts of the Apaches, in your vicinity, the possibility of your employing reliable guides and packers for the troops and any other matters which you may consider it desirable for him to know.
> Until Major Lynde communicates with you, it will be advisable that you should undertake no operations, which may interfere with his plans.
> The remoteness of Fort Buchanan from these Hd. Qrs. renders it necessary to act upon the prescription, that you will at

once avail yourself of the Leave of Absence, granted to you on your application of December 4, 1860; as soon as you do so, please direct the senior officer you may leave in Command of Fort Buchanan, to report to Major Lynde for orders.[6]

Maury advised Morrison to leave Fort Buchanan as soon as possible. He was to conduct no operations but was to prepare his troops for a campaign that he would not lead. The order to leave quickly Lieutenant Colonel Morrison obeyed to the letter. The preparations he was ordered to make before leaving were left to others. In other words they were not acted on. Morrison left Isaac Lynde hanging, no matter the excuse or reason for his leaving. When he arrived back East he used his influence to obtain an immediate promotion to colonel. Pitcairn Morrison, who may have expected a general's stars, had to wait until 1865 to attain them. Back in New Mexico his regiment muddled along without him.

Brevet-Lieutenant Colonel George Bibb Crittenden, then at Fort Union, was issued orders on March 1 to lead an expedition against the Mescalero Apache bands east of the Rio Grande. Crittenden, a future Confederate general officer, was given far better instructions than Major Lynde. He was told to establish his base of operations at Fort Stanton. He was to operate from Fort Stanton and Fort Fillmore with a depot to be set up in the mountains south of Fort Stanton before the troops moved. Adequate supplies would be sent.[7]

On that same day 1st Lieutenant Lane at Fort Fillmore was informed that he was to consider himself and his post under the command of Brevet-Lieutenant Colonel Crittenden, not Major Isaac Lynde's command, who had few horse soldiers. Of course, Lane was theoretically already under Crittenden's command, being a member of the Regiment of Mounted Rifles, with Crittenden as acting commander until Colonel Loring returned. Lane was to report to Crittenden by letter at Fort Stanton, informing him of all available resources ready for field service, such as rank and file, pack saddles, horses, mules, wagons, subsistence and ordnance stores. Lane was also to provide Crittenden with information related to known haunts of the Apaches in the region of Fort Fillmore. The campaign, whatever its outcome, would pull the last of the mounted resources in southern New Mexico away from the Texas border during the period when Texas was just beginning to send troops to garrison the abandoned western Texas military posts.[8]

Word was sent in early March to Colonel Lorenzo Thomas of the upcoming expeditions against the varied Apache bands. An account of Canby's Campaign against the Navajos during the fall and winter of 1860-61 was included, as well as Brevet-Lieutenant Colonel Crittenden's successful campaign against the Kiowa and Comanches in January. Colonel Fauntleroy informed Colonel Thomas, and through him General-in-Chief Winfield Scott, of the coming campaigns to be conducted by Lynde and by Crittenden.[9]

Colonel Fauntleroy also informed Thomas of a practice of trading with the Comanches which he found repugnant. Acting on information provided by Brevet-Lieutenant Colonel Roberts of the Mounted Rifles, Fauntleroy stated that Indian Agent Kendrick, then with the Pueblo Indians in the north, was giving passes for the Pueblos to trade ammunition and information of troop movements with the Comanche in exchange for mules and horses the Comanches had stolen from citizens in the U.S., in Texas and elsewhere. It is to be noted that Fauntleroy deliberately separated Texas from the United States in this correspondence, indicating he was well aware that Texas had seceded from the Union.[10]

Second Lieutenant Joseph Wheeler, on receiving news that he was denied leave because of the troubles with the Apaches, immediately resigned his commission and notified Santa Fe of that fact. In response, on March 3, Brevet-Captain Maury reminded him that the Department Commander could not grant his resignation. Wheeler would have to state that the resignation was "unconditional and immediate" as per Paragraph 29, General Regulations of the Army. Wheeler's departure left Fort Fillmore with only one officer, at a time when the troops were expected to be in the field.[11]

The reason for Joe Wheeler's leaving, or at least the excuse for his home state of Georgia's secession, was sworn in as President of the United States on March 4, 1861. Most people forget that it was not an Abraham Lincoln in office that triggered the rapid secession of the Southern States, including Texas, but his election. The surrender of the Army's public property in Texas took place while James Buchanan was still in office.

Abraham Lincoln was born in Hardin County, Kentucky, February 12, 1809. His parents were Thomas and Nancy Hanks Lincoln. The family moved to Indiana on the Ohio border in 1816 and Lincoln grew up there. At six-feet four-inches, he was unusually tall for that period. Lincoln served as a private in one of the fights with Indians in his area. After mustering out he served as postmaster of New Salem, Illinois for three years after 1833. About that time he was appointed deputy county surveyor and was elected to the Illinois State Legislature in 1834. In 1837, he moved to Springfield, Illinois, and, in 1842, married Mary Todd, daughter of Robert S. Todd, of Kentucky. Lincoln was elected to Congress in 1846, serving only a single term. In 1858, he was chosen by the newly constituted Republican Party to run for the United States Senate. His opponent was Steven A. Douglas, and the resulting campaign became famous for the debate between the two men. Douglas won the contest if not the debate. In May 1860, Abraham Lincoln was nominated for President on the third ballot by the Republican Party. On November 6, 1860, he was elected President. The electoral vote was Lincoln 180; John Breckinridge (the Southern favorite) 72, John Bell 39, and Steven A. Douglas 12. The process toward secession and Civil War began officially on November 7.[12]

Lincoln was not ready for a civil conflict on the day he took office. During his inaugural speech the new President, taking a very moderate stance, clearly tried to stave off a breakup. He said, "I have no purpose, directly or indirectly, to interfere with the institution of slavery in the States where it exists. I believe I have no lawful right to do so, and I have no inclination to do so."[13]

On March 10, 1st Lieutenant Lane notified Santa Fe by express that he had received the orders to put himself under Colonel Crittenden's command. He noted:

I have the honor to acknowledge the receipt of your letter of the 1st Inst. In regard to placing Lieut. Col. Crittenden in command of an expedition against the Apaches east of the Rio Grande, and making this post & garrison subject to his command—and directing me to report by letter to him at Fort Stanton, & give all necessary information, as to the resources of the post, and ability to employ suitable guides & packers for the troops, etc. etc.

I will as soon as possible communicate with Col. Crittenden on these subjects, but my success here in the small matter of employing guides & packers, will be very much embarrassed, on account of the want of funds in the Quarter Master's Dept. At this post, [it is] almost [an] impossibility to get funds on the credit of the Quarter Master's Dpt. But I will do my utmost, to get some person with money to stand as security, for the Government, for the small amount that will be required to pay these men.

When I first came to this post, it was understood that I wished to have a guide for the post, & formerly, for such a position, there were plenty of applicants, but in this instance there were none—& I think it was altogether from account of the uncertainty of securing pay for the service.

I will at once get all information possible in regard to the Indians, and report accordingly to Col. Crittenden.[14]

In the matter of securing guides for service in the field, the criterion was not loyalty to any Union of States, but cash on the barrel-head for services rendered. Times, and respect for the American Government's authority, were eroding.

More oddly worded orders were issued to Major Lynde at the newly named Fort McLane as of March 10. He was told he "will not until further orders make any contract for lumber, adobes or other building materials for the construction of Fort McLane." This cryptic message to cease work on construction is very puzzling. Did the Department already know that Fort McLane was to be abandoned at this early stage? Or were they concerned with the upcoming campaign against the Apaches being more urgent? Other questions immediately arise. Was Fort McLane only a tent city or were buildings actually constructed there during the time Lynde commanded?

This order from the Department came some six months after the founding of the post. Chances are, if there were any buildings, they were crude and haphazard structures of a temporary nature.[15]

On March 11, politeness over the upcoming civil conflict ended and reality set in, even with the correspondence that normally took place between commands. In a letter to the Department, Major Lynde, having received word that he was to be in charge of a significant Indian campaign, changed the face of the enemy from Apache warrior to secessionist agitator, telling a tale of threats from secessionists and potential thieves living in the mining camp of Pinos Altos to the north, a hotbed of hatred and sedition directed at American authority. Lynde warned:

> I have the honor to report that the Public Ox Train of fifteen wagons from Albuquerque that I reported as having been attacked by Indians at Cooks Spring, arrived at this place and after refitting left for Fort Buchanan on the 25th of February. On the 5th of March I received reliable information, that a party of separate men from the mines at the instigation of Mr. Kirk, Wagonmaster, had left for the purpose of taking the train and running it into Sonora and selling it. I have ascertained beyond a doubt that they have succeeded, that the train took the road to Janos, the nearest point in Mexico and had crossed the line before I received the first report.
>
> I have also received information that the inhabitants of the mines have formed a plan to attack this post, to capture the public property, take all the arms, etc., from us.
>
> They hope to surprise us, but in that, they will be mistaken. Their object is plunder, and the report states, that when they have captured us, they intend to take all the stock of the Overland Mail. I believe such an attack will be made and they may get some of our animals as we must send them out to graze.
>
> I shall keep my command here, and cannot furnish escorts, as I shall have no men to spare if this attack is made with their whole force. I consider the preservation of the public property of the first importance.[16]

This is the first time that the growing climate of insurrection appears to have impacted the Department correspondence of a field commander of the United States Army in New Mexico. Although Major Lynde did not mention Confederates or the coming of civil war (he may not even have heard such words used as yet) he was quick to realize that many miners at Pinos Altos were hostile to the Federal Government, as represented by his command. The Apaches were not the only enemy, and at this point, perhaps not even the most important.

In line with what was to happen later at Fort Fillmore, Major Lynde's comment concerning, as he saw it, his most important duty as a commander, is extremely relevant. Lynde stated emphatically, "I consider the preservation of the public property of the first importance." An officer of the antebellum United States Army would definitely think in that fashion, especially one who served in post duties rather than out on the campaign trail. After all, the designated officer signed for everything; a career could be lost if every nut and bolt, saddle, rifle, horse, nail, etc., under their control, were not accounted for. To lose public property in a raid by Pinos Altos Miners would be as bad as having his whole command wiped out by Indians.

"Saving the public property," that indeed was Major Lynde's first and foremost priority, as taught him during a career of service of over thirty years. As one Army regulation of the period clearly stated, "Any commissioned officer of the Army, having charge of a military post, temporarily or otherwise, will be held accountable that all public property, of every description whatsoever, be properly secured and taken care of." To the antebellum Army, there was no more important duty. Equipment and supplies were simply too vital to the mission, and so very hard to replace. Lynde could think in no other fashion given how he had been trained. Infantry protected forts and public property, and Major Isaac Lynde was first and foremost an infantryman.

Given this trained mind set, Major Lynde's worries were about to increase many times over, as the commands (and all the public property) at Fort's Buchanan and Breckinridge were to be placed under his care. Lynde must have gone almost insane with worry over the prospect. Such responsibility was rarely, if ever, placed upon a major. Confederates coming up from Texas? Apaches raiding from the Chiricahua Mountains? What would that do to the 7th Infantry Regiment's stock of public property of all kinds? Major Lynde's reaction to either possibility was to state emphatically that he was not even going to provide escorts for the mail stages. Let them protect themselves. Major Lynde had a higher duty.

The coming dissolution of the nation was more obvious to national-level business interests than to the military. Financial strains put an end to the Butterfield Overland Mail Company by March. The Texas route would have to be renegotiated if secession was recognized and Texas was part of a new nation. The last stage from the west, traveling through Apache Pass without being attacked, reached Fort Fillmore safely in mid-March. Cochise and other Apache leaders believed it was the Indians that brought the stages to a halt. Like the U.S. Army commanders, the Apache leaders had trouble understanding the concept of an American civil war. Perhaps, had the war not come, a quick campaign by Major Lynde, properly conducted with adequate preparation, including Mounted Rifle or dragoon contingents, may have snuffed the fires of war quickly, ending before it began the long and costly battle between Americans and Apaches.

A group of Southern sympathizers met in Mesilla on March 14, adopting a resolution declaring in part that "the people of New Mexico would not recognize the present black administration [in Washington]," and that they "would resist any officers appointed to the Territory by said administration with whatever means in our power." Whether 1st Lieutenant Lane at Fort Fillmore was aware of what was happening in Mesilla is not known. One has to assume he was, but he was also in no position to do anything about mere words, and no actions against the government had yet taken place. It would be months yet before freedom of speech would be suppressed through the negation of habeas corpus by President Lincoln.[17]

The approbation and appreciation of the New Mexico Department commander was extended to Dr. Irwin and 1st Lieutenant

Bascom for what was, in effect, a badly handled confrontation with Cochise at Apache Pass. Colonel Fauntleroy may not have been privy to all that happened there, and certainly was provided a biased account by Lieutenant Colonel Pitcairn Morrison. The Colonel seemed unable to believe that a major Indian War would result. Dabney Maury wrote, "He [Fauntleroy] approves of Lieutenant Bascom's decided action in executing the Indian warriors after the atrocious murders which have been committed by the tribe." Colonel Fauntleroy notified the commanding officers at Forts McLane and Buchanan that he was aware that a wagon train filled with government stores, sent from Albuquerque, was highjacked by a Wagonmaster named Kirk and taken to Mexico. Fauntleroy said nothing about Kirk being a Confederate sympathizer, out to do whatever damage he could to the Federal Army in New Mexico. It was as if the climate of secession, so rampant among the miners at Pinos Altos, and in the town of Mesilla, was a subject which might not be discussed in official Army channels. Fauntleroy must have known there was an underlying political problem. Lydia Lane discussed the fact that the subject of secession and the growing movement in New Mexico was a major topic among the officers at that time. Colonel Fauntleroy did order the commanders of the two posts to try to locate the stolen train, request the arrest of the wagonmaster, and recover the goods from Mexico.[18]

In fairness, the Army was hardly prepared to curtail a civil conflict. Perhaps that is why Colonel Fauntleroy made no mention of the interrelationship between the current climate of secession and the theft of government stores. Although open insurrection was what led to the theft of that train, officialdom was not yet prepared to say the words. The United States Regular Army, at the beginning of the Civil War, had 183 of its 198 infantry, dragoon, Mounted Rifles and artillery companies dispersed among seventy-nine frontier posts. Even if the up to 16,000 Regulars could have been concentrated rapidly, there would not have been enough troops to control even one southern state. Also, of approximately 1,080 officers, 313, almost one-third of the force, resigned their commissions at the beginning of the war. This percentage was higher in the Department of New Mexico, a military entity overloaded in 1861 with sons of the South.

Initially, Major Isaac Lynde responded positively to the order to conduct a sweeping campaign against the Apaches. He advised the Department in early March:

> I have the honor to acknowledge the receipt of your letter of the 25th of February with the accompanying papers. As soon as I receive the reports of the other posts, so as to know the resources of those posts, I shall organize the expedition against the Apaches. At this time there is less than thirty days provisions for two Companies at this post, but I have sent three wagons to Fort Buchanan and if they return safely, we shall have a supply for the additional Companies ordered here.
>
> The men at the mines have not attempted to molest this post yet, though they are very anxious to do so. I am informed of all their movements. These <u>Land Pirates</u> are many of them in a starving condition and may be guilty of any outrage at any time.[19]

It is fascinating that Major Lynde did not use the terms secessionists or Confederate sympathizers, but instead used the phrase "Land Pirates" when referring to the Pinos Altos miners. Of course, this period was very early in the civil conflict, before Fort Sumter, and the later familiar terms may not have been in common use yet. If Lynde was able to get a copy of the Mesilla newspaper from a traveler, he must have known of the hotbed of sedition and hatred which surrounded him in all directions. He surely knew of the movement to create an independent Arizona from the land on which his fort stood. The oblique references to the obvious must have roots in his unfamiliarity with new terminology.

Colonel William Wing Loring replaced Colonel Thomas Turner Fauntleroy as New Mexico Department Commander on March 22. The Virginian Fauntleroy returned immediately to the East where, on May 17, 1861, he resigned his commission and accepted a commission as brigadier general in the Virginia Volunteers. Colonel Loring was also a Southerner, from North Carolina, a state which as of March 22 had not yet seceded. In fact, North Carolina did not secede until May 20, after President Abraham Lincoln called for troops to fight those states which had left the Union. Lincoln's action infuriated the people of North Carolina, many of whom were said to support the Union until that point. Colonel Loring did not resign his post until May 13, about a week before North Carolina seceded. He remained in New Mexico and at Fort Bliss for a while after his resignation, a point we will examine in some detail later. Loring obviously held deep Southern sympathies while he was in command in New Mexico, as had Fauntleroy before him, which leaves open the question of what he did to serve the Confederate cause before his resignation.[20]

Loring's arrival did not change previous obligations and orders, at least not immediately. By March 23, the campaign against the Mescalero Apaches east of the Rio Grande was being conducted from Fort Stanton by Brevet-Lieutenant Colonel George Bibb Crittenden. Crittenden ordered 1st Lieutenant Lane and Company 'A,' R.M.R., to Dog Canyon, to search for Indians there. Before his departure Fauntleroy notified Crittenden that the dearth of transportation in the Department would make his campaign difficult to complete. He hoped that Crittenden's transportation assets, then on hand, would be sufficient. Although Colonel Fauntleroy did not mention it, the fact that he had sent the 8th Infantry companies into the unsettled and disturbing situation in Texas added to the transportation problems. All of those wagons and animals which were desperately needed in New Mexico were now in the hands of the new secessionist government in Texas.[21]

Loring did change some of the orders Fauntleroy issued. Half of the 7th Infantry battalion, under Brevet-Major Paul, then at Albuquerque, was formerly to be sent to Major Lynde at Fort McLane. Orders were changed on March 23. Company 'I' was ordered to Fort Fillmore at once, to protect the fort and the public property. Company 'A,' 7th Infantry, was ordered to Fort McLane to reinforce Lynde's command in its upcoming campaign on the west side of the Rio Grande, as per previous orders. Thus it was that three companies of the 7th Infantry Regiment, 'D,' 'I,' and 'K,' were ordered out onto the road south as quickly as possible. Like

Colonel Fauntleroy, the old dragoon commander, the cavalry-man Loring sent no mounted troops south.[22]

Colonel Loring's first formal response as commander of the Department of New Mexico was to write Assistant Adjutant General Thomas concerning the New Mexico situation. For the first time in any official correspondence yet encountered from the Department, the secession of Texas was mentioned. Loring said:

> I have the honor to report for the information of the General-in-Chief, that I arrived here and assumed Command of this Department on the 22nd instant.
>
> I feel it to be my first duty to call his attention at once to the condition of affairs, which I find existing throughout this Territory.
>
> The expeditions against the Comanches and the Navajos have caused the loss of a very large portion of the means of transportation; and the secession of the State of Texas has involved an additional heavy loss to this Department, of Subsistence Stores, of transportation and of funds.
>
> By the mail today I have received a Report from Major Lynde, commanding Fort McLane, a copy of which I enclose, for the information of the General-in-Chief. And by the same mail, I am informed of a plan, by the people about Albuquerque, to possess themselves of the Government Stores at that Depot.
>
> The people in every portion of the Territory are becoming uneasy and restless about their pay. And unless they can be assured of a very early day, that they will be paid off, very serious consequences may result.
>
> The great scarcity of means of transportation and the difficulty of hiring it must necessarily cramp the [current] operations against the Apaches, and render long marches impossible, except for a small body of troops.
>
> I earnestly request therefore, that I may receive at the earliest possible moment the means of paying off the troops & other creditors of the Government, or instructions for my guidance and additional means of transportation in case it may not be possible to send the funds now imperatively required.[23]

No matter how Colonel Loring behaved in the future, he told the truth at this point. The situation in New Mexico was growing desperate. Funds for paying the troops and contractors were not available. Loring may not have known that the Texas Commission was confiscating other funds which should have been available in New Mexico. Future transportation of goods and every kind of supply would soon be limited to the Santa Fe Trail, out of the State of Missouri, a state whose secessionist tendencies were obvious.

Even if Colonel Fauntleroy did overstep his authority in respect to actions which one might consider aided the secessionist cause, his replacement by Loring in no way changed the situation. succeeding Confederate officers held firm control over the Department of New Mexico in late March 1861, and would continue to do so for some time, long past the firing at Fort Sumter. Colonel Loring and Brevet-Captain Maury held the Department reins. Brevet-Lieutenant Colonel Crittenden, soon to join them in Confederate general officer grade, controlled Fort Union, the main supply base, and the activities of Fort Stanton, Fort Craig and Fort Fillmore. Brevet-Major Henry Hopkins Sibley, the future Confederate general who later led an Army to invade New Mexico Territory from Texas, commanded a squadron of cavalry at Taos. At Fort Fillmore, 1st Lieutenant Lane, a Kentuckian, sympathetic to the Southern cause, and certain to leave if Kentucky seceded, held command there. Of the paymasters who would be paying the troops at Loring's insistence, at least two of them, Major James Longstreet and Major Thomas Grimke Rhett, were soon to become Confederate officers as well. The only field grade officer in Southern New Mexico and Arizona who did not have Southern sympathies was Major Isaac Lynde, who had, in March, no idea that everyone in a command position above him was about to give their loyalty to the South. When they did so, the news of their disloyalty to the Union must have filled Lynde's whole being with paranoia. Who could be trusted? If his superiors were not loyal, what about those who served with him in his own command?

On March 30, 1st Lieutenant William Lane departed Fort Fillmore for Dog Canyon and a hoped for fight with the Mescalero. He left behind his wife, Lydia Spencer Lane, and a small detachment of fifteen men (Lydia reported only ten). Fort Bliss was abandoned and Fort Fillmore had no infantry contingent to protect the public property. In effect, Lydia Lane was in command of the post for a period of about five days, from March 30 to April 4, when Company 'K,' 7th Infantry, finally arrived from Albuquerque. Lydia Lane wrote of her experience years later:

> A sergeant and ten men, all that could be spared from the little command, were left behind to guard the post and our small family, and they were picked men. Those in the guard-house were taken on the scout. I was left in command of Fort Fillmore. All public funds were turned over to me, and the sergeant reported to me every day. He slept in our house at night, heavily armed, which gave us a sense of security.
>
> There was a flag-staff on the parade ground, but no flag. Husband sent to Fort Bliss for one before he left for Dog Canyon. I knew I would feel safer to see it floating above us, and it was run up at reveille every morning through the summer before the post was abandoned. When was the flag ever more needed than in those anxious days before the war was declared, to cheer the weak-hearted and bid defiance to its enemies.
>
> The public money in my hands gave me considerable uneasiness, and I hid it away in what I considered a secure place; then it seemed to me that would be the first spot searched, and I found a safer one. I was determined no one should have that money while I was alive to defend it. Just how I would act circumstances must decide; if I lost my life in protecting it, I would have done my whole duty.[24]

Mrs. Lane later added her thoughts that the state of affairs at Fort Fillmore and the surrounding country had been misrepresented at Santa Fe, and the folly shown of sending all the troops away from the post, when right in their midst was a real danger to be dreaded. She did not say what that danger was. According to post records the length of her "command" could have been as many as four days. On April 4, 1861, Captain Augustus H. Plummer, commanding Company 'K,' 7th Infantry Regiment, arrived at the post, the first of three companies then on the route of march.

Should Lydia Lane be credited as commanding officer of Fort Fillmore, regardless of having no official authority? In theory, she should. There are a finite number of days in the post record where she was in charge of the public funds, in the name of her husband. That she gave orders to the small remaining command should also not be doubted. Of course, she bore no military title in carrying out the command function. The old rule of he (or she) who holds the purse strings has the power fits here.[25]

Her husband was back in garrison by April 7; he was to formally relinquish command of the post soon after. Company 'A's' part in the Mescalero campaign was rather uneventful. The Apaches quickly pleaded for peace and, given the degrading position of the military at that time, their pleadings were accepted with relish.

On March 31, as Lydia Lane was being watchful of the company funds at Fort Fillmore, larger amounts of money were being discussed in a letter from Colonel Loring to Colonel Lorenzo Thomas at Army Headquarters in New York City. Apparently, Major-Paymaster Thomas Rhett, Paymaster for Fort Fillmore, Fort Bliss and Fort Quitman, had disappeared without a trace, and there was no sign of the money Rhett held in trust. Colonel Loring added that no resignation by Paymaster-Major Rhett had arrived at his headquarters. In fact, Major Rhett's money was already in Confederate hands in El Paso. Rhett next appeared during the Battle of Bull Run, in the uniform of a Confederate Army Major.[26]

NOTES - Chapter 5

1. Lynde to Assistant Adjutant General, Santa Fe, February 19, 1861, M1120, Rolls 13/14.
2. Edwin Sweeney, *Cochise*, p. 164.
3. Maury to Wheeler, February 24, 1861, M1012, Roll 2.
4. Maury to Canby, February 24, 1861, M1012, Roll 2.
5. Maury to Lynde, February 25, 1861, M1012, Roll 2.
6. Maury to Pitcairn Morrison, February 25, 1861, M1012, Roll 2.
7. Maury to Crittenden, March 1, 1861, M1012, Roll 2.
8. Maury to Lane, March 1, 1861, M1012, Roll 2.

9. Fauntleroy to Thomas, March 2, 1861, M1012, Roll 2.

10. Fauntleroy to Thomas, March 3, 1861, M1012, Roll 2.

11. Maury to Wheeler, March 3, 1861, M1012, Roll 2.

12. James D. Richardson, *Messages and Papers of the Presidents*, pp. 3204, 3205.

13. Ibid.

14. Lane to Maury, March 10, 1861, M1120, Rolls 13/14.

15. Maury to Lynde, March 10, 1861, M1012, Roll 2.

16. Lynde to Maury, March 11, 1861, M1120, Rolls 13/14.

17. *La Posta*, Volume II, #6, November-December 1970, p. 4.

18. Maury to Fort McLane and Fort Buchanan commanding officers, March 17, 1861, M1012, Roll 2.

19. Lynde to Assistant Adjutant General, Santa Fe, March 20, 1861, M1120, Rolls 13/14.

20. *Historical Times,* pp. 536, 537.

21. Maury to Crittenden, March 23, 1861, M1012, Roll 2.

22. Maury to Paul, March 23, 1861, M1012, Roll 2.

23. Loring to Thomas, March 23, 1861, M1012, Roll 2.

24. Lydia Spencer Lane, *I Married A Soldier*, p. 101.

25. Fort Fillmore Post Returns, March 1861.

26. Loring to Thomas, March 31, 1861, M1012, Roll 2.

6

A RESPONSE TO TEXAS BELLIGERENCE

Lieutenant Colonel Pitcairn Morrison was in Tucson seeking a way east on April 1, 1861. Morrison's departure at so curious a point in time indicates the Army high command either did not appreciate a Confederate threat to New Mexico or they did not intend to oppose that threat with Federal troops.[1]

A short note, written in early April by J.L. Donaldson, reported that the stolen wagon train that was headed from Albuquerque, through Fort McLane, to Fort Buchanan, had been carrying a new stock of shoes for the soldiers of Forts Buchanan and Breckinridge.[2]

Major Isaac Lynde had more problems in the first days of April than just a stolen wagon train, although the missing stock of shoes was certainly important. A paucity of military shoes helped end the Bonneville campaign of 1857 just when it was truly accomplishing its goals. Lynde's first report on the condition of his new field command was totally negative. There were severe problems at Fort Buchanan, the main supply depot for his post, Fort Mclane, and Fort Breckinridge. Lynde said:

> I have the honor to report that I have received the report from Fort Buchanan, by which it appears that the troops at that post are in no condition to take the field. The men are without shoes, and none for issue. That Post is the depot for provisions for this Post and Fort Breckinridge yet they have not more than

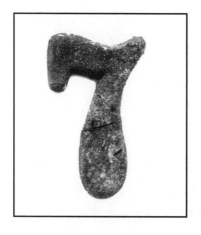

A brass 7th Infantry Regiment insignia for hat or collar that was left behind at Fort Fillmore when Isaac Lynde abandoned the post on July 26, 1861. *Courtesy: Author's collection.*

thirty days of some of the most important part of the rations (bacon particularly) for their own command. I have not received the report from Fort Breckinridge but am informed that it is in no better condition. We have not more than thirty days rations at this post for the companies now here.

It will be impossible to take the field until supplies are received from some point.[3]

While Lynde fretted over the state of readiness in the 7th Infantry companies in the western forts, Company 'K,' commanded by 1st Lieutenant Augustus H. Plummer, was the first unit of the 7th Infantry to arrive at Fort Fillmore that April. Plummer was the number two officer in the company. Company 'K' was recently commanded by Brevet-Major David P. Whiting, a very experienced soldier, who transferred to the 10th Infantry for a promotion. Whiting was another of the 7th Infantry officers who, like Marmaduke, should have been with their company at this point in history, and weren't.

First Lieutenant Plummer was an 1853 graduate of West Point, born in Ohio in 1832. Unlike 1st Lieutenant Lane, who was his senior and still retained, temporarily, command at Fort Fillmore, Plummer had no concerns over whether his state might choose to secede from the Union. He was commissioned a brevet-2^d lieutenant in the 6th Infantry on July 1, 1853 and was unable to find a permanent assignment until March 3, 1855, when he found his place in the 7th Infantry. A 1st lieutenant's promotion came on

January 2, 1858. Plummer was the first of the 7th Infantry officers to arrive at Fort Fillmore who would be involved in the Battle for Mesilla, the abandonment of Fort Fillmore, and the 7th's surrender at San Augustine Springs, three months after he arrived.

First Lieutenant Plummer, after surrendering Company 'K' at San Augustine, became a prisoner of war from July 1861 to August 1862. Plummer was promoted captain in the 19th Infantry on May 14, 1861, but the notice of promotion did not reach him in time to prevent his participation in the final events at Fort Fillmore. After gaining an end to his parole he became the operations staff officer in the 4th Division of the 20th Corps and served in that capacity for the remainder of the American Civil War. At the end of the war he was assigned as a captain to the new 37th Infantry Regiment, but became ill while on duty in Texas, dying on November 18, 1866 at the age of thirty-four.[4]

Plummer was assisted in performing company duties at Fort Fillmore by a second officer who arrived in April. He was 2^d Lieutenant Francis Crilly, from Pennsylvania, and the 1859 Class at West Point. Had 2^d Lieutenant Wheeler remained, he and Crilly might have had a fine reunion, both being from the same class. But Wheeler was gone and Crilly, a northerner, stood firm with the Union. The blue-eyed, blonde-haired Academy graduate was commissioned a brevet 2^d lieutenant in the 5th Infantry Regiment on July 1, 1859 but, before he could join, a slot opened and he came to the 7th Infantry Regiment on July 31, 1859. Like Plummer, he was taken prisoner at San Augustine Springs and eventually paroled. Back East, and once again with the 7th, he served as regimental quartermaster from September 1861 to February 9, 1863. Remaining in the quartermaster field he received brevets to major, lieutenant colonel, and colonel on March 13, 1865, for faithful and meritorious service during the Civil War. Crilly was general manager for United States Military Railroads from 1865 to 1867. He resigned from the Army on February 8, 1869.[5]

The Consulate of the United States still had an office in the Mexican town of Paso del Norte in the Spring of 1861, even though

Texas had seceded. No down-state Confederate authorities had yet arrived in the region by April. The Consulate was responsible for locating the stolen wagon train intended for Fort Buchanan. On April 5, the Consul appealed to Mexican authorities for assistance in finding the train and arresting the thieves. A Mexican, D. Pablo Rico, was authorized to make the arrests when the thieves were found. Rico found the thieves and the wagons in the town of Galiano, where he arrested the Confederate sympathizers. Rico took possession of the United States Army stores and moved them to Casas Grandes where another ripple in the story took place. A Captain of the Mexican Army, Miguel Avila, arrested Rico upon his arrival, stating that the wagons were to be confiscated because they had been illegally smuggled into Mexico to avoid payment of dues. Captain Avila then deposited the stolen stores at Casas Grandes and took his prisoners, Kirk and Rico, to the Governor of Sonora. When the American Consul wrote his letter the whole business was still up in the air, and Major Lynde's shoes were in the unfriendly hands of yet another potential enemy.

On April 7, Company 'D,' 7th Infantry, commanded by 1st Lieutenant Edward J. Brooks, arrived at Fort Fillmore, the second of the companies to arrive safely and without incident. Brooks is one of Fort Fillmore's most enigmatic and mysterious officers. Without him, the entire history of the next four months at Fort Fillmore might have changed drastically. Edward Brooks was appointed as a 2d lieutenant direct from civilian life in his home state of Michigan on June 30, 1855. He was assigned to the 7th Infantry Regiment and participated in both the Utah Campaign of 1858 and the Navajo Campaign of 1860, under Brevet-Lieutenant Colonel Canby. His actions against the Navajos were commended. Promotion to 1st lieutenant came on February 26, 1861. Of most importance to 7th Infantry Regimental history, 1st Lieutenant Brooks, while moving back and forth between Fort Fillmore and Fort McLane on duty, became Major Isaac Lynde's adjutant as of April 24, 1861. Although not a Southerner, Brooks chose to tender his resignation on May 16, but did not leave New Mexico Territory or the regiment. Instead, awaiting his resignation's approval, he somehow retained his adjutant's appointment under Lynde. His influence over Isaac Lynde and the decisions made in July 1861 appears to have been very significant. Brooks probably returned to Michigan after his parole. A gentleman named Edward J. Brooks, who may have been the mysterious former Fort Fillmore officer, is said to have served in the 10th Michigan Regiment during the Civil War, but not necessarily in combat. The most detailed reference available on Civil War officers' careers carries no further references for Brooks following the surrender at San Augustine Springs.[6]

On the day 1st Lieutenant Brooks and Company 'D' arrived, 1st Lieutenant Lane reported to Captain D.H. Maury in Santa Fe that the troops under his command had not been paid since August 1860, almost eight months before. This situation was due partly to the perfidy of Major Thomas Rhett, the former R.M.R. captain once stationed at Fort Fillmore. Lane didn't know why, or who did it; he was simply worried about the morale of his troops.[7]

That same April 7, Colonel William Wing Loring, now firmly in command of the Department of New Mexico, sent a status report to Assistant Adjutant General Thomas, stating:

> I have the honor to call the attention of the General-in-Chief to certain changes in the Department which have become desirable.
>
> The Post of Fort Breckinridge was established last year by order of the War Department, chiefly I believe with a view to the better protection of the Overland Mail route. That mail service has now been discontinued and Fort Breckinridge is a most unhealthy, comfortless, and expensive station. I request authority to break it up.
>
> The Point on the Canadian River which has been selected for the establishment of Fort Butler is an excellent one, on account of the influence it will give us over the Comanches, whose favorite haunts are upon that River and within striking distance of where Fort Butler is to be.
>
> [Reports] and my own knowledge of the Country have satisfied me that there is nowhere in that vicinity a suitable point for the establishment and maintenance of a General Depot for the Department. I request authority therefore to select a site for the Depot where timber, grass, fuel and water can be found at hand and from which supplies of all kinds can be conveniently

distributed. If this authority be granted to me at an early day, I believe I can find such a point.

When Albuquerque and Fort Craig are broken up there will be no post on the line of the Rio Grande between Fort Fauntleroy and Fort Fillmore. The establishment of Fort McLane renders Fort Fillmore no longer necessary. I therefore request authority to retain Fort Craig and to break up Fort Fillmore.

There will then be seven authorized Posts in this Department, which, a glance at the map will show you, are well planned for the general defense of the Territory. And so soon as I can I shall distribute the troops so as to occupy only these posts. There can be no doubt that discipline and efficiency will be naturally benefitted by this arrangement while there will also result from it a considerable diminution of the expenses of the department.[8]

It is easy with hindsight to believe that Colonel Loring was in the camp of Confederate Texas when this letter was written. If all his requests were satisfied, including the closing of Forts Breckinridge and Fillmore, there would have been no troops in southern New Mexico which could have challenged Confederate authority at Fort Bliss. The closest Federal force would have been hundreds of miles away, at either Fort McLane or Fort Craig. The border area with Mexico would have been under total Confederate influence. Was Loring really intending to construct a wide arc safety zone in the south in order to protect those Confederate interests? We can only conjecture. He did maintain Colonel Fauntleroy's strategy of keeping mounted troops at a minimum close to the Texas border. Of twelve mounted companies in New Mexico at the time, only two were south of Albuquerque. It is true Loring did acquiesce in the decision to send three companies of the 7th Infantry to reinforce Fort Fillmore. Why would he reinforce if he intended to protect Confederate interests south of the Jornada? There are two possible answers.

First, the reinforcing 7th Infantry companies were initially intended for use in the quelling of Indian troubles in the south. They were a warning to the Mescalero and other Apache bands that the Army was not going to tolerate open criminality.

A second possibility exists that Loring wanted to concentrate the 7th Infantry on the single route which would have allowed that regiment to leave New Mexico Territory, should the order come to depart. Was Colonel Loring already aware of the move back East to transfer all Regular Army regiments then on the frontier closer to Washington? That is very possible. He had been in the East only recently and must have attended strategy meetings related to what might happen as the result of secession. If the 7th Infantry units were concentrated at Forts Fillmore, McLane, and Buchanan (after the abandonment of Fort Breckinridge as Loring requested), then they would lie along a well-traveled route permitting quick concentration of the companies at Fort Fillmore for a regimental march to the East as a body. This, in fact, was what eventually happened.

Fort McLane was now the headquarters of the 7th Infantry Regiment. Isaac Lynde was the regimental commander. The transfer of the 7th Infantry Regimental Band from Fort Buchanan on April 8, 1861, signaled that transition of power. The regimental band went wherever the commander of the regiment had his headquarters.

On a lighter side, Lydia Spencer Lane mentioned attending a bullfight in the town of Mesilla in April, in a period when relations between the fort and the community across the river were still amicable. She also mentioned a flash flood on a sunny clear day caused by rainfall in the distant Organ Mountains. She said the water flowed all the way from the mountains, by means of who knew how many changes of direction, and into her quarters. Theirs were the only quarters flooded, so they had to change to a vacant dwelling nearby. As Fort Fillmore artifacts attest, the fort is in a spot where runoff water tended to gather. The greenish buildup of corrosion on brass and the poor quality of iron finds at the post attest to the truth of Lydia Lane's tale. During the 1986-87 New Mexico State University excavation at the ruins, participating students, on finding a possible path for water through an officer's quarters back adobe wall, were quick to believe they had found the actual route of Lydia Lane's flood. Lydia Lane also mentioned finding a rattlesnake in her quarters during this period. During the 1970s, when this author was often at the old ruins, rattlesnakes were a constant problem, as were tarantulas, scorpions and centipedes.[9]

Company 'I' was the next company from the 7th Infantry to arrive at Fort Fillmore that April. Company 'I's' arrival brought the total number of troops in the Fort Fillmore garrison to six officers and two hundred forty-one enlisted men, almost as many as in the best of the old days when the 3[d] Infantry Regiment headquartered there. The young men must have had a time putting the old fort back in a presentable and livable condition, given Lydia Spenser Lane's previous description. Lydia did not mention their arrival, but future writings indicate that the 7th Infantry was well accompanied by wives and children.

The commander of Company 'I' was Brevet-Major and Captain Gabriel Rene Paul. As senior officer, Paul officially took over command of the post after April 13, 1861, replacing 1st Lieutenant Lane who had outranked the earlier 7th Infantry officers. The fifty-year-old Paul was an 1834 graduate of West Point in his twenty-seventh year of service when he arrived at Fort Fillmore. Future career attainments indicate he was highly thought of by his compatriots. Commissioned a brevet-2[d] lieutenant of the 7th Infantry on July 1, 1834, he never left the regiment during his long career to that point. Promotion to 2[d] lieutenant followed on December 4, 1834, 1st lieutenant on October 26, 1836, and captain on April 19, 1846. Gabriel Paul earned a brevet to major on September 13, 1847 at the Battle of Chapultepec Castle, the final battle of the Mexican War. A Missourian by birth, he was honored with a special award by the people of St. Louis following that war. While at Fort Fillmore Brevet-Major Paul received a promotion to actual major of the 8th Infantry on April 22, 1861. Of course, there was no question of his reporting for duty with his new regiment. They were about to be made prisoners of war down in Texas. Major Paul was transferred in late June to Santa Fe where, on December 9, 1861, he was commissioned colonel of the 4th New Mexico Volunteer Infantry Regiment. Promotion to lieutenant colonel of the 8th Infantry Regiment, Regular Army, followed on April 25, 1862, which led to Paul being mustered out of his New Mexico Volunteer position on May 31, 1862. In September 1862, he became a brigadier general in the Federal Volunteer Service. At

Gettysburg, in early July 1863, he was severely wounded, losing sight in both eyes. Honors still kept coming. Gabriel Paul was officially retired from the Volunteer Service on February 16, 1865, receiving a brevet to major general for gallantry and meritorious service at Gettysburg. As a final reward he was temporarily activated, then retired once more, this time in the rank of brigadier general, Regular United States Army, with full pay, and by a Special Act of Congress. General Paul died in Washington D.C. on May 5, 1886, at the age of seventy-five, one of the most honored of those who once served at Fort Fillmore.[10]

Gabriel Paul's second in command of Company 'I,' Brevet-2^d Lieutenant Lyman Mischler, took over command of the company when Paul took over the post. Lyman Mischler was one of the youngest officers in the regiment, if not the youngest. He graduated from West Point in 1860. Born in Pennsylvania in 1839 Mischler was closing in on his twenty-second birthday when his life was snuffed out at Valverde Mesa in February 1862, in battle with the Texans who had dishonored the reputation of his first regiment. Mischler was at Fort Fillmore only a very short time, having earlier received a promotion to 2^d lieutenant of the 5th Infantry Regiment, which caused his immediate transfer to northern New Mexico to join his new unit. Hastily promoted to 1st lieutenant in the 5th Infantry on May 14, 1861, he posthumously received one final award, a brevet to captain for gallantry and meritorious service at the Battle of Valverde in February 1862. 1st Lieutenant Mischler was one of those young men who died fighting to save McRae's artillery battery during the battle, perhaps the single most famous incident in Civil War New Mexico history. Not far from Mischlers' body was that of 2^d Lieutenant George Bascom, whose temper and actions at Apache Pass Station were the reason Mischler had a chance to be at Fort Fillmore, brief as that service was.[11]

The six officers at Fort Fillmore in early 1861 included Brevet-Major Gabriel Paul, 1st Lieutenant William B. Lane, 1st Lieutenant Augustus H. Plummer, 2^d Lieutenant Edward R. Brooks, 2nd Lieutenant Francis Crilly and Brevet-2^d Lieutenant Lyman Mischler. All, save possibly Lane, were absolutely Union men. That situation was soon to change.

*   *   *

On the day Fort Sumter was fired upon in far away South Carolina, April 14, 1861, duties of a mundane nature seemed to be the order of the day in the Department of New Mexico. In Santa Fe, Brevet-Captain Maury wrote 1st Lieutenant Chapin, 7th Infantry, commanding Fort Buchanan, that the delay in paying the troops at the fort was of concern to the Department, and efforts were being made to see that the troops were paid. Fort Fillmore's commander received similar reassurances. This failure to pay the troops could, and did, cause problems with discipline and increased the rates of desertion within the commands. As the situation worsened, the credit of the Federal Government came into question and merchants would no longer accept payments for goods which were not made in cash. Federal vouchers, the normal manner of attaining credit in peace-time, became unacceptable.[12]

On April 15, 1861, the United States flag that flew over Fort Sumter during the bombardment was lowered. The bay fort surrendered to South Carolina militia under the command of General P.G.T. Beauregard, a former Regular Army officer. President Abraham Lincoln quickly called for seventy-five thousand volunteers to put down a potential insurrection in the states of South Carolina, Georgia, Alabama, Florida, Mississippi, Louisiana, and Texas. It is unclear when the command at Fort Fillmore found out about the fall of Fort Sumter. Lydia Lane stated there was no improvement in mail facilities, and a month was still required to receive a civilian letter from the East, if it arrived at all. It is doubtful that the news would have taken that long to reach them, coming by means of the pony-express-like official government service.[13]

As Fort Sumter hauled down the flag of the United States in surrender, Companies 'A' and 'E' of the 7th Infantry arrived at Fort McLane. Major Isaac Lynde notified the Department of their arrival, mentioning that of the three forts under his command (Breckinridge, Buchanan, and McLane) there were only 1,767 pounds of bacon at Fort McLane, 3,000 pounds at Fort Buchanan and 3,000 pounds at Fort Breckinridge. Major Lynde considered this amount of bacon, the soldier's staple meat, to be very insufficient for the campaign he was still intending to conduct against the Apaches. Additional supplies of bacon were requested on February 24, 1861, but there had been no response from Albuquerque, the point of shipment.[14]

In addition, Lynde reported that all the mules at Fort Buchanan were broken down—an army term meaning they were unfit for service. Lieutenant Colonel Morrison had not advised higher authorities of the true situation there before going on leave. In fact, both the Fort Buchanan and Fort Breckinridge commands advised Lynde that the current strengths of their posts were barely adequate for interior defense, let alone trying to support a long and arduous campaign against the Apaches.[15]

The two infantry companies sent to Fort McLane arrived in the most shabby condition possible. They were destitute of proper clothing and Major Lynde had on hand only the amount necessary to clothe his own companies over the next half year. The two companies brought no usable transportation and were in such a state that Isaac Lynde considered them a burden on the command, rather than a reinforcement. Colonel Loring and Brevet-Captain Maury may or may not have been responsible for increasing Major Lynde's burden by sending unfit and poorly supplied troops into a situation that would make matters worse for all concerned. Major Lynde, frustrated at being given a totally ridiculous task without proper supply and support, firmly stated the obvious. He could not conduct a campaign against the Apaches under such conditions.[16]

On April 19, Brevet-Captain Maury ordered Major Lynde, in the name of Colonel Loring, to establish a system of express riders and/or wagons to carry the mail between Forts Fillmore, McLane, Buchanan and Breckinridge—the Butterfield Overland Mail was closed for operations. No mention was made of Mesilla or any other civilian community being involved in the mail route.[17]

Although he was in the middle of an expedition against the Mescalero, Brevet-Lieutenant Colonel George Bibb Crittenden, then at Fort Stanton, requested leave of absence from his command in early April, presumably to go East and check his prospects with the Confederacy. By October 1861, he was appointed to the rank of major general, Confederate States Army. On April 24, Colonel Loring had refused Crittenden's request for leave. According to the refusal letter, the Department was swamped with requests for leave for various officers and "does not feel authorized to accede to your request." Even at this date, Loring must have been considering the time of his own departure as well. Can Loring have wanted Crittenden to hold his position for the South? Whatever the case, Crittenden immediately resigned his commission upon receiving Loring's refusal and departed New Mexico.[18]

The Department of New Mexico was falling apart. Second Lieutenant Jackson, R.M.R., Crittenden's second in command, requested leave at the same time. Jackson was also refused leave, forcing his resignation.

Indications of a coming collapse of military goals in New Mexico were obvious by mid-April. Had there been no American Civil War, Colonel Loring would no doubt have established a fort named Fort Butler near Hatch's Ranch at Mesa Rica, in the Comanche country. He was already calling the site by that name when he requested 1st Lieutenant Alexander McRae to urge the Comanche tribal leaders to meet with him at the future fort site.[19]

A freight (wagon) train leaving Fort Buchanan for the Rio Grande was ambushed by Cochise's Apaches on May 3 at the now-abandoned San Simon Station on the former Butterfield Mail Stage route. San Simon Station lay eighteen miles northeast of Apache Pass. The attack was fought off by the soldier escort but the Indians escaped with seventeen head of cattle.[20]

Virginia seceded on April 17. By April 27, officials in Richmond requested that consideration be given to making Richmond the capitol of the Confederacy. At that time the capitol was still located at Montgomery, Alabama.

On April 28, Captain Morris, Mounted Rifles, at Fort Craig, was ordered to furnish an escort for the mails from Fort Craig to Fort Fillmore. The journey was no longer safe. The mail agent assured the Department that a spring wagon would be provided by the mail company for the transportation of the escort. Whether Mounted Rifles or infantry, the mail escort was to ride in wagons on the journey, vehicles with springs being much more comfortable over the rough dirt tracks through the Jornada and below. At Fort McLane, Major Isaac Lynde waited in vain for the quartermaster and commissary supplies he was expecting, so that the campaign against the Apaches could begin. Measures to gather the goods were supposedly being taken at Santa Fe and Albuquerque, although they were never sent.

The means to uncover hidden secessionist sympathizers within the Army was drafted in Washington by April 30. War Department General Order No. 13 stated:

> The President directs that all officers of the Army, except those who have entered the service since the 1st instant, take and subscribe anew the oath of allegiance to the United States of America, as set forth in the tenth article of war.
> Commanding officers will see to the prompt execution of this order, and report accordingly.[21]

No wonder so many resignations took place in May 1861. The hidden Confederates could not stay beyond the point of reception of the order to take the oath, not if they had any honor, which at least one former New Mexico post commander at Fort Craig apparently didn't have, not joining the Confederate cause until 1862, a year after the war started. Given about two weeks for the loyalty oath message to arrive in New Mexico and be distributed, a significant number of officers were about to give up their careers, or be dishonored through taking the oath of loyalty without intention to obey that order.

Later, at a point when there was a definite threat from Confederate Texas, Colonel Edward Canby stated that in early May the Federal troops at Fort Fillmore began receiving encouragement from secessionist forces in Texas and at Mesilla to desert to the Texas camp. There was no official notice of such a threat in Fort Fillmore correspondence. On May 3, 1st Lieutenant Lane was notified that the War Office had rescinded the contracts with Taliaferro & Grant for the delivery of supplies to Arizona. This may have been an indication that private contractors were not fulfilling the needs Major Isaac Lynde required. There was no mention of who might replace the contractors; at this point probably nobody did. Lieutenant Lane was assigned to the Subsistence Department, along with his Company 'A' duties, and followed the orders of the Department chief of commissary. The commander of the single mounted company below the Jornada was ordered to take his mind off Indian problems and concentrate on getting supplies to where they were needed.[22]

At Fort McLane, Major Lynde had more wagon train trouble, possibly from Confederate sympathizers among the teamsters, or maybe as the result of the growing Apache conflict. Everything was going wrong, everywhere, as Lynde's May 5 letter to the Department indicates. He said:

> By the last mail I received an extract from the proceedings of a Board of Officers held at Albuquerque N.M. on the 17th of April 1861. I have only to say, in explanation, that when the train arrived here, a part of the teamsters asked to be discharged, in consequence of which the train was detained four or five days to supply their places. When the train was ready to start and just hitching up to start some more of the teamsters refused to go on, and I ordered them marched out of the garrison by a file of the guard, which was done.[23]

Lynde may have wondered whether anyone around him was still loyal. Pinos Altos miners threatened to take his public property; secessionist wagon masters stole his trains; Apaches were vigilant and ready for a fight on every side; teamsters, the key to survival and the safety of public property, refused to move the goods. Might Major Lynde have wondered what next?

Captain Richard Stoddard Ewell, sometimes a visitor to Fort Fillmore and many times a campaigner with Fort Fillmore-based companies while serving at Forts Thorn and Buchanan, resigned his commission on May 5, 1861, leaving for the East at once. By June he was a brigadier general in the Confederate Army. Ewell was supposed to be in Arizona at the time of his resignation but, as civil war rhetoric began to rise, he was on sick leave in his native state of Virginia.

May 13 was the date on which Colonel William Wing Loring officially tendered his resignation as Colonel of the Regiment of Mounted Rifles and as Head of the Department of New Mexico. One can only wonder if this was not also near the date when the loyalty oath order arrived from the East, unmasking those who had previously hidden their Southern attachments. May 13 was not the date in which Loring gave up effective command of the Department, however. He controlled Department of New Mexico affairs until he was replaced by Brevet-Lieutenant Colonel Edward Canby on June 11. The intervening period has to be credited for decisions made by Loring. There certainly were some interesting ones.

Brevet-Captain Dabney Maury resigned his position in May also, although the date is not sure. His initial resignation was not accepted and, like Colonel Loring, he remained in the Department until late June, when, because of known and vocal Southern sympathies, he was dismissed from the Army. By early 1862, he was a colonel on the staff of Earl Van Dorn in Texas.

The incoming Department commander, Brevet-Lieutenant Colonel and Major of Infantry Edward Richard Sprigg Canby jumped two ranks to the grade of Colonel of the 19th Infantry Regiment, as of May 14, 1861. An unprecedented promotion, Canby's rise can only mean that the coming civil war was beginning to affect the careers of many Regular Army officers. By 1862, he would be a general officer.

In early May, Captain Cadmus Wilcox, commanding officer of Company 'K,' 7th Infantry, arrived at Fort Fillmore for duty. Wilcox replaced Augustus Plummer in command. He was, like Maury, another interesting character with strong secessionist leanings. Wilcox, born in 1825 in North Carolina, attended West Point, where he was commissioned a brevet-2d lieutenant in the 4th Infantry Regiment on July 1, 1846; advancement to 2d lieutenant in the 7th Infantry came on February 6, 1847. Wilcox was awarded a brevet to 1st lieutenant on September 13, 1847, for gallantry at the Battle of Chapultepec Castle in Mexico City. Promotion to 1st lieutenant came on August 24, 1851, after which he was assigned to duties in the tactics department at West Point for five years. His final Federal promotion, to captain, came on December 20, 1860. This officer was one of the young bright lights of the United States military establishment of his day. He was to resign his commission on June 8, 1861, at exactly the moment he was most needed by his company at Fort Fillmore. Wilcox was the fourth 7th infantry line officer, after Marmaduke, Whiting, and Paul, who would not be there in July when experience and leadership counted most.[24]

Cadmus Wilcox was appointed a brigadier general in October 1861, as Isaac Lynde and the other paroled members of the 7th Infantry, including soldiers from his own company, made their way across the great plains in disgrace. General Wilcox commanded a brigade at Gettysburg and, although the outcome was a defeat of immense proportions, was promoted to major general in August 1863 as a result of his bravery. He was a division commander thereafter in battles from the Wilderness Campaign to Appomattox. After the war, Cadmus Wilcox became a Federal government employee, working in the post of Chief of the Railroad Division in the U.S. Government Land Office.[25]

While Wilcox wrestled with his decision as to when to tender his resignation at Fort Fillmore, Cochise struck at Fort Buchanan. At Monkey Springs, about two miles south of the fort, Apaches killed one soldier and stole two mules.[26]

On May 17, 1861, a most important order was dispatched from Headquarters of the Army. The commander of the Department of New Mexico was to gather all Regular Army troops into their regimental commands, in preparation for their leaving the Department as quickly as possible. They were not to defend the forts but to abandon them or turn them over to New Mexico volunteers. Colonel Edward Canby, who was in command at the time the order arrived at Santa Fe on June 14, 1861, went into immediate action, ordering the massing of the 7th Infantry at Fort Fillmore and elements of the 5th Infantry at Fort Union. We do not want to get ahead of ourselves here, but this order is so important to what eventually happened at Fort Fillmore that special note of its sending must be taken.[27]

On May 17, an order went out to all posts stating that thirty-four companies of New Mexico Volunteers were to be enlisted to protect the Territory in any upcoming conflict. Three days later, on May 20, the state of North Carolina, its many pro-Union citizens angered by Abraham Lincoln's call for volunteers, seceded from the Union.

While authorities in Texas prepared their troops for garrison duty along the old line of forts stretching from Fort Clark to Fort Bliss, Major Isaac Lynde had his share of troubles at Fort McLane. Apaches attacked the post herd, running off a number of animals. Lynde notified the Department of his response to the attack in a letter written on May 25. At the same time Lynde asked once again how the Department of New Mexico could order him to conduct a full campaign against the Apaches and yet provide him with nothing with which to conduct it. Lynde said:

> I have the honor to report that on the 22nd instant a party of Apache Indians attacked our herd of mules about three miles from the post, returning from the herding ground in the evening, and killed one of the herders Private Robert Crawford of "A" Company 7th Infantry and run off 22 public mules belonging to this post and 5 belonging to Fort Fillmore that have not been recovered besides a large number of private animals. They were immediately pursued by a party mounted on mules but could not be overtaken. A mounted force is much needed here, for it is almost useless to pursue these Indians with troops on foot or mounted on poor mules. The mules left here are much broken down, as the grazing is very bad there having been no rain since last summer, and we have no forage. The a.a.q.m. [quartermaster] has no funds except drafts which he can neither get cashed or use to purchase with. If we don't receive forage soon or get rain to start the grass, the mules that we have will soon be totally unfit for service, in fact are nearly so now from the constant labor of escorts and other duties required of them.
>
> This loss of mules will cripple me very much if supplies are received to enable me to send troops into the mountains against the Indians, we are still without bacon.
>
> The Indians are getting very bold and are constantly committing the most cruel outrages. The whole Apache nation seem on the watch for any opportunity to commit depredations on any party that is not strong enough to defend themselves. I have daily applications for protection and am unable to supply it for the want of provisions and a mounted force. I have to request that at least two companies of mounted troops may be

ordered to this Post if supplies can be sent here for them and that the a.a.q.m. may be authorized to purchase mules to supply the place of those lost and funds in coin for the purpose may be sent immediately.

I am ordered to conduct an expedition against the Apache Indians, yet nothing is supplied to enable me to do so; there has not been a pound of salt provisions for issue at this post for more than a month. Three months has passed since <u>bacon</u> and other provisions were ordered here from Albuquerque, as reported by the Chief Commissary of the Department [Grayson], yet not a pound has been received. A train from Albuquerque came here a few days since with Sugar, Coffee, etc. which we did not need but no bacon. We have but a few days flour, but we expect some soon from Fort Fillmore. When it will come I can't tell. There has been a gross neglect of duty on the part of either the Quartermaster or Subsistence Departments which is unpardonable.[28]

Was there actually an intent for Lynde to conduct an expedition against the Apaches, or were the future Confederates who still headed the Department of New Mexico simply giving him something to do while the problems in the East could be sorted out? It appears there may have been deliberate sabotage of this campaign, either from Department or in collusion with others, such as officers working for the commissary. Neither Department commander, Fauntleroy or Loring, seemed disturbed that Lynde was unable to conduct his campaign. There were no urgent messages demanding action, and Lynde's requests for supplies remained unanswered by the gentlemen of the quartermaster and commissary. Major Lynde had to wonder what was going on, yet he laid no blame on the Department commander for what may have been incompetence at least, if not downright treachery. Was a too-trusting nature also part of Isaac Lynde's personality? Was he rendered inactive when he found so much treachery around him, with the Apaches, the miners, the people of Mesilla, even the officers in his command?

Such questions are important to raise because of what happened in July 1861. At this point Lynde acted very much as any other New Mexico commander might have. He refused to send infantry out alone to conduct a hapless pursuit of mounted warriors.

NOTES - Chapter 6

1. Fort McLane Post Records, April 1861.
2. Donaldson to Assistant Adjutant General, Santa Fe, April 1861, M1120, Rolls 13/14.
3. Lynde to Assistant Adjutant General, Santa Fe, April 3, 1861, M1120, Rolls 13/14.
4. Heitman, Augustus Plummer.
5. Heitman, Francis Crilly.
6. Heitman, Edward Brooks.
7. Lane to Maury, April 7, 1861, M1120, Rolls 13/14.
8. Loring to Thomas, April 7, 1861, M1012, Roll 2.
9. Lydia Spencer Lane, *I Married A Soldier*, pp. 102, 103.
10. Heitman, Gabriel Paul.
11. Heitman, Lyman Mischler.
12. Maury to Chapin, April 14, 1861, M1012, Roll 2.
13. Lydia Spencer Lane, *I Married A Soldier*, p. 100.
14. Lynde to Assistant Adjutant General, April 16, 1861, M1120, Rolls 13/14.
15. Ibid.
16. Ibid.
17. Maury to Lynde, April 19, 1861, M1012, Roll 2.
18. Maury to Crittenden, April 24, 1861, M1012, Roll 2.
19. Loring to McRae, April 25, 1861, M1012, Roll 2.
20. Edwin Sweeney, *Cochise*, pp. 173, 174.
21. James P. Richardson, *Messages and Papers of the Presidents*, p. 3219.
22. Maury to Lane, May 3, 1861, M1012, Roll 2.
23. Lynde to Assistant Adjutant General, Santa Fe, May 5, 1861, M1120, Rolls 13/14.
24. Heitman, Cadmus Wilcox.
25. Ibid.
26. Edwin Sweeney, *Cochise*, p. 174.
27. Thomas to Canby, May 17, 1861, M1102, Rolls 13/14.
28. Lynde to Assistant Adjutant General, Santa Fe, May 25, 1861, M1120, Rolls 13/14.

7

THE ENEMY WITHIN

A nother of the key characters in the Fort Fillmore final days' story arrived at the fort on May 29. He was Captain Robert R. Garland. Garland, a Virginian, was probably aware when he arrived at Fort Fillmore that his state had seceded (April 17). Garland was not a West Point officer, having been appointed directly from civilian life as a 2^d lieutenant in the 7th Infantry on December 23, 1847. Promotion to 1st lieutenant came on March 3, 1855 and to captain on March 23, 1861. Captain Garland had an interesting, if brief, one-month career at Fort Fillmore. When the time came to take up the cause of the South, rather than resigning, he simply deserted. Garland became a colonel in the 6th Texas Volunteer Infantry, so it is easy to tell which side he was on while at Fort Fillmore. Unfortunately, Isaac Lynde trusted Garland implicitly, rejoicing when he found Captain Garland was to be in command of the post just before his arrival there. Here, as at Fort McLane during the Apache campaign, is a further example of Isaac Lynde trusting too much in the honor of those around and above him, only to be disappointed by their treachery and incompetence. Robert Garland signed the June 30, 1861, monthly report while serving as commanding officer of Fort Fillmore, and then deserted just before July 4, the day Lynde arrived.[1]

Companies 'D,' 'I,' and 'K,' 7th Infantry, and Company 'A,' R.M.R., were at Fort Fillmore on May 29 when Captain Garland arrived. Brevet-Major Gabriel Paul was still in command. The situation in Texas had not changed. The 8th Infantry companies were gone but there were as yet no Confederate troops on the scene. Federal artillery pieces, with ammunition and powder, as well as other public property, remained at Fort Bliss. This equipment would be of immense value to the Texans. No move was made by Brevet-Major Paul to recover the property; as was the custom in New Mexico Territory, no action could be taken unless the Department commander permitted that action. Future Confederate General William Wing Loring was still in command at Santa Fe, despite of the fact he was in the process of resignation. Loring was not about to order Paul to advance on Fort Bliss. Thus it was that the Federal artillery eventually fell into the hands of the Texans, who later turned it on its former owners.

Resignations were becoming a problem within the 7th Infantry Regiment. Trained company officers abandoned their commands in May and June in significant numbers, permitting their troops to come under the command of officers who did not know the men. Like Marmaduke, Whiting, Wilcox, and Garland, Captain Lafayette McLaws, then at Santa Fe, was supposed to be at Fort Fillmore commanding Company 'D.' Instead, Captain McLaws resigned his commission, another future Confederate general-to-be. McLaws was the fifth 7th Infantry troop commander to leave the regiment before Isaac Lynde arrived at Fort Fillmore. McLaws's abandonment was critical, as his company, which would have been part of any force advancing toward Fort Bliss if called upon, no longer had any officers available for duty.[2]

The lone Southern sympathizer who did not resign in the end was 1st Lieutenant William Lane. Lane, a Kentuckian, had sympathies with the Southern cause, but he would never serve it. Kentucky chose by a narrow margin to stay in the Union, although many of its sons fought for the South. Why slave-owner Lane stayed loyal is not known. He took the loyalty oath when offered. Whatever his thoughts, there were soon to be other actions that would eliminate Lane's training as a company commander from being of any use to Isaac Lynde.

There were still loyal Union officers at Fort Fillmore in late May and into June 1861. Besides Brevet-Major Paul on the Union side there were 1st Lieutenant Plummer, Assistant Surgeon McKee (not a troop leader) and young 2^d Lieutenant Francis Crilly. Once Brevet-Major Paul left in June, under somewhat clouded circum-stances, Lynde was reduced to using junior officers with little command experience to command companies whose soldiers did not know their leaders. Also, of the three officers supposed to be assigned to each company only one was available at most. Such was a recipe for disaster.[3]

There were problems of a disciplinary nature within the ranks as well. An unusual total of four enlisted men deserted in the month of May from Lane's Mounted Rifles company. More left in the days to come, but not the flood that some might have expected.

Although there had yet to be a major battle, the schism between the Northern and Southern States was fully rent by June 1, the day the Confederate States postal system began operations. It must be assumed postal business went on as usual in southern New Mexico. The main route for mail was north, then across the Santa Fe Trail to Missouri. George Frazier, a Southern sympathizer, remained postmaster at Mesilla and George A. Hayward, also a Southerner, at Fort Fillmore. Frazier somehow managed to stay on as Mesilla postmaster throughout the Confederate period and the Union reoccupation, not leaving the position until December 26, 1867. The Fort Fillmore post office closed when the fort fell in July 1861.[4]

June 1861 was a most interesting month in Fort Fillmore history, perhaps even more interesting in some ways than the following month of July, when the post was abandoned and the troops surrendered. Brevet-Major Paul theoretically held the command until the last days of the month. Wilcox and Garland, ardent secessionists, stayed on for most of the month of June as well, being joined by fellow secessionists such as Colonel William Wing Loring, who, although resigned from the Army, decided to retain command in southern New Mexico until President Lincoln accepted his resignation. As we shall see, Canby commanded north of the Jornada del Muerto, unable to do anything about Loring's continued presence. Because the dates on which Colonel Loring arrived and departed Fort Fillmore in the month of June were between monthly reports, his presence was not included in post end-of-month records, even though he was there into the fourth week. We have to trust to Colonel Canby's dating as to when Loring left Santa Fe and may have arrived at Fort Fillmore. There is no record of his having taken temporary command from Brevet-Major Paul, although Loring must have done so.[5]

Several other future Confederate officers passed through Fort Fillmore that June after resigning their commissions. Lydia Lane remarked on their passing, but seemed confused at the later date of her writing as to who was there when. She said:

> Many of our oldest and truest army friends resigned and went South, several of them passing through Fort Fillmore on their way out of New Mexico. Among them were General Longstreet [then a major-paymaster], who came into post driving his own ambulance, en route to Texas; Cadmus Wilcox, Colonel W.W. Loring, Lawrence Baker, Major Sibley [Henry Hopkins Sibley, the future invader of New Mexico], and others [such as Marmaduke and Garland] whose names I have forgotten. Colonel George B. Crittenden, one of our best friends, also went down to Texas, and I never saw him again.[6]

The rebel officers-to-be must have found a warm welcome at Fort Fillmore, since the commanding officer, whether it was Loring, Wilcox, or Garland at different times in that hectic month, was one of their own. Fort Fillmore had become a Rebel stronghold, save for the enlisted men. The post was apparently used as a way station on an underground railroad moving Confederate sympathizers out of the Territory. The fact that Texans didn't capture the post at this point indicates a sufficient force from Texas was not yet on the scene. Besides, it took a Baylor and a Sibley to convince Confederate authorities that New Mexico had any value at all in their overall scheme. That time was not yet come.

Cochise returned to the warpath in Arizona in early June. His large band stole forty-four mules at the San Pedro Station, then swung south along the Santa Cruz River. Estimates are that eighty to one hundred warriors were in the band. During one battle the Apaches ran off four hundred cattle and killed four men. There were no mounted troops in the region to oppose them. The road from Mesilla to Tucson was often cut by Apache raiders during this period, and as often closed to traffic. On June 3, 1861, a wagon train was ambushed at Cook's Peak with two Mexicans killed and two mules stolen.[7]

First Lieutenant Lane wrote the Department on June 7. He reported the potential for a total breakdown of morale and discipline at Fort Fillmore, the result, he said, of the failure of the Federal Government to pay the troops. Lane pointed to eighteen or twenty desertions in his command, only eleven of which were listed in the Post Returns of the period, as having been caused by the failure to receive pay. He made no mention of the disharmony caused by the presence of so many ardent secessionists, although no doubt some enlisted men deserted out of loyalty to their longtime Regiment of Mounted Rifle's commander, Colonel Loring. Lane said:

> I have the honor again to call the attention of the Dept. Commander to the great length of time it has been since my Company has been paid. I have lost by desertion since about the middle of Feby. last eighteen or twenty men & I believe it has been almost solely on account of the impression that they were not to be paid. The men that have deserted were all recruits but it has been with the greatest difficulty that I have satisfied some of the "old men" of the Company that they were certain to receive their pay. I have [given them] our [word]. Again to be assured that there was no doubt about their getting all that was due by the government, but it has become such an old story, that I am not sure but they think I am a party to the wrong that is being done them. The majority of the Company was paid in August 1860 but a great many have not been paid since April of last year.
>
> I would also call the attention of the Department Commander to the fact that it is almost impossible for an officer to dispose of his pay accounts to pay his debts, & is not at all [improbable] to hunt the country over, [if] it was to discount a

pay account. In [view] of these facts, I would most earnestly request that money, if not a paymaster, be sent to this post to pay the troops.[8]

If any enemy wanted to lower morale, the easiest way would be to ensure that the opposition's troops were not paid. Failure to pay the troops at Fort Fillmore led to desertion, lower morale, and an inability to properly perform their mission. The troops were not paid until Canby took full command and could overcome the policies of his predecessors. It is difficult to see how Colonel Fauntleroy, Colonel Loring, and Brevet-Captain Maury were not involved in the pay debacle, as well as Major James Longstreet and Major Thomas Grimke Rhett, both paymasters. The failure to pay the troops, which created a high desertion rate and a lowering of morale, as well as a mutinous condition among the troops, is the clearest sign that treachery was afoot in New Mexico and at Fort Fillmore before Isaac Lynde got there.

The only surviving major-paymaster in the Department at this point was Augustus Henry Seward. Paymaster Seward, then at Santa Fe, was notified by Canby that the condition of affairs in the Department were such that he was to be retained for the present at Santa Fe—he was to execute his official bond as paymaster in the Army of the United States and would enter upon his duties in that capacity. The cryptic nature of this message is not clear across the years. Indeed the Department was now in the midst of disaster. Was it feared that Seward would also defect with the funds necessary to pay the troops, if he were allowed to leave Santa Fe?[9]

With Fort Fillmore infested with Southern sympathizers, could the situation in Mesilla have been any better? Lydia Lane stated, when speaking of one of the wives of a southern-born officer, that the woman "made a flippant remark" when mention of the flag of the United States was raised in conversation. The woman stated she had made the remark "just to tease Doctor McKee," an ardent Unionist. W.W. Mills, a Union sympathizer then residing briefly in Mesilla, stated, "I assure you that I find matters here in a most deplorable condition. A disunion flag is now flying from the house in which I write, and this country is now as much in the possession of the enemy as Charleston [South Carolina] is." One can only wonder what a disunion flag was. Was it a Texas flag? Was it some kind of "Don't tread on me" type of secessionist banner created by the locals? The *Historical Times Illustrated Encyclopedia of the Civil War* states that the Confederate Congress, in March 1861, hastily adopted a flag which looked something like the flag of the United States with a canton in blue in the upper left corner but with only seven stars, one for each of the seven states in the Confederacy. There were but three stripes, red at top, white in the center, and red on the bottom. This is the flag that flew over secessionist units during the 1st Battle of Bull Run. It is possible that such a flag was flying at Mesilla in June. The flag definitely was not the currently popular Confederate Battle Flag, which was not adopted by the Confederate Congress, although most of the people in the South adopted it by popular acclamation.[10]

Major Lynde, at Fort McLane, was still acting as if he had an Indian campaign to conduct that June, rather than having to deal with a civil war just on the horizon. He seemed completely out of the political loop. One reason for his attitude could have been that Fauntleroy and Loring kept him in the dark, save for rumors, about the situation in the East and in the rest of New Mexico. On June 7, a perturbed Major James L. Donaldson, Chief Quarter Master of the Department of New Mexico, responded briefly to Major Lynde's charge that there may have been gross neglect on the part of the Quarter Master or Commissary in equipping his units for a field campaign. Donaldson said:

> I must again call Major Lynde's attention to par. 441 of the Regulations. If he has any complaint to make it should be to this office agreeably to that Para.
> Major Lynde's charges against the Quartermasters Dept. are not warranted by the facts. He had authority to call upon the Depot at Albuquerque for whatever stores he needed to make a Campaign against the Apaches. In that reference to this office, and if all he called for was not sent, it was because it was not in depot and could not be purchased in the Territory. No bacon

was sent to Fort McLane for the reason that the Depot Commissary had none on hand for transportation. Bacon has since arrived, and will be promptly transported when ready.[11]

If Donaldson and the Quarter Master Department could so easily slip their responsibility, allowing that bacon, the staple of the troops, was not at the Albuquerque Depot and could therefore not be shipped, then the failure to take the field against the Apaches could be laid at the feet of the former Department commander, who gave the order to begin the campaign. Fauntleroy was gone when Donaldson reported, but when he was in command did not seem to care if Lynde was able to carry out his mission or not, only that he be kept busy. There remains the potential that the whole episode was contrived to appear as if activity wase taking place, when in fact actual events rendered such campaigning difficult if not impossible. Drought, a pending civil conflict, internal friction within the Officer Corps, Indian depredations, all occurring at the same time, brought a breakdown in Department capability that was impossible to overcome.

When news of North Carolina and Virginia's secession arrived in New Mexico Territory, Colonel William Wing Loring did the right thing, finally and immediately tendering his resignation. On June 11, soon-to-be private citizen Loring left Santa Fe for the South. Loring headed for Fort Fillmore, where he is known to have stayed for several days before going on to Fort Bliss.

The record is not as clear as to whether former Brevet-Captain Dabney Maury was with Loring at the time. One can only wonder if Maury was among those "others whose names I have forgotten," mentioned by Lydia Lane when referring to future Confederates who visited Fort Fillmore that June, "en route to Texas."[12]

Brevet-Lieutenant Colonel Edward Canby took command of the northern portion of the Department on Loring's departure. Fortunately for the Union forces, Canby immediately began to change Loring's spider-like hold on Department affairs. Canby contacted the Assistant Adjutant General at once, detailing the state of affairs in the Department he now commanded in all but name. Canby said:

I have the honor to report that Colonel Loring, Regiment of Mounted Riflemen, in anticipation of the acceptance of his resignation, left this place today after placing me in the general charge of the affairs of the Department and in the immediate command of the Northern District. He has not formally relinquished the Command and will await at Fort Fillmore the action of the President upon the tender of his resignation.

I have no reason to apprehend any immediate political trouble in this Department, and in the future this will be contingent upon the action of Missouri with which the people of this Territory are more intimately connected in their commercial relations and associations than with Texas or the States of Mexico. The disaffection in Arizona is, in my judgement, confined to a small portion of the population of that Territory and the disaffected are believed to be without the means of effecting anything against the Government as they have earnestly and expectantly applied for the assistance of the troops in settling their local difficulties.

A demonstration against Arizona by the people of Texas may be apprehended, although there is nothing known here of any movement, in that direction. I will take measures to increase materially the force at Fort Fillmore by withdrawing and transferring a portion of the troops from the interior part, and if possible an additional mounted force from the upper country.

The long deferred payment of the troops aided by the mischievous efforts of some individuals in that country have created some dissatisfaction among the troops at some of the posts, but this will be removed by the payment at an early period of a portion of the arrearage now due. The funds in the hands of the paymasters will not be sufficient to pay the whole amount, but will leave for the troops in Arizona about four months arrearage. It is hoped that a sufficiency of funds to meet these may soon be received.

Major Reynolds will pay the troops at Fort Fillmore, Major Seward those at Forts McLane, Buchanan and Breckenridge [sic], and Captain Wainwright (Ord. Dept.) those at Fort Fauntleroy. Major Reynolds I think contemplates resigning which will leave but one paymaster Major Seward (now under orders for Washington) in the Department. It is respectfully recommended that additional paymasters should be sent out as soon as practicable.

I think it proper to refer to the disabled condition of the mounted Companies for the want of horses, and of the Quarter Master Department for the want of draft animals.

The past two years have been years of great scarcity almost famine throughout the whole of New Mexico. The scarcity of water, grass, and forage and constant hard service have destroyed a large proportion of the animals in the service of the Government. The same causes have operated to reduce the number of animals in the possession of private individuals, so that the supply necessary to place the troops in this Department in an effective condition—cannot be procured here, and I respectfully recommend, that the estimates for remounts and for draft animals may be filled from the East.[13]

All was immediate action once Canby took command. Missions were performed and jobs done which had been put off for months by the foot-dragging of the secessionists. Troops were ordered paid; an additional mounted force was targeted for the southern New Mexico region; additional troops were to be sent to Fort Fillmore. Canby used the word mischievous when he might have used the word treasonous when referring to the problem of non-payment of troops. No doubt there were many hands involved in that disgraceful action. Unfortunately for the Union forces, Canby's changes came too late to save either the 7th Infantry or Major Isaac Lynde.

The fact that Colonel Loring gave Brevet-Lieutenant Colonel Canby command of the Northern District of the Department only, while he kept command of the Southern District, including Fort Fillmore, is confirmed by this letter. Loring may have kept the command so he could not be arrested for any disloyal acts by Canby until he could leave the Territory safely.

During Loring's tenure at Fort Fillmore he had the opportunity to join in the collusion to render ineffective the only mounted force remaining in the south, Lane's Company 'A,' R.M.R.. On June 22, 1861, all of the horses of Company 'A' were stolen while Loring was still at the post. According to Canby, Loring did not leave for Fort Bliss until June 23. Did Colonel Loring direct that the horse herd of Company 'A' be stolen by "friends of the

Confederacy," as Lydia Lane reported? The possibility certainly exists, though the exact proof does not.

Major Henry Hopkins Sibley, a Confederate brigadier general as of June 17, 1861, contacted Colonel Loring at Fort Fillmore, while Loring still wore the green-trimmed blue uniform of the Regiment of Mounted Rifles. Sibley's letter was written from Hart's Mill, El Paso, Texas, on June 12, 1861. In this treasonous letter, Sibley welcomed Loring into the Southern fold, saying:

> We are at last under the glorious banner of the Confederate States of America. It was indeed a glorious sensation of protection, hope and pride. Though it folds most modest and unpretending, the emblem was still there. The very Southern verdure and familiar foliage, as we progressed on our journey, filled us with enthusiasm and home feeling.
>
> We shall have no trouble from here down to San Antonio. The stage runs regularly semi-weekly, carrying five passengers and a reasonable amount of baggage, reaching San Antonio in six days; thence to Berwick Bay in stages, and to New Orleans by rail.
>
> Van Dorn is in command at San Antonio. He has ordered four companies of Texas troops to garrison this post. They cannot be expected to reach here, however, before the 1st proximo. Meanwhile, Colonel Magoffin, Judge Hart, and Crosby are very much exercised and concerned on account of the public stores here in their present unguarded condition.
>
> There are full supplies of subsistence and ammunition here for two or more companies for twelve months. The loss of these supplies by capture or destruction would occasion serious embarrassment to the cause. The gentlemen I have named have applied to me for advice in the premises. I have promised to hasten on from below by forced marches that cavalry force en route here. Meanwhile you may, by delaying your own departure a week or two, add much to the security of this property.
>
> I regret now more than ever the sickly sentimentality (I can call it by no other name) by which I was overruled in my desire to bring my whole command with me. I am satisfied now of the disaffection of the best of the rank and file in New Mexico, and that we are regarded as having betrayed and deserted them. I wish I had my part to play over again; no such

peace scruples should deter me from doing what I consider a bounden duty to my friends and my cause. I do not advocate the meeting of duplicity and dishonesty by the like weapons, but if I capture the treasury buildings I shall certainly not send back to my enemy the golden bricks.

Should you be relieved from command too soon to prevent an attempt on the part of your successor to recapture, by a coup de main, the property here, send a notice by extraordinary express to Judge Hart. Your seat in the stage may at the same time be engaged.

Movements are in contemplation from this direction which I am not at liberty to disclose. You will arrive here in time for everything and to hear everything.

Rhett, I fear, has shamefully betrayed his money trust. My love to those who love me.[14]

When taken out of context some believe this letter a forgery. Yet it fits perfectly with a Colonel Loring temporarily in charge at Fort Fillmore, seconded by future Confederate subordinate Captain Robert Garland, and perhaps Maury and others. The Federal supplies and cannon at Fort Bliss were safe. Loring ensured that they were by keeping the blue-coated Federal troops at Fort Fillmore in their barracks as Sibley requested. The comment concerning Major Rhett is Sibley's attempt at wry humor. He was delighted that Rhett absconded with the funds needed to pay the troops at Fort Fillmore. Sibley could not know of Brevet-Lieutenant Colonel Canby's order to send another paymaster out.

If Loring was by then Rebel enough to protect Fort Bliss arms and munitions from falling into the hands of his former troops, who could doubt that he may have set in motion the plan which led to the horses of Company 'A' being stolen. Loring possibly used former deserters from his own Regiment of Mounted Rifles who had joined the Texan cause. There were plenty of secessionists in the region to help. By dismounting Company 'A,' Loring ensured there would be no mounted unit capable of reaching Fort Bliss in quick fashion, for confiscation or for assault. He had no knowledge that Canby was ordering other mounted units south of the Jornada, something both Fauntleroy and Loring refrained from doing while Department commanders. All Colonel Loring knew was that when he passed through Fort Craig earlier in the month the post had only parts of two Mounted Rifle Companies—'F' and 'G'—with about one hundred men total on duty.

Historically, Edward Canby has been judged the right man for the right post at the right time. It is interesting how many small events had to happen for him to take that post. Loring's resignation was only one. Specifically, Brevet-Lieutenant Colonel and later Major Edward Richard Sprigg Canby was born in Platt's Landing, Kentucky on November 9, 1817. In June 1861, he was forty-four years old, some thirteen years younger than Major Isaac Lynde. Canby was an 1835 graduate of West Point, who, in his early career, served in Florida and assisted in the removal of the Creeks, Cherokees, and Choctaws to the Indian Territory, now called Oklahoma. During the War with Mexico he served as chief of staff of a brigade and received two brevets, to major and to lieutenant colonel. This final brevet made all the difference to his career. Coming out of the Mexican War, Canby participated in the recruiting service and served in the Territory of Washington on the Pacific Coast, where he was promoted to major in the newly formed 10th Infantry in 1855.[15]

Special attention has been paid in the last paragraph to Canby's exact rank and title. The reason is that Major Canby, excusing his brevet title for a moment, was not in terms of years of service the senior major in the Department of New Mexico at the time of his appointment. The senior major was Isaac Lynde, 7th Infantry, who had eight years more service than Canby. Canby gained control of the Department based on a brevet rank attained during the war with Mexico. On May 14, when he replaced Loring in the Department command, Canby was also given a promotion to colonel of the 19th Infantry—a regiment not yet formed. The jumping of two grades allowed Canby to become a colonel and Department commander at the same time.[16]

Had a seniority-type of promotion policy, based on years of service, been followed, Major Isaac Lynde would have been the

Department commander as of June 1861. One can only wonder what such an appointment would have brought to the events that followed. Going back one step further, what if Lieutenant Colonel Pitcairn Morrison, the officer whose resignation forced Isaac Lynde into command of the 7th Infantry, had not resigned. Morrison certainly would have been senior and the command would have devolved on him without question. Morrison's departure for the East, which may have been for the purpose of attaining a higher rank, given the coming civil conflict, gave Canby his chance at fame and glory. All mentioned here—Canby, Morrison, Loring, Sibley, McLaws, Maury, Wilcox, Garland, etc.—went on to higher commands, great honors and praise. For Isaac Lynde, commanding an ill-equipped and widely scattered regiment, having lost many of its most capable company officers and forced to conduct an Indian campaign with the military structure falling apart around him, there was no pro-motion to be attained, only a sure and lasting historical infamy.

NOTES - Chapter 7

1. Heitman, Robert Garland.
2. Fort Fillmore Post Returns, May 1861.
3. Ibid.
4. La Posta, Volume II, #6, November-December 1970, p. 6.
5. Fort Fillmore Post Returns, June 1861.
6. Lydia Spencer Lane, *I Married a Soldier*, pp. 105, 106.
7. Edwin Sweeney, *Cochise*, p. 170.
8. Lane to Assistant Adjutant General, June 7, 1861, M1120, Rolls 13/14.
9. Magruder to Seward, June 1861, M1102, Rolls 13/14.
10. *La Posta*, Volume II, #6, November-December 1970, p. 4.
11. Donaldson Memorandum, June 9, 1861, M1120, Rolls 13/14.
12. Lydia Spencer Lane, *I Married a Soldier*, p. 105.
13. Canby to Assistant Adjutant General, New York City, June 11, 1861, M1012, Roll 2.
14. Sibley to Loring, June 12, 1861, M1120, Rolls 13/14.
15. Ezra J. Warner, *Generals in Blue: Lives of the Union Army Commanders*, p. 67.
16. Heitman, Canby.

8

SPECIAL ORDER NUMBER 134

Special Order Number 134 from the Headquarters of the Army arrived at Santa Fe on June 14, 1861. This order directed that all Federal troops were to leave New Mexico as soon as possible and return to the East. A New Mexico Militia was to be raised to protect the Territory as best it could. Brevet-Lieutenant Colonel Canby's response to the order was immediate and affirmative. He ordered the troops out at once. In the case of Fort Fillmore that meant abandonment, but not before the 7th Infantry companies had mustered there for departure as a regiment. Canby hinted at some delay being unavoidable. His major problem was the scarcity of wagons for transport of public and private property. He said:

> I have the honor to acknowledge the receipt on the 14th instant of Special Orders from the Head Quarters of the Army of May 17, 1861, directing the movements of troops, Recruits, etc.
>
> The preparatory arrangements for the movement of the troops from the Department are being made with as much rapidity as possible, but the scarcity of transportation (both public and private) in the country will occasion some delay. The Companies at the interior posts that can be spared before the volunteers are mustered into the service have already been ordered in, those of the 5th Infantry will be concentrated at Albuquerque and Fort Union, until the necessary transportation for the march can be provided, and those of the 7th Infantry at Fort Fillmore.

Since my report of the 11th instant, information has been received giving greater consistency to the rumored invasion of Arizona by the people of Texas, and I have in consequence taken measures to hasten as much as possible the concentration of troops at Fort Fillmore and hope to have in a few days a sufficient force there to secure the interests of the United States against attack from any quarter.

The Head Quarters of the 7th Infantry will be temporarily established at that post, and the troops in Arizona placed under the orders of the same officer [Major Lynde] with instructions that will enable him to meet any emergency.

This information applies also to the supply trains that are understood to be on the road to the country from the Missouri river, and I have given instructions to prepare a mounted force to move in the direction of the Arkansas river, for the protection of the trains. If necessary, I shall anticipate the orders of the War Department by calling for a portion of the volunteers immediately to replace the troops detached for this purpose.

The commanding officers at Forts Wise and Larned will be furnished with the information in relation to these anticipated movements of the Texans in order that they may be on their guard.[1]

Canby later spoke of the receipt of the withdrawal order in an August 16, 1861, letter to the Western Division Headquarters in St. Louis, long after events at Fort Fillmore had come to a conclusion. He explained his interpretation of the order and his subsequent actions:

On the 14th of that month the instructions of the General-in-Chief to withdraw the infantry force from the Department were received, and measures were immediately taken to bring them in from the interior and most distant posts. By the same instructions the commander of the Department was instructed to post the regular troops remaining in the Department and such volunteers as would be presented to him so as to best protect the United States.[2]

This order was Brevet-Lieutenant Colonel Canby's authorization to do two things, at least. First, he was permitted to start the withdrawal of all Federal troops from the Department. They were to be sent East as quickly as possible, hopefully after a local volunteer militia had come into being. That allowed for the abandonment of Forts Breckinridge, Buchanan, McLane, and Fillmore, orders for each of which to do so were eventually issued. Second, this order allowed him to mass the 7th Infantry at Fort Fillmore in preparation for being withdrawn.

In that same letter to St. Louis, Canby stated firmly that on July 15 the commanding officer at Fort Fillmore was advised that the fort would be abandoned, and was instructed to remove the public property, so as to abandon the post as soon as the troops from Arizona had passed through; the regular troops from Fort Stanton and Fort Craig were to be withdrawn as soon as volunteers could be raised to replace them.

This incredible admission by Canby that he ordered Isaac Lynde to prepare to abandon Fort Fillmore explains much of what happened there and why. Lynde would be castigated first for abandonment of Fort Fillmore. The fact that he had orders to do so are never mentioned. This omission was part of the need to place all blame for what happened with Isaac Lynde.

In fact, the Federal Government had every intention of abandoning all of New Mexico and placing its fate in the hands of untested volunteer militia. This decision was fully understood as early as June 15, 1861, as indicated in a letter to Brevet-Major Gabriel Paul, then still at Fort Fillmore. The Department Adjutant informed Paul:

> The Department Commander instructs me to say to you, in reply to your letter of the 10th. instant, that, as the 5th, 7th and 10th Infantry are to be replaced by volunteer troops, your services will probably be required to aid in instructing these troops into service, for a short time after notice of your promotion has been received.[3]

On June 16, Major Lynde was informed of the situation in Texas. He may not have been surprised, although the level of the debacle in Texas should have given him concern for his own future. He was also told officially, for the first time, that an invasion from Texas was possible. Canby stated:

Information from private but reliable sources indicate the possibility of a demonstration by the people of Texas, aided perhaps by some disaffected individuals in Arizona against the posts and property of the United States in that Territory and Colonel Canby desires that you will at once concentrate such a force at Fort Fillmore, as will enable you to resist an attack from any quarter. To do this, Fort McLane will at once be abandoned and the troops & public property transferred to Fort Fillmore, The transportation at both posts, and any that can be hired in the neighborhood of either, will be employed for this purpose. When this concentration is affected it is believed you will have under your command a sufficient force to prevent or defeat any attempt of this character. If satisfied of your ability to do this, the transfer of the companies of the 1st Dragoons to Fort Buchanan will proceed as indicated in Spl. Orders No. 85 of the 14th instant, the four Companies constituting the garrison of Fort Buchanan until further orders, but if these posts should be threatened by a force, which in your judgement cannot be resisted, you will take such measures for abandoning them as will best subserve the interests of the Government, transferring the troops and property to other posts in this, or in the Department of California [Fort Yuma] as may be determined by circumstances. It is of course important that both troops and property should be transferred to Fort Fillmore, or other posts in this Department, if it can be done, without endangering the loss of one or both, but in no event will stores of any kind be allowed to fall into the hands of the invaders, if it be possible to remove or destroy them.

It is understood here that Mr. Grant, late a contractor for supplying the posts in Arizona, has a train of waggons [sic] at Tucson, which may probably be hired or purchased, if these movements become necessary. It is probable that Fort Buchanan is the only post in the interior of Arizona, that will be retained and the effort to maintain that will be contingent upon the loyalty of the neighboring population.

You are desired to keep yourself as fully informed as possible of the movements of the Texas troops at and below Fort Bliss, the strength of the garrison at that post and Fort Quitman; of any reinforcements that they may receive, and of any movements that may be made in the direction of any part of New Mexico, keeping these Head Quarters advised, as frequently and as speedily as possible.

The extent of the disaffection in the Mesilla Valley is not fully known here and probably will not be fully developed there, until the civil authorities enter upon their duties. The action of the civil authorities will not be anticipated by the military authorities, but any active opposition to the Government of the United States, any measures that would be likely to endanger the safety of your Command, or any efforts to furnish assistance to Texas, by raising troops, or sending supplies of any kind, will be quietly but effectively frustrated.

Efforts have been made and will no doubt continue to be made to induce the men to desert and to carry with them into Texas public property of every description and particularly arms and ammunition. Every effort will be used to defeat these attempts and particularly to prevent the transfer of this ammunition into Texas.

It is stated here upon good authority that the Collector of Customs at Las Cruces who is also the sutler at Fort Fillmore, has openly expressed his determination to turn over the funds of the United States in his possession to the State of Texas. It will be the duty of the military authorities to prevent this, and similar theft of public funds and property by any measures that might be in their power.

Colonel Canby desires that you will not consider yourself trammeled by instructions, but will do whatever in your judgement will best serve the interest of the United States and maintain the honor of the flag, and he wishes you to feel assured that you will be supported by all the means in his power.

A copy of this communication will be sent, from these Head Quarters to Major Paul at Fort Fillmore for his information, and for such action as may be necessary before your arrival at that post.[4]

On what authority did Canby purportedly order Lynde to mass his forces and defend Fort Fillmore—certainly not on the authority of Washington. On what authority did he tell him to "... not consider yourself untrammeled by instructions, but will do whatever in your judgement will best serve the interest of the United States ... ."? This chain of instructions was like a three-headed snake. At this point a terrible confusion must have arisen in Isaac Lynde's mind. Was he to obey Canby and fight to the death at Fort

Fillmore, or was he to obey his orders from Washington, in which he was to first mass his forces and then leave for the East? Third, was he to do what he wanted, regardless of orders? Hardly. Canby had no authority to issue such instructions to Lynde, nor did he mention doing so in any later correspondence. Canby acted as if he had simply given Lynde Washington's order to converge on Fort Fillmore, mass the regiment and prepare to leave for service in the East. In other words Canby covered his own backside. On that same June 16, a letter went out to Brevet-Major Gabriel Rene Paul at Fort Fillmore, who was notified of the instructions given Major Isaac Lynde to move the 7th Infantry Regimental Headquarters to Fort Fillmore. Paul was ordered to prepare to receive the troops from Fort McLane. In response, Paul informed the Department concerning the local situation. This letter is proof that news of the ignominious surrender of the 8th Infantry and parts of other regiments was known by the officers at Fort Fillmore. Brevet-Major Paul said:

> I have the honor to report that the bad faith of Texas in capturing the United States troops who were within the limits of the State, after having made a solemn agreement that they should be permitted to leave the country unmolested; also the invasion by Texas militia of the Indian Territory, and the occupation by them of Forts Washita and Arbuckle, and again, the expected occupation of Fort Bliss by four companies of Texas militia, renders this frontier peculiarly important.
>
> In connection with the above, it may be proper to state that a Convention was held in Mesilla on the 16th of March, 1861, purporting to be a "Convention of the people of Arizona," acting separately from the government of the Territory of New Mexico, repudiating the United States, and attaching themselves to the Confederate States. I consider the whole transaction as a farce, and treated it with silent contempt, determined, however, if they attempted to carry out any of their resolutions by resisting or interfering with any of the United States civil officers, that I would protect the latter and punish the former.
>
> Yesterday Mr. L. Labadi, the United States agent for the Indians near Tucson, showed me a paper (a copy of which is enclosed), saying that it was handed to him by Mr. Kelly, editor

of the Mesilla Times, who was accompanied by three other citizens of Mesilla, who threatened to tar and feather him if he attempted to exercise the duties of his office. I promised Mr. Labadi military protection should any attempt be made against his person.

The paper referred to is the sixth resolution of the convention, in which they do not recognize the United States Government, and bind themselves to resist any officer appointed by said Government with any means in their power. The signatures of the document are also appended to the governor of New Mexico begging him to use his influence to have United States troops stationed in Mesilla for the protection of its citizens. Now that their fears are allayed with reference to an alleged invasion of New Mexico, they are secretly engaged in fomenting opposition to the United States and when the four companies of the Texas militia reach Fort Bliss difficulties may be reasonably apprehended, and I therefore recommend that a stronger force be stationed here to overawe any attempt on this post. Two additional companies would probably be sufficient.

I think it proper to state that inducements are held out to our men to desert, with their horses, arms, etc., by secret agents of Texas. They are told that it is not desertion to quit the United States Army and to join the South, and that they will be paid all arrearages due them, etc.

Thus far I am happy to report that there has been no discontent among the men, and the discipline of the command is perfect. They are now engaged in target practice.[5]

It would seem the threat to Agent Labadie would have at least allowed Andre Paul to move against the town of Mesilla, if he would not move against Fort Bliss. Of course Paul had no orders to do either. Freedom of action at this time could have changed history significantly. Certainly, the quick and easy taking of Fort Bliss and its stores should have been a first act of war.

The commanding officer at Fort Stanton was notified on June 16 of the possibility of an invasion by Texas troops, and to take this possibility into account. He was to be especially watchful of the approaches from the Pecos River route, using loyal Mexicans and Indians whenever possible to scout the region of approach. He was allowed to hire these men as guides and spies, paying them accordingly. Volunteer units were to be raised in that region also. It is interesting that the Fort Stanton commander was directed to raise a native volunteer militia, while Major Lynde was not advised of this new mission about to be given his command. By the time Lynde received the order to raise a local militia it was far too late to do so; this failure was simply added to the list of accusations made against Lynde that should have fallen upon others.[6]

While a change in Department strategy from studied unaware-ness of coming civil conflict to preparations for a fight were taking place, the Indian problem continued to escalate. A hay camp near Pinos Altos was struck by Mangas's group. One man was killed and another wounded. With Mangas and Cochise now raiding throughout eastern Arizona and western New Mexico, a state of war existed in their minds between themselves and the Americans, much as was true in the minds of the Texans as well. For the Army officer remaining loyal to the Union the way to war was less clear in both cases. Response to Indian depredations would now have to wait, but when that time did come it would be shattering for the freedom of the Apache peoples.

On June 20, a large band of Chiricahuas raided the Thompson Ranch south of Fort Buchanan, stealing every head of cattle they could find. Two days later they ran off another cattle herd grazing only a mile south of the fort. They killed one soldier and one Mexican. Although pursued by 2[d] Lieutenant Bascom, they eluded his chase. Bascom and Cochise had another fight, with Bascom forced to retire on this occasion after reinforcements reached the Apache leader. The day was coming when Fort Buchanan would be abandoned, a sign Cochise took to be reflective of his victory over the soldiers.[7]

While the Apaches raided in Arizona and believed they were the cause of the disruptions in the United States, Army Brevet-Lieutenant Colonel Canby addressed a subject that should have been a major topic months before. He spoke of occupying Fort Bliss in a letter to the Assistant Adjutant General in Washington.

This, at a time when Confederate militia were on the road north to garrison the post. Why did Canby not order an immediate take-over of Fort Bliss? Did he honor Loring's false declaration of holding command in the southern part of the Territory? Or did Canby need the permission of the Adjutant General and General-in-Chief Winfield Scott to occupy Texas land, a precedent-setting action at the time? Whatever the reason, it was too late. Canby informed the assistant adjutant general's office that, in his opinion:

> Fort Fillmore, or preferably Fort Bliss, on the south and Forts Union and Stanton, on the east, will be strategical points, and should be strongly garrisoned with, if possible, a large portion of each command—regular troops, both infantry and cavalry. Fort Garland [Colorado] and Fort Craig are of sub-ordinate importance, but their garrisons should be determined by the same considerations. The principal depot [Albuquerque] should also be guarded by regular troops.

He added that Forts Fillmore, Stanton, and Union were at exposed points and "it will not be well to trust either entirely to new and undisciplined troops." Canby was referring to New Mexico militia.

Was Canby asking the General-in-Chief to countermand the order to remove all Federal troops from the Territory? Although he didn't use those words, the implication is obvious. No counter-manding order was issued, however. The removal of Federal troops was to go forward unimpeded, save for transportation problems and a possible Confederate invasion creating a short delay. Canby also wanted one of the two infantry regiments, 5th and 7th, to be retained in the Territory while the volunteers were trained, and that the total force, Regular Army and volunteer, remaining in the Territory be forty-two companies, to include one Regular Army infantry and one Regular Army cavalry regiment. Canby requested that, since the volunteers would draw heavily on the Territory manpower assets, consideration be given to bringing in volunteers from Colorado as well. Canby did not ask for volunteers from California, although that was the force which eventually arrived to save the day.

Just before the Fort Fillmore horse herd was raided and the animals stolen, there was supposed to have been at least one foray to the south, in the direction of El Paso. This scout was made on June 22, 1861, as reported by Lydia Lane. Virtually any remarks she made years later when writing her book, *I Married a Soldier*, have been validated somewhat through cross-verification, but there is confusion in dates. The events she described may have happened, but often not in the chronological order she indicated. The supposed June 22 scout could not have taken place on that date, but may have taken place on July 22, just before the fort's abandonment. The new Department adjutant replacing Dabney Maury, 2[d] Lieutenant A.L. Anderson, 5th Infantry, confirmed on June 30 that on June 22 the horse herd at Fort Fillmore was stolen; no horses were available at the post after that for a scout to use until the first week of July. Here is how Lydia Lane described the incident even though the date is incorrect:

> The scout left Fort Fillmore June 22, and went down the Rio Grande towards El Paso, a rumor having been brought in that the Texans were advancing four hundred strong. First Lieutenant W.B. Lane was in command of the United States troops, and with him were Second Lieutenant C.H. McNally and Second Lieutenant E.J. Cressy [sic], Regiment Mounted Rifles, and seventy men.[8]

McNally did not leave Fort Craig with Company 'F,' R.M.R. until June 30. Cressey started out from Fort Stanton with a small portion of Company 'B,' R.M.R. at about the same time. If there was a scout to the south as she described it had to have taken place in July. This crucial mistake in dating by Lane is but one of many that will be mentioned in this book. Many accusations against Major Lynde were based on just such errors and misstatements; the erroneous information continues to be used to this day.

Rene Paul immediately reported the theft of the horses to the Department commander, after they were stolen on June 22. Paul blamed Texans for the act and also indicated that the theft may have been planned as early as June 12, at Hart's Mill in El Paso. He did not place any blame on Colonel William Wing Loring by name. The latter was supposed to have been at Fort Fillmore up to the day after the horses were stolen, June 23. Whatever the case, Company 'A,' the only mounted company then available in the south, operated on foot after June 22, and hence could not have made the scout Lydia Lane mentioned. Her reporting of the theft of her husband's horses is exaggerated and has been too long taken as gospel as to what actually happened. She observed, almost offhandedly,

> Late in June, or the beginning of July [it was June 22], the post herd was stampeded, but by whom was not known. It was suspected the friends of the Confederacy could tell a good deal about it. The stampede dismounted one or all the companies of riflemen at Fillmore, and made them foot soldiers for the time being.[9]

This confusing statement must have been written a long time after the events and is indicative of how memory fades with time. Lane's husband's company was, in fact, the only mounted company at Fort Fillmore in June—the only mounted force able to engage the Texans in battle or serve as a reconnaissance force.

The stealing of the R.M.R. horse herd was a blow of incalculable importance to what was about to happen. The raiders took away the eyes of the Fort Fillmore garrison. After that the only intelligence received at Fort Fillmore from the south was from rumor and innuendo brought by persons passing by and through the post. Scouting was curtailed until almost the last days of the fort's occupation. Lydia Lane was right about one thing: the theft did dismount her husband's company.

Mrs. Lane also was confused in that she had Major Isaac Lynde at Fort Fillmore during this period. He was not. She said, "The commanding officer, Major Lynde, seemed utterly oblivious of the danger, and took no means to strengthen the place, nor to put his small force where it would be most efficient in case the Texans carried out their plans to make a raid on the garrison."[10]

Lynde was still at Fort McLane when Company 'A's' animals were stolen, the single most important event to occur before the

Battle of Mesilla in July. Her husband was responsible for the safety of those horses. That they were stolen points to 1ˢᵗ Lieutenant Lane's level of watchfulness, or rather the lack of it. If another officer besides the phantom Colonel Loring was to receive any blame it would be Brevet-Major Paul. Of course, it served Lydia Lane's purpose, and that of other officers involved in upcoming events, if all blame for the coming tragedy at Fort Fillmore fell on Major Lynde's shoulders. Therefore, she put Lynde conveniently in command when the R.M.R. horse herd was stolen.[11]

Mrs Lane's memories were sometimes not even her own. She took whole sections of her memory as it pertained to Fort Fillmore from the work of Doctor James Cooper McKee, the Fort Fillmore assistant surgeon. In 1886, twenty-five years after the events, McKee wrote a slanderous book which blamed Isaac Lynde for just about everything accept the assassination of Abraham Lincoln. Unfortunately for history, his savage attack has been taken as absolute proof that Isaac Lynde was an incompetent, cowardly, bungler who was the absolute last man who should have been commanding at Fort Fillmore. The main criticism about McKee and his work is that, if one wishes to savage the reputation of another person, the data used should at least be accurate. It was from McKee's work, *Narrative of the Surrender of a Command of U.S. Forces At Fort Fillmore New Mexico In July, A.D., 1861*, that Lydia Lane took her memory of the June 22, 1861, scout, with McNally and Cressey present.[12]

McKee had it wrong. Lydia Lane propagated McKee's wrong. In fact, Assistant Surgeon McKee had it wrong on more than one occasion, as we shall see. Lynde may have been at least partly as McKee viewed him, but the doctor's hatred for the man disallowed any objective viewing whatsoever.

As an example, Assistant-Surgeon McKee stated:

> On or about the 20ᵗʰ of June, I took my buggy and horses, and got Major Lynde to drive over the river with me to the town of Mesilla. I took him around the store-rooms and houses, pointing out such as I thought would do best for troops to occupy in case of the necessity of occupying the town.[13]

What McKee says here is not important. He is just showing what a wonderful tactician he thought he was and how unseeing and moribund Lynde was. He continued praising his own advice in the following paragraph.

The point is that Major Lynde was nowhere near Mesilla or Fort Fillmore on June 20. Lynde was at Fort McLane, trying to orchestrate the abandonment of three military posts simultaneously—Breckinridge, Buchanon, and McLane, as per Department orders. He did very well for such a supposedly incompetent person when performing this task. If McKee took anybody across the river on June 20 it was Brevet-Major Rene Paul, not Major Isaac Lynde. Curiously, Assistant Surgeon McKee had nothing to say about the most important event that did take place around June 22—the stealing of the Company 'A' horse herd.

By June 23, preparations were in full swing for leaving New Mexico in the hands of a volunteer militia and pulling the Regulars out. On that date Brevet-Lieutenant Colonel Canby informed Governor Rencher that he was calling for four companies of foot volunteers to rendevous at Albuquerque. An additional company of foot and one of mounted troops to rendevous at Fort Craig, and one company of foot and one mounted at Fort Stanton. The post records at Fort Craig indicate that a New Mexico militia company with three officers was present at about the time of the fall of Fort Fillmore in late July. All were to be mustered into the service of the United States in conformity with War Department regulations.

While Canby told Governor Rencher of his plans for New Mexico volunteer militia units on June 23, he also sent word to Major Isaac Lynde to get his 7th Infantry Regiment out of New Mexico as expeditiously as possible. This, after he had earlier advised Lynde on June 16 to defend Fort Fillmore with all his capability—simply more confusion in orders. The 7th was to proceed from Forts Breckinridge, Buchanan, McLane, and Fillmore on the long journey to Fort Leavenworth, Kansas, and then to the East for service there as needed. We cannot be sure when Lynde received either order, but he must have had them both at some point. Certainly, the order to abandon trumped the order to defend, the abandonment order being issued from Washington.[14]

On the same day Canby was ordering Lynde to get the 7th Infantry out of the Territory, he addressed the Mexican Governor of the state of Chihuahua on the matter of the wagon train which had been stolen while en route to Major Lynde at Fort McLane. In this letter, he mentioned 1st Lt. Donald C. Stith, 5th Infantry, who would soon be at Fort Fillmore. Stith may even then have been a Confederate agent, unbeknownst to Canby, so any mention of his visiting Fort Fillmore is of interest. Canby noted:

> The bearer of this communication, First Lieut. Donald C. Stith, of the U.S. Army, has been commissioned by me to visit your excellency, for the purpose of asking your assistance in effecting the restoration of a train of wagons and a large quantity of stores, the property of the Government of the United States, which were carried into the State of Chihuahua in the month of March last, by William D. Kirk, then a wagon-master in the U.S. Army. This flagrant robbery and breach of faith will be fully reprobated by your excellency, and I have the fullest confidence that you will at once, in the exercise of your powers, direct the restoration of the public property and the delivery of the robber [Kirk] into the hands of the accredited agent of the United States. Lieutenant Stith takes with him, for the information of your excellency, a full statement of the circumstances connected with this robbery, so that you can see at once the true history and merits of the case. He will also take inventories of the stolen property, in order that everything may be verified. When this property is restored to Lieutenant Stith I have the honor to request that your excellency will cause him to be furnished with any assistance that may be necessary to facilitate his return to this department , and if it should be needed that you will direct the train to be escorted to the frontier of Chihuahua, where an escort from the troops of this department will meet it. I beg to assure your excellency that the action that you may take in this matter will be fully recognized and appreciated by the Government of the United States.[15]

June 23, 1861, was certainly one of Brevet-Lieutenant Colonel Canby's busiest days for correspondence. Having addressed Isaac

Lynde, the Governor of the Territory of New Mexico, and the Governor of Chihuahua, he took time to pen a few important words on the New Mexico situation for the General-in-Chief. Canby informed the Headquarters of the Army, now located in Washington due to the coming civil conflict, concerning his current thinking:

Since my report of the 16th instant the statements in relation to a contemplated invasion of the Territory appear to be confirmed by information received from various sources, and it is positively known that a considerable force of Texan troops is now on the march for El Paso or that neighborhood, with the ostensible object of garrisoning Forts Quitman and Bliss. I feel assured, however, that a sufficient force will, in two or three days be concentrated at Fort Fillmore to render that portion of the country entirely secure, and enable the commanding officer to suppress any revolutionary movements that may be set on foot by the people of the Mesilla Valley.

I hope, too, that Major Lynde will find himself in sufficient force to reoccupy Fort Bliss and recover the public property now at that place. Two mounted companies have been ordered to report to him at Fort Fillmore as soon as practicable, and he has been authorized to call for volunteers if he should find it necessary.

The next point of importance is Fort Union, and to enable the commanding officer of that post to guard the depot, protect the trains on the road, and watch the approach by the Canadian [River] I have called upon the governor of the Territory for four companies of foot volunteers, who will rendevous at that place in two or three days. Four companies of foot volunteers have also been called for the purpose of relieving the companies of the Fifth Infantry now at Fort Fauntleroy. They will rendevous at Albuquerque. One company of foot and one of mounted volunteers will rendevous at Fort Stanton, and one company of foot and one of mounted volunteers at Fort Craig, making in all ten companies of foot and two of mounted volunteers. These requisitions have been made in anticipation of the orders of the War Department calling them into the service, and for the purpose of defending exposed points and facilitating the concentration of the regular troops that are to leave the department.

Our Indian relations are still unsatisfactory. The Apaches of Arizona are still actively hostile, and have committed many depredations during the past month, and the Comanches are openly at war with us.[16]

A second letter went out to Major Isaac Lynde on June 23. He was given further instructions on the need to raise volunteer companies, recruited locally. Lynde's mind must have been confused by the multiple missions he was given to do virtually all at once. He was to abandon three forts, gather the entire 7th Infantry at one post, raise local volunteer companies, be wary of secessionist activities in the area, provide intelligence on Rebel activities in Texas, watch out for traitors in his own ranks, fight the Indians and take Fort Bliss by force. In addition, Lynde was to leave New Mexico Territory at once for the East, but he might stay long enough at Fort Fillmore to defeat the Texas insurgents should they invade. Canby also introduced the man who was carrying the letter to Lynde, John Watts, an individual who knew Mesilla well, and was loyal to the Union. Canby informed:

> The bearer of these communication, Judge John S. Watts, of this city, is thoroughly acquainted with the inhabitants of Mesilla, of Dona Ana County, and will be able to render you valuable assistance in organizing volunteer companies, if you should find it necessary to call for any, or in any event in which you may require his aid. His intimate knowledge of the people in that part of the country will enable him to indicate to you those upon whose fidelity you can rely, and this, at the present juncture, will be a matter of the utmost importance. I have requested him to take charge of these communications, for the reason that I do not feel assured that they would reach you if sent through the post office, and for the same reason a triplicate of the instructions of the 16th inst., is also sent. My own knowledge of Judge Watts and his reputation here warrant me in saying that you can rely upon him for any service in which you may require the assistance of an active, zealous, and faithful man.[17]

More information for Major Lynde was included in a third letter written on that same, busy, June 23. This time it was Captain Anderson addressing Lynde in Canby's name. The subjects were reinforcement of Fort Fillmore and the arming of volunteers.

I am instructed to say that your communication of the 14th instant and Major Paul's report of the 16th Instant, in relation to affairs in the Mesilla Valley, have been received. The orders and instructions heretofore given you anticipate the recommendations made by Major Paul and yourself. Duplicates of these orders and instructions will be sent herewith. I am instructed to state, for your information, that your command will be reinforced by two mounted companies: one from Fort Craig and one from Fort Stanton. A requisition has been made upon the governor for volunteers to strengthen the garrisons at Forts Stanton and Craig, and keep open the communication between these posts and Fort Fillmore.

You are authorized, if you should consider it necessary, to call into the service of the United States two or more companies of volunteers from the neighborhood of your post. Three hundred rifles and muskets and 12,000 cartridges will also be sent for the purpose of arming any volunteers that you call for. Twenty thousand rations of subsistence have been ordered from the depot at Albuquerque for the use of your force. Assistant Surgeon Alden will be ordered to report to you for duty with your command. You are requested to transmit, at as early a period as possible, your requisitions for any supplies that may be needed for your command, basing them upon the supposition that there will not be less than 2000 men to be provided for, in order that arrangements may be made for filling them as rapidly and as fully as possible.

It is impossible, at this distance, and with the imperfect knowledge of passing events in your neighborhood, to give you definite instructions, but the lieutenant-colonel commanding relies upon your zeal and judgement to give the greatest effect for defense or for offense to the means that will be under your control. The present strength of Fort Bliss and the period of the expected arrival of reenforcements from Texas are not known here, but it is scarcely necessary to suggest to you that the frontier in charge could be more permanently secured from invasion by the seizure of that post and the property of the United States now there than by any other course and before the reenforcements have arrived. You must judge whether the means under your control will be sufficient to accomplish this object without hazard to the more important object of maintaining your position at Fort Fillmore.

It is represented that there are many loyal men in the Mesilla Valley who would readily volunteer their services, and as the organization of volunteer companies in their midst would tend greatly to paralyze the disaffected, this course is suggested in calling for any volunteers you may consider necessary.

The promotion of Major Paul to the Eighth Infantry has been received here, but as his services will be necessary in organizing and mustering volunteers into the service of the United States, you are authorized to retain him for the present, and will please give the same directions at other posts within your district where the immediate change would leave a company without an officer or occasion other serious embarrassments to the service.[18]

Words don't mean much when they are ignored. Major Paul did not stay on to help Lynde muster the regiment. Instead, he left him without an officer for Company 'I,' Paul's own company. Gabriel Paul simply up and left, ignoring Department orders, before Isaac Lynde arrived. Paul was the sixth experienced company officer to leave his duties in the 7th Infantry Regiment at this crucial time, after Whiting, Wilcox, Garland, Marmaduke, and McLaws. Nor did the Department of New Mexico ensure that suitable officers were made available to fill the vacant slots in Lynde's ranks.

On the day after Colonel William Wing Loring supposedly left Fort Fillmore for Fort Bliss, according to Canby's calendar of events, the matter of Loring's loyalty was for the first time openly discussed. Canby warned Lynde:

Information has been received here that some movement is in contemplation from Fort Bliss against the interests of the Government in this Territory, at the head of which are Magoffin, Hart and Crosby. Sibley is also said to be associated with them. It is alleged that Colonel Loring is in communication with these parties, and that he will remain in the department long enough to prevent any measures being taken to frustrate these designs. When Colonel Loring left this place every officer here had implicit confidence in his integrity, but I am sorry to say that some information received since he left has shaken that confidence. It is a long step from confidence to absolute distrust, but it is necessary that you should be on your guard against any betrayal of the honor or interests of the United States. I send this communication by Dr. Alden.[19]

On June 25 1861, Captain Robert M. Morris, commanding about one hundred soldiers at Fort Craig, was directed to furnish escorts for public property being sent south to Fort Fillmore, as that post was being expanded. One company of infantry from the newly organized New Mexico Militia and one of cavalry were sent to Fort Craig. Morris was told that Mr. Robert H. Stapleton, who lived near Fort Craig at the time, was to raise a mounted company, and Colonel M.E. Pino, appointed by the president to command the 2[d] Regiment of New Mexico Volunteers, was to designate the infantry company. That company was to be mustered in for three years' enlistment. Morris was charged with "organizing, inspecting and mustering these companies into the service." An oath of allegiance was to be taken to the government of the United States, and all who refused to take the oath were to be rejected. The mounted company was to be armed with rifles and the infantry with muskets. These arms were to come from the depot at Fort Union. Morris was also warned that the actions of the state of Texas and the people of Mesilla made it necessary to strengthen the garrison at Fort Craig. Communications with the south had to be kept open.

Canby stated, through Anderson, that it was known that the Texans intended to invade New Mexico, organizing at Fort Bliss. Texas reinforcements were expected early the next month. Anderson said that "it is known privately" that the invasion would come soon. Who was in on the secret? We don't know. What is known is that within two months the sleepy post at Fort Craig became a bustling hive of Union activity, with the troop strength raised to almost a thousand soldiers.[20]

On June 26, Brevet-Lieutenant Colonel Benjamin Roberts, commanding at Fort Stanton, was informed that two companies of volunteers, a cavalry unit enlisted for three months, and an infantry company selected by Colonel M.E. Pino, commanding 2[d] Regiment,

N.M. Volunteers, were to be sent to Fort Stanton. The infantry company was enlisted for three years' service.[21]

Fort Fillmore was not the only source of friction Brevet-Lieutenant Colonel Canby was dealing with in late June. William Chapman, commanding at Fort Union, was told to interrogate captive Comanche women in the hopes of obtaining information but, that if they would not cooperate they were to be sent back to their tribe. The women were to take the message that the United States Army did not want war with the Comanches, but an armed force was being gathered that would enter Comanche country if the Indians did not keep their agreements. Chapman was also ordered to raise a force of at least one hundred mounted men and two companies of New Mexico volunteers to be placed under the command of Captain Duncan, R.M.R., for the protection of the trains on the road from the crossing of the Arkansas to Fort Union. The units were to be lightly equipped and to take rations for thirty days in the field. The commanding officer at Fort Lyon, Colorado was requested to advise wagon trains passing that post to keep tp the Arkansas and come into New Mexico by the Raton route, presumably to avoid Texan patrols.[22]

Fort Buchanan was ordered to be abandoned. On June 30, 1861, that order was clarified. Anderson stated:

> I enclose an extract from special orders directing the abandonment of Fort Buchanan, which should be done with as little delay as is consistent with the proper disposition of the property at your post and other interest in your charge. If the abandonment of Fort Buchanan has not yet been completed, it will be hastened as much as possible. The command will move in one body, if it be possible to procure the necessary transportation for the whole command, and prepared to resist attack from any quarter. Your artillery may possibly be needed, and should be put in a condition for service. If there should be any loyal citizens in the neighborhood of your post that wish to occupy the improvements that have been made at Fort Buchanan, you are authorized to turn it over to them.
>
> At this distance, and under the circumstances, no special instructions can be given to you, but you will exercise your own

judgement in carrying out this object in the manner that will best subserve the interests of the United States. This communication will be sent to you by express from Fort Craig, and you will please advise the commanding officer of the receipt by the return of the expressman.[23]

One historical note to the Fort Buchanan abandonment was not brought to light until the last decade of the twentieth century. Artifacts uncovered near the old post were quite different from the usual finds. These consisted of belt buckles of the smaller Mexican War infantry type, cross-belt plates, cartridge-box plates and epaulette scale pieces. The lead had been melted out of the buckles and plates (presumably to keep the lead and the accouterments out of the hands of secessionists and Indians) and all the brass pieces cut with shears into relatively large chunks. The retiring 7th Infantry units obviously used this method to eliminate any public property they could not carry away. The destroyed materials at Fort Buchanan remind one of the destruction of the medical bottles at Fort Fillmore at the time of its abandonment, though there was no sign the Fort Fillmore troops took measures such as cutting up their small brass decorative pieces.

Brevet-Lieutenant Colonel Canby mentioned the perfidy of Colonel Loring, his Confederate predecessor, as well as that of the Texas authorities in El Paso in a letter to the Assistant Adjutant General in Washington on June 30, 1861. He informed them he was taking responsibility for defending Fort Fillmore, even though he had no orders to do so other than the order to withdraw all forces to that point for evacuation from the Territory. Canby stated:

Since my report of the 23rd instant positive information has been received of the contemplated movements of the Texans against the interests of the Government of this Territory. This was naturally to have been expected, and measures were taken at an early period after Colonel Loring left this place to concentrate a sufficient force at Fort Fillmore to defeat any measures of this kind and to cover the movements that would be necessary in withdrawing the troops from the interior of Arizona. Several resigned officers who have left the Territory through Texas have aided and counseled in these contemplated movements, and my information implicates one or more who have not yet left the department. The commanders interested have been warned, and if the mischief has not already been accomplished it will be prevented.

Major Paul's report of the 22d instant undoubtedly chronicles one of a series of robberies that have for some time been in contemplation, and I cannot comprehend how the officers at Fort Fillmore can still place any faith in the protestations and disclaimers of the Texan authorities at Fort Bliss. It is notorious that for two months past they have been tampering with the enlisted men at the posts in the South and offering them large bribes to induce them to desert.

Indian depredations still continue; one near Socorro of some magnitude. The others are generally of but little importance. Several proved upon investigation to have been committed by citizens, several of whom have been caught by the troops and are now in jail at this place.

The most assailable point in this department is the approach from Arkansas and Texas by the Canadian, and rumors indicate the probability of an invasion from that quarter. If it should be made in large, serious difficulties may be apprehended, as the Mexican population will not furnish, for some time at least, a reliable force to resist invasion. To meet this possibility I am hastening as much as I can the organization of the volunteers called for, in order to concentrate as large a force of regulars as possible.[24]

Major Lynde, still commanding at Fort McLane as of June 30, was sent notification of the theft of the forty-one horses of Company 'A,' Regiment of Mounted Rifles. Lynde may not have received this letter until he arrived at Fort Fillmore. If he did get the letter he was made aware that he was heading toward a situation in which all loyalties, especially among the officer corps and the surrounding citizenry, were in question. Lynde was now being addressed as the Commanding Officer, Southern District New Mexico, Colonel Loring having quit the Territory officially. Anderson, the adjutant at the Department of New Mexico, said, in the name of Colonel Canby:

Major Paul's communication of the 22d instant, reporting the loss of 41 horses, of Company A, Mounted Rifles, and other communications from Fort Bliss in relation to the same subject, have been received, and I am instructed to say there is sufficient evidence here to show conclusively that this robbery was not the unauthorized act of a band of robbers, but was planned at Hart's Mill as early as the 10th or 12 of this month, and is only one of a series that will be undertaken if prompt measures are not taken to defeat them. The horses were stolen for the purpose of mounting one of the companies of Texas troops now on their way to Fort Bliss. The reward offered by Magoffin and the disclaimers of the Texas authorities are mere blinds, to throw you off your guard and keep the troops inactive until Fort Bliss is re-inforced. When this object is secured there will be demonstrations against your post, the trains that supply it, or against Fort Stanton.

The movements of the Texans at Fort Bliss have been watched, and although the precise object and the details of their contemplated movements cannot be ascertained, it is positively known that movements against New Mexico are on foot; that officers who recently left the country by that route have aided and counseled in the plans, and it is alleged that others still in the service are implicated in these transactions. There is no doubt that these movements will be undertaken the moment that the instigators feel assured of a probability of success. The leading secessionists in Mesilla are apprized of these plans, and to the extent of their ability will assist in carrying them out.

The State of Texas is avowedly at war with the Government of the United States. The character of the enemy you have to deal with has been fully exhibited in the last few months, and they now expect to be able in a few days to carry the war into New Mexico. It is hoped that before this time you have a sufficient force under your control to make them feel that the war is not to be entirely upon one side.

The surplus horses at Fort Craig will be sent down as soon as possible to Fort Fillmore for the purpose of remounting a part of Company A, but it will be very difficult to procure a sufficient number in the department to remount the whole company. As many as can be procured will be sent [none were].

Orders have been sent direct to-day for the abandonment of Fort Buchanan; the garrison to report to you at Fort Fillmore as soon as possible.

The lieutenant-colonel commanding directs me to repeat his assurance that you will be supported in any measures that you may undertake by all the means that he can control, and that there is no intention of withdrawing any portion of the regular force under your command until the affairs within the limits of your command are placed upon a satisfactory footing. He desires that you will keep him fully advised of matters that transpire in your neighborhood, and that you will keep the commanding officer at Fort Stanton advised of any matters that may affect this post.[25]

Note that Anderson, in the name of Canby, stated that "Texas is avowedly at war with the Government of the United States." He did not say that the United States was at war with Texas, because it was not. Lincoln had not yet formalized the state of insurrection he was already training troops to quell. It was not until the very day that Major Isaac Lynde arrived at Fort Fillmore, July 4, 1861, that Lincoln called a special session of Congress and allowed that branch to declare the existence of a state of insurrection and call for 500,000 volunteers. During the events at Fort Fillmore, Mesilla, and at San Augustine Springs in July, Isaac Lynde was acting without knowledge of the actual war situation. As far as he was concerned belligerent Texans might be a threat but he had no official basis on which to seek a fight with them. Only Lincoln and Congress could have given him that standing through a declaration of war. Given the slowness of the mails, Lynde did not receive word of Lincoln's actions until after his tribulations at San Augustine Springs. As far as his official authority was concerned, Major Isaac Lynde had no right to assume the nation was at war when he arrived at Fort Fillmore in July.

Lynde was also told there was no intent to "withdraw the units" under his command until the situation in the south had been stabilized. Did Isaac Lynde ever read this letter? He certainly left Fort McLane while the Anderson/Canby letter was in transit, but it could have caught up with him somewhere. If it did, his conduct in the upcoming days is open to question, although interpretation of the letter can be deceptive. One reading might be that Lynde was ordered to defend Fort Fillmore with all 7th Infantry forces converging on him, includ-ing those troops abandoning Forts Breckinridge and Buchanan. Another way of reading the order is that Canby was not speaking of defending Fort Fillmore at all, but was telling Lynde that he, Canby, was not going to remove troops for use elsewhere. The 7th Infantry would come together at Fort Fillmore without any interference from him. Lynde had freedom of action and would be "supported in any measures you may undertake."

Splitting this hair, it is easy to see that in July 1861, Major Isaac Lynde may have decided to operate under the order, never revoked, and never to be revoked, that all Federal troops were pulling out of New Mexico Territory as their first priority. Every action he took thereafter points to an early decision to save what he could for a later fight on another battlefield back East, should civil war fever continue to build.

First Lieutenant Charles Hely McNally left Fort Craig on June 30 for duty in the south at Fort Fillmore. McNally's Mounted Rifle Company 'F' was not his normal home. He was assigned to Company 'G,' R.M.R. McNally was no stranger to Fort Fillmore, having served there in September and October 1856, after the Rifle Regiment arrived in the Territory from Texas. Of interest is that McNally then served under Captain Thomas Grimke Rhett who, as a Major-Paymaster in the Spring of 1861, absconded with the money needed to pay the troops at Fort Fillmore and handed it over to Southern authorities. McNally was almost a total stranger to the men he would lead into battle while at Fort Fillmore. As was often typical of the antebellum Army, no officers of Company 'F' were then in the Department.

The situation at Fort Fillmore was similar to that of Company 'F' at the end of June. There were three infantry companies, 'D,' 'I,' and 'K.' Of these, only Company 'K' had a troop commander now that Captain Garland had taken control of the post after Brevet-Major Rene Paul left for Santa Fe, and Garland was soon to desert his post.

The Captain of Company 'D,' Lafayette McLaws, resigned to join the Confederate Army in the East. The second in command of Company 'D,' 1st Lieutenant Edward Brooks, was with Major Lynde, serving as adjutant of the 7th Infantry Regiment. Company 'D' was therefore without officers of any grade.

Company 'I' was formerly commanded by Gabriel Paul, who left that company without an officer to serve with Canby as head of the volunteer recruitment program. Canby had previously ordered Paul to stay with his company so that Major Isaac Lynde would not be short of trained company officers with a possible fight coming. Major Paul ignored that order, and Company 'I' was abandoned and leaderless when Lynde arrived.[26]

Company 'K' was in the best condition, having two officers, Plummer and Crilly, although Company 'K' was not without turmoil. Captain Cadmus Wilcox, the Company 'K' Commander during much of June, left post before Isaac Lynde arrived.

Thus, of the three infantry companies then at Fort Fillmore all were impacted in some fashion by the coming civil conflict and were not led by the officers who normally directed them.

The last company at the post, Company 'A,' Regiment of Mounted Rifles, was dismounted, its horses having been stolen. There were only thirty-six men remaining in the company. First Lieutenant Lane had suffered a very high desertion rate over the last several months, the result of the troops not being paid.

On paper, the Fort Fillmore strength consisted of five officers and two-hundred and three enlisted men as the post entered the last month of its service as an antebellum Army installation. These numbers were to grow as Major Isaac Lynde brought in the companies previously serving at Fort McLane. But numbers do not make an Army. There are many definable qualities that lead to a proud and victorious force, foremost among them good and *familiar* leadership. The soldiers of the 7th Infantry Regiment gathering at Fort Fillmore were demoralized, unsure of their commanders, and filled with suspicion. That situation was about to degrade even further.

NOTES - Chapter 8

1. Canby to Assistant Adjutant General, Head Quarters of the Army, New York City, June 16, 1861, M1012, Roll 2.

2. Canby to Assistant Adjutant General, St. Louis, August 16, 1861, M1012, Roll 2.

3. Anderson to Paul, June 15, 1861, M1012, Roll 2.

4. Anderson to Lynde, Santa Fe, June 16, 1861, M1012, Roll 2.

5. Paul to Assistant Adjutant General, Santa Fe, June 16, 1861, M1120, Roll 2.

6. Anderson to Roberts, June 16, 1861, M1012, Roll 2.

7. Edwin Sweeney, *Cochise*, pp. 176, 177.

8. Lydia Spencer Lane, *I Married a Soldier*, p. 107.

9. Ibid.

10. Ibid., p. 106.

11. Ibid., p. 106,107.

12. James Cooper McKee, *Narrative of the Surrender of a Command of U.S. Forces at Fort Fillmore New Mexico in July, A. D. 1861* (Houston: Stagecoach Press, 1960), p. 10. (Hereafter cited as McKee.)

13. Ibid., pp. 11,12.

14. Canby to Lynde, June 23, 1861, M1012, Roll 2.

15. Various editors, *Confederate Victories in the Southwest - Prelude to Defeat* (Albuquerque: Horn & Wallace Publishers, 1961). (Hereafter cited as Horn & Wallace.) This particular reference was to a letter written by Colonel Canby to the Governor of Chihuahua, pp. 58, 59.

16. Canby to Assistant Adjutant General, June 23, 1861, M1012, Roll 2.

17. Canby to Lynde, June 23, 1861, M1012, Roll 2.

18. Horn & Wallace, Anderson to Lynde, June 23, 1861, pp. 60, 61.

19. Canby to Lynde, June 24, 1861, M1012, Roll 2.

20. Horn & Wallace, Anderson to Morris, June 25, 1861, pp. 61, 62.

21. Anderson to Roberts, June 26, 1861, M1012, Roll 2.

22. Horn & Wallace, Anderson to commanding officer, Fort Union, pp. 63, 64.

23. Horn & Wallace, Anderson to Fort Buchanan commander, June 30, 1861, p. 64.

24. Horn & Wallace, Canby to Assistant Adjutant General, Washington, D.C., p. 65.

25. Anderson to Lynde, June 30, 1861, M1012, Roll 2.

26. Ibid.

9

LYNDE ARRIVES AT FORT FILLMORE

In 1856, upon his return from Europe, ex-President Millard Fillmore gave a speech at Albany, New York, which appears prophetic to a future audience. The former President said:

> We see a political party presenting candidates for the Presidency and Vice Presidency, selected for the first time from the free states alone, with the avowed purpose of electing three candidates by suffrage of one part of the Union only, to rule over the whole United States. Can it be possible that those who are engaged in such a measure can have seriously reflected upon the consequences which must inevitably follow in case of success? Can they have the madness or the folly to believe that our Southern brethren would submit to be governed by such a Chief Magistrate? ... Suppose that the South, having a majority of the electoral vote should declare that they would only have slaveholders for President and Vice-President, and should elect such by their extensive suffrages to rule over us in the North. Do you think we would submit to it? No, not for a moment. And do you believe that your Southern brethren are less sensitive on this subject than you are, or less jealous of their rights? If you do, let me tell you that you are mistaken. And therefore you must see that if this sectional party succeeds, it inevitably leads to the destruction of this beautiful fabric reared by our forefathers, cemented by their blood, and bequeathed to us as priceless inheritance. I tell you, my friends, that I feel deeply and therefore I speak earnestly upon this

subject, for I feel that you are in danger. I am determined to make a clean breast of it. I will wash my hands of the consequences, whatever they may be, and I tell you that you are treading upon the brink of a volcano, that is liable at any moment to burst forth, and overwhelm the nation. I might by soft words inspire delusive hopes, and thereby win votes. But I can never consent to be one thing to the North and another to the South. I should despise myself, if I should be guilty of such duplicity. For my conscience would exclaim, with the dramatic poet,

> Is there not some chosen curse,
> Some hidden thunder in the stores of heaven,
> Red with uncommon wrath, to blast the man
> Who owes his greatness to his country's ruin!

That was 1856. The year was now 1861 and Abraham Lincoln, the very type of leader Fillmore warned against, was president. The above quote was from the *Mesilla Times* newspaper of August 24, 1861, almost two months after Major Isaac Lynde surrendered his command of the 7th Infantry Regiment at San Augustine Springs, and while Mesilla was then the capital of the Confederate Territory of Arizona. Former President Fillmore's words went unheeded, of course. In November 1861, the Republican Party joyfully celebrated doing exactly what President Fillmore advised them never to do. The fort in New Mexico, his namesake, paid one of the first great prices for the onset of radical rule in the North. We tend to overlook the fact that Abraham Lincoln was con-sidered, by Southerners, to be the greatest of radicals, his election comparable in many ways to Lenin taking over in Russia in 1917, or Hitler being given power in Germany in 1933. Lincoln was Millard Fillmore's perfect choice for being the wrong man in the wrong spot at the wrong time.

On July 2 Major Isaac Lynde abandoned Fort McLane and, with all troops and the public and private property of four companies, along with the women, children, dogs, and other animals, began the journey to Fort Fillmore. Major Lynde led the way, accompanied by the regimental band and his adjutant, Edward J. Brooks. Lynde was also accompanied by Company 'E,' 7th Infantry, under the command of 1ˢᵗ Lieutenant David Porter Hancock, a Pennsylvanian, and hence loyal to Lynde and to the Union.[1]

More major players who would have roles in the drama soon to unfold were on their way to Fort Fillmore from several directions in late June-early July 1861. Mounted Rifles detachments were sent from Forts Craig and Stanton. The main body of troops, under Major Lynde, prepared to leave Fort McLane.

David Hancock was an 1854 graduate of the United States Military Academy. He had been on the frontier since his graduation, following a posting to the 7ᵗʰ Infantry as a brevet 2ᵈ lieutenant on July 1, 1854. Promotion to 2ᵈ lieutenant came on March 3, 1855, 1ˢᵗ lieutenant on April 20, 1858, and captain on May 27, 1861. At the time he was leading Company 'E' out of Fort McLane, Hancock may not yet have received word of his promotion to captain. Involved in the surrender of his company at San Augustine Springs in late July 1861, Hancock was paroled and returned East. He was assigned to the Army of the Potomac in 1862 and received a brevet to the rank of major on July 2, 1863, and lieutenant colonel on March 13, 1865, for gallantry and meritorious service at the Battle of Gettysburg. Hancock did not get a majority in the Regular Army until October 24, 1874, when he was serving once again on the frontier with the 2ⁿᵈ Infantry. He served in that rank and regiment until 1880. David Porter Hancock died on May 21, 1880 at the age of forty-seven, while still on duty.[2]

David Hancock didn't disparage the reputation of his regimental commander Major Isaac Lynde, after the surrender at San Augustine Springs. Did he agree with the need to surrender? If he did Hancock never said a word in any surviving record. If he had a family with him when he left Fort McLane, or if he had private property, no doubt he fully understood what Lynde did and why. Had Company 'E' been attacked by Indians on the route from Fort McLane to Fort Fillmore, Hancock would have fought ferociously. Had he been attacked by troops guaranteed to represent the state of Texas, he probably would have surrendered for the same reasons the 3ᵈ and 8ᵗʰ Infantry Regiments surrendered in Texas, and without a fight. When the dragoons, infantry, and Mounted Rifles went out to fight the Apaches they did not take their families and public or private property along. They did not bring their cattle herds and the tools necessary to perform tasks around a military post. In fact, the very weakness of the Apache lay in their inability to withstand attacks on their families and public and private property. The Apaches usually made peace when the soldiers neared their homes. United States soldiers on the march with everything they owned or held dear were not a fighting force either, no matter the arms they carried.

There is no surety as to where the other three Fort McLane 7th Infantry companies were in the line of march. Lynde, Hancock, and Company 'E' may have been some distance in front, perhaps even a day's travel. No matter, three other companies, 'A,' 'B,' and 'G' followed behind. They arrived at Fort Fillmore shortly after Major Isaac Lynde.

First Lieutenant George Ryan commanded Company 'A' on the march. Ryan, a West Point graduate, Class of 1857, was from Massachusetts and an ardent Unionist. A picture of George Ryan taken during the period shows a handsome baby-faced young man in West Point uniform just before being commissioned as a brevet 2[d] lieutenant of the 6th Infantry on July 1, 1857. A slot opened for a 2[d] lieutenant in the 1st Infantry Regiment on October 31, 1857, and he was transferred to that regiment. Ryan didn't begin serving in the 7th Infantry until June 24, 1858. He served in Utah in 1858 and 1859 during the Mormon troubles and in New Mexico thereafter. Ryan was promoted to 1st lieutenant on April 22,1861. The twenty-five-year-old officer surrendered his Company 'A' at San Augustine Springs in late July, thereafter becoming a prisoner of war. Sent East on parole he served as regimental adjutant of the 7th Infantry from September 1, 1861, to July 19, 1862, when he was promoted to captain. On August 29, 1863, Ryan accepted a colonelcy of the 140th New York Volunteer Infantry Regiment. He served with that regiment until he was killed at the Battle of Spottsylvania on May 8, 1864, at the age of twenty-eight.[3]

Following the surrender of his company at San Augustine Springs, 1st Lieutenant George Ryan did not respond with negative comments on Major Isaac Lynde's decision to surrender.

Captain Mathew Rider Stevenson commanded Company 'B,' 7th Infantry, on the march from Fort McLane to Fort Fillmore. Stevenson was an 1846 graduate of the Military Academy at West Point, receiving a commission as a brevet 2^d lieutenant in the 1st Infantry Regiment on July 1, 1846, just in time for the Mexican War. Born in New York in 1826, Stevenson accepted a captaincy in the New York Volunteers at the same time he was to join the Regular Army. He served with the New Yorkers in Mexico from 1846 to 1848, meanwhile receiving an appointment to 2^d lieutenant in the 7th Infantry on February 16, 1847, but he did not join the regiment at that time. Whenever he joined the 7th Infantry, by August 24, 1851, he was a 1st lieutenant. For an unknown reason Stevenson was dismissed from the Army on September 20, 1856, and not reinstated until June 14, 1858, when he was given a captaincy in his old regiment. Stevenson, a married man with his wife and children near him, surrendered Company 'B' at San Augustine Springs in July 1861, becoming a prisoner of war and parolee. He did not serve actively thereafter, dying in New York City at the young age of thirty-seven in January 1863. Stevenson's wife was one of the heroines at San Augustine Springs, doing her duty by helping keep the 7th Infantry colors out of the hands of the Rebels. Her story will be told later.[4]

Following the surrender of his company at San Augustine Springs, Captain Mathew Rider Stevenson did not respond officially with negative comments on Major Isaac Lynde's decision to surrender.

Captain Joseph Haydn Potter commanded Company 'G,' 7th Infantry, the last of the companies to arrive at Fort Fillmore early in July 1861. Next to Major Isaac Lynde, Potter was the senior officer of the 7th Infantry then present. A future general officer during the American Civil War, Joseph Potter graduated from West Point in 1843 and accepted a commission as a brevet 2^d lieutenant in the 1st Infantry Regiment on July 1, 1843. A Yankee from New Hampshire, Potter was a loyal Unionist. He served with the 7th Infantry Regiment from October 21, 1845, when he was appointed a 2^d lieutenant. Potter received a brevet to 1st lieutenant on September 23, 1846, for gallantry and meritorious conduct at the Battle of Monterrey in Mexico, where he was wounded. Promotion to 1ˢᵗ lieutenant came on October 30, 1847, after which he served as adjutant of the 7ᵗʰ Infantry Regiment from November 1853 to January 9, 1856. He was promoted to captain on that day and assigned to the command of Company 'G.' Captain Potter surrendered his company at San Augustine Springs, becoming a Confederate prisoner of war and parolee.

Returning to the East, Joseph Potter commenced a brilliant career in the Volunteer Corps of the Union Army. On September 22, 1862, after his parole time expired, he was appointed colonel of the 12ᵗʰ New Hampshire Infantry. Regular Army promotion to major of the 19ᵗʰ Infantry Regiment followed on July 4, 1863. Potter was breveted to lieutenant colonel on December 13, 1862, for gallantry in the Battle of Fredericksburg, Virginia. A brevet to full colonel followed on May 3, 1863, for gallantry and meritorious conduct at the Battle of Chancellorsville, where he received a second wound, and became a prisoner of war for a second time. Paroled again, Potter was placed in command of a brigade and given a brevet to brigadier general on March 13, 1865. He was promoted to brigadier general of Volunteers on May 1, 1865, and received a second Regular Army brevet, this time to major general, on March 13, 1865, for gallantry and meritorious service in the campaign terminating with the surrender of Robert E. Lee's Army. Potter was mustered out of the Volunteer Service on January 15, 1866.

After the Civil War Joseph Haydn Potter returned to duty with the Regular Army, being appointed lieutenant colonel of the 30ᵗʰ Infantry Regiment on July 26, 1866. During his Indian War career, from 1865 to 1886, Joseph Potter was the second of the former Fort Fillmore officers to serve as a colonel in an all-black regiment, in this case the 24ᵗʰ Infantry. He was promoted to colonel of that regiment on December 11, 1873. His next promotion, to Regular Army brigadier general did not come until April 1, 1886, his retirement following shortly thereafter on October 12. Potter died in Ohio on December 1, 1892 at the age of seventy. He had served the Army for forty-three years.[5]

Following the surrender of his company at San Augustine Springs in late July 1861, Captain Joseph Haydn Potter did not respond with any public negative comments on Major Isaac Lynde's decision to surrender.

Two other officers either traveled with Lynde or preceded him to Fort Fillmore. The first of these was 1st Lieutenant Charles Bryant Stivers, the regimental quartermaster and commissary officer of the 7th Infantry Regiment. Stivers was a Kentuckian and had a choice as to whether to go to the South or stay with the Union. Like William Lane, Charles Stivers stayed in blue, although we have no idea of his views. He was an 1856 graduate of West Point and was commissioned a 2^{d} lieutenant of the 7th Infantry on July 1, 1856, without having to endure a period in brevet rank before a slot opened. Participating with the 7th in the Utah Campaign he came to New Mexico in 1860 and was stationed at Fort McLane. A promotion to 1st lieutenant came on April 20, 1861. Stivers was part of the surrender at San Augustine Springs, where all of his quartermaster and commissary goods were surrendered to the Texans. He was made a prisoner of war and then paroled, along with the rest. His career during the rest of the Civil War is sketchy. After a long period of parole he was available for active service after August 1862. He was dismissed from the Army on July 14, 1863, and reinstated on August 11, 1863. A final retirement for disability was granted on December 30, 1864, in the rank of captain. By a special act of Congress thirty years later, in 1894, Charles Stivers was made a captain and retired once again in that rank. He died in Ohio on June 10, 1907 at the age of seventy-three.[6]

Following the surrender of his quartermaster goods and commissary supplies at San Augustine Springs in late July, 1st Lieutenant Charles Stivers did not respond with negative comments on Major Isaac Lynde's decision to surrender.

Assistant Surgeon Charles Henry Alden was the last of the officers to arrive at about the same time as Major Isaac Lynde. Alden was sent by the Department to provide a second medical officer, with James Cooper McKee, for the large force then concentrating at Fort Fillmore. Assistant Surgeon Alden was commissioned from Pennsylvania on June 23, 1860. Little else is known about him other than Canby sent him to assist in whatever way he could.

Assistant Surgeon Charles Henry Alden.
Courtesy: US Army Military History Institute.

Alden was involved in the surrender at San Augustine, became a prisoner of war and was paroled. He served as a surgeon on the eastern battlefields where, on March 13, 1865, he received a double brevet, first to brevet-major-surgeon, then brevet-lieutenant colonel-surgeon. On July 26, 1866, he was appointed major-surgeon, followed by lieutenant colonel-surgeon on November 14, 1888, and colonel-surgeon on December 4, 1892. Charles Henry Alden retired on April 28, 1900.

Doctor Alden had no negative comments related to the conduct of Major Isaac Lynde during the surrender at San Augustine Springs.

The other 7th Infantry officers then at Fort Fillmore, 1st Lieutenant Augustus Plummer and 2[d] Lieutenant Francis Crilly also had no negative comments on the conduct of Major Isaac Lynde officially recorded immediately after the surrender, on the conduct of Major Isaac Lynde during the surrender.

Lynde's march from Cook's Peak to Fort Fillmore was observed closely by the Apaches. Believing they had driven the Americans out of their lands the Apache leaders, Cochise and Mangas Coloradas, made a temporary camp at Cook's Peak, a mountain called by the Apaches *Dziltanatal*, "Mountain Holds Its Head Up Proudly." Here they hoped to cut off the former Fort McLane-protected Pinos Altos region from the town of Mesilla. What pride the Apaches must have felt, watching the long train of bluecoats finally leaving their lands.[8]

As Major Lynde's infantrymen trudged toward Fort Fillmore on July 3, Perry E. Brocchus advised the Honorable Simon Cameron, the new Union Secretary of War, concerning mounted volunteers in New Mexico. Brocchus pointed out that infantry were "not well adapted to active service in the field in New Mexico" and there should be an additional regiment of mounted volunteers, providing their own horses. These cavalry troops were to protect both the northern and southern parts of the Territory and defend it against Indian depredations and the "rebellious domestic foe."[9]

Major Isaac Lynde's four Companies, 'A,' 'B,' 'G,' and 'E,' arrived at Fort Fillmore from Fort McLane on or just after

Independence Day, July 4. On July 7, while Lynde tried to situate the troops at the post, probably in tents in and around the decaying Fort Fillmore adobe buildings, Brevet-Lieutenant Colonel Canby addressed the Adjutant General in Washington on the matter of former Department commander William Wing Loring's perfidy while in office. Loring was probably still at Fort Bliss during this period and working against Isaac Lynde. One has to wonder why Canby wrote of Loring's actions to the far away Adjutant General in Washington, but sent no official word to Lynde. Canby wrote:

No information, except the special orders of May 17, has yet been received in relation to the volunteers to be called into the service in this department, and as the organization of the regiments cannot be postponed without delaying the concentration of the regular troops or hazarding important interests, I have informed the governor of the Territory that, in addition to the requisitions that have already been made, I would at once accept and muster into service the companies that are required to complete the organization of Colonels St. Vrain and Pino's regiments.

The organization of the companies already called for progresses very slowly, and I entertain such serious doubts of the ability of the Territory to furnish all, that I have made a requisition on the governor of Colorado Territory for two companies of infantry for the garrison of Fort Garland. The state of affairs at the South and the increasing Indian hostilities will render it inexpedient to detach any of the force now in this section.

Fort Bliss has been re-enforced by four companies of Texas troops. The movements of these troops have no doubt been hastened for a special purpose, in connection with enterprises against this department. Colonel Loring left the department on the 23rd instant, but I had previously, for reasons that have already been assigned, exercised the command of the department without reference to him. There is reason to fear that his influence, coupled with other causes, may have been productive of evil in that quarter, but I hope that a sufficient force was concentrated at Fort Fillmore in season to counteract the designs of the Texans upon that post. Major Lynde, with a portion of the command from Fort McLane, was expected on the 5th instant, and I think that there are by this time eight or ten companies at that post, which will be sufficient, I think, to resist the threatened invasion, and give time and cover for any movements that may be necessary to protect the interests of the United States in that quarter.

A command of about 300 men, regulars and volunteers, will be detached from Fort Union for the protection of the trains coming into this country from the Missouri frontier. This force will be sufficient to secure them against the attacks of Indians or marauding parties, but not against a large organized force from the frontiers of Arkansas or Texas.

The enclosed papers will give the General-in-Chief some idea of the state of affairs in the South, but I hope that the measures that have been taken and are in progress will be sufficient to defeat these designs.[10]

The discussion of the perfidy of former Colonel Loring, although important, is not the most critical part of this message with regard to the history of what was to happen at Fort Fillmore. In the opening paragraph Canby reported, "the organization of the regiments [New Mexico Volunteers] cannot be postponed without delaying the concentration of the regular troops." This statement proves Canby, regardless of his rhetoric to stand and defend against Texas incursions, fully understood that General Winfield Scott's order to get Federal troops out of New Mexico Territory had first priority.

The commander at Fort Fillmore at the end of June was Captain Robert Garland. Soon after receiving news of Major Lynde's imminent arrival, Garland deserted. We cannot be sure of the exact date since the Fort Fillmore Post Return for July was never written. Near the time Garland left, 1st Lieutenant John McNally arrived from Fort Craig with a portion of Company 'F,' Regiment of Mounted Rifles. In addition, a small command under 2d Lieutenant Cressey was on the road from Fort Stanton. Cressey's command consisted of troopers from Company 'B,' R.M.R.

Second Lieutenant Edmund Potter Cressey was nearing twenty-five years of age when he arrived at Fort Fillmore, a West Point graduate of the Class of 1858. A New Yorker, Cressey was commissioned a brevet 2d lieutenant in the Regiment of Mounted Rifles on July 1, 1858 and a 2d lieutenant on November 22, 1859. He was promoted to 1st lieutenant on May 14, 1861 but may not yet have heard of that promotion when he came to Fort Fillmore. Cressey surrendered with his troops at San Augustine, served for a short period as a prisoner of war and was then paroled. He stayed on after the Regiment of Mounted Rifles became the 3ᵈ Cavalry Regiment in 1861, being promoted to the grade of captain on July 17, 1862. He received brevets to major and lieutenant colonel on March 13, 1865. After the war he continued in service until retiring on January 1, 1871, as a brevet-lieutenant colonel. Edward Cressey died in California on June 21, 1899 at the age of sixty-three.[11]

Canby addressed the state of recruitment of New Mexico Volunteers in secessionist-minded Mesilla and the region surrounding Fort Fillmore in a letter written July 7. One cannot be sure that Lynde received it before abandoning the post. Canby wanted names of loyal militia officers, and an immediate creation of militia units. To Major Lynde this would simply have been another task on an already overloaded schedule. Canby stated:

> In the organization of the volunteer companies in this part of the department I have endeavored to secure at least one American who could be relied upon among the commissioned officers of each company. It is desirable that the same principle should be observed in organizing the companies that you may call for in your neighborhood. The names of the commissioned officers should be sent to this office in order that they may be reported to the governor of the Territory for commissions. Dr. Steck, Mr. Labardine, and Mr. Mills have been suggested to me as suitable persons for these positions. It will be advisable that the companies now organized by you should be mustered in for the period of three months. Such of them as desire it may hereafter be mustered in for the period of three years.[12]

Did Lynde make any effort to obey this order? He was at a new and overcrowded post—no doubt in disrepair—among officers and enlisted men most of whom he did not know, trying to coordinate the activities of a regiment which had rarely been gathered in one place since the Mexican War. Confederates were to the south, his officers were an unknown quality, and the local citizens were hostile to the Union. Adding all these together, when did Lynde have time to set up volunteer companies? Why didn't Canby have Major Paul do it earlier? That mystery begs an answer that is simply not available. Perhaps the most interesting person mentioned in this letter was Dr. Michael Steck, who was recommended to Isaac Lynde as suitable for a commission. Steck must have been concerned over the closing of Apache Agency and the war being waged by the Apaches. Though of little impact on the general conditions caused by the coming Civil War, someone, perhaps the militia, was going to have to address the Indian problem. There was no better man than Dr. Steck to lead that militia.

While Canby was writing Lynde on July 7, Lynde was also writing to Canby, informing him of his arrival at Fort Fillmore:

> I have the honor to report that I arrived at this position on the 4th instant with the regimental staff, band, and Company E, Seventh Infantry, and found that no demonstration from Texas had been made on this post. The remaining companies of the Fort McLane command, viz., B and I, Seventh Infantry, will be here to-day. I shall then have very little fear of the result of any attack that will be likely made from Texas. From the best information that I can obtain, there are four companies of Texas troops at Fort Bliss, with two 18-pounders and four or more small guns. It is stated that they are fortifying for their own defense. It is probable that there are two companies now at Fort Stanton. With the force that I shall have at this post in a few days I do not think that the enemy will attempt to attack us, but if they do, I think we shall give them a warm reception.[13]

In a second letter written July 7, Major Lynde addressed the treachery of Colonel Loring and Major Sibley. Lynde obviously had seen the intercepted letter that Sibley sent but Loring apparently did not receive. Lynde said:

> I received your dispatches yesterday by Lieutenant Hall, and was very much astonished to receive such proofs of treachery against Colonel Loring. I had always believed him to be a man of the most unflinching honor and integrity. I was not so much disappointed in Major Sibley. I think the extracts enclosed do great injustice to the officers at this post. I fully

believe that every officer at this post will do their whole duty as long as they retain their commissions in our Army, though some may intend to resign soon. I believe that if the post had been attacked before my arrival, Captain Garland would have fought with his command to the last extremity.

This fort is very badly situated for defense. It is placed in a basin, surrounded by sand hills, at least half the circumference of the circle, and they are covered by a dense growth of chaparral. These sand hills completely command the post, and render it indefensible against a force supplied with artillery. A force of a thousand men could approach it within 500 yards under perfect cover.

As yet I have not been able to make myself acquainted with the surrounding localities, but I am now of the opinion that if Texas should make a strong effort to overcome Arizona, it would be policy to withdraw our force beyond the Jornada to Fort Craig, as I do not think this post or the valley worth the exertion to hold it. If no more troops reach Fort Bliss I do not think they will attempt any aggressive movement against this Territory other than theft or robbery, yet I shall be on my guard at all times. I shall make an effort to raise a company of volunteers, but I am not able to say with what success. I presume you are informed before this of the departure of Colonel Loring prior to my arrival. P.S.—From what I have just learned, I think I can raise one or two companies of volunteers, and they are the kind of troops I want to act as spies.[14]

Lynde's words on the subject of Robert Garland show, to this author, a misplaced faith and trust in a U.S. Army Officer Corps which would not, and perhaps could not, live up to the standard he set for them. This character flaw, if it is one, of having too much faith and trust in his fellow officers, was demonstrated once more on the way to San Augustine Springs. Lynde believed that an American officer, when given an order or job, would obey an unwritten code of honor, and do the expected job assigned, no matter which side of a political issue he might be on. He expected Robert Garland, when wearing the blue, would fight the Texans if they attacked. Would Garland ever have done so? Such a question lies at the very heart of Lynde's guilt or innocence at San Augustine Springs. Lynde believed in the duty-consciousness of his junior officers. This belief, however noble and admirable in the abstract, was the fatal flaw in Lynde's character.

No truer words were spoken than those Lynde used in this letter concerning the physical situation and defense capability of Fort Fillmore. The fort had no wall, was easily approached from the east, if not the south, by mounted troops or infantry with artillery. If an infantry company was placed on the ridge south of the fort, which dominates the approach from the south, the fort could be said to be better defended from that direction than any other. There was no way, and is no way today, to defend a low-lying post from the gradually rising sand hill heights to the east and north. A right envelopment from the south (out of Texas) cutting and passing north of the Soledad Canyon road could have allowed a cavalry force to approach Fort Fillmore unseen. That Baylor made no attempt to come that way may mean he either had no reconnaissance of the area or was not originally intending to attack Fort Fillmore. He may have always sought Mesilla as his primary goal. No matter what Baylor's intent, Major Isaac Lynde was absolutely right in judging Fort Fillmore indefensible. Had Apaches determined to run through the place screaming and firing off arrows, which they never did, they could easily have done so. The fort was, if anything, a liability to a defending commander. A regiment would not be enough to overcome the obvious defects.

One of Isaac Lynde's other responsibilities, the abandonment of Forts Buchanan and Breckinridge, and the transfer of their troops to Fort Fillmore, was partially accomplished on July 10, 1861. Fort Breckinridge, once named for John Breckinridge, former Vice President under President Buchanan, and also a future Confederate general, was burned to the ground, the troops having begun to withdraw earlier. Fort Buchanan, south of Fort Breckinridge, was still preparing for the withdrawal of its troops and public property as Lynde arrived at Fort Fillmore.

The New Mexico volunteer militia program seemed to be the most important job on Lynde's mind as of July 14, only twelve days before San Augustine Springs. He had seven companies of infantry, one dismounted Rifles Company ('A'), 1st Lieutenant

McNally's Company 'F,' RMR, as well as 2ᵈ Lieutenant Cressey's small detachment of Company 'B,' R.M.R., from Fort Stanton. On July 14, Major Lynde appeared to have few concerns about an invasion from Texas, which was only days off. He said:

> The state of affairs is much the same at this post as when I last reported. It is rumoured that they have raised a Company of Volunteers at Fort Bliss as spies for the purpose of stealing the animals from the different Posts in this Department—strength about 40 men.
> They bluster very much about attacking us here, but have made no effort to do so as yet.
> I received your communication by Mr. Mills. He had rendered himself so obnoxious to many of the officers here that he declines taking any part with the volunteers. I have employed him as a Confidential Agent in El Paso. I think by the time the arms arrive from Fort Union I can muster at least one Company of Volunteers. Am I authorized to mount one Company? They would be very useful here ... .[15]

On July 14, Brevet-Lieutenant Colonel Canby informed the Adjutant General in Washington that seven companies of infantry and two of Mounted Rifles were then at Fort Fillmore. Canby stated that these troops were being used to cover the ordered withdrawal of the Federal forces from Arizona. There was absolutely no mention of a stand and fight order being issued to Lynde. Canby said:

> I have the honor to report that there has been no material change in the state of affairs in this department since my report of the 7th instant.
> The garrison of Fort Fillmore has been increased to seven companies of infantry and two of rifles, relieving the anxiety that had previously been felt for the security of the post. Under cover of this force the troops and public property in the interior of Arizona are now being withdrawn. Arrangements are being made as rapidly as possible for the withdrawal of the regular troops and disposition of public property, as required by the special orders (Headquarters of the Army) of May 17 and June 12, 1861. The organization of the volunteer regiments, particularly the Second (Colonel Pinos), progresses very slowly.

Our relations with the Comanche Indians and the Fort Stanton Apaches are more satisfactory than they were at the date of my last report.[16]

On July 17, at Fort Craig, Captain Alfred Gibbs received an order directing him to take part of Company 'I,' Mounted Rifles, and escort a herd of one hundred cattle to Fort Millard Fillmore from Fort Craig. Thereafter he was to report to Major Lynde and serve under his command. Gibbs left for Fort Craig the next day from Albuquerque.[17]

First Lieutenant Donald C. Stith reported to Lynde at Fort Fillmore that he was a prisoner of Colonel Baylor at Fort Bliss. Stith, a future Confederate officer, pretended he was still loyal to the Federal cause when, in fact, he was soon to be a colonel in the Confederate Army in Texas. Stith said:

I have the honor to report, for the information of the commanding officer of the Department of New Mexico, the circumstances connected with my arrest and being brought to this place. While on my way to Chihuahua, in pursuance of instructions from the Department, having proceeded as far as one mile beyond the town of Guadelupe [sic], Mexico—which place is about 40 miles distant from the town of El Paso, Mexico—and while encamped, a party of men from 12 to 15 in number came up; and one, representing himself to be Lieutenant Adams, told me he had orders to arrest me and take me to Fort Bliss.

I asked him by what authority he did so. He replied, "By authority of the Southern Confederacy." I told him I did not recognize any such power, and that it was a violation of the law of nations—[I] being on the soil of a foreign power. He replied that he was acting under the orders of his commanding officer, Colonel Baylor.

As I had not sufficient force to resist him, I obeyed the order under protest, and was brought to this place, together with those who had accompanied me the whole way from Fort Fillmore, which we reached on the morning of the 18th instant.

I was brought into the presence of Colonel Baylor, who told me I was a prisoner of war. I told him in substance the same as

I did Lieutenant Adams, saying that I acknowledged no such power as the Southern Confederacy, and that it was a violation of the soil of Mexico. He replied that he had not given any orders for my arrest, but that as long as I had been brought to the garrison, he did not see fit to release me; he, however, acknowledged that his command had exceeded their authority in arresting me on the soil of Mexico. He then offered me a parole, which I signed, the only alternative being close confinement.

I have given the full particulars of the matter, with my regret that my mission has been so abruptly terminated. I beg leave to state that I have been treated by Colonel Baylor and his officers with the utmost kindness and consideration.[18]

One cannot be sure what 1st Lieutenant Stith intended to accomplish with his letter. Was he seeking re-entrance to the Federal community at a later date, or was his entire purpose to state firmly to Federal officers who might wish to surrender that he was well treated by Baylor? Given his future Confederate career the latter reason may be the correct one. He may have been trying to convince his former tentmates that the Texans were really nice guys who did not torture or abuse prisoners.

Apaches attacked a party of seven Americans near Cook's Springs in mid-July. Two hundred Apaches were said to have been involved in the attack. All seven Americans were killed but not before causing a great number of Indian casualties. Cochise is later to have indicated that with twenty-five such men, he could whip the whole United States Army.

At Fort Fillmore on July 21, Major Isaac Lynde notified the Department that a letter was received in Mesilla to the effect that 1st Lieutenant Donald C. Stith, 5th Infantry, and his party, had been arrested at Guadalupe, Mexico (twenty-five miles below Fort Bliss). The letter had been sent to Messrs Hayward and McGrorty in Mesilla, both Confederate sympathizers.[19]

A second letter written that day described activities Lynde ordered performed by his garrison. He stated:

Since my last weekly report no material changes have occurred in affairs at this Post, or in this valley. Scouting parties from Fort Bliss penetrated this country as far as the Cotton-woods (22 miles below this place) and on one occasion, I detached a column of Infantry from this side and a column of Rifles for the other side of the river, to capture or drive back a party said to be at the Mesa, a town ten miles below this Post. The command returned without finding any suspicious bodies of men. On the 18th Inst. I detached two Companies of Infantry under command of Captain J.H. Potter 7 Inf. and occupied the town of San Tomas, on the opposite side of the river and distant about 2 ½ miles. From its location, the town commands the road from El Paso to Mesilla. A [line] of Lagunas between the town, and hills prevents the passage of artillery or wagons, and only horsemen could pass over the lava ridge in rear of the town. A detail of one Non Com officer and ten mounted men is sent to Captain Potter daily, for such service as may be necessary.

Information has reached me that ammunition is being sent from Fort Bliss to Mesilla. I have accordingly ordered all wagons from that direction to be stopped and searched.

The Apaches have commenced operations in our immediate vicinity—as on the night of the 19th inst they killed two peons 2 or 3 miles in rear of the Post, and stole a pair of horses and harness, and the next morning killed two men and drove off 2000 sheep. Application was made to me for mounted troops to pursue them. I declined furnishing any but stated that when the volunteers called for [are] forthcoming I would then assist them as far as was in my power.

In compliance with instructions received yesterday from Department Head Quarters the enlistment of Volunteers is suspended. About 50 names were on the list up to that time.

Capt. J.M. Jones, 7 Infy. is still absent.

Contradictory [estimates] are in circulation as to the number of troops at and en route to Fort Bliss. From the best information I can obtain, the number all told will not exceed five hundred.

The effective force at present under my command is 450. Exclusive of sick (38). There are 98 men on detached service, nearly all of whom will [return] within a week.

Nothing has been heard of the troops from Forts Buchanan & Breckinridge, since the acceptance of the order requiring the abandonment of those Posts.

Enclosed I transmit Oaths of Allegiance of Lieuts. Lane Rifles and Stivers 7 Infy.[20]

Lynde sounds like a very busy man, not an incompetent unable to do anything, as later accusations stated. He was involved with thwarting Texan adventures, with evaluating the Apache threat, and also concerned with the volunteer militia program thrust upon him. He responded to each as expeditiously as he could. Mounted Rifles soldiers crossed the river to investigate La Mesa while infantry advanced on the east side of the river as far as the Cotton-woods camping ground (near present-day Canutillo) to chase any Texans there. They found none. This must have been the foray described by Lydia Lane and Doctor McKee as having occurred back on June 22. It is important to examine how McKee viewed this troop movement. We need not look at Lydia Lane because she took her recollection straight from McKee's book. Of course, McKee was at least a month off in his remembrance, and forgot the infantry presence entirely. He stated:

> On or about the 22d of June [Just before July 18 in actuality], 1st Lieutenant W.B. Lane, commanding, 2d Lieutenant C.H. McNally, and 2nd Lieutenant Ed. J. Cressey, Regiment of Mounted Riflemen, with about seventy men, were ordered to make a scout down the Rio Grande toward El Paso, a rumor having reached the post that the Texans were advancing, and said to be four hundred strong.[21]

At this point in his narrative McKee was busy elevating the reputation of 1st Lieutenant Lane, so that later he could use Lane's leaving post as a reason for saying Major Lynde wanted to get rid of the fighting men then at the fort, keeping only the cowards and traitors who would not fight. There are several errors in this brief but crucial paragraph. McKee forgot to mention Lynde's sending of an infantry force down the east side of the river. To mention them would have detracted from building up Lane's reputation as an aggressive fighter. The infantry advance might also have made Isaac Lynde appear to be a commander who was thorough in this planning, sending forces to investigate both sides of the river for any enemy scouts who might be coming. In addition, McKee erroneously reported a rumor that four hundred Confederates were advancing. This also was intended to heighten Lane's reputation as a fighting man. Only Lane, the cavalryman, went out to face four hundred Rebels. The cowardly infantry, by McKee's implication, remained at the fort protecting the incompetent Major Lynde. McKee continued, "Lieutenant Lane, a hot-headed Kentuckian, had his own way of being loyal, which did not suit the extremists; but I had confidence in his determined bravery as a soldier, and his integrity as a man."[22]

Who were the extremists McKee referred to in this insulting comment? At this point in the Fort Fillmore drama all the secessionists, save possibly for Lane himself (if Kentucky seceded), had resigned, deserted, or in other ways left the post. Not one single officer who remained as of July 21, 1861—Lynde, Lane, Plummer, Brooks, Crilly, Stevenson, Potter, Ryan, Hancock, Stivers, Alden, Cressey, or McKee—was a Confederate sympathizer. All were from the North save for Lane and Stivers, both Kentuckians. McKee was either exaggerating in this statement, or lying in order to build a case that could not be made any other way. Captain Robert R. Garland, whom McKee never mentioned in his writing, was the last Confederate sympathizer (extremist) to depart. McKee's timeline of events is very poorly put together, and quite erroneous.

Lydia Lane passed on the story of her husband as the martyred and only hero of the Fort Fillmore drama. She noted, "About the middle of July it was decided to send some of the surplus commissary stores to Fort Craig, and the company Lieutenant Lane commanded was ordered to escort the wagon train. Doctor McKee writes, 'He [Lane] was a fighting man, and had to be got rid of.'"[23]

Here in these words lies the essence of Doctor McKee's message to posterity. Only cowards and traitors, save for McKee and a few others he liked, remained to uphold American honor at Fort Fillmore once Lane departed. Dr. McKee has been successful in having his version become history. McKee actually said a bit more on the matter than Lydia Lane chose to relate in her book:

> I hope I'll be pardoned for relating an incident. On one of those wretched nights I was excited, unable to sleep, and

dreading treachery and cowardice from the apathy of the garrison, I went to Lane's quarters about two A. M., wakened him up, and asked him what he would do if the Texans attacked the post? Whether he would fight or surrender? He assured me that he would fight, and not think of surrendering. My anxiety was allayed and my confidence restored. I went home and slept soundly until morning. Lane was shortly after this ordered to Santa Fe, N.M., with his company, and escaped the deep mortification of our surrender. He was a fighting man, and had to be got rid of.[24]

This two a.m. visit to Lane's quarters may have happened on or about June 20, when Colonel Loring was still at Fort Fillmore, along with Garland and possibly Wilcox and others of a secessionist bent, if it happened at all. Loring may indeed have wanted to simply hand the garrison over to the Texans. This event McKee describes did not happen on July 21 or immediately before the time Lane left on July 24. McKee was way off in his time-line, and mixing events to make points as he wanted to make them. Dr. McKee hated Isaac Lynde. He built his case around that hate. We have no direct quote from McKee as to why he hated Lynde so deeply, other than the fact of the surrender at San Augustine Springs. Major Lynde was briefly restored to his old rank in 1866, by President Grant, then retired in recognition of thirty-four years of honorable service before San Augustine. Dr. McKee is on record at that time as vehemently opposing that reinstatement. Perhaps that was the act that pushed him over the edge.

The quote that Lydia Lane used so proudly, that, "He [Lane] was a fighting man and had to be got rid of" is rendered doubly disgusting by the records of so many of the 7th Infantry officers during the American Civil War. In fact, most of the officers involved in the San Augustine surrender later fought on many of the major battlefields of the Civil War, George Ryan giving his life, others suffering wounds. The "fighting man" Lane stayed away from the combat of battlefields, spending his wartime service recruiting volunteers for the various fields of slaughter.

Oaths of allegiance were required for all officers by the order of the President of the United States Abraham Lincoln. In a July 21 letter, Major Lynde referred to 1st Lieutenant Lane and 2d Lieutenant Stivers taking the oath. At this point, whether or not Lane had flirted with secession in the past, taking of the oath ended any thought of his disloyalty. Although he did not fight on Civil War battlefields he seems to have conducted his career thereafter in a manner beyond reproach. It is only this author's suspicion that he may have had sympathy for the South, by virtue of his birth in Kentucky, and his loyalty to so many Southern friends serving in the Mounted Rifles, as his wife admits.

Captain Alfred Gibbs arrived at Fort Craig on July 22, following a four-day trip from Albuquerque, averaging about twenty-five miles per day of travel with his mounted unit. He picked up a herd of cattle at Fort Craig destined for Fort Fillmore and almost immediately headed south onto the Jornada del Muerto. Gibbs had about thirty-five men of Company 'I,' Regiment of Mounted Rifles, with him.[25]

Fort Buchanan was evacuated and burned on July 23, 1861. Mining, ranching, and all parts of the economy in what was then the western part of New Mexico Territory were at a standstill.

On that same day Colonel John R. Baylor, commanding the 2d Texas Mounted Rifles, prepared to march 258 Texas troops north out of Fort Bliss along the east bank of the Rio Grande, destination Fort Fillmore or Mesilla.

As Baylor made his departure on the night of July 23-24, preparations were made at Fort Fillmore to dispatch a wagon train loaded with personal or public property to Fort Craig. The remainder of Lane's dismounted Company 'A' went along in the wagons as escort. Lane, his wife, and his dismounted soldiers, left the post before any threat from Lieutenant Colonel Baylor and his Texans became known by the military command at Fort Fillmore. The wagon train bearing the Lanes was well up the road past Las Cruces, and past Doña Ana before Baylor's column arrived unexpectedly in front of Fort Fillmore on the night of July 24-25.

Lydia Lane reported on their leaving and the reason for it. "About the middle of July it was decided to send some of the surplus commissary stores to Fort Craig, and the company Lieutenant Lane commanded was ordered to escort the wagon-train."[26]

At that point she should have stopped writing, for she had told the truth. That was why she and her husband left Fort Fillmore. But Lane, caught up with praise for her husband, continued. She repeated Dr. McKee's comment about her husband being a "fighting man, and had to be got rid of." Unwittingly, however, she reveals the true nature of the incident. The departure of the wagon train had been anticipated since the "middle of July." The train was a sound and normal precaution Isaac Lynde took. He was clearing out some crucial but unnecessary supplies which could later fall in the hands of an enemy, if the situation deteriorated. Lydia Lane continued:

> On the 24th of July, 1861 we left for Fort Craig; our escort of riflemen was distributed among the wagons, as there were no horses to ride. We had travelled but a short distance when the wagon-master insisted on halting to rest the mules, preparatory to a night march across the Jornada del Muerto, the eighty miles's stretch without water.[27]

Neither Lydia Lane nor Dr. McKee were involved in the military decisions being made concerning the post, he being a doctor and responsible for the health of the troops and the hospital, and not privy to the meetings of the 7th Infantry staff, and she the wife of one of the post officers. Neither may have known that Major Isaac Lynde received an order from Brevet-Lieutenant Colonel Canby, which led to the wagon train leaving Fort Fillmore just before Baylor's unexpected arrival on the scene. Then again, perhaps Lydia Lane and Dr. McKee did know of the order and, since it reflected positively on Lynde, made no mention of it. On August 16, 1861, in a letter to the Division Headquarters at St. Louis, Colonel Canby told of sending that order:

> In consequence of the anticipated arrivals of Texan reenforcements on the line below Fort Fillmore, that post was

re-enforced by two additional companies of mounted troops, and Forts Stanton and Craig were strengthened. On the 15th of July the commanding officer at Fort Fillmore was advised that Fort Fillmore would be abandoned, and was instructed to remove the public property, so as to abandon the post as soon as the troops from Arizona had passed up; the regular troops from Forts Stanton and Craig to be withdrawn as soon as volunteers could be raised to replace them.[28]

In accordance with Canby's orders the wagon train took excess public property out of the fort in anticipation of an abandonment of the post as soon as the remaining 7th Infantry companies came in from Forts Buchanan and Breckinridge. It was not known that Baylor was on the scene until after the wagon train left. Clearly, Isaac Lynde did not send Lane away because "He was a fighting man, and had to be got rid of."

NOTES - Chapter 9

1. Lynde was to take four companies of the 7th Infantry to Fort Fillmore and still maintain control over the regimental assets at Forts Buchanan and Breckinridge. There were three companies of the 7th at those posts, with no mounted units present, the dragoons having moved out of western New Mexico Territory, another example of needed assets being moved away from the Texas border at the time of secession.
2. Heitman, David Hancock.
3. Heitman, George Ryan.
4. Heitman, Mathew Stevenson.
5. Heitman, Joseph Haydn Potter.
6. Heitman, Charles Stivers.
7. Heitman, Charles Henry Alden.
8. Edwin Sweeney, *Cochise*, pp. 180, 181.
9. Horn & Wallace, Brocchus to Cameron, July 3, 1861, p. 68.
10. Canby to Assistant Adjutant General, Washington, D.C., July 7, 1861, M1012, Roll 2.
11. Heitman, Edward Potter Cressey.

12. Horn & Wallace, Canby to Lynde, July 7, 1861, pp. 72,73.

13. Horn & Wallace, Lynde to Canby, July 7, 1861, pp. 73,74.

14. Ibid.

15. Lynde to Canby, July 14, 1861, M1120, Rolls 13/14.

16. Canby to Assistant Adjutant General, Washington, D.C., July 14, 1861, M1012, Roll 2.

17. Anderson to Gibbs, July 17, 1861, M1012, Roll 2.

18. Stith to Assistant Adjutant General, July 20, 1861, M1120, Rolls 13/14.

19. Lynde to Assistant Adjutant General, July 21, 1861,M1120, Rolls 13/14.

20. Lynde to Acting Assistant Adjutant General, July 21, 1861, M1120,Roll 13/14.

21. McKee, p. 10.

22. Ibid., 11.

23. Lydia Spencer Lane, *I Married a Soldier*, p. 108.

24. McKee, p. 11.

25. Horn & Wallace, Statement of Captain Gibbs, pp. 24,25.

26. Lydia Spencer Lane, *I Married a Soldier*, p. 108.

27. Ibid.

28. Canby to Assistant Adjutant General, St. Louis, August 16, 1861, M1012, Roll 2.

10

THE TEXANS

O n the night of July 23-24 Lieutenant Colonel John Baylor's Texas cavalry force left Fort Bliss, taking the road to Fort Fillmore forty miles away. In September 1861, long after the coming events transpired, Baylor reflected on his reasons for moving north that evening. There was as yet no bloody civil war, although one might certainly have been anticipated, especially by Baylor and his Texans. Baylor's troops wanted Yankee blood. In fact Baylor's actions in moving north made him an aggressor without cause, unless one considered he was anticipating renewing Texan claims to New Mexico lands, now the statehood agreements were abrogated through secession. Perhaps John Baylor wanted to begin the American Civil War himself, not knowing that it had already begun, a few days before, on a field in Virginia. He said:

> On assuming command at Fort Bliss I ascertained that the United States forces were concentrating in strong force at Fort Fillmore, and from a proximity of that post I supposed that the object of the enemy was to attack the forces under my command at Fort Bliss. I was satisfied that if I permitted them to concentrate, my command was too weak to maintain my position. I therefore determined to attack the enemy in detail, and prevent, if possible, the contemplated concentration. For that purpose I sent a detachment, under Major Waller, to reconnoiter Fort Fillmore and see the position of the enemy's

Lieutenant Colonel John Baylor
Courtesy: Gernomino Springs Museum,
Truth or Consequences, New Mexico.

pickets, also whether the fort could be approached without discovery. The report of Major Waller satisfied me that I could easily in the night gain a position between the fort and the river [Rio Grande], and cut off the animals as they went to water; then the enemy would have to attack me in a strong position, thus rendering the protection afforded by the fort of no use. I accordingly took up the line of march in the night of the 23rd of July with 258 men, and in the night of the 24th succeeded in taking a position on the river near Fort Fillmore. The surprise of the enemy would have been complete but for the desertion of a private from Capt. Teel's company, who reported to Major Lynde our strength and position. The long-roll was distinctly heard, which apprized us that our approach was known to the enemy.[1]

Baylor wanted a surprise attack, knowing full well that the Federal commander had no orders to attack him. Isaac Lynde confirms Baylor's account of the detection of the Confederate force being the result of a deserter's raising the alarm. Unfortunately, neither man mentioned who the deserter was and why he chose to act in such a fashion. Baylor simply referred to him as a private from Teel's Company of artillery. Lynde described the detection as follows in a July 26 letter to the Department of New Mexico:

> I have the honor to report that on the night of the 24th instant a deserter from the Texas troops was brought in by our Picket, and he informed me that a large body of mounted men between 3 & 400 under Command of Lt. Col. Baylor, Texas Troops, were moving up the river, and that he left them at Willow Bar about 12 miles below the Post. Presuming their object to be an attack on the Post, I immediately ordered the two Companies of the 7th Infantry from San Tomas and kept the garrison under arms until after daylight, when mounted parties were sent out to reconnoiter.[2]

Having detected the Texan presence on the eastern side of the river, numbering by estimate some three hundred to four hundred troops (258 by Baylor's count) Lynde did exactly as he should have done given that numbers estimate. He pulled Potter's two companies from their defensive positions at Santo Tomás on the other side of the river, and brought them back to the fort. This was the correct strategy given what Lynde perceived to be the situation. He now had seven companies on the east bank, enough to counterbalance the Confederate Texas strength as he believed it to be. Should the Confederates have chosen to attack, the "perceived" odds would have been 1:1.5 or better in favor of the defender. It was, after all, Baylor's initial strategy to attack the post directly while cutting them off from the river water they needed in order to survive. Had Lynde left the two companies at Santo Tomás, and Baylor followed his initial plan of attack, Lynde would have been at a disadvantage, having divided his forces and, with Texans between himself and the river, suffered a tactical reverse at the least.

Though more colorful and chaotic in his wording, Assistant Surgeon McKee backs up the basic assertions made by both Baylor and Lynde. McKee says of the arrival of the Texans:

> The Texans, under command of Lieutenant-Colonel Baylor, C.S.A., to the number of four hundred men, had on the 24th of July advanced from El Paso (distant forty Miles) and were quietly encamped within (600) six hundred yards of the fort, intending to surprise us at daylight, on the morning of the 25th, kill or capture the officers in their quarters, and then take the men prisoners in their barracks. A perfectly feasible plan, as the men, without any officers to give orders, would readily have submitted. Luckily for us, one of the Confederate pickets, composed of two old discharged soldiers, deserted from their posts, came in, and alarmed the garrison, otherwise their success would have been complete, as they intended storming the place at the break of day. Drums beat the long roll, the command turned out, and we were saved for the time. Lynde took no further active steps, not sending out any scout to see where the enemy were. All was left to Providence. The mistake he made here was, in not sending out immediately a flag of truce, and surrendering us at once. Some lives would have been saved, and much public property saved for the use of the enemy.[3]

Putting aside McKee's hate-filled rhetoric throughout, his words actually confirm the statements of Baylor and Lynde as to what happened. McKee noted he too believed four hundred

Confederates were out there. McKee hinted there were no guards posted on watch when in fact Lynde clearly stated that the deserting Confederate was "brought in by our Picket," an implication that more than one 7th Infantry soldier was on lonely watch in the night. The word picket, as defined, means a group of soldiers or a single soldier stationed, usually at an outpost, to guard a body of troops from surprise attack. Since Lynde had pickets out he was doing what he had to do, what thirty years of experience taught him to do. It worked. The Confederate defector was detected and taken into custody by the guard.

McKee later accused Lynde of violating this most basic of military procedures, saying, "Such a brilliant method of defense, with no pickets out in front, deserves to be immortalized." McKee was an assistant surgeon, not a line officer. It would have been none of his business how Lynde managed the affairs of the regiment, or posted the guard. McKee saw only what he wanted to see, which was laxness and incompetence. He knew well how to build a case against a defenseless military man years after the event. Simply accuse him of not performing even the most basic of military procedures. At the time he wrote his July 26 letter Lynde obviously used the term "picket" matter of factly, not expecting that later someone would accuse him.

If one can believe the enemy, in this case the *Mesilla Times*, McKee's assertion that pickets were not "out in front" is made doubly ludicrous. On July 7, and just after the arrival of Major Isaac Lynde, the newspaper reported:

> The U.S. troops at Fort Fillmore have commenced fortifying the post. The troops are drilled daily and a picket guard is kept out some three miles. The companies now known to be on the way to this fort will increase its garrison to eleven companies, nine of infantry and two of mounted rifles. The concentration of so large a force at this point, the receipts of supplies, and every preparation being apparently made to permanently locate them here, excites considerable anxiety in the valley.[4]

According to this article, the intelligence operatives in Mesilla, all loyal to the Confederate cause, had better information about

Fort Fillmore than McKee did at the post. They may have known where each picket post was. Even the newspaper's estimate of future troop strength was correct. On July 7, there were seven infantry companies and parts of three Mounted Rifles companies at the post. Had the companies from Forts Buchanan and Breckinridge arrived as expected, there would have been exactly the number of troops at Fort Fillmore that the *Mesilla Times* postulated.

In fact, secessionist intelligence appears excellent. On July 20 the *Mesilla Times* also reported:

War Movements.

The U.S. force ordered to the Mesilla Valley, we are informed from Santa Fe, is fifteen companies of Regulars, eleven of infantry and four of horse, 10 companies of volunteers, 6 of Infantry and 4 of Cavalry.

"B" Company of the Mounted Rifles, arrived this week from Fort Stanton.

Lieut. Lane's company of Rifles has been ordered from Fort Fillmore to Fort Craig.

The troops in abandoning Fort Breckinridge burnt up all the government property they could not carry away, amounting to many thousand dollars, consisting of provisions and clothing. Some little property was sold. The garrisons of Forts Buchanan and Breckinridge are expected to arrive here next week.

A company of infantry have been stationed at Santo Tomas, with the intention of keeping a line of pickets to cut off all communication with El Paso by ordinary citizens.

Three companies, it is reported, are to be stationed in Mesilla, on the arrival of the troops from the west

Two pieces of artillery have left Fort Union for Fort Fillmore.

It is reported at Santa Fe, by the knowing ones, that the cause of so large a force at this point, is to recapture Fort Bliss and subjugate Arizona.[5]

The *Mesilla Times* indicated they had an agent from Santa Fe providing much of their news, but one might conclude they had friends inside the Fort Fillmore garrison, possibly among the Post Sutler's store employees or among the enlisted men. Whatever the case, their intelligence was excellent. They picked up Cressey's arrival with his few troops, knew of Lane's departure well before he left on July 24. They even knew of the burning of stocks of public property at Fort Breckinridge. They did get the number of companies at Santo Tomás wrong by one. The *Mesilla Times* failed to make any mention of a possible thrust by Colonel John Baylor, if they knew of it beforehand. They were Confederates, after all.

John Baylor was born in Kentucky in 1822 and was thirty-nine years old at the time he left Texas for Mesilla. He was the son of an Army officer and had been raised in Army camps and forts on the western frontier, much of it in the Indian Territory. Baylor had once been an Indian agent to the Comanches, and tried to remove all Indians from Texas onto reservations in Indian Territory, now the state of Oklahoma. An ardent secessionist, Colonel Baylor put the Texas secession decree into practice immediately. That decree had been passed by the people of Texas on February 23, 1861, and made firm on March 5, 1861, with Texas joining the Confederacy. Visiting the small towns surrounding San Antonio, Baylor collected men for what he called, "a buffalo hunt on the plains." In fact, he meant to invade the Territory of New Mexico. His ardor for secession and for conquest may have been one reason, personal glory another. His views on secession were far different from those of Isaac Lynde and most northerners at the time. Baylor's was an aggressive secessionist philosophy which included making war on northern interests before a war was ever declared. His immediate seeking of a militia to engage Federal interests in 'Arizona' demonstrates that attitude.

Contrast with Baylor the attitude of most of the non-Southern Army officers. Unless they had a personal problem with this rebel or that, chances are good they were not sure what they were fighting for, or why. Isaac Lynde's state of Vermont was not seceding, nor was its way of life being challenged daily in a hostile Congress over the issue of slavery. Chances are good Lynde hardly understood all the commotion. What he knew was that no war had been declared. The Texans were enemies only if they chose to attack him, just as the Apaches or the Pinos Altos miners would have been. Lynde would fight if the War Department told him to fight, else he would only fight if attacked. The presence of Rebel forces to the south, at Fort Bliss, did not equate with a formal declaration of war. In effect, should the Rebels attack him Lynde would have to decide, in the absence of such a declaration of war, and with the precedent of Sibley and Reeve in Texas to follow, whether he should be the man to begin the bloodshed.

Baylor's next move forced Lynde to respond, whether he wanted to or not. Blocked by a force equal to or greater than his own, Colonel John Baylor chose to avoid an immediate armed con-frontation. On the morning of July 25, he crossed what may have been a mostly summer-dry Rio Grande and took the road to the town of Mesilla. Baylor noted on September 21, with brevity:

> On the morning of the 25th I determined to occupy Mesilla, and prevent, if possible, the enemy from getting a position there, as it was one that would be easily held, and would enable them to hold the country. I reached Mesilla in the afternoon of the 25th, and was soon informed that the enemy was marching to attack us. I posted my men in position and awaited the arrival of the enemy.[6]

Baylor knew he would receive a friendly welcome in Mesilla, given the open support provided secessionist views by that town's newspaper and most of its American citizenry. His move across the river was unopposed, Potter's two companies having already crossed the river at Lynde's command to help protect the fort. Baylor makes no mention whatsoever of any knowledge that there had been, or were, Federal forces on the Mesilla side of the river. Lynde's option on deciding what to do with Potter had been a fifty-fifty decision. He could take a chance on imperiling his whole force by splitting the command in the face of a perceived enemy strength equal to or greater than his own, or he could pull Potter back to ensure he had the greatest possible defensive force on the correct side of the river, and undivided. Hindsight indicates that Baylor required surprise before he would attack the fort on the night of July 24-25. Having lost the element of surprise he took his second option, which was to go to Mesilla. Lynde had no idea Baylor did not intend to attack if surprise was lost.

Years later Colonel George Armstrong Custer was blamed for dividing his forces in the face of an enemy strength he did not yet know. After the debacle at Fort Fillmore, Major Isaac Lynde was blamed for uniting his forces in the face of an enemy strength he did not yet know. Some reviewers are always on the side of the victor. It is easy to see the correct decision once all the cards have been played. Had Baylor attacked Fort Fillmore with Potter still in Santo Tomás, and Lynde was forced to surrender, he would have been blamed for not pulling Potter in.

Isaac Lynde was almost matter-of-fact when he reported on Baylor's movement across the river, stating:

> Presuming their object to be an attack on the Post, I immediately ordered the two Companies of the 7th Infantry from San Tomas and kept the garrison under arms until after daylight [the 25th], when mounted parties were sent out to reconnoiter. In the meantime the Enemy passed up the opposite of the river through the town of San Tomas where they captured seven men of my Command left behind by the Battalion of the 7th Infantry in the hurry of departure. After extracting from them what information they could in reference about the probable time of the arrival of the troops of Forts Beckinridge & Buchanan they were released and joined the Post. All property public and private belonging to the command was seized and carried off or destroyed.[7]

Baylor, as the aggressor, had the advantage of changing position or posture as he wished. He may not have moved across the river for any strategic reason whatsoever, such as knowing that Lynde no longer had the Paso del Norte-Mesilla road guarded. His words indicate he either didn't care about a guard force, intending to attack them if present anyway, or he never even considered the presence of such a force. There is a third option. Baylor may have received intelligence that Potter had been removed. If so he didn't care to include that piece of information when writing his superiors.

He flippantly said that, faced with an alert Federal garrison, he simply crossed the river and went to Mesilla. This was the worst possible move for Isaac Lynde. Had Baylor attacked, the 7th would have defended the fort and probably won. Infantry against cavalry was no contest at all, not if the infantry was dug in and ready to fight. The problem with Baylor's move to Mesilla is that it cut off the natural escape route of the troops from Forts Buchanan and Breckinridge, the only reason Isaac Lynde and the 7th were still in the area. Whether he wanted to or not Lynde had to attack Mesilla to open the road west. If he didn't, the woefully unprepared companies then on the march from the Arizona posts would no doubt be forced to surrender, as they could not get past Mesilla to safety at Fort Fillmore.

It should be remembered that Baylor was writing on September 26, 1861, some months and a possible fading of his memory later. Major Isaac Lynde's words, or whoever wrote them in his name, were written on July 26, 1861, soon after these events transpired. The move bringing Potter back across the river was proven wrong by Baylor's acts, intentional or not. What looked correct when first tried now opened options that Lynde could not possibly have wanted. He had to try to take Mesilla, and that meant a bloodletting.

Assistant Surgeon McKee had a different and, as usual, more extreme view of the Baylor crossing incident. He wrote:

> He [Lynde] ordered Captain Potter to abandon San Tomas, with his two companies, and hasten to the fort. The Mesilla Times published a statement shortly afterwards, that clothing, provisions, ammunition, and supplies were left behind in considerable quantities, that eight prisoners were said to have been taken by the Confederates, disarmed and sworn not to serve against them. How it happened that these eight men were left behind their companies, I never heard explained. I presume that they took advantage of the confusion, chose to remain, and take their chances with the enemy.[8]

The discrepancy between Lynde's version, written on July 26, 1861 and McKee's, written many years later, concerning the men left at Santo Tomás is a minor point, but interesting nonetheless. Lynde reported the soldiers were interrogated then released, returning to Fort Fillmore. Lynde also accurately reported that any and all public property left behind during Potter's ordered withdrawal, was captured. McKee said roughly the same thing but used the well chosen words "in considerable quantities" to make the seizure out to be as bad as possible for future readers. To Baylor, the taking of prisoners and captured equipment at Santo Tomás was so unimportant that he didn't mention the incident at all.

NOTES - Chapter 10

1. Horn & Wallace, Baylor to Washington, September 26, 1861, pp. 34-37.

2. Lynde to Assistant Adjutant General, July 26, 1861, M1120, Rolls 13/14.

3. McKee, p. 11.

4. The *Daily Picayune* (New Orleans), Volume 25, #165 (August 6, 1861), p. 1, column 6.

5. *Mesilla Times*, July 20, 1861.

6. Horn & Wallace, Baylor to Washington, September 21, 1861, pp. 34-37.

7. Lynde to Assistant Adjutant General, July 26, 1861, M1120, Rolls 13/14.

8. McKee, p. 15.

11

THE BATTLE OF MESILLA

Once Major Isaac Lynde knew of the presence of the Texas forces in Mesilla on July 25, he appears to have called his officers together and planned a march on that town. No surviving document exists telling exactly why he went to Mesilla. Perhaps it was as simple as the fact that he could not permit the occupation of a United States town by a government growing openly hostile to United States interests. More likely, Lynde wanted to clear the road west so the troops from Forts Buchanan and Breckinridge could pass through Mesilla as per his July 15 order to secure their arrival. As a third reason, his honor dictated that such a foray be made. Baylor was, after all, an invader, even if, as Lynde well knew, the Mesilla Americans wanted the invasion. Lynde reported:

> About 4½ O'Clock P.M. yesterday, I moved in the direction of the town of Mesilla, where the Texas troops then were, with six Companies of the 7th Infantry, one acting as artillery with the Howitzer Battery of the Post, and two Companies of Rifles. One Company of Infantry with the Band and convalescents were left to garrison the Post under Lieut. Stevenson and Ryan, 7th Infantry. Dr. Alden also remained behind. My command numbered about 380 men. About two miles from Mesilla, I sent Lieut. Brooks 7th Infantry a.a.a.g. forward with the white flag, to demand the surrender of the town. He was met by Major Waller & Col. Herbert on the part of Texans, who replied that if I wanted the town I must come and take it.[1]

Colonel Baylor was very brief in his description of the approach of Federal troops, not even addressing the fact that he had his troops ready to fight and in good defensive positions. His estimates of the number of Federal troops involved were as inaccurate as were Lynde's estimate of his forces. He is completely unresponsive as to the number of Mesilla Americans who took up the cause of the South, with arms. He merely noted:

> At about 5 o'clock I discovered their cavalry approaching the town by the main road, and soon after the infantry came in sight, bringing with them three howitzers. They formed within 300 yards, and were, as near as I could tell, about 600 strong. A flag was sent in to demand the unconditional and immediate surrender of the Texas forces, to which I answered that we would fight first and surrender afterward.[2]

Doctor McKee sat on both sides of the fence in his attempt to portray Isaac Lynde's incompetence and cowardice at Mesilla. He first surmised the Texans wanted to capture Fort Fillmore as their primary goal, then reverted to a different theory after Baylor crossed the river. McKee noted, in changing his theory from the capture of Fort Fillmore to the occupation of Mesilla, that, "My object in getting the town of San Tomás occupied by troops was to guard the ford, and prevent the enemy from gaining the town of Mesilla, where most if not all the Americans were rebel sympathizers."[3]

Being always right (in his mind), McKee continued after Potter had been brought into the fort, and Baylor had changed his mind about a direct attack:

> The Confederates, meeting with no resistance at the ford, crossed on the morning of the 25th into San Tomas, and then leisurely marched into the town of Mesilla, distant some two miles, where they arrived about 10 A.M. and if the Mesilla Times is to be credited, they were received with every mani-festation of joy. Vivahs and hurrahs greeted them at all points. Forage and supplies were freely offered by the over-joyed citizens, who declared they were weary of Yankee tyranny and oppression. What was remarkable, these same much abused

citizens had been supported by money received from Yankee officers and soldiers.[4]

Assistant Surgeon McKee was certainly right in his last comment. The American population of Mesilla was predominantely Southerners. Neither Lynde, Baylor, McKee, nor the *Mesilla Times* indicates if any civilians took up arms in the Southern cause, although some must have gone beyond verbal support. Were some of the businessmen and employees who served the Fort Fillmore population in the past in the ranks with weapons? McKee, who despised them almost as much as he hated Isaac Lynde, never made the connection. Perhaps Baylor made little or no use of them. McKee then discussed in some detail Lynde's approach toward Mesilla, of course using his own adjectives to attack Lynde as "our venerable commander," no doubt meaning someone too old and infirm to hold a command. McKee noted:

> On the morning of the 25th of July it was really known by us that the enemy had occupied Mesilla that morning. Our venerable commander ordered out the command with the exception of a guard for the post, for the purpose of crossing the river, and, as I supposed, attacking the enemy. The latter part of my supposition was erroneous, as it afterwards turned out.[5]

McKee went along with the force headed for Mesilla, leaving Assistant Surgeon Charles H. Alden at the post. McKee claimed:

> No braver or more determined command ever marched to meet an enemy. It made my despondent heart glad as I rode along and looked at the glittering array of muskets, well-drilled men, and trained horses. Now I fondly hoped, we would at last certainly redeem ourselves, and make a successful blow for the honor of the old flag, which fluttered in the breeze at the head of the column.[6]

Lynde, Baylor and the *Mesilla Times* did not place McKee in the role he defined for himself next. Perhaps he actually did what he says he did. Whatever the case, McKee stated he was involved with 1ˢᵗ Lieutenant Brooks's white flag confrontation with the Texans, in which Brooks demanded the surrender of the town and was told, according to Lynde, "if I wanted the town I must come and take it." Baylor used other words for the message, saying, "We would fight first and surrender afterward."

McKee remembered the words close to how Lynde learned of them. When the column was within five hundred yards of the post, Lieutenant Brooks suddenly rode up to where McKee stood, the white flag of parley in his hand. McKee went on to describe how he participated in the meeting between Brooks, himself, and either Waller, Baylor or both on the other side. McKee reported:

> Lieut. Brooks, the Adjutant, came riding up with a flag of truce in his hand, and said that the Major desired me to accompany him [Brooks], as I was better acquainted with the people on the other side than any other officer. To hear was to obey. I mounted and rode with the flag toward the enemy's lines. Two mounted men advanced to meet us; both were armed with double-barreled shot-guns carried on the front of their saddles ... . Lieut. Brooks, in the name of his commander, demanded, 'An unconditional surrender of the forces and the town.' The reply was, that 'if he wished the town, to come and take it.' At this time, thinking that we would certainly have a fight in which many men would be wounded on their side, I kindly offered to Herbert, as a matter of humanity, that, in case they had any wounded on their side, I would be happy to render all the assistance in my power. This was abruptly rejected with the remark that they had surgeons of their own.[7]

Why McKee should have known the Confederate commanders better than the rest of the 7ᵗʰ Infantry command was not addressed. There is, in fact, no reason he should have, unless he was referring in some way to the townspeople of Mesilla, who were in no way involved in the negotiations. Brooks and McKee supposedly rode back to their lines, reporting what had been said. Lynde immediately deployed for battle.

The question now is what was the state of Major Lynde's mind? He may have thought he had a rattlesnake by the tail, both in the deployed forces of the Texas army and from the possibility that he was about to take a step that could irrevocably begin the bloodletting of civil war. Not a single round had yet been fired between any Texas force and a Federal force. What was Lynde thinking as he deployed the small mountain howitzers he had with him, and readied the troops to make the assault once the howitzers had their range? On his shoulders alone may have rested the deaths of hundreds of thousands of young men afterwards. After all, he had orders to abandon Fort Fillmore, not to waste lives in defending it against an enemy whose blood had yet to be shed in battle. Still, there was the need to serve honor. That required a demonstration of force. Was Lynde wondering whether to fire those cannon even as he deployed them? We will never know. We only know he gave the order for one volley, and that fell short. Lynde reported the rest of the battle from his standpoint:

> I moved the battery forward and fired two shells at long range but they burst in the air short of the object. The command continued to advance slowly towards the outskirts of the town while the Battery which had to be moved by hand was working through the heavy sand. From a cornfield and house on the right, we received a heavy fire of musketry, wounding two officers and 4 men and killing three men; as night was coming on and the fields and houses on both sides of the road filled with men and the Howitzers useless except as a Field Battery, owing to the difficulty of moving them through the sand, I decided to withdraw my force and return to my Post.[8]

Lynde spoke of only firing two rounds from the four mountain howitzers that were present, perhaps from the same pair that Lieutenant Colonel Dixon Miles used for salutes in the good old days at Fort Fillmore before American fought American. Why did he only fire two ineffective rounds, then quit? He may have halted his attack for the simple reason that the little weapons were out of range of the Confederate positions and could not easily be wheeled forward to provide the support required. Major Lynde did say he could not roll the mountain howitzers through the soft sand to get them into proper range to support an attack. For Lynde this was

Twelve-pound brass mountain howitzer as used
in the Mesilla battle.
Courtesy: Author's collection.

sufficient reason to break off and withdraw, along with the coming of darkness. Without the support of the howitzers he would be sending the infantry forward into a slaughterhouse. These were adequate tactics on any battlefield, even to the present day. Without artillery support to hold the Rebels' heads down, there would have been a free fire zone for the Texans against the oncoming line of 7th Infantry soldiers. Lynde was attacking a force of unknown strength in strong defensive positions. Without explanation of the tactical use of those howitzers, his actions may have appeared to some as cowardice. They were not. The main question is why was he not able to get those howitzers in range in the first place?

The range question is also tied to the type of shoulder weapon Lynde's soldiers carried. Were they the old short-range .69 Caliber smoothbore muskets (effective range one hundred yards) or the long-range .58 Caliber Rifle/Musket (effective range six hundred yards)? Either arm was available in that period of weapon changeover within the Army. Some regiments had the new arms and some didn't. If Lynde had the longer range weapons, one would think he would have volley-fired them at Mesilla to make use of their range. This author suspects the 7th Infantry were still armed with the short-range weapons at the time of the battle. If Lynde had the older weapons he would have found it necessary to have artillery support for a much longer period of time as the infantry crossed hostile ground. If he could not maneuver the artillery in the sand, the necessary artillery support would have been unavailable.

Doctor McKee savagely attacked Major Lynde's decision to withdraw. It is obvious McKee's main concern was with his view of honor, not with the tactics that might be necessary to prevent a slaughter. McKee was not a trained soldier. Perhaps the doctor would have attacked regardless of casualties to his own forces simply because the Rebels were to his front. That type of tactic, so often used in the Civil War, led to the mass slaughters at Shiloh, Antietam, Gettysburg, etc. Regardless of McKee's cruel words, what he says helps us understand the range problem and how Lynde might have viewed the situation tactically. Dr. McKee noted:

The line of battle having been formed the two field-pieces were on the road in the center of the column, one half of the infantry on the left, and the other on the right. Our left was in a cornfield, with a large acequia (or irrigation canal) on its left, and in their front, some two hundred yards, an adobe house, which proved to be occupied by Texas troops. Here Lynde made one of the most extraordinary military movements. Instead of throwing out infantry skirmishers in the cornfield to feel the enemy and protect his column, he ordered Lieut. McNally to deploy his company mounted in front of the infantry, with the result of making the mounted men conspicuous targets for the Texans, lying, as they were, concealed in the adobe house, and with the result, that, when fired upon, Lieut. McNally was shot through the apex of one of his lungs, four men killed and several wounded.[9]

If McKee is right about the two-hundred-yard range, the 7th Infantry companies did not have the new Minie ball firing rifle-muskets. Armed with the old .69 caliber smooth-bore muskets, Major Lynde's infantry could not reach the Texans and would have required artillery support to suppress the enemy in order to cross the ground and reach effective one-hundred-yard range. We don't know when the 7th was scheduled to receive the new arms. The regiment had been en route for Utah at the time the new longer-range weapons were issued in New Mexico to the 3[d] and 8th Infantry Regiments. Provided the shorter-range weapons were all that were available, McKee's comment about the use of McNally's troops as skirmishers was precisely what any sensible commander would have done. McNally's R.M.R. troopers had .54 caliber Minie-ball-firing rifled-muskets, with a range of about six hundred yards. This fact is well proven by artifact finds at Fort Fillmore and by Ordnance Corps data. They could reach the enemy with those weapons. Naturally Lynde would have sent them to the front to do what damage they might, especially if his infantry was limited by range.

During the 1970s, a full case, some seven hundred rounds, of .69 caliber buckshot-and-ball munitions was found buried in the sand at Fort Fillmore. These smooth-bore musket rounds may have been secreted by 7th Infantry troops when Lynde abandoned

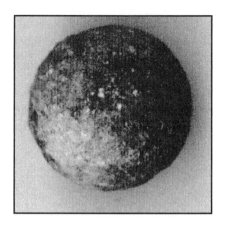

left: .69 round ball (smooth-bore musket - range one hundred yards.
right: .58 conical bullet (rifled musket - range 600 yards).
Courtesy: Author's collection.

the post. Had the box of cartridges belonged to the 3[d] Infantry they would have been turned back in to the Ordnance Office in Albuquerque at the time the new .58 caliber rifle-muskets were exchanged in 1859, being valuable public property. This ammunition find may be all the proof needed to point to the 7th Infantry being equipped with the shorter-range weapon. This certainly would answer many of the questions related to the Battle of Mesilla. The presence of shorter-range muskets would also help explain what happened on the road to San Augustine Springs at a later date.

Several other problems with McKee's account must be pointed out. He said there were two howitzers in the road with infantry on both sides. Lynde indicated there were more than two, perhaps even all four howitzers available to him, a battery, deployed in soft sand. McKee said Lynde did not deploy skirmishers. In fact, since Lynde did not advance toward the enemy with his infantry there was as yet no need to deploy infantry skirmishers. As to casualties, McKee was simply venting his hatred against Lynde one more time. In fact, the R.M.R. did not suffer the greatest number of casualties during the battle. The 7th Infantry did. McKee hinted that four R.M.R. troopers died and several more were wounded in the volley which wounded McNally. In fact, only three soldiers were killed, not four, during the brief engagement, and two of these were 7th Infantry,

one R.M.R.. Six were wounded in the engagement, four 7th Infantrymen and two R.M.R., including McNally.

A third version of the Battle of Mesilla was included in the
overall report of 1st Lieutenant Charles Hely McNally, wounded in
the battle, who received a brevet for his bravery in action that day.
McNally, like Assistant Surgeon McKee, had no love for Isaac
Lynde. An officer of the Regiment of Mounted Rifles, McNally
appears to have had little use for infantry in the first place. His
version is full of the activities of McNally and McKee, so much so
that they must have at some point cooperated in their versions of
the story. Neither wasted any words of praise or, in the case of
killed and wounded, mentioned infantry casualties. Whatever his
personal prejudices or beliefs McNally was an obviously brave
man, whom Major Lynde seemed to bow to for suggestions in the
use of his horsemen for surveillance and attack. Did McNally
recommend his horsemen be at the front, a suggestion Lynde
accepted? McNally's portrayal of the brief battle is included
below. He uses his own last name, a form of the royal "we" when
referring to his personal activities that day. McNally stated:

> At daylight [July 25] McNally went to Major Lynde, and
> asked him to let his company of 32 men, and Cressey's of 22
> men, go over to Mesilla and see if the Texans were there. He
> said: "Yes; mount your command and go, and give me all the
> information you can collect." I took the command, crossed
> the Rio Grande, and went over as fast as possible to Mesilla,
> halted the command, gave it to Mr. Cressey, and rode into the
> town with three men, first sergeant, corporal, and a private.
> Gave orders to Cressey, if we were not back by a certain time,
> either to take the town or send back for re-inforcements, as he
> saw fit. Rode through the town; found everything quiet; the
> flag was not flying. Went back and reported to Major Lynde
> no Texans present, and everything appeared to be quiet. Then
> McNally mounted his 32 men; again started out with Dr.
> McKee to find their trail. Found their camp within 2 miles of
> Fillmore, about 300 or 400 men, who had left shortly before
> and crossed the river to Mesilla. Went back and reported to
> Lynde. They had gone in by the San Tomas road, abandoned

by his order the night before. Lynde told him to dismount his men and put his horses in the stable. This was at 9 a.m. on the 25th. At the same time positive word was brought back that the Texans were in the town of Mesilla. After that we laid quietly in garrison until 4 p.m., when he moved the whole forward, putting McNally, with 22 men, in front, with the order to go on and feel the way. He had four 12-pounder mountain howitzers. He first fired two shells at long range. Ordered McNally to form and go ahead. McNally kept ahead until he got within 60 or 70 yards of the Texans. Halted, and reported in person that they were in the jacals and cornfields. First McNally knew they fired one shot, that cut away his saber; the second struck him. Then fired a volley of about 80 shots. (They confessed to seventy men.) They had no artillery. McNally dismounted, and fired at random. They fired another volley. Remounted, not being supported. Sent to Major Lynde, who could not be found, and not being supported by infantry or artillery, ordered his men to retreat. In this fire one sergeant and one corporal were wounded and one man killed. In retreating, the Seventh Infantry fired into us. I retreated behind the battery, and found the infantry still in the rear. There McNally fainted from loss of blood, and was carried from the field. The last he heard was an order from Major Lynde to retreat. The command reached Fillmore about 10 p.m. on the 25th.[10]

The Texans were not well armed; many of them had only shotguns. No doubt they did have some longer-range hunting rifles. If the situation was as McNally indicated (there is doubt of that) then he should have stayed outside their nominal range and covered the approach of the infantry with his long-range weapons. Perhaps he did, since there were more infantry casualties than R.M.R.. There is another possible answer to the question of the R.M.R. companies being forward. This answer may lie in the simple explanation McNally gives without any apparent thought to the situation. Lynde could have ordered McNally to take the lead, as cavalry certainly would, on the march to Mesilla. McKee's "extraordinary military movement" was only common sense. The column approaching Mesilla had McNally's and Cressey's horsemen in the front, the mountain howitzers (McNally said four, Lynde hinted at four, McKee said two) following the cavalry, with the infantry column coming next, followed by McKee and the medical staff and ambulance. When the column encountered the Confederates, McNally's troops formed a natural skirmish line, the infantry deploying behind them on the left or right side of the mountain howitzers as directed.

With this formation facing the enemy, Brooks and McKee (if they were truly together) went forward with the white flag to demand surrender. Lynde could have ordered the cavalry back of the infantry, their normal battle place if not strung out in a column. The R.M.R. would then have served as the breakthrough or envelopment force should the infantry, with artillery support, have broken the Confederate line. But, because the R.M.R. was already in front, and possibly with longer-range weapons, Lynde did not remove them. In theory, he was totally correct in what he did. The R.M.R. were designed as mounted infantry when formed during the Mexican War. They were to ride to battle, then dismount and fight on foot as infantry. What Lynde did in using the R.M.R. troopers as skirmishers hearkened back to their true purpose. McKee might have known this if he had been a line officer. Had these horsemen been dragoons, their function as skirmishers would have been difficult to justify. As Mounted Rifles, they were in the right place at the right time. If they were not dismounted that would have been McNally's fault, not Lynde's. He should have dismounted to fight his unit as it was designed to fight. In fact, McNally stated that he was himself, at one point, dismounted.

According to McNally, there was no attempt made by the 7th Infantry companies to advance to his position. That statement was true, and was explained by Lynde. When he could not move the mountain howitzer battery forward, to advance the infantry would have been to court disaster. McNally also said the 7th Infantrymen fired on his troops as they retreated. They may have fired over his position and toward the Confederates, since McNally did not claim any casualties as the result of friendly fire.

The most startling part of McNally's report is that the Federal cavalry, parts of two companies, 'F' and 'B,' R.M.R., were in Mesilla earlier that same day and reported the town quiet. This was before Baylor crossed the river. There were no rowdy demonstrations going on in the town and the Rebel flag was not flying. McNally, who at that point owned the place, instead chose to return to the fort and report what he saw. He was able to cross the river and return to Fort Fillmore without encountering any of Baylor's force or pickets. This is a strange story that no other report confirms, but certainly could have happened.

Doctor McKee embellished his account of the battle with stories neither Lynde nor McNally confirm. Lynde indicated he fired two rounds of artillery, tried to advance the guns, couldn't, and decided to pull back as night was approaching. His infantry casualties were suffered as his men tried to slowly advance at the pace of the bogged down artillery. He may have fired more artillery rounds. If so, he didn't mention them. Doctor McKee spoke of other rounds fired that day, in the direction of women and children, rather than at Confederates. McKee added the following slur on Lynde's reputation:

> The company [McNally's] at this surprise retreated behind the infantry. Lieut. Crilly was ordered to fire shells into the town full of women and children; indeed, I heard Lynde order Crilly to fire a shell at a group of women, children and unarmed men, on one of the sand-hills to our left front; a shell was so fired; luckily it fell short, and no harm was done. The frightened crowd dispersed rapidly. So, without having, in accordance with the humane role of civilized warfare, given notice to remove the women and children to a place of safety, shells were thrown into different parts of the town, fortunately injuring no one.[11]

If any of the events described happened, they are so twisted by bias that every word has to be viewed through McKee's hatred to determine what really happened. What McKee says about the women, children, and unarmed men on top of a sand hill has a ring of truth. These were the opening moments of the Civil War. At Bull Run, on July 21, people from Washington and the surrounding towns came out in droves, some bringing picnic baskets, in hopes of watching a battle unfold. The opening cannon shots, some aimed in their direction, scattered civilians far and wide. Unfortunately for McKee, we know where he got this fallacious story of Lynde firing on civilians. The words came directly from a column in the *Mesilla Times* newspaper, written after the battle. McKee hated Lynde so much he believed enemy propaganda first.

A fourth observer reported on the Battle of Mesilla. He was Colonel John Baylor, who commanded the Texas forces. Baylor's report was almost as short as Isaac Lynde's. He said:

> The answer [to Brooks's demand for a surrender] was followed by the enemy opening up on us with their howitzers. After four or five rounds of bombs, grape and cannister, the cavalry formed and marched up within 250 yards, preparatory to making a charge. Captain Hardeman's company, being in position nearest the enemy, was ordered to open on them with his front rank, to see if they were within range of our guns. The fire was well directed and proved effective, killing 4 of the enemy and wounding 7. The cavalry was thrown into confusion and retreated hastily, running over the infantry. In a few moments the enemy were marching back in the direction of their fort; but supposing it to be a feint, intended to draw me from my position, I did not pursue them, but kept my position until next morning, the 26th, expecting that they would attack us under cover of night.[12]

Baylor has the R.M.R. under McNally panicking under fire and running over Lynde's infantry in their haste to get to the rear. Lynde, McKee, and McNally do not mention such an incident. Baylor thought there were four or five rounds fired by Lynde's howitzers. He mentioned no Texas casualties during the brief battle, believing his forces had killed four of the enemy and wounded seven. The actual figure was three killed and six wounded, most among the infantry. Baylor's estimates were closer to the truth than the figures Lynde used for casualties on the Texas side. Time was not critical to Baylor so he did not indicate there was a significant delay between Lynde's arrival, the first casualties, and the final withdrawal.

The last source to report on the Battle of Mesilla was the *Mesilla Times* newspaper. Biased toward the cause of the Texans, the *Times* had only good news to report, so perhaps the words of the editor can be taken as close to what happened from the Mesilla American citizen's point of view. The *Times* said:

> The United States troops were reported crossing the river about noon of the 25th. About five o'clock clouds of dust indicated the enemy were advancing for an attack towards the Southern part of the city. The whole force was moved to that point and every preparation made to give them the warmest of receptions. Several of the principal streets of Mesilla converge at the Southern end of the town, the old houses forming an angle and are quite scattered, old corrals and the proximity of corn fields, make the position an advantageous one for defence. The companies were stationed on the tops of the adobe houses and behind the corrals. Capt. Coopwood's company was mounted. The citizens posted themselves on the tops of the houses on the principal streets prepared to render their assistance.
>
> The enemy advanced to within 500 yards of our position and halted and formed in line of battle with two howitzers in the center and the infantry, and on the wing cavalry, the whole force appearing to be about 500 men. A flag of truce was then sent to our position with the modest demand to surrender the town unconditionally, the reply was 'that if they wished the town to come and take it.' They unmasked their guns and commenced firing bombs and grape into a town crowded with women and children, without having in accordance with an invariable rule of civilized warfare given notice to remove the women and children to a place of safety. Several shells were thrown in different parts of the town, fortunately without doing any injury to a single individual. Two companies were ordered to take their positions on the top of the houses on the main plaza. The first shell thrown struck on the top of a building on which was stationed a portion of Captain Teel's company and exploded.
>
> After firing a couple of rounds of grape at the more advanced position of our force, the cavalry of the enemy made a charge and had advanced to within three hundred yards of a corral behind which Capt. Hardeman's company were stationed. From 40 to 60 shots were fired by this company, killing four and wounding four of the enemy, throwing them into confusion and finally into retreat, their

officers vainly trying to rally them. The order was given to charge four times to no purpose and they retired in confusion carrying with them the dead and wounded.

Capt. Coopwood's company had been continually employed in deploying among the houses and corrals, first appearing mounted and then on foot, and appearing in may different directions. This and other movements, and the appearance of men both far and near, at many different points, succeeded in greatly deceiving the enemy as to our real force. They were disheartened by their ill success in the charge, and as night was falling they drew off their whole force in good order, in the direction of Fort Fillmore.[13]

How many Battles of Mesilla were there? There seem to be almost as many as the number of observers who reported on the battle. Many facts in the *Times* account are confused, including the number of artillery pieces used, the shots fired by artillery, whether there was a cavalry charge or a slow walk, how many were killed and wounded, the ranges mentioned, etc. Taking all the reports together, what do we really know? We know that Baylor's Texans crossed the Rio Grande on July 25, 1861. At some point during the day, after the Texans were safely in Mesilla, an undetermined number of troops under the command of Major Isaac Lynde crossed the river and headed toward Mesilla. Upon arriving, the Federal representative(s) asked the Texans to surrender the town, were refused, deployed their forces, and opened the battle with artillery. The Rebels responded, killing and wounding some of the Federal soldiers, one of whom was 1st Lieutenant McNally. This maneuvering and firing took time and darkness began to fall. The Federal force then fell back on Fort Fillmore.

Of the several officers of the 7th Infantry involved in the battle none gave an account of the action, save for Major Isaac Lynde's brief version. Second Lieutenant Cressey of the Mounted Rifles gave no account. We have only the enemies of Major Isaac Lynde to turn to for further information on the battle, and they are at cross purposes most of the time. McKee seems to have taken much of his account of the battle from the Rebel *Mesilla Times* newspaper, rather than from his own personal observations. Lydia Lane took her account from McKee. Once casualties occurred one hopes McKee was back in the rear tending to the wounded. One of the wounded he tended was 1st Lieutenant Edward J. Brooks, whom McKee supposedly rode forward with into the Texan ranks to deliver Lynde's surrender ultimatum. McKee hated Brooks almost as much as he hated Isaac Lynde. There was quite a difference in how McKee described the wounding of McNally and the wounding of Brooks during the battle. On treating McNally he said:

> The wounded were all brought to me. Lieut. McNally pluckily rode up on his gray horse, and said that he was shot. I helped him off his horse, when he fainted, and fell on the sand. I opened his coat and shirt, saw the bullet hole, ran my finger into it, detected at once the pulsation of the subclavian artery, and saw that he was safe for the present.[14]

How different were his words for the wounded Brooks, whom McKee had brought to him by Isaac Lynde himself. Here is how McKee treated Brooks's wound and reported Lynde's order to pull out of the fight. McKee said:

> At this time Major Lynde and Lieut. Brooks rode up to me from somewhere on our right front, where they had been fired on. Brooks had a slight scratch from a bullet on one of his forearms, and his sword had been struck. They were the worst scared men I ever saw. The gray beard and hair of Lynde were a fitting frame for that pale face and cowardly soul. On riding up he said, 'Doctor, get your wounded ready to retreat.' I, thinking that the fight had only commenced, innocently asked, 'where to, sir?' He replied, 'To the fort.' My soul sank within me and I thought, 'Is this to be the disgraceful finale of an attack by as good and true a set of soldiers as ever fired a musket?' Had any of the senior officers present at this time, stepped forward, put Lynde in arrest, and taken the command, his fortune would have been made.[15]

Neither side wanted a further battle that night. The withdrawing 7th Infantry troops safely crossed the river and entered the

Fort Fillmore area. We know little of the next day, July 26, perhaps the most important day of all. This was the day the decision was made to abandon Fort Fillmore, yet all we have of this day are increased words of hatred from Doctor McKee, who was in hospital tending his wounded, and not a part of the decision-making process. What led Major Isaac Lynde to the decision to withdraw from Fort Fillmore? Lynde explained his decision quite clearly at a later time. However, the words best remembered are McKee's:

> We reached the fort about 10 p.m., and although since then I have passed many a sad, dreary, and gloomy night among dying and wounded men on the battlefield and in hospitals, yet that night left a lasting imprint on my memory. My friend McNally lay in my front room in great pain. The wounded in the hospital had to be attended to. I confess that I shed many bitter tears, cursing my luck that I had been born to the misfortune of being in the command of such an imbecile and coward. Again and again was the hour and the time for some one of the elder line officers to step to the front, and yet save us from an inevitable fate. But all were silent; had anyone done so, the whole command would have sustained any kind of determined action.[16]

The only two officers who might have stepped forward and risked a mutiny charge would have been Captain Potter or Captain Stevenson. These had some experience. The rest of the 7th were completely inexperienced. It should be said once again that no 7th Infantry officer laid any blame at Isaac Lynde's feet for what happened at Fort Fillmore in the period after the event. If they did so in private, their words have not survived. If his own officers did not fault Isaac Lynde's decisions at the time, how can we trust the words of those, like Assistant Surgeon McKee, who were not part of his infantry command or part of the decision-making process? The only words against Isaac Lynde's decisions were those of one doctor and two Mounted Rifles' officers, one of whom was not even there at the time. We will continue to provide the words of his detractors but, from this point on, we will examine Isaac Lynde's decisions with a view toward their correctness.

McKee described the night and morning to the absence of any other reports. Right or wrong, his words are all we have, and we will use them. He continued:

> The morning of the 26th of July came in all its loveliness and freshness. The grand old 'Organ Mountains' to the east loomed up in all their magnificent majesty. Their rugged, clear-cut sides stood out in bolder relief than usual, as if in mockery at the pitiable military farce going on at their base.
> At about 9 A.M. Lieut. Brooks, Adjutant, came to my house and said that the Major ordered me to destroy my hospital property, preparatory to a retreat that night in the direction of Fort Stanton, N.M. I declined to receive any such verbal orders, as I was personally responsible to my department for the valuable property, and would have to make showing what disposition I had made of it, to the Surgeon-General, U.S.A.[17]

Anyone who visited Fort Fillmore before the 1980s is probably familiar with the low piles of broken glass which filled the area near the hospital, proof that Dr. McKee received a written form of the order to destroy much of his public property. Calling out his hospital steward, Charles E. Fitzwilliams, he ordered the man to bring all bottles from the storeroom and line them up around the edge of the hospital placita. Fitzwilliams was a southern sympathizer and, with great hindsight, McKee claimed he had always suspected the man of supporting the enemy cause. Fitzwilliams did join the Texas army after the surrender at San Augustine Springs but, on July 26, he worked alongside Dr. McKee to destroy all of the bottles, leaving none untouched, or so McKee believed. In the early 1970s, from among that pile of broken glass, one whole bottle was extracted. It was a soft green-colored bottle about seven inches tall, with a stopper of the same color. This one bottle had survived McKee's assault. Perhaps the ghost of Doctor McKee could not stand the thought of that bottle unbroken. Almost as soon as it arrived at its new El Paso home a freak accident saw it fall and break. The destruction of the Fort Fillmore hospital bottles was at last complete.[18]

McKee said the officers serving in the quartermaster and commissary roles probably received the same instructions, but they failed to carry out a similar destruction of their public property. Indeed much of it did fall into the hands of the Texans, as we shall see. Quoting the *Mesilla Times* again, McKee noted:

> The Mesilla Times next day reported that the hospital stores, medicines, and furniture were most completely broken up. A great deal of valuable commissary stores and other property were unharmed, to the amount of several thousand dollars. That the Mexicans, eager as ever for plunder, entered the fort soon after it was evacuated, and commenced a general pillage, carrying off property on their backs, on animals, and by the cart-loads. They must have pillaged property to the amount of several thousand dollars.[19]

The fort must have been a beehive of activity that day—some of it observed by the forces from Texas. McKee believed there was no way a large column of wagons, loaded with soldier's equipment, women, children, quartermaster and commissary supplies could vanish undetected in the direction of Fort Stanton. In that he was partially right. The Federals escaped detection in darkness, but not in sunlight.

Isaac Lynde gives short shrift to the day he decided to abandon Fort Fillmore and move his whole command out onto the road to Fort Stanton. Below is all he said of the matter. From this brief statement we must determine the why of what he did. McKee didn't fault the decision. Heaven knows why he allowed Lynde that reprieve. On July 26, Lynde wrote two letters, excerpts from one of which we have already included. In his first writing he spoke briefly of the events which followed the Battle of Mesilla, listing the casualties within his force. He said:

> The march back was uninterrupted and today I am fortifying with sand bags etc. in anticipation of an attack. I have sent an express to Capt. Gibbs directing him to return to Fort Craig with his Command as he can not join this Post now. They have possession of the road above. Orders will be sent if possible to the commandant of the troops from Forts Breckinridge & Buchanan, to take the nearest route to Fort Craig from a point where the orders reach them.

List of Killed

Private Lane Company "F" R.M.R.
    "   Jenkins   "   "I" 7th Infty.
    "   Sherwood "   "G" 7th Infty.

List of Wounded

Lt. Brooks 7th Infantry Slightly
    " McNally R.M.R.   Severely
Sergeant Callaghan Co. "F" Rifles, Mortally
Private   Myers Co. "E" 7th Infty Slightly
    "   Farber   "I"   "   "   "
    "   Goss   "D" "   "   "
"F" Co. R.M.R. 4 Horses Wounded
"B" "   "   1   "   "

A re-enforcement of 100 men joined the Texans from Fort Bliss last night. There [sic] force at present with the addition of the citizens of Mesilla is nearly 700 men. I am hourly expecting an attack. The loss of the enemy is reported eleven killed and wounded. Part of their horses were stampeded by one of our shells.[20]

This letter tells much about the situation on July 26, if one is permitted to read between the lines. First, there were a total of three killed and six wounded in the battle. One of the men killed, Private Lane, was part of McNally's R.M.R. Company 'F.' Another, Sergeant Callaghan, Company 'F,' was mortally wounded. This term usually meant that Callaghan was expected to die of his wounds. There is no corroboration that he did or did not. McKee never mentioned his case at all. The two infantrymen who died, Jenkins of Company 'I' and Sherwood of Company 'G,' 7th Infantry, belonged to Potter's Company 'G' and Crilly's Company 'I,' the latter responsible for the movement of the brass mountain howitzers, which as Lynde indicated they were unable to manage. Second Lieutenant Crilly was as good a choice as any by Lynde to manage the artillery. He was a member of Potter's Company 'K' but, Company 'I' not having a commanding officer, Crilly was assigned there.

Francis Crilly was the youngest officer on post and the freshest from West Point. At West Point all cadets were taught to maneuver and use artillery in the field. Being the freshest, Crilly was more likely

View of Fort Fillmore from the cemetery.
The fort is in the cleared area to the left of where
the blue field of the flag meets the bars.
Courtesy: Author's collection.

to remember his instruction. Having no artillerymen on post, Major Lynde had to use him. Crilly's inability to maneuver the howitzers in the soft sand at Mesilla may have caused his side to come out second best in the battle. He was an infantryman trained to maneuver artillery in an emergency, not an artilleryman working daily at his trade. Second Lieutenant Crilly could not be expected to be familiar with the fact that the twelve-pounder bronze mountain howitzer, mounted on a wooden carriage studded with heavy iron accouterments, would sink of its own weight in the soft sand, once off the hard-packed road.

The casualties Lynde reports conflict with McKee's estimates, Baylor's estimates and those of the *Mesilla Times*. What can be judged from this data is that, wherever the Texans were deployed with respect to the Federal force, they were able to reach all of the infantry companies but one, the artillery and McNally's Mounted Rifles. They did not engage Plummer's Company 'K,' 7th Infantry, or Cressey's Company 'B,' R.M.R.. No report states where each company was in the line, especially not Cressey's, whose presence was completely ignored. Cressey's troopers may have been merged with McNally's company, but he just as well may have been on the side with Plummer, where no casualties were taken.

One thing is certain based on this data. Isaac Lynde was no coward as McKee claims, afraid to face the fire. His adjutant, Brooks, was with him the whole time, as it was his responsibility to be. Brooks was struck twice, once on his sword and once on his arm. A bullet could just as well have reached Lynde, who was in firing range with Brooks.

One of the between-the-lines facts implied here is there may have been three hastily conducted funerals at the Fort Fillmore Cemetery that day for Privates Lane, Jenkins, and Sherwood. The cemetery lay on a ridge south of the fort near the El Camino Real, the old Spanish road to El Paso. The cemetery was established in 1851 by Lieutenant Colonel Dixon Stansbury Miles. At the time of the Battle of Mesilla, there were seventy to ninety earlier burials in unmarked graves. There exists the possibility that the bodies of Lane, Jenkins, and Sherwood were not brought back from Mesilla.

If they were brought back, their graves were not marked. The only marker in the cemetery was wooden with the name Captain Henry Stanton inscribed, and the date of his death in January 1855. Stanton, for whom Fort Stanton was named, was killed by Mescalero Apaches. He was the only officer to be buried at Fort Fillmore during its occupancy.

Some of the final acts before Fort Fillmore was abandoned are known. Lynde sent an express rider out to intercept Captain Alfred Gibbs and tell him to not come to Fort Fillmore, but to return to Fort Craig with the cattle. The same rider carried a message to Fort Craig, for the commander there to send a rider to warn the Fort Buchanan and Fort Breckinridge commands to turn north and head for Fort Craig. Of these two messages sent from Isaac Lynde, the one for Gibbs did not find him on the normal road. The reason for that will be explained shortly. The other message was received and acted on at Fort Craig. The troops coming in from the west did not fall into Baylor's clutches, as Major Lynde's prompt action saved them.

Lynde must have made up his mind to abandon Fort Fillmore as he dictated a letter to this effect, although he did not say so directly. He was fortifying the post, a fact noted by spies serving Baylor's cause, and part of the reason Baylor was so late in detecting the pullout of the 7th Infantry Regiment during the night. Lynde's fortifications appear to have been along the edge of the parade ground toward the west, the most vulnerable and open area on the post, hundreds of yards wide. He was probably attempting to delay an assault from that quarter until sufficient troops could be brought to bear on an attack. At that point the road from Mesilla seemed the most likely approach. While a few troops, perhaps one company, were left to defend the Mesilla approach, the rest of the soldiers, women and children prepared to leave on a moment's notice.

Why did Major Lynde finally decide to pull out? He clearly indicated why in a letter written later that day. First, Fort Fillmore was indefensible—especially if artillery were brought to bear, or there was an attack from the east out of the sand dunes. The enemy could not even be seen until they were on the post, so high were the dunes and tall bushes in that direction. In fact, the only two defensible directions were to the west and south. An attack from the west by a force with artillery would be difficult to repel. Did he know that the Texans had no artillery? That is unimportant. He knew they had artillery forty miles to the south at Fort Bliss, if they didn't yet have it in Mesilla. If the 7th remained at Fort Fillmore, Lynde would soon face that artillery, with his women and children in the midst of it. Doctor McKee savaged Isaac Lynde for not getting the women and children out earlier. He said:

> The command was hampered with the wives and families of five officers, and the wives and families of soldiers, numbering about one hundred souls. Lynde had his family with him, and had been warned repeatedly of this encumbrance, but was too weak to act. No move or effort was made to send them north to Santa Fe, N.M.—a place of security.[21]

McKee, the bachelor surgeon, never understood that a military unit operated under orders, not at the whim of the commander. The 7th Infantry Regiment was ordered out of New Mexico Territory. That meant officers, soldiers, wives, children, personal, and private property. The force at Fort Fillmore was never a fighting force such as could later be found on every American Civil War battlefield, stripped for action and waiting for an enemy assault.

The Fort Buchanan and Fort Breckinridge commands were not fighting forces either. They were encumbered with all the public and private property from their posts, as well as their own women and children. They were a large enough command to scare off any Indians who might wish to attack them, but they could not stand up to a well-armed and fielded force. Baylor's troops were a force stripped of encumbrances and ready for action. Had Baylor encountered the Arizona column, a second surrender of the 7th Infantry in New Mexico would have immediately taken place.

McKee certainly knew better than to chastise Lynde over the families. Movement of an entire regiment did not mean sending the well-armed military in one direction and their families and personal property by a separate route. They traveled together, as one would expect. The families had to make do. If chasing Apaches, the families stayed home at whatever post they settled. If abandoning a post as per orders, everybody went along. Of course, this meant that while en route the 7th Infantry column was vulnerable. If either of the assigned front or rear guards failed, the whole column, families included, were extremely vulnerable to an enemy attack.

Besides, the extra wagons which might have been used to haul the women and children to safety as McKee wished were performing other duties, as per orders from Colonel Canby in Santa Fe. Lane's column, dispatched on July 24 before Baylor came north, took the last of such available transport. With the families there at the post vulnerable to a four-sided attack and to an artillery bombardment, and having an order in his pocket which he believed gave him discretion to abandon the fort, Major Lynde decided it would be folly to mount an effective defense. Lynde would have had to spread his troops over an amazingly large area in order to get minimal ground coverage. Baylor could easily have probed for the holes that had to be there and then simply walked through them and into the post. Fort Fillmore, with no wall, was wide open to any invader. The modern-day visitor can easily make that judgment while standing on the two-hundred yard long parade ground. The post was long and narrow and absolutely indefensible. There were no wells for attaining water at the post. Given what he saw around him, Lynde said of the place:

> On the 26th of July I had the honor to report the fact of an unsuccessful attempt to dislodge the Texan troops from the town of Mesilla ... . On that day I had reliable information that the enemy would in the course of the night receive a battery of artillery, and if I moved to intercept it with a sufficient force for the purpose they were ready to attack the fort in my absence, and, as I have previously reported, the fort is indefensible against artillery, being perfectly commanded by sand hills for at least half the circle, and the only supply of water at the distance of one and a half miles. Other officers, with myself, became convinced that we must eventually be compelled to surrender if we remained in the fort, and that our only hope of saving the command from capture was in reaching some other military post. I therefore ordered the fort to be evacuated,

and such public property as could not be transported with the limited means at the post to be destroyed as far as time would allow.[22]

Unfortunately for him, and his legacy in history, Isaac Lynde apparently believed, or was led to believe, that he was then outnumbered and soon to be out-gunned in artillery as well. Lynde later noted, "A re-enforcement of 100 men reached the Texans from Fort Bliss last night. Their force at present, with the addition of the citizens of Mesilla, is nearly 700 men. I am hourly expecting an attack. The loss of the enemy is reported 11 killed and wounded. Part of their horses were stampeded by one of our shells."[23]

Major C.C. Sibley and Brevet-Lieutenant Colonel Reeve, in Texas, and Major Isaac Lynde, in New Mexico, justified their actions based on a "perceived" estimate of the threat. All three believed the enemy strength to be superior. In Lynde's case he believed, or was led to believe by intelligence estimates, that he was outnumbered about seven or eight hundred to six hundred, a disparity of about 1.2: 1. Given that he could not defend the indefensible Fort Fillmore, and given the presence of so many women and children in the line of fire, abandonment was the only option.

The only other officer with something to say about that day's activities was Colonel John Baylor. He remarked very briefly that, while waiting for a second attack on Mesilla on the morning of July 26:

> The enemy not appearing, I sent my spies to reconnoiter, and discover, if possible, their movements. The spies reported the enemy at work at the fort making breastworks, and evidently preparing to defend themselves. Upon hearing this, I sent an express to Fort Bliss, ordering up the artillery to attack the fort on the arrival of my reinforcements.[24]

Baylor was fooled by attempts to fortify the Fort Fillmore parade ground into believing Lynde intended to make a stand there. Lynde was not fooled by Baylor. Lynde believed if he made that stand Baylor would do exactly what he did, bring up the artillery from Fort Bliss and pound the fort into submission from long range. Hence, if Baylor is to be believed, Isaac Lynde was correct in abandoning Fort Fillmore, although some, such as McKee, believed he should have chosen to stand and die.

The 7th Infantry force at Fort Fillmore was a combination of savage deadliness for its day, and a total military command fiasco. One went hand in hand with the other. The weaponry was good, but may have included only short-range muskets. The soldiers were well trained, and numerous for that time period, but they had never faced major combat. The officer situation was well below standard. Unfortunately, the fort was not defensible against existing American arms and cannon, even the often poor armament of the Texans. There were over one hundred women and children camped essentially in the open, without walls to protect them, or water and subsistence to fill their needs, if Baylor managed to cut the post off from the river. The troops had to be brought to a place where these amenities were available and where the power of the 7th Infantry formations could be brought to bear in all their strength. That place was not Fort Fillmore. Unfortunately, it was not to be the dusty dirt road to San Augustine Springs either.

NOTES - Chapter 11

1. Lynde to Assistant Adjutant General, July 26, 1861, M1120, Rolls 13/14.
2. Horn & Wallace, Baylor to Washington, September 21, 1861, pp. 34-37.
3. McKee, p. 14.
4. Ibid., p. 15.
5. Ibid., pp. 15,16.
6. Ibid., pp. 16,17.
7. Ibid.
8. Lynde to assistant Adjutant General, July 26, 1861, M1120, Rolls 13/14.
9. McKee, pp. 18,19.
10. Horn & Wallace, Statement of Capt. C.H. McNally, Third Cavalry, pp. 28-31.
11. McKee, p. 19.

12. Horn & Wallace, Baylor to Washington, September 21, 1861, pp. 34-37.

13. *Mesilla Times*, Number 41, Saturday, July 27, 1861, p. 1.

14. McKee, pp. 19, 20.

15. Ibid., p. 20.

16. Ibid., pp. 20, 21.

17. Ibid.

18. Ibid., p. 23.

19. Ibid., p. 24.

20. Lynde to Assistant Adjutant General, Santa Fe, July 26, 1861, M1120, Rolls 13/14.

21. McKee, p. 8.

22. Lynde to Assistant Adjutant General, August 7, 1861, M1120, Rolls 13/14.

23. Horn & Wallace, Lynde to Acting Assistant Adjutant General, pp. 19, 20.

24. Horn & Wallace, Baylor to Washington, September 21, 1861, pp. 34-37.

Proposed Line of March
Over San Augustine Pass[*]

Head of Column
Major Isaac Lynde with Crilly's Cavalry

Front Guard
Captain Joseph Haydn Potter's Battalion
(Two companies - 100 men)

Color Party
Regimental Flags, Band,
Medical Wagons, Officer's Wives

Front Mid-Column Protection Party
One infantry company

Regimental Public Property Wagons
Foodstuffs, quartermaster good, etc.

Rear Mid-Column Protection Party
One infantry company

Regimental Public Property Wagons
Foodstuffs, quartermaster goods, etc.

Lieutenant Crilly's Infantry Company Serving as Artillerymen
At least four wagons towing artillery
and families

Rear Guard
Two infantry companies,
possibly under Captain Stevenson

---

[*]   This author's interpretation of the line of march is based upon information gleaned from various reports and commentaries.

12

A DAY TO MAKE DECISIONS

On July 27, of the year 1861, seven companies of the 7th Infantry Regiment, horsemen from parts of two Regiment of Mounted Rifle companies (four after Gibbs joined), and their accompanying wives, children, servants, civilian employees, personal and public property, and animals, slowly made their way up into the Organ Mountains and down to a place called San Augustine Springs.

While examining the site modern maps refer to as San Augustine Springs the author turned over a thirty-six by forty-one inch board and discovered wording on the other side. The lime green colored surface with white painted edges was badly faded and cracked after suffering years of sun, wind, and rain, although the white painted letters on the front were still readable. The words said:

San Augustin Pass
Divide between Tularosa Basin to east, and Jornada del Muerto to west, cut between Organ Mountains to south and San Augustin-San Andres Mountains to north. White gypsum sands glisten to northeast. Roadcuts in tertiary monzonite. Organ mines yielded copper, lead, silver, gold, zinc and fluorite. Elevation 5710 ft.

This old wooden road sign, is similar to the new metal one on the four-lane road above, but the new sign spells San Augustine with an 'e' in white on glittering dark green. Someone obviously tossed the old sign into the ravine below when the new sign was raised. Fortunately, it landed paint side down, or the intervening period would have left little, if anything, to read. Even at over a mile high (5710 feet) the New Mexico sun is hot and, when mixed with infrequent rain and even snow at this altitude, lettering on the best of signs does not last long.

There is no marker (July 2002) indicating that on such-and-such a spot, on July 27, 1861, the pride of the United States Army in southern New Mexico surrendered to an equally proud force from Texas. There is little at this gorgeous site to hint that such an event happened near there. There is a spring near the sign, but it is generally dry. The spring lies at the base of a sloping hill that is part of the approximately fifty feet of rock and soil supporting the current roadway through the pass. This 'San Augustine Springs' is the one modern maps show. If the spring hasn't shifted from the original point due to the pressure of the roadway, it may have been there in 1861. If one stands at the rail of the observation point above—near a Nike Hercules missile the Government placed here to honor the Whites Sands Missile Range just down the road—looking down, one can still see a few water plants in a small area next to the gravel base of the roadway.

The first time this author saw it the thought came, "How could that tiny flow of water be the famous San Augustine Springs where Lynde surrendered hundreds of thirsty soldiers?" This small, almost minuscule, few feet of water-requiring plants, covering an area of perhaps two hundred square feet, simply didn't seem right. If it was, then no wonder Major Isaac Lynde arrived there that hot July day to find little in the way of water for his troops, families, and horses to drink. What a small group of Apache warriors on the move might delight in would not satisfy the terrible thirst of hundreds of parched and terrorized people, who had just climbed a mountain to get to water that was in no way sufficient to meet their needs.

No, this could not be the San Augustine Springs where Major Isaac Lynde surrendered his command. If this was ever the spring Isaac Lynde sought, time and conditions had certainly changed it.

No contemporary 1861 description of the surrender at San Augustine Springs fits the spot lying off the roadway below the shell of the old Nike Hercules missile. But if this was not 'San Augustine Springs,' then where were those springs?

Lynde's suffering soldiers may or may not have noticed that they were at one of the world's most beautiful spots when they arrived at the crest of San Augustine Pass. Suffering in the heat, beautiful scenery was far from their minds. San Augustine Pass and the surrounding region has few rivals for natural beauty, especially when one arrives at dusk, with the sun going down, or on a cloudy or even rainy day, when the surrounding countryside is bathed in the soft light of the sun rather than its blinding heat. The visitor comes up and over the pass to view a truly stunning panorama, a view encompassing fifty miles and more. Standing on the top and looking east lies the great Tularosa Valley with the white gypsum sands of the White Sands National Park on the left and an area of vast desert sand hillocks to the right. One seems to see forever. Looking downward to the right one can see the buildings and houses of the White Sands Missile Range, some four miles off in the distance, where the government has tested many military weapons systems over the years, and where the author spent thirty-two years of enjoyable work.

The absolutely breathtaking Organ Mountains, so called because the mountains look somewhat like a set of organ pipes to those with good imaginations, are at the far right when looking toward the east from the small spring. The dark green/blue hue the Organs take on at times hints of the distant merging of pine trees and other growth with the light of day. To the north, the San Andres Mountains do not give off this hue, their countenance showing the shades of brown and black that the non-forested mountains of southern New Mexico display. Looking right and back toward the west from the Nike missile there is a large cleft in one of the pipes of the Organs. It is a canyon. The canyon cannnot be seen from the San Augustine crest, but it is there when the viewer is close enough. Maps name the canyon as Baylor Pass, hinting that it was named for Colonel John Baylor, and also hinting, because of the name, that he may have come through that canyon at some time in the past.

An unconfirmed rumor is that Baylor Pass has nothing whatsoever to do with John Baylor, but may instead be associated with Baylor University in Texas and some work that university did there. Whatever the source of the name, there is a possibility that 'Baylor Pass' may have been the route Isaac Lynde and the 7th took, rather than what is now called San Augustine Pass. An old trail, possibly associated with Baylor Pass, linked early Las Cruces and Doña Ana with the road to Hueco Tanks in Texas, and with the old salt road south to Paso del Norte. There were other possible routes as well. The clear trail through Soledad Canyon must be considered, although this pass through the mountains was far south of San Augustine Pass. The author considered each of these as possibly being the route Lynde took, but only San Augustine Pass fit the descriptions given after the surrender.

After much initial confusion, and a number of trips, it was an electronic trip on the Internet that provided the final answer as to the location of the surrender site. A journey into the minutiae published on that growing web of world knowledge uncovered a previously unknown document from one of the officers in Isaac Lynde's command. That officer's description made the route determination easier to make. As the story of the surrender unfolds the location of the surrender site unfolds as well. For now we need to return to July 26, 1861, and the last hours before the abandonment of Fort Fillmore.

Some time in the early morning of July 26, 1861, Major Isaac Lynde decided to abandon Fort Fillmore. Public property, such as Dr. McKee's hospital bottles, was destroyed; other items, including some hospital beds and possibly a crate of .69 caliber cartridges, were simply left behind. Much of the soldiers' private property was also left behind. Lynde explained, "Other officers, with myself, became convinced that we must eventually be compelled to surrender if we remained in the fort, and that our only hope of saving the command from capture was in reaching some other military post."[1]

At least three routes were open to Lynde to reach safety. The first of these was the most obvious, and the closest. He might have followed the route of 1st Lieutenant William Lane and his wagon train across the Jornada del Muerto to Fort Craig. About that route Lynde had this to say: "I have sent an express to Captain Gibbs directing him to return to Fort Craig with his command as he can not join this Post now. They have possession of the road above." Why did Lynde believe the Confederates held the road north? He had to travel on that very road, at least as far as Las Cruces, before turning right onto the dirt track headed east. Whatever the reason, Major Lynde believed, perhaps because he was fed false information, that the road above Doña Ana was in Confederate hands.[2]

There was a second route, the character of which is unknown today. One of the favored routes used by the Apaches when raiding into southern New Mexico below Fort Fillmore was by way of Soledad Canyon, a well-known point some twenty miles directly east of Fort Fillmore. The dragoons and Mounted Rifles favored this route with their presence on several documented instances. The Soledad Canyon route led to the old Spanish Salt Road, which led up past the Organs, San Augustine and San Andre's Mountains. At one point, on what is now the White Sands Missile Range, a dirt track branched off and headed for San Augustine Pass. Lynde never mentioned knowing of this Soledad Canyon route. Perhaps none of his officers were familiar with it. Perhaps the route was so bad that only mounted horsemen could traverse it, although it looks wide enough today. The Soledad Canyon route, however, offered complete safety from Confederate observation. The track into the mountains was more level and would have put less strain on troops and animals. Lynde may have believed that because the Soledad Canyon route was closer to Fort Bliss, a second Texas column could cut that route off as well, via the salt road north from Paso del Norte.

Whatever the reason, Major Isaac Lynde chose a third alternative, the steep rising mountain road to San Augustine Pass, then down to San Augustine Springs, a point he believed was only twenty miles distant. This was the shortest, if not the best, route to

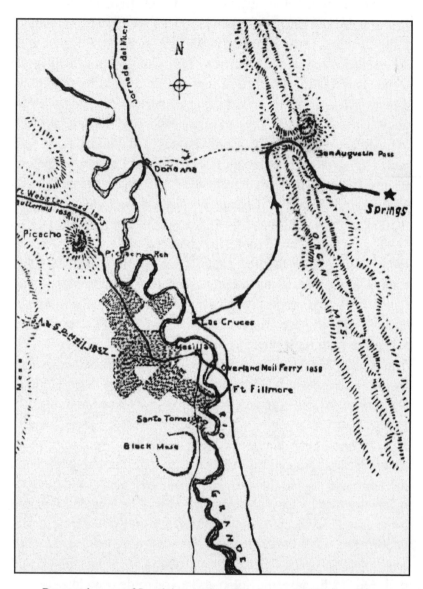

Proposed route of Lynde's march to San Augustine Springs from
Fort Fillmore. Route is shown passing through San Augustine Pass.
Note: This map is a modification of an original map created for
Colonel Joseph Mansfield's 1853 inspection report. Roscoe Conkling,
in his book *The Butterfield Overland Mail 1857-1869, Volume II*,
altered Mansfield's map by updating terrain features to the late 1850s.
This updated version includes the proposed route Lynde took
to San Augustine Springs.

Fort Stanton, his intended destination. Lynde believed that post to be threatened by the Confederates as well, but that a stand, if necessary, might better be made there than at Fort Fillmore. Lynde had never been to Fort Stanton, or Fort Craig. The route may have been chosen because 2^d Lieutenant Cressey had brought his few troopers of Company 'B,' R.M.R., over that route from Fort Stanton only a few weeks previously, and theoretically knew the route, and the places where water might be found in sufficient quantity.

Another piece of the puzzle needs to be resolved before returning to Lynde's decision-making on that fateful day. There is more to learn about the Fort Craig route, and the question of its safety for travel. On July 24, before Baylor made his presence known, Lynde had dispatched the Lane wagon train, loaded with excess quartermaster and commissary goods destined for Fort Craig. This train, commanded by 1st Lieutenant Lane and protected by his dismounted R.M.R. troops, escaped the clutches of the Texans just in time. Although well past Doña Ana, and into the beginnings of the Jornada del Muerto before Colonel Baylor rode into Mesilla, the train, and especially Lydia Lane, were not safe by any means. She poured her feelings concerning their plight into her writing:

> On the 24th of July, 1861, we left for Fort Craig; our escort of riflemen was distributed among the wagons, as there were no horses to ride. We had travelled but a short distance when the wagon-master insisted on halting to rest the mules, preparatory to a night march across the Jornada del Muerto, the eighty miles's stretch without water. Lieutenant Lane thought the halt so early in the day entirely unnecessary, but agreed to it, never dreaming the man had any other motive than the one given, the good of the animals. After events seemed to prove he was playing for high stakes, but he lost, that time.[3]

Lydia Lane was attempting to throw suspicion after the fact on the train's wagon-master for possibly being in the pay of the Texans, whom she could not at that time have known were in Mesilla. Her writing seems natural and true here. Her husband had no reason to suspect the man, nothing yet having happened to the south. The train broke camp early in the evening, intending a night march across the eighty miles of desert called the Journey of Death. Unfortunately, Lydia made no attempt to describe the wagon train's journey through Las Cruces and Doña Ana, two small valley towns of which we have little idea as to their reactions to the coming conflict. Nor are we sure of who had control over them during these critical days. Not far out on the Jornada the train was overtaken by a group of galloping riders. This was the point at which the news of a Texas invasion reached the Lanes, although the exact date and time are unknown. Lydia Lane said:

> Suddenly we were roused by the noise of galloping horses coming from behind us, and in a few moments several men rode up and asked for 'Lieutenant Lane.' The ambulance was stopped at once, and the strangers hurriedly told their story. One of them was Doctor Steck, an Indian agent and a strong Union man, whom we had known in Mesilla. He came to warn us that two hundred and fifty Texans were ready with horses saddled to leave the lower country, overtake us that night, and capture our train! I felt as if turned to stone, and did not speak for some time. Then I asked, 'What are we to do?' 'Fight,' answered the lieutenant. 'we will corral the wagons, use the sacks of flour and bacon for a fortification, put you, the children, and servants inside, and do our best to defend ourselves.[4]

If this incident happened at all, it did not happen on July 24 when Lydia Lane indicated it did. The Texans were undetected at Fort Fillmore until the night of July 24, and no word seems to have reached Mesilla of their approach till the next day, July 25. Of course, some people in the town may have known by prior notice. Lydia Lane did not say where Doctor Steck came from. If he came from Mesilla, and this depiction really happened, then the night of July 25 is more likely. That date seems right. The wagon train could have been on the lower edges of the Jornada by the evening of July 25, but certainly not on July 24. Time and events do blur dates in everyone's mind. Unfortunately, exact dating is often the key to truth when presenting history. What is most important here is that Lydia Lane reported a rumor from Doctor Steck that Texas cavalry were coming after them. What Michael Steck probably reported was that the Texans were in Mesilla and could easily be coming up behind the train. For his part, Colonel John Baylor never hinted in his correspondence that he even knew Lane's train existed. If he did, he made no attempt to overtake it.

The Lane wagon train was in no danger from Confederates at that point, although they could not know this for sure. We are following their course because of what happened next. Lydia Lane indicated that her husband was aware that Captain Alfred Gibbs and a herd of cattle were heading along their same route, destination Fort Fillmore. First Lieutenant Lane expressed a wish to do exactly what Isaac Lynde intended to do at a slightly later time, warn off Gibbs and have him turn back for Fort Craig. Lydia Lane described meeting Gibbs and his cattle herd on the road:

> When a cloud of dust in the distance heralded his approach, I was greatly relieved: and as help was in front and no sign of an enemy in the rear, I began to feel bold, and tried to convince myself I was not so very badly frightened after all, but I think any woman under the circumstances would have been quite as much alarmed as I was. I could not run away, lest I should meet a foe far worse than the Texans. The Indians were always somewhere in the neighborhood, so that I would have been safer to stay where we were than to fall into their clutches.
>
> Lieutenant Lane tried to induce Captain Gibbs not to go on to Fort Fillmore, but he decided to obey orders, taking a round-about way to reach the post, and so avoid, he hoped, the expected enemy.[5]

Lydia Lane's comments in this case, as least with respect to Gibbs's mission, agree with other accounts for the most part. Captain Alfred Gibbs, with his herd of cattle, supposedly arrived at the Point of Rocks on the southern end of the Jornada del Muerto by July 23, 1861. There is a time gap between his arrival there and his meeting with 1st Lieutenant Lane, which had to be on July 25 or early July 26. If the meeting was on July 26, 1st Lieutenant Lane's wagon train must have been further south, and nearer Fort Fillmore, than one might believe from Lydia Lane's account. Perhaps to her the Jornada was all the desert land in the area above Doña Ana, rather than just the cutoff above San Diego Crossing.

The information Lane gave Gibbs on July 25 or 26 did not change Captain Gibbs's mind about getting through to Fort Fillmore, but did cause him to turn toward the San Andres Mountains and head for the Organs, possibly intending to reach the San Augustine Pass wagon road, which was a back door into Fort Fillmore. Gibbs stayed with Lane's convoy the day and evening, then set out on an alternate route, not the road to Doña Ana. Where did Lane meet Gibbs? We only know it was south of the Point of Rocks, and may have been somewhere in the desert between Doña Ana and San Diego Crossing, at the entrance of the actual Jornada del Muerto.

Wherever they met, Gibbs left the main road at that point and headed up what must then have been another dirt track in the direction of the San Andres or San Augustine Mountains. Doing so, he never received the express Isaac Lynde sent him ordering him back to Fort Craig and safety. Instead, in a most unfortuitous meeting, Gibbs's command and that of Lynde's joined on the west side of San Augustine Pass, with most disagreeable consequences for both.

As to the fate of Lydia Lane and her husband, they arrived safely at Fort Craig. Lydia failed to record their arrival date in her book. Her most important comments after she reached safety were related to how she viewed Isaac Lynde many years later, and also after she had her mind filled to the brim with Dr. McKee's hatred, the result of reading his book. She said of Isaac Lynde:

> Major Lynde was tried and dismissed from the army; but after the war he was reinstated and placed on the 'retired list.' It was never proved, I believe, that he sympathized with the South, as many were inclined to think. He seemed utterly incompetent and unfitted for his important command, and it was freely discussed, after it was too late, that he was not the man for the place.[6]

Indeed, given what eventually happened, Isaac Lynde may not have been the man for the place, as Lydia Lane noted, but to accuse him of Southern sympathies seems a bit much, especially when one remembers all of Lydia's Confederate friends who passed through Fort Fillmore in the days before Lynde's arrival and stopped to visit and talk. Her husband's Kentucky birth, her use of black servants who may have been slaves (at least one such was a free black woman), as well as the theft of her husband's command's horses at a time when the need to watch over them carefully was most desperate, call Southern loyalties to mind in the case of her own family.[7]

Lydia Lane was very wrong in one assumption: Major Isaac Lynde was never tried, never given a hearing by the United States Army he served so faithfully.

At Fort Fillmore the time of post abandonment finally arrived late on the night of July 26-27. The departure time of the extensive wagon train and troop columns from Fort Fillmore has not been firmly established. Major Isaac Lynde provided one time, Doctor McKee, another. Doctor McKee said:

> About eleven o'clock, P.M., on the evening of the 26th I got into my two-horse buggy with my wounded friend, McNally, leaving and abandoning all my books, beds, bedding, carpets, pictures, kitchen utensils, cooking ware, etc., in my home, to the value of several hundred dollars. I was most reluctant to part with my books, most of which were of a scientific character, and had been my inseparable companions during many a lonely day at Fort Massachusetts, Col., Fort Defiance, N.M., in campaigns and on the road, and their loss to me was like a parent parting with his children.[8]

How angry Doctor McKee must have felt later when he read the comments in the *Mesilla Times* stating, "the Mexicans, eager as ever for plunder, entered the fort soon after it was evacuated, and commenced a general pillage, carrying off property on their backs, on animals, and by the cart-loads." McKee certainly must have reflected that many of those pillaged items might have been his personal property.

Dr. McKee mentioned the severely wounded 1ˢᵗ Lieutenant McNally as being with him in his buggy, but made no mention at that time of the mortally wounded Sergeant Callaghan, of McNally's Company 'F,' being under his care. Perhaps he left Callaghan in the hands of Medical Orderly Fitzwilliams, or with Dr. Alden.

Major Lynde gave a different time for the column's departure in an August 7 letter to the Department of New Mexico:

> ... at 1 O'clock a.m. on the 27th of July I took up the line of march for Fort Stanton, which was believed to be the most practicable point to reach, and was reported to be threatened by the enemy. I had no personal knowledge of the road, but it was reported to me that the first day's march would be 20 miles to San Augustine Springs, where there would be abundance of water for all the command.[9]

A third report on the time of departure was made some thirty years later, far after the time of the events. The writer was 2ᵈ Lieutenant Francis J. Crilly, the only 7ᵗʰ Infantry officer ever to make an unofficial report on the San Augustine surrender. In 1892, Crilly reported:

> The order for the abandonment of the post was issued by Major Lynde about eight o'clock P.M., on the evening of July 26, 1861, and was in terms as follows: "In accordance with the orders of the Department Commander, this post will be abandoned this evening." Many of the officers and their families were at supper when they received the order.
>
> They got up from their tables, leaving nearly everything in their houses. Only one or two wagons were allowed each company for officers and men. The laundresses and their children were concentrated in a few wagons at the head of the train. The terms of the order left it beyond the power of the senior officers to dispute it. The command started about one A.M., following the road along the Rio Grande to Las Cruces, and thence easterly to the Organ Mountains, ...[10]

We will take up the last part of Crilly's story later when what he says will be most applicable to the overall situation. At this point several items of importance are to be noted. Crilly agrees with Isaac Lynde's version rather than McKee's, that the march began about one o'clock on the morning of July 27. He adds a further detail which is helpful. It appears as if the officers may not have known of the abandonment before eight o'clock on July 26. Second Lieutenant Crilly has them rise from their dinner tables and immediately prepare to leave, packing up their families, their children, and what household goods they could take. Of greater importance is the fact that Crilly states emphatically that the command took the road to Las Cruces, then turned eastward from there in order to reach the Organ Mountains, rather than continuing on to Doña Ana before making the turn. Roads ran into the Organs from both places. The road Lynde took is unknown but could have been along the track of modern Highway 70. More likely the route was to the south, in the area where University Avenue runs today through the city of Las Cruces. A road in that region went to Soledad Canyon, Baylor Pass, and eastward. If he took that route, one can only wonder why Isaac Lynde didn't go through Soledad Canyon.

The appearance of the column at the starting point at Fort Fillmore is crucial to what would happen, yet we have only a vague idea as to how it was configured. We can assume Major Lynde was toward the front of the column, with his adjutant, 1st Lieutenant Edward Brooks. His presence there is well documented.

The colors of the 7th Infantry Regiment, the blue background regimental flag with its embroidered eagle, and the 7th Infantry Regiment lettering across the bottom, plus the thirty-three-or thirty-four-star United States flag, both huge and hard to handle, were probably furled for this night march. We do know the colors reached San Augustine Springs with Lynde, so they must have been toward the front of the column as well. Lynde may have ridden in his personal buggy, as Doctor McKee did, or in one of the ambulances which were public property of the regiment. It is also possible, because of Lynde's later words indicating he had a mount at some point, that he rode out of Fort Fillmore on a horse.

The clearest statement as to who was where in the column comes from the fact that we know Major Lynde assigned two companies of infantry as the rear guard and one additional infantry company just in front of the rear guard with the wagons towing the artillery. During the hardest part of the march, when men were falling out of ranks in droves due to heat and thirst, Major Lynde reported, "... they had driven in or captured our rear guard and the men that had given out in the rear. Three of the four mountain howitzers that we had with us were with the wagons in the rear and captured. They were guarded by one company of infantry acting as artillery [Crilly's Company]."[11]

The single company identifiable by name that we can be sure was back there in the rear was Company 'I,' 7th Infantry, Major Paul's old company, which he left officerless when he removed himself from Fort Fillmore in June. Company 'I' was under the command of young 2[d] Lieutenant Francis J. Crilly, whose men were marching near the howitzers for which they were responsible. There were two other companies, identification unknown, to the rear of Crilly's. These two companies, the actual rear guard, were crucial factors in whether Major Lynde would gain San Augustine Springs with safety or fall prey to a Confederate attack. If the rear guard did its job, as Army regulations defined that job, there is no way John Baylor's Texas horsemen could gain access to the rest of the column from the rear, at least via the road on which the column was travelling. Formed infantry trumped cavalry every time.

We know something about the rear of the column through the words of Captain Albert Gibbs, R.M.R., whose presence with the column was almost totally fortuitous. Gibbs said:

> Four of Major Lynde's baggage wagons, filled with stores, and women and children, completely blocked the road. I requested Lieutenant Brooks to try to get a couple of the 12 pounder mountain howitzers that were fastened behind these wagons, and gave him men from my command for that purpose.[12]

Thanks to Captain Gibbs, we have a second witness that places at least four of Crilly's wagons towing mountain howitzers just in front of the two infantry companies forming the rear guard. The women and children in these wagons may have been the wives and children of enlisted men assigned to those companies, and hence would have been close to their fathers and husbands.

We have now accounted for Major Isaac Lynde at the front of the column and three infantry companies and the artillery wagons in the rear. That leaves us with four infantry companies, the two Mounted Rifle companies, the medical command, and the other women and children to account for as to position in the column.

It would seem that both Mounted Rifle Companies 'B' and 'F' were at the front of the column with Major Lynde, his adjutant Brooks and others. One of the brief and cryptic comments Major Lynde made when approaching San Augustine Springs seems to clearly indicate that Lynde had all the R.M.R. horsemen with him at one point. He said, "I now determined to push forward with the mounted force to the Springs, and return with water for the suffering men in the rear."[13]

Both partial companies of the R.M.R. were under the command initially of 2[d] Lieutenant Cressey, the only mounted officer available for duty when the wagon train left Fort Fillmore on the night of July 26-27, McNally being wounded. Cressey's troopers numbered approximately thirty-one from Company 'F' and twenty-two from Company 'B.'

The other man to confirm that Lynde had Cressey up front with him, at least at the start, was Doctor McKee. He said:

... drove after Lynde 6 miles in a buggy with two horses on a full run. He was then 5 or 6 miles in front of his whole command, with a company of Mounted Rifles under Mr. Cressey.[14]

Two other infantry companies probably marched immediately behind Lynde and Cressey's mounted force. These Lynde later referred to as the "100 men of the infantry battalion," who formed ranks with him at San Augustine Springs. These foot companies would have served as the advance-guard force to protect the front of the column from attack, just as the two infantry companies in the back provided the rear guard.

Just behind these two forward infantry companies were the ambulances carrying the wounded. Doctor McKee at first said he left Fort Fillmore with a two-horse buggy and the wounded 1st Lieutenant McNally with him. If that was true, at some point he transferred McNally to a hospital ambulance, perhaps under Hospital Steward Fitzwilliams' care. He next encountered the ambulance at San Augustine Springs, where it rested with the remnants of the advance guard, some of the R.M.R. troops, and several wagon-loads of women and children. McKee said, "After getting into camp at San Augustine Springs, [I] asked McNally and the sergeant (wounded) what they wanted—if he should hang out a hospital flag to protect him, thinking there was to be a fight. They both requested him to put out a flag, which he did on his buggy."[15]

We know there were several vehicles carrying civilians and possibly personal property, quartermaster and commissary goods which arrived safely at San Augustine Springs that day. They may have arrived with or just behind the ambulances carrying the wounded. These wagons/buggies also carried some of the officers' wives and families, with their servants, including Major Isaac Lynde's wife; these persons would probably have been separated from the enlisted men's wives and families as per custom. We have one vivid cut of their presence at the Springs. On the Internet web site of the 7th Infantry Regiment, titled 'Adjutant's Call,' is the story of the saving of the 7th Infantry colors. We will say more about the story later, but for the present a small section of the tale confirms the presence of the officers' families at San Augustine Springs. In referencing the fate of the 7th's colors at the Springs a sergeant noted, "Sections of the colors were cut up and given to such ladies as were nearby. The Union of one was given to the wife of Captain Matt Stevenson who wore it apron style and kept it."[16]

The only acceptably titled 'ladies' at Fort Fillmore were probably the wives of the officers, or their family members. That title was often reserved for them, not always for enlisted men's wives or servants. In this brief comment we have verification that several, perhaps all, of the officers' wives and families were at the Spring, their lives in mortal danger if a Rebel attack reached the front of the column.

This leaves the center of the column undefined. There were two infantry companies remaining, whose position in the column we cannot ascertain, plus an undetermined number of wagons hauling quartermaster and commissary goods. We can be fairly certain that no wagons were spared to transport large personal items such as furniture, etc. We have already noted McKee's comments about having to leave his books and other private items behind. Lydia Lane, although not involved in the loss of personal goods, commented after the fact about a matter which was of great interest to her. She said, "Before leaving Fort Fillmore we sent all our furniture, china, etc. to Mesilla, to be sold at auction, and, strange to say, realized remarkably good prices for everything. We were more fortunate than those friends who remained at Fillmore and lost their all later on."[17]

In a second comment concerning the loss of private goods by the men and women of the Fort Fillmore garrison, she added, "On the 26th Major Lynde ordered a great deal of public property destroyed, which was done, preparatory to a hasty retreat in the direction of Fort Stanton. The officers and families lost everything they owned, as they could not take their property with them, beyond a change of clothes."[18]

There is a problem with this statement, though only of a minor nature. It is true there were not enough wagons to haul all the private property, but many small personal possessions must have been loaded into the wagons carrying the families. That seems clear given what happened later at San Augustine Springs at the time of the surrender. In general, however, one can be assured the furniture and other larger pieces of private property were undoubtedly hauled off by the looters who came to the fort just after the abandonment, and before the troopers from Texas arrived to secure the post.

Having attempted to define the makeup of the 7th Infantry column which left Fort Fillmore late on the night of July 26-27, it is time to return to the point of leaving and take up the march based on what we know. In review, the column Lynde led toward the mountains appeared as follows, with allowances for error in the exact positioning of some of the pieces. Major Lynde was toward the front of the column, with his adjutant 1st Lieutenant Edward J. Brooks. Brooks had a horse at Mesilla so there is little doubt he rode it to San Augustine Springs. Lynde also rode a horse at Mesilla, as McKee reported, and is known to have been mounted at some point on the journey.

Lynde and Brooks were accompanied by the fifty-three members of the combined R.M.R. mounted force, parts of Companies 'B' and 'F,' commanded by 2d Lieutenant Edward Potter Cressey. Immediately in front of the wagons carrying the officer's wives and families was the best location for the two companies of the 7th Infantry Regiment advance guard, the two companies Lynde referred to at San Augustine as "the infantry battalion," commanded by Captain Joseph Haydn Potter. These troops numbered about seventy to one hundred men.

The next part of the wagon train is the least definable, but there are reasons for suspecting a pattern. This would have been the best place for the quartermaster and commissary wagons, perhaps interspersed with the two other infantry companies guarding these wagons from any attacks from the side of the column. We cannot be sure how many wagons were available for hauling, but there had to be some. The Texans reported, following the surrender, the capture of immense quantities of flour, rice, coffee, soap, hay, bacon, beans, candles, and even fifty-four head of beef cattle.[19] The Texans did not say what was surrendered where, or whether the goods were left at the abandoned Fort Fillmore or on the road to San Augustine Springs. The best guess for this middle section of the train, which did not make it to San Augustine Springs with the front of the column before the surrender, would be that it consisted of an indeterminate number of wagons, followed by an infantry company, followed by other wagons and a second infantry company.

Whatever the exact mix of the center section of the train, the picture once again becomes more clear as the end of the column is approached. We know for sure that wagons hauled the four mountain howitzers and the families of the enlisted men, as well as servants and other non-military in this part of the train. Crilly's Company 'I' was with these artillery pieces and families, as both the guard for the women and children and for serving as artillerymen if needed.

At the end of the column, and in the most important position as far as any attack from Mesilla would be concerned, were the two infantry companies making up the rear-guard battalion. Unfortunately for this study and for students of military history, we do not know who these two companies were, or who was in command. They were the last to leave Fort Fillmore and should have included the best and most experienced officers. We cannot be assured that such was the case. Within the 7th Infantry at that time the rear guard should have been commanded by senior Captain Joseph Haydn Potter's Company 'G' or Captain Mathew Ryder Stevenson's Company 'B.' If there is one single place to fault Major Isaac Lynde's decision-making process, the choice of command for the rear guard is that place. Yet, extant records tell nothing of who was back there.

Army Regulations of the period pertaining to the rear guard of a column of troops on the march state:

> The advance and rear-guards are ordinarily formed of light troops (infantry). Their strength and composition, in different arms, are regulated according to the nature of the country, and the relative position of the enemy. These guards are destined to cover the movements of the troops to which they belong, and to hold the enemy in check ... .[20]

"To hold the enemy in check." How critical these words are to the fate of the 7th Infantry Regiment marching upward toward San Augustine Pass that hot July day. In 1951, as part of a movie produced by the 20th Century Fox Company, *Fixed Bayonets*, the objective of a rear guard was defined by one of the actors, portraying a member of an Army infantry company assigned to hold back Red Chinese hordes in Korea. He said, "The object of the rear guard is to check every pursuit and harassment and thus allow the main body to retire unmolested." The accusation will be made in these pages that the 7th Infantry rear guard did not follow this injunction, or Army regulations, on the road to San Augustine Springs, and hence the force they were supposed to protect was lost. Not once did the rear guard form up to stop the enemy. Not once was a round fired toward the enemy. Here we have the actual reason for the surrender at San Augustine Springs. Was it Lynde's fault his orders were not followed by the officers in command of that rear guard? Was it the fault of the boiling New Mexico sun, or were the soldiers all drunk, as so many modern storytellers choose to believe? That is yet to be determined.

Back to the night of July 26-27. The column now defined as closely as possible, we turn to the conditions as they were when Major Lynde took the first tentative steps toward his final destiny. Before the first soldier stepped out onto the dark road at about 1:00 a.m., Major Lynde must have been aware of the warning given in Army regulations, "As night-marches are always performed with difficulty, they ought never to be undertaken, unless on the most urgent occasions."[21]

Recalling these words concerning night marches, one has to wonder what the rising sun found when it struck the blue-coated column the next morning. The situation at Fort Fillmore was indeed an "urgent occasion" but that did not stop natural forces from breaking down column discipline in the darkness. The military wagon train described on these pages had one firm characteristic. It was not, under any circumstances, a fighting formation. Two basic stingers could cause an enemy to pause, one in the front and one in the tail, two armed contingents who had to do their job or the safety of the wagon train was imperiled. The cavalry and infantry at the front of the column protected the point and drew the first fire of any Indians or Texans encountered in that direction. They had to be able to deploy quickly to form their shield. In the rear the safety of the entire column from the direction of Mesilla and Las Cruces would be at peril if the rear guard broke down.

Another important condition to be met was holding the wagon train formation as tightly together as possible. This was always a difficult proposition, especially in the dark and especially under the conditions Lynde encountered. During the 1850s, the essence of the military unit was the company. The company—infantry, cavalry, etc.—lived together, traveled together, fought together. The concept of the regiment as the primary unit existed, but rare were the occasions when a regiment joined together and moved as one unit. In the entire 1850s, the arrival in New Mexico of the complete Regiment of Mounted Rifles in 1856 was one of the few instances of a regiment on the march together that is recorded. Isaac Lynde's 7th Infantry Regiment, then leaving Fort Fillmore, had seven of the ten companies of the regiment at the post. Three others were on the way from Fort Buchanan and Fort Breckinridge. Even with only seven companies, this was the first time the 7th had moved anywhere in that level of strength since their move to Utah in 1857—if they were complete at that time. Lynde, the fourth-ranking man in the regiment had, at most, moved four companies from Fort McLane to Fort Fillmore, and then not while under a threat. His normal size unit of command, as a Major, was two companies, which formed a battalion.

Protect the front! Protect the rear! Keep the column tight! Had these tasks been performed to perfection the column Major Isaac Lynde led into the mountains might have been saved. That they were not was due to two other conditions which were beyond any man's control. The two greatest allies of Colonel John Baylor's Texan force were the simple condition of fatigue among the Federal troops while on the march and the presence of the bright sun and clear sky of a boiling hot July day in New Mexico. If one hasn't experienced that sun let it be known that there are few more torturous events a human can experience. On a truly hot day, as the dawn of July 27, 1861 promised to bring, the torture could be almost exquisite.

Since the evening of July 24, the garrison had had little time for rest, and especially for sleep. The remainder of the night of July 24-25 was spent in watchful suspense, expecting an attack at any moment. The day of July 25 was spent in that same state of watchfulness with the additional burden of preparing a move towards Mesilla in the late afternoon. The Battle of Mesilla followed, with all its tension and fright, in addition to the taking of casualties, and the ignominious necessity of a march back to the fort without having taken the town. The night of July 25-26 was not a restful night either as watchfulness was redoubled for fear of a Confederate attack and what would happen next.

Then came July 26. That entire day must have been spent in trying to catch a little sleep, mixed with intense activity in preparation for abandoning the fort and gathering together what must be taken, and deciding what had to be left behind. If one examines the Fort Fillmore situation closely there appears little possibility of rest for any of the command. It is conceivable that there were officers and men who did not sleep throughout the entire three-day period. Whatever the case, nerves or lack of rest, the Federal column that left Fort Fillmore in the dark after midnight on July 26 was hardly fit for the journey it was about to undertake.

They had to march twenty-five miles, about half of that distance over fairly level ground, the last part up a steady rise until a much steeper rise was encountered about six miles from San Augustine Springs. Lynde believed it to be a twenty-mile march with adequate water at the end for the whole command. His information was wrong. He was to have five extra miles to cover in the heat, and the worst part of the landscape to traverse over that distance.

The officer most familiar with the route to San Augustine Pass and beyond was 2^{d} Lieutenant Cressey. If Lynde believed Cressey had first-hand knowledge of the springs and the route, perhaps that is why he placed Cressey's combined R.M.R. unit in the front of the column, forming the point of the advance. The choice to put cavalry up front seems a little odd. There were two reasons for doing so. In a twenty-mile distance, even up a mountain, the cavalry could run the legs off the infantry as per their rate of march. The heavily laden infantry could not keep up with the horses and there would be a tendency for the slower moving to fall behind. Not a good idea, unless Lynde was operating under the assumption that they needed to move fast and far, and as quickly as possible. Cavalry to the front would have put the burden on the heavily burdened infantry to move faster, if they could.

Sometime near 1:00 a.m., perhaps a little later, the long column of men and wagons slowly departed Fort Fillmore on the old Camino Real route north. Orders were probably given to travel as quietly as possible, but no column on the move can be totally quiet. Equipment creaked and groaned; clanging sounds of metal striking metal could be heard in the night; animals called out their sounds for all to hear. The men must have spoken to each other, complaining, grousing, discussing, much as soldiers have always done when on the march. Perhaps these men talked less because they were simply bone tired from all that had happened the past few days. They had a long march before them; none of them knew what was at the end, or what might happen if they were discovered.

Nights could be warm in southern New Mexico in July, as the days could be scorching hot. The soldiers wore much of what they owned on their backs. If they were allowed they wore some form of shirt, pants, and long tan underwear, the kind that stretched from collar to feet and made of the light materials used in summer. Depending upon their officers, however, and the availability of wagons, they may even have been wearing their heavy woolen frock coat, rather than carrying it with their pack. One thing was sure: they carried all the public property they could, for no company officer wanted to leave anything behind that he had signed for if it could be carried. Perhaps some of the wagons bore excess uniforms and property but, on this kind of march, the soldiers bore more than the regular field load on their backs, plus carrying a musket, a cartridge box with up to fifty cartridges, a bayonet, canteen, and pack.

Finally, it was the turn of the two rear-guard companies to leave. The rear guard should have been a senior captain's responsibility, with that officer at hand and leading them in person, but we cannot be sure that this happened. There were very few officers with the regiment, only one per company, and there should have been at least two with the rear guard. Potter was the most experienced officer, followed by Stevenson. The best clue that Captain Potter was not in the rear comes from a statement made by Doctor McKee, while at San Augustine Springs. McKee reported:

> Just after that Captain Potter came to the medical camp and said, "its no use; we are all surrendered; that d--d old scoundrel has surrendered us! I am going to protest against it. Who'll go along?" I said, "I'll go." McNally, with his bloody shirt on, said he would go with Dr. McKee and Lieutenant Ryan (he thinks). Dr. Alden and the officers around said they would go too.[22]

One can only assume Captain Potter was in command of the advance guard. Who were the "officers around" McKee referred to? Why weren't they with their companies? Was McKee exaggerating, or suffering faulty memory so many years later? One would hate to think the rear guard was commanded by NCOs while the officers stayed at the head of the column with their families. If that was true, defeat was inevitable from the start, and Isaac Lynde to blame. There is no proof such was the case. No mention was ever made of Captain Stevenson being at San Augustine Springs during the surrender. Perhaps Stevenson *was* in command of the rear-guard, as would be expected because of his rank.

Seven companies of infantry marching up to a mountain pass, according to Army regulations, should have had twenty-one officers with the roughly five hundred troops. Save for Lynde and Brooks there were in fact only seven, one-third of the leadership that should have been available. Such a situation was normal for the antebellum Army in New Mexico Territory, but was totally unsuited to a force facing a battle. In addition, several of the officers served with a company whose men were not known to them or, in the case of one infantry company, there was no officer on hand at all, the one assigned officer performing quartermaster and commissary duties. This was not a fighting formation, although it was certainly not a mob either, or at least it shouldn't have been.

Making as little noise as possible, the troops of the rear guard passed Tortugas Pueblo some time after two 'clock, unless they were delayed by that common problem of companies on the march, the tail of a column always running to catch up with the rest, or stopped in place as the head of the column advanced farther and farther away. It was dark, perhaps with moonlight, with only the light from a few flickering candles to be seen within some adobe structures they passed. Some time later they neared the village of Las Cruces, perhaps awakening a few citizens in that small community, who peeked out their windows to watch the procession pass by. Obviously, there were no Confederate troops yet in the town, as none sought to engage the 7th in battle. At the next divide in the road, a cutoff at a now indeterminate location, they turned to the east and the Organ Mountains.

None in the Federal or Texas commands chose to say anything of the night march, save for the briefest of comments by Major Lynde. With this comment we pick up the chain of events at dawn, July 27, 1861, somewhere on the Fort Stanton road, as Lieutenant Colonel Baylor later called it. Lynde reported with the greatest brevity, "Until daylight the command advanced without difficulty, but when the sun arose the day became intensely hot, and soon after the men and teams began to show signs of fatigue, and I found that the distance was greater than had been represented."[23]

NOTES - Chapter 12

1. Lynde to Assistant Adjutant General, August 7, 1861, M1120, Roll 13/14.
2. Ibid.
3. Lydia Spencer Lane, *I Married a Soldier*, p. 108.
4. Ibid., p. 109.
5. Lydia Spencer Lane, *I Married a Soldier*, p. 109.
6. Ibid., p. 115.
7. Ibid., p. 81.
8. McKee, p. 25.
9. Lynde to Assistant Adjutant General, July 7, 1861, M1120, Rolls 13/14.

10. Francis J. Crilly, Appendix I, Circular Publication Committee, The Military Service Institution, Governor's Island, N.Y.H., November 10, 1889, p. 10. (Hereafter cited as Francis Crilly.)

11. Lynde to Assistant Adjutant General, August 7, 1861, M1120, Rolls 13/14.

12. Horn & Wallace, Statement of Captain Gibbs, November 7, 1861, pp. 24-26.

13. Lynde to Assistant Adjutant General, August 7, 1861, M1120, Rolls 13/14.

14. Horn & Wallace, McKee to Canby, August 16, 1861, M1120, pp. 26-28.

15. Ibid.

16. The Internet, 7th Infantry Regiment Web Site. This site contains much information about the 7th Infantry Regiment, and includes music which is known to have been used at parades of the Regiment in the 19th Century. The song, "The Girl I Left Behind Me," is the regimental song. Major Lynde had the regimental band with him at San Augustine Springs, but it is doubtful that they were playing their instruments.

17. Lydia Spencer Lane, *I Married a Soldier*, p. 108.

18. Ibid.

19. The *Daily Picayune* (New Orleans), Volume 25, #183 (August 27, 1861), p. 2, col 3.

20. War Department, *General Regulations for the Army of the United States-1847* (Washington DC: J. & G.S. Gideon, 1847), pp. 120, 121.

21. Ibid., p. 121.

22. Horn & Wallace, Statement of Assistant Surgeon J.C. McKee, August 16, 1861, pp. 26-28.

23. Lynde to Assistant Adjutant General, August 7, 1861, M1120, Rolls 13/14.

13

A JULY NEW MEXICO SUN

The troops marched some indeterminate distance, perhaps fifteen to eighteen miles, when the light of a July New Mexico sun rose on the scene. Colonel Baylor's most ferocious ally was present. The great orange cavalry, bugle-like rays blaring forth heat, attacked Lynde's column. With the coming of the sun, and the promise of the hottest of hot days, the infantry, especially in the rear, who were exposed to the speed-up/slow-down motion of a column on the move, began to truly suffer. Lynde remarked, on the head of the column approaching the final steep two-mile rise to the crest of the San Augustine Pass, that, "About 6 miles before reaching the Springs commences a short ascent to a pass in the Organ Mountains, and here the men and teams suffered severely with the intense heat and want of water, many men falling and unable to proceed."[1]

Lynde did not say how long they marched after dawn broke before trouble truly set in. The hour may have been approaching noon when a crisis situation developed. Certainly by that time of day the temperature could have risen to intolerable levels, far too hot for tired soldiers on the march, many of whom may already have emptied their canteens. If it were an average July day the temperature could be hovering near 100 degrees, even by noon. If above average, temperatures up to 109 degrees are not uncommon. The *Mesilla Times* backed Lynde's comment on the day's heat, saying proudly,

"The road lay over the tablelands and mountains to a pass in the Organos chain, by way of San Augustine Springs, over a route where there was no water, and the day was excessively warm."[2]

The sun and the desert on a clear July day—imagine it. Imagine being an already tired soldier marching in the Federal rear guard. There had been three days of intense activity, followed by a long night march loaded down with full equipment. After a few moments of delight in looking east to watch the day break over the beautiful Organ Mountains reality must have quickly set in. A rising hot sun on a July New Mexico morning is something to experience, especially for the uninitiated. We moderns look at the sky and say, "the blue is going to be white today," referring to the fact that on the hottest of July days the blue of the sky washes out into a blue-tinged white, the worst of days for someone to be outside. How their blue wool coats or shirts must have itched when the sweat began to reach their eyes! By ten o'clock in the morning they must have been in agony, and the hardest part of the journey, and the greatest heat, still lay before them.

We don't know where the column was when John Baylor's forces first saw them. Baylor's words on the sighting are confusing because of how he chose to phrase them. Unfortunately, we have no others. Baylor said:

> On the morning of the 27th, a little after daylight, my spies reported a column of dust seen in the direction of the Organ Mountains, distant 15 miles, on the Fort Stanton road. I could from the top of a house with a glass see the movements of the enemy. I immediately ordered the command to saddle and mount, for the purpose of intercepting them at San Augustine Pass.[3]

With a spy glass Baylor must have been able to see the dust cloud the soldiers raised up on the march, a cloud that choked the men in the column as they marched through it. It is assumed John Baylor was still at Mesilla when he climbed a roof to look in the direction of the mountains. If the distance of fifteen miles was correct he was perhaps closer, or the troops had not yet advanced to San Augustine Pass. Whatever the case, just after dawn, the

Confederates became aware that Major Isaac Lynde and the 7th Infantry had escaped from Fort Fillmore and passed by unnoticed in the night. Baylor's cavalry was likely bedded down when he got the news, as he mentioned ordering them to saddle their horses and mount.

Learning only at dawn that Lynde had abandoned Fort Fillmore meant it would take some hours for him to reach the rear guard of the column. The blue-coated soldiers would have trudged up the mountain through the dust and heat for some time before he caught up to them, and that raises another interesting possibility. If Baylor's spies had done their job properly and detected Lynde's movements when they should have, Baylor might have attacked the column near dawn, when the Federal soldiers still had some portion of their normal fighting instinct. The sun, the dust, and the steeply rising road up the mountain would not yet have sapped their strength.

The next piece of documented information does not pick up the Federal column until some hours after dawn. The time is not known, but discipline and order had already collapsed before the Confederates made their appearance at the back of the column. Doctor McKee noted:

> At daylight on the morning of the 27th of July, we were some eight or ten miles east of Las Cruces; the road lay over the table lands and foot hills to a pass through the Organ Mountains to San Augustine Springs. The day was excessively warm, and there being no water, many men dropped out of the ranks almost dead from fatigue and thirst.[4]

McKee's words are backed up by his nemesis, Major Isaac Lynde, who noticed the breaking down of discipline and order at about the same time, and well before the Confederates came on the scene. At a point about five or six miles from San Augustine Springs Lynde said, "Up to this time there was no indication of pursuit. I now determined to push forward with the mounted force to the Springs, and return with water for the suffering men in the rear."[5]

Lynde was not simply defending his action of moving forward, rather than trying to ensure that the rear guard was stable and operational. It was not his job to monitor the entire column personally. He had other officers to do portions of that job and report to him. The right move was for him to go forward, get water, and send it back to the "suffering men in the rear."

Second Lieutenant Francis Crilly, with Company 'I' and the wagons towing the artillery, was even more pointed in his comments, providing a time by which he felt discipline had collapsed, especially at the rear of the column where the crucial rear guard was supposed to be maintaining watch. Crilly said, "Shortly after sunrise, the heat became so oppressive that many of the men fell out of ranks exhausted. The water in their canteens was soon used up, and the mesquite bushes afforded no protection from the frightful heat. By eleven o'clock there was practically no organized command."[6]

No "organized command," at least at the back of the column, where the most important position as regards the Confederate approach was. Here was supposed to be the column's most powerful reactive force, the two infantry companies of the battalion forming the rear guard. If Confederate horsemen were seen to be approaching, these men were to deploy and defend. If they did not, or could not, do their job, the column in front of them was to all purposes lost. It would be simply rolled up by an attacker. And that is exactly what happened.

The first of those to arrive on this tragic scene were Colonel John Baylor and his 2[d] Texas Mounted Rifles, who, riding hard, at last arrived in range of the back of the column. These Texans are to be admired, if only because they traveled through the same heat and dust as the Federals and arrived in a reasonable condition to fight. In fact, the cavalry on both sides performed well. It was the infantry force that collapsed, and that was due to the fact that they were on foot and carrying an inordinately heavy load in the oppressive heat. Baylor relayed his thoughts on first spying the Federal rear.

> I reached the river, distant 1 mile, when I received intel-
> ligence that a messenger had arrived from the fort, and stated
> that the enemy had fired the buildings; that it had been

extinguished, and that but little had been destroyed. I at once ordered Major Waller to take a detachment of men and go to the fort, and save, if possible, the property therein, and to leave men enough to guard the post, and then overtake me as soon as possible. On reaching the foot of the mountain, distant about 15 miles, I could see the rear of the enemy, composed chiefly of famished stragglers, endeavoring to make their way to water. I disarmed and collected a number of them, and finding most of them dying of thirst, we gave them the water we had, and were compelled ourselves to go to a spring in the mountain for water. Lieutenant Baylor, and Mr. Barnes, a citizen of Las Cruces, who acted as guide, found 24 of the enemy at the spring, who had from exhaustion gone to sleep, whom they captured.[7]

Baylor never detected what he could call a rear guard. As he approaches the stragglers from two companies, he mentioned seeing no officers, nor capturing any, though he may have done so. Surely he would have mentioned capturing a Yankee officer if he found one. In addition, no residue from an infantry rear guard deployed to give him a moment's pause. The column's main defensive force was in total collapse, though Major Lynde couldn't, and didn't, know that until much later. Baylor's cavalry rode through and around the prostrate bodies to get to their next destination, a spring off the side of the road near where the bluecoats still moved in the direction of the San Augustine Pass rim. This spring could be the site underneath the Nike missile where modern maps say the San Augustine Springs lie, or it might have been a spring near what is now the town of Organ.

Then again, if Baylor's fifteen-mile estimate from Mesilla is correct he may have been much farther to the south. There is no way to know for sure. According to modern topographical maps the only other natural springs, other than the one below the Nike Hercules missile (on the eastern side of the pass) are to the south along the western edge of the Organs. In 1861, there may have been a road traversing this very area in the direction of San Augustine Pass. One could either go to San Augustine Pass, Baylor Pass, or Soledad Canyon by this route. One other contemporary report will confirm this possibility existed.

Doctor McKee was the first of the Federal officers to report seeing the Texans coming, according to an August 1861 document he signed. At that time he still believed there was at least one infantry company acting as rear guard. He panicked immediately upon seeing the Texans, putting the whip to his buggy and swiftly heading in the direction of the crest of the hill. There he met Dr. Alden, who appears to have been tending the wounded in their ambulances. McKee reported:

> On getting within 6 or 7 miles of the Springs the Texans were reported in the rear. Ascending to the summit of the pass, asked Dr. Alden, of the Army, "Shall we go forward and bring back Major Lynde because the Texans are in our rear, or shall we stay back with our wounded and be taken prisoners?" On consultation, we concluded to go forward and tell Major Lynde, and try and get him back and protect his command. There was then but one company in the rear. Concluded to go after him. Drove after Lynde 6 miles in a buggy with two horses on a full run. He was then 5 or 6 miles in front of his whole command, with a company of Mounted Rifles under Mr. Cressey. Reported to him the Texans in our rear. He grinned in an imbecile way and said, "Ah, indeed!" and ordered the troops back. Drove back after him. Then I heard that Captain Gibbs was coming with a company of cavalry. McNally and his ambulance came up at this time. Order was then given to move into camp [at San Augustine Springs].[8]

Did McKee really believe one officer controlled the actions of all the rest? True, Major Lynde had overall authority. He alone was responsible for the success or failure of the overall mission. Yet, no commanding officer can be in all places at all times. The commander must have faith in the capabilities of his subordinates to obey orders and regulations as required. Lynde's subordinates had authority delegated to them to perform specific tasks in that column to the best of their abilities. Second Lieutenant Charles Stivers was in charge of the quartermaster and commissary wagons; 2[d] Lieutenant Cressey commanded the cavalry contingent; Captain Potter was responsible for protecting the front of the column with his two companies; Dr. Alden or Assistant Surgeon McKee was in charge of the medical supplies and the wounded; Lieutenant Crilly was responsible for the artillery, and for the safety of the wagons toward the rear. Whoever it was, Captain Stevenson or another, had responsibility for the rear guard and safety of the column from that direction.

Another witness saw the same sight and reported on it to Major Lynde only slightly later. He was Captain Alfred Gibbs, whom fate brought to this tragic scene. Gibbs arrived at the northern junction with the San Augustine road after Lynde and the front of the column had passed over the crest. He could scarcely believe what he saw, saying:

> On arriving at San Augustine Springs, or rather the Pass of La Cueva, 5 miles this side, I found Major Lynde's command in full retreat for Fort Stanton. I reported myself, with 35 men of Company I and 10 of Company G, Mounted Rifles - the last the escort to the mail I met upon the road, and which I ordered to join me—to Lieutenant Brooks, Major Lynde's adjutant, and with him proceeded 5 miles to the front, to report myself to Major Lynde, as directed in your instructions. I also reported to the Major that I had seen a force of Texans approaching, and that I thought they would molest our rear. Major Lynde asked what force I had, and I replied 70 men, all told. He said that there were two companies of infantry on rear guard in addition, and that would be sufficient. He then turned back and returned to San Augustine Springs.[9]

Gibbs's statement of meeting the column at the Pass of La Cueva is the only time this place is mentioned in any account. Down toward Soledad Canyon, some three or four miles from San Augustine Pass, is a very famous cave, called locally La Cueva. Can Alfred Gibbs have been referring to that well-known landmark? If he was, then Lynde's route was skirting the Organs rather than coming up from Las Cruces in the manner of Highway 70 today. Gibbs's comment also opens up the possibility that Baylor Pass could have been the route Lynde took to San Augustine Springs. For this account it is only important to note where the surrender

Regiment of Mounted Rifles Brevet-Captain Alfred Gibbs,
photographed in the rank of Brigadier General
U.S.A., American Civil War.
Courtesy: Massachusetts Commandery,
Military Order of the Loyal Legion and the
US Army Military History Institute.

site was rather than exactly how the troops got there. Using the Baylor and Gibbs data, Baylor Pass, if traversable by wagons in that day (it is not at present), could have been Lynde's route into the mountains. That pass fits Baylor's fifteen-mile distance and Gibbs's La Cueva designation much better than does San Augustine Pass. In addition there are natural springs in the area which Baylor might have diverted toward, whereas at San Augustine Pass there is only the spring near the Nike missile.

Unfortunately, the distance from the entrance to Baylor Pass and the distance from the crest of San Augustine Pass to the actual San Augustine Springs where Lynde surrendered is about the same. A ground examination of the two routes provided no clear winner, although Baylor Pass is more rugged and harder to imagine as being the route. A wagon road on the east side of Baylor Pass leads to a spring, but it was not the spring where Lynde surrendered. According to sources, that spring was not developed until the twentieth century. All in all, when the two possible routes are considered, San Augustine Pass has to be favored. Baylor Pass has too many unfavorable features, but it is hard to say what the Pass might have looked like in 1861.

If Isaac Lynde's column did not go through Baylor Pass, did Baylor, or part of his force, go through that pass, possibly cutting off the Federal column as a result? There are those who ardently subscribe to this theory. Some of the Texans may have gone through Baylor Pass. Baylor, however, is clear in saying he was following the tail of Lynde's column. Other sources, Gibbs, Crilly, and McKee, appear to say that the Rebel forces were seen at the rear of the column. There is not enough evidence to make an absolute statement one way or the other about Baylor Pass. This author can only say that, from visits to the pass, the topography would have to have been very different in 1861 to make that route viable.

In a second statement, given at Jefferson Barracks, Missouri, during a hearing into Gibbs's conduct, which he requested to clear his reputation following the surrender at San Augustine Springs, Captain Gibbs was a little clearer on the circumstances of his first meeting with Isaac Lynde. He said:

At noon on the 27th, when within 5 miles of the Springs, met Major Lynde's command, which had abandoned Fort Fillmore the night before. Rode forward and reported to Major Lynde's adjutant, Lieutenant Brooks, who told me that Major Lynde was encamped 5 miles in advance, at the Springs. Rode forward with the adjutant, and sent on an express that a party of the enemy were approaching from the rear. Came up to Major Lynde a quarter of a mile this side of the Springs with Lieutenant Cressey, returning to the rear with 40 men of the Mounted Rifles. Reported to Major Lynde and asked for orders. He told me that there were two companies of the Seventh Infantry in rear guard, and that they, with the Rifles, would protect the rear. Filled my canteen at the Springs; rejoined Major Lynde about 2 miles from it, returning to the front without his escort, which had gone to the rear. He told me to protect the rear with the infantry rear guard and the mounted force as long as I saw fit, and then return to the camp at the Springs. Rejoined the mounted force, then consisting of 70 men, and formed at the foot of the hill in front of the enemy. I found that the infantry rear guard was completely broken down by their long march and want of water; that I had nothing but the mounted force to rely upon.[10]

Lynde's memory of the arrival of Gibbs is different from either Gibbs or McKee, though perhaps reconcilable. His account may explain the presence of 1st Lieutenant Brooks on the Las Cruces side of the mountain at that time. Lynde said:

When I had nearly reached the Springs word was brought me that a mounted force was approaching in our rear; but it was believed to be Captain Gibbs, R.M.R., with his command, and soon after that supposition was confirmed by another express. On reaching the Springs I found the supply of water so small as to be insufficient for my command. After procuring all the water that could be transported by the men with me I started back to the main body. After riding some distance I became so much exhausted that I could not sit upon my horse, and the command proceeded without me, under the command of Lieutenant Cressey, R. M. R., and I returned to the Springs.[11]

Captain Gibbs might have been mistaken or misleading in his statement, when he said they personnally communicated on that first occasion. He may have forgotten that an express rider was the first communication. Conversely, Lynde could have forgotten a first meeting with Gibbs, which would make his memory faulty and Gibbs's correct. Whatever the case, it is sure that neither Gibbs, McKee, or Lynde knew the rear guard had collapsed into disarray due to the heat, rather than enemy action, when they first contacted each other. Gibbs did not question Lynde's opinion that the rear guard and Gibbs's horsemen should be able to save the day for the Federal column. They certainly should have been strong enough to do so. The R.M.R. horsemen Gibbs and Lynde referred to were Cressey's troopers, now combined with the newly arrived troopers of Gibbs's party. Alfred Gibbs, as a captain, immediately took command of all R.M.R. soldiers. Gibbs marched them toward the Confederates and the rear of the Federal column.

From his description we don't know where Captain Gibbs's force was when they first encountered Baylor's Texans. His words can be interpreted two ways. He was either on the west side of San Augustine Pass, where it starts to rise, or on the east side, some three to four miles from the location where Lynde was camped, which we will now for the first time begin to identify as the true San Augustine Springs. Baylor placed a Federal cavalry force, presumably that of Gibbs, at the crest of San Augustine Pass, retreating before him.

During the interval in which Captain Gibbs arrived on the scene, reported to Lynde in some fashion, then went back to the mountain, Baylor seems to have gone off to the secondary spring for water. How many of his troops he took there he does not say. What he did say is that after an interval at the secondary spring, where he captured some of what was probably the rear guard, he returned to the scene of disaster at the rear of the Federal column. Here, Baylor had to wait for Waller's troops to come all the way from Fort Fillmore. After their arrival, Baylor continued his mission of pressing the Federal column. Baylor stated:

After getting water for my men, I started in pursuit of the enemy, who had passed through San Augustine Pass. I was delayed for some time here waiting for Major Waller, who, mistaking my orders, had carried with him the whole command, except Captain Hardeman's company, to Fort Fillmore. So soon as they joined me I started in pursuit, and found the enemy's cavalry drawn up to cover the retreat of the infantry through the Pass. These I charged with Captain Hardeman's company. They retreated in haste, leaving behind them their wagons and artillery and all their supplies. Upon gaining the summit of the Pass, plain view of the road to the San Augustine Springs was presented. The road for 5 miles was lined with the fainting, famished soldiers, who threw down their arms as we passed and begged for water.[12]

Major Isaac Lynde was already on the other side of the mountain, perhaps even at the springs, when Baylor charged Gibbs's cavalry, and no doubt sure in his mind that all was still well with the rear. And why should he not have thought that? His strong rear guard numbered almost two hundred troops, including the cavalry, and should have savaged the Texas cavalry long before the charging horsemen, who had to ride uphill, reached them. All the rear guard had to do was form ranks and fire, reload and fire again, reload and fire again, when Baylor charged with Captain Hardeman's company. The slaughter to the horses alone would have been incredible. Two companies of infantry and a strong cavalry contingent armed with long-range rifles firing downhill at charging horsemen— not even a close contest if the infantry were properly led. The bloody American Civil War battles back East proved the logic of such tactics. Cavalry did not charge ready infantry willingly, not if they valued their lives.

Of course we now know the infantry rear guard was nowhere to be found. Where were the officers and NCOs of the rear guard when the time came for the guard to perform its simple military mission of slaughter? Where were the men? According to Baylor he found only confusion in the Federal ranks, basically an undisciplined, leaderless, rabble. There was no determinable infantry rear guard. Nor did Gibbs and his cavalry stand and fight Baylor, and that cavalry force was Lynde's last remaining hope.[13]

In his statement given at Jefferson Barracks in November 1861, Captain Alfred Gibbs added details about the moments before he made the decision to leave his rear-guard position and fall back on the springs, the sight of which Baylor commented on earlier. Captain Gibbs said:

> Four of Major Lynde's baggage wagons, filled with stores, and women and children, completely blocked the road. I requested Lieutenant Brooks to try to get a couple of the 12 pounder mountain howitzers that were fastened behind these wagons, and gave him men from my command for that purpose. It was found that the ammunition for these pieces was not in the wagons to which the pieces were fastened, and the effort failed. Finding that my force of 70 men, armed with rifles and pistols only, was opposed to the enemy's force of 300 men, similarly armed, with the addition of sabers, [which] was rapidly approaching, and the ground was favorable only for a single charge, I sent another message to Major Lynde, telling him of the enemy's near approach and their strength.[14]

Gibbs, in the tone of these statements, implied that an incompetent Major Isaac Lynde was merely waving aside any helpful suggestions and placing all his hopes on an infantry rear guard that, as Gibbs later noted, had disappeared. The artillery was also unusable, no ammunition being stored with the weapons. No doubt that was true as 2[d] Lieutenant Crilly, who was responsible for those wagons, also used them to haul the enlisted men's wives and children. There were not enough wagons to serve every need. Gibbs apparently made no attempt to find out where the ammunition was. Here it must be said that every officer involved in this hopeless fiasco had a stake in ensuring that Isaac Lynde took all blame for what happened on the road to San Augustine Springs. Their military reputations were on the line.

Major Lynde was to take responsibility for the infantry rear-guard not doing its job. Major Lynde was to take responsibility for 2[d] Lieutenant Crilly having no artillery ammunition handy. Major

Lynde was to take responsibility for Captain Gibbs abandoning the last strong rear-guard cavalry position and racing back down the hill without engaging the enemy with a single volley. Lynde was responsible, although he had no idea how many of his officers and men had failed in their duty. Yes, in respect to overall command, the commander is always responsible for the faults and failures of his subordinates.

The Army seems to have thought so. By crucifying Isaac Lynde, the United States Army avoided a situation which previously ruined the career of another of the Army's most promising officers, though not to the extent that Isaac Lynde suffered. That officer was J.V. Bomford, and he went on to have a distinguished, but unnoticed, career in the Regular Army after the Civil War. Lieutenant Richard H. Wilson, writing of Bomford about the year 1890 said:

> This distinguished officer, who had spent almost a lifetime in the Eighth, was one of the best known and most esteemed of the officers of the old [a]rmy. To a bravery in battle never surpassed by any one, he united a peculiar kindness and urbanity towards all those, of whatever rank, with whom he came in contact. With his high reputation in the old army and his estimable personal qualities, his failure to attain distinguished prominence in the War of the Rebellion has always been a matter of surprise and a subject for comment among those who knew and admired him. An explanation of this may, however, be found in the fact that, having surrendered in Texas in 1861 as a major of the 6th Infantry, his loyalty was for a time unreasonably suspected by the authorities.[15]

Bomford was held back during the Civil War because he was suspected of disloyalty due to his surrender in Texas at a time when there was no Civil War. Not treated as horribly as Isaac Lynde, Bomford's promising career was put on hold. He did not make colonel, let alone general, as most of his other promising contemporaries did. Captain Alfred Gibbs became a major general in the Union Army. So did Captain Joseph Haydn Potter. They were both deserving officers and had meritorious careers. Had

Major Isaac Lynde not taken *all* the blame, these officers would have faced conditions similar to those faced by Bomford. Lynde had to be the scapegoat for an Army command that did not do its job up and down the line from Winfield Scott and Abraham Lincoln, back down to Canby, Gibbs, and the commander of the infantry rear guard. Lynde was a convenient scapegoat for them all.

Our last view of the scene on the road to San Augustine Springs, through the eyes of the Confederate commander Colonel John Baylor, spoke of five miles of road "lined with the fainting, famished soldiers, who threw down their arms as we passed and begged for water." Baylor mentioned no rear guard of troops, their officer with sword raised preparing to give the command to fire as he charged. Baylor encountered no opposition as he rode through the ranks of the dispirited and broken-down troops. It is during this ride of victory that Captain Gibbs and others of rank in the column noticed the hard-charging Texans. Gibbs spoke of their presence in words of disdain aimed at Major Lynde, while Lynde had no idea that the rear guard had not obeyed his orders, nor in fact performed their duty as required under Army regulations governing a column on the move. That they were savaged by the sun and their weariness does not matter to Army regulations. Only the order matters, or at least it should when brought before a military court. This rear guard did not even try to perform their mission. Gibbs excused them by saying:

> It will be well here to mention that the infantry had been marched up to noon 20 miles without water, and that under the bushes by the side of the road over 450 men were lying, unable to rise or to carry their muskets, and useless and disorganized in every way. This was the rear guard on which I was ordered to rely. Major Lynde had not seen it for several hours.[16]

Lieutenant Francis Crilly provided some idea of how early in the day it really was when all this took place. He places the time at about 11:00 a.m. when discipline began to collapse and the troops, in effect, deserted in their craze to get out of the sun. Second Lieutenant Crilly must have known that eleven o'clock was very

A July New Mexico Sun   295

First Lieutenant Francis Crilly in 1893..
Courtesy: US Army Military History Institute.

early in a New Mexico July day. That sun was going to be a god deal hotter by afternoon. There was no Texas presence when he made this observation. Crilly continued:

> The writer [Crilly] with I Company, had charge of the train, and succeeded in getting the loaded wagons more than half-way up the mountains. Major Lynde's wagons, and those used by the laundresses, being light, got to the Springs early in the afternoon. The mules hauling the loaded wagons, being utterly used up, were unhooked and sent forward to water.[17]

Crilly may have confused the laundresses with the officers' wives, the years between the march and the early 1890s when the letter was written having brought confusion in his mind as to who was where. There may indeed have been laundresses at the head but there were also the wives and children of the principle leaders. If Crilly is to be credited, he observed the collapse of the rear guard without comment. Surely he realized what he saw. He did not mention that collapse, or the officers responsible, but he must have realized what it meant if the Confederates came upon them. If he did understand the consequences, he did not report the matter to Major Lynde. Instead, Lieutenant Crilly unharnessed the mules from at least some of the wagons and took them up the hill to seek water. The wagons were left in the road, abandoned, to be recovered at a later time when the mules were no longer broken down. If Crilly could move, and the mules could move, why couldn't the soldiers, or at least some of them, move toward water as well?

Captain Gibbs and his horsemen moved toward the rear of the column after his meeting with Lynde, in the direction of Baylor's oncoming force, according to his somewhat confusing words. Gibbs reported sighting the Confederates:

> On arriving at the mouth of the canyon I assumed command of the cavalry force, consisting of Companies F, B, and I, and a part of G, Mounted Rifles—70 men strong. The Texans, under Colonel Baylor and Major Waller, and about 320 strong [all cavalry], with some dismounted men, and what seemed to be a couple of pieces of artillery, at this time debouched from behind

the point of the hill below me to the left, and captured the beef cattle and my two wagons. I deployed 50 men as skirmishers, with 20 men as a reserve; but finding that I was entirely outflanked, I formed column of sections and prepared to charge with drawn pistols.[18]

Gibbs uses the figure of seventy men, but there may have been as many as ninety according to a later count. One can only wonder what he thought he was outflanked by. Of course this is standard military terminology when an officer is about to order a retreat. As with being outnumbered, having one's flank turned is the best possible excuse for backing up. Colonel John Baylor noticed Gibbs's cavalry about the same time but noted little attempt by Gibbs to impede the Texans' progress. Baylor said that when he charged, the cavalry rear guard simply fled. His words were:

> So soon as they joined me [Waller] I started in pursuit, and found the enemy's cavalry drawn up to cover the retreat of the infantry through the Pass. These I charged with Captain Hardeman's company. They retreated in haste, leaving behind them their wagons and artillery and all their supplies. Upon gaining the summit of the Pass, plain view of the road to the San Augustine Springs was presented.[19]

In effect Alfred Gibbs and his R.M.R. rear guard collapsed, as had the infantry. Captain Gibbs may have ordered pistols drawn but he never charged, never defended, and never fired a shot. The real truth may have been as Baylor said. The cavalry simply withdrew in haste. Why didn't Gibbs fire? Why didn't he dismount and use his long-range rifles against the inferior weaponry of the Texans? Such a response might have galvanized the fleeing column into some kind of action. Instead, he retreated—slowly as Gibbs puts it—quickly as Baylor tells it. In fact, during his after-action report Captain Gibbs placed the blame for his haste in withdrawing squarely on the shoulders of Major Isaac Lynde, those same shoulders where every other officer in the command was looking for a clean spot. Gibbs said:

Before doing this I sent back word to Major Lynde, by an intelligent man, the exact state of affairs. He brought back word to protect the wagons, if possible, and then to fall back on the camp. As most of the men had thrown away their muskets and gone to the front [toward San Augustine Springs], I retreated slowly and in good order, forming in line three times, and keeping the Texans in check by causing them also to form line. On arriving at the crest of the Pass I galloped into camp and reported myself to Major Lynde as ready for action, and asked where I should take position.[20]

Captain Gibbs had to gallop over three miles, past panicked and thirsty soldiers, to reach Major Lynde and the lead elements. Gibbs should have taken his rear guard position up on the crest of the ridge, where he belonged. In effect, Lynde ordered Gibbs to fight for the wagons and, only then, fall back to the camp at San Augustine Springs. There was not a single cap popped on a single pistol. Gibbs fell back, racing his seventy to ninety troopers down the hill to the Springs where Lynde waited, perhaps wondering why he heard no firing. Gibbs reported he was simply looking for new orders and to explain the tactical situation to his commander. By abandoning the crest of the ridge and the last place where a rear guard might have been able to hold off the Texans until Lynde could determine what to do, *as Army regulations required him to do*, Captain Gibbs in effect drew the Texans downhill with him to their glorious victory.

Second Lieutenant Francis Crilly was witness to the Texas approach as well, but made no mention of Captain Gibbs's headlong retreat down to the Springs. The last mention of Crilly, who was nowhere near his Company 'I' troops as he was supposed to be, said he was leading mules to the springs to get water. He had plenty of soldiers to do that job. After arriving at the springs he too chose to gather up canteens and take them to the rear for the thirsty soldiers. Crilly noted many years later:

I got about a hundred canteens, with which I went forward in an old buggy. Having filled them, I returned and gave them to the half-dazed men stumbling on their way to the Springs. When I arrived, about a half a mile from the crest of the mountain, the head of the mounted Texas force appeared. I turned back down the mountain with the horses at a run, and found about ten men of my company who had already aligned themselves with the other companies.[21]

Can Gibbs have passed Crilly in his headlong flight, perhaps causing Crilly to flee as well? It is certainly odd that Crilly made no mention of Gibbs. Of course he wrote his story some time in the early 1890s; the event may have slipped his mind. It would have been soldierly had he fired at least one shot at the approaching enemy, but, like Gibbs, he chose not to do so.

Doctor McKee didn't fire any bullets either, for all his talk, although he reached a low point in defending Captain Gibbs's abandonment of his rear-guard position. McKee lauded the action of Captain Gibbs and stated for the first time that he couldn't fire at the Texans. Lynde had ordered him not to fire. In fact, no such order was ever given to anybody. Regardless, McKee stated:

> Captain Alfred Gibbs, with his company of Regt. Mounted Riflemen, on his way down to Fillmore from Fort Craig with beef cattle, seeing our dust off toward the mountains, unfortunately joined us at this time, fell into the trap, and was compelled to accept our fate. Everything was in unutterable and indescribable confusion. Ruin was on every side. The enemy was steadily advancing. The only temporary security and intervening guard was that Captain Gibbs kept his company deployed every now and then in the line of skirmishers, as he covered our retreat, retarding the advance of the enemy. Not a shot was fired, and I understood afterwards that this was Lynde's positive order.[22]

Gibbs reported no order not to fire. Crilly reported no order not to fire. No officer reported an order not to fire. Canby never mentioned it in all his correspondence concerning the surrender. Baylor and the *Mesilla Times* newspaper never mentioned learning of such an order There was no order not to fire, except in the hate-filled mind of Doctor McKee. Here Doctor McKee wanted to praise Gibbs, and to ignore the fact that he abandoned his rear-guard position, and to once again lay all the blame on Major Isaac Lynde. In his official report after the incident McKee was more calm and made no mention of any order given by Isaac Lynde not to fire on the enemy. He said, "Went back to camp, Captain Gibbs protecting the rear. He came up on our left, and but for him every man would have been taken before we reached camp."[22]

Baylor observed the headlong flight of the R.M.R. rear guard led by Gibbs. He even commented on the fact that when he charged them, the rear guard "retreated in haste." Baylor made no comment on having to deploy his cavalry following a deployment by Gibbs. As the Confederates rode over and through the San Augustine Pass, the last natural defensive obstacle on their way to reaching San Augustine Springs, Baylor reported:

> At the Springs the enemy had drawn up in line of battle some 200 or 300 strong. I ordered Major Waller to charge with Captain Hardeman's company until he reached the end of the line of straggling soldiers, then to form and cut them off from the main body. I followed, disarming the enemy, and as fast as our jaded horses would go.[24]

This was a good order. Baylor made sure the soldiers, an indeterminate number of whom had thrown down their arms while still moving toward the springs, were cut off from Lynde's command. Had these columns of defeated men continued forward toward the springs they would either have impeded the line of fire or in other ways become a nuisance. By stopping their progress forward Baylor could better assess what was waiting for him at the springs. He must have been nervous at this point. If his estimate of two hundred or three hundred effectives was correct, such a force was fully able to repel a charge by his lightly armed cavalry command. In fact, there were only some one hundred effective troops at the springs and, as Baylor approached, these troops, at last, rapidly formed a line of defense. The extra people in Baylor's estimate must have been the many women and children at the front of the column, the hospital wagons, and wounded, Gibbs's now dismounted and out of action R.M.R. horsemen, and scattered ineffective and heat-prostrated infantrymen who had managed to get to the springs but were by then unarmed.

And what of the man who was to be blamed for this total disaster, the man called "imbecile," "coward," and even "traitor" for what was about to happen. Major Isaac Lynde was at San Augustine Springs when the last of his covering rear guard of cavalry suddenly rushed into camp, with the Confederates close on their heels. Even at this late stage, Lynde reacted correctly, bringing his remaining infantry force to the proper formation to fight. How surprised he must have been to find out so late that the entire rear guard failed to do what they had to do if the column were to survive. Lynde said:

> Soon after it was reported to me that a part of the teams had given out and could not be brought up, and that large numbers of the infantry had become totally overpowered with the intense heat. At this time an express from Captain Gibbs reported that eight companies of mounted men, supported by artillery and a large force of infantry, were approaching our rear guard. I had the "Call to arms" sounded, and found that I could not bring more than 100 men of the infantry battalion on parade. Captain Gibbs, with a mounted force, now rode into camp, and stated to me that eight companies of mounted Texans (supported by a regiment of infantry, more or less) were approaching; that they had driven in or captured our rear guard and the men that had given out in the rear. Three of the four mountain howitzers that we had with us were with the wagons in the rear and captured. They were guarded by one company of infantry acting as artillery. Captain Gibbs also reported that his company, men and horses, had been without water for twenty-four hours.[25]

At last Isaac Lynde knew what happened in the rear of his column. Should he personally have been back there in the rear whipping the men into order and forcing them to do their job? Of course not. Other officers should have been there. The question which is no longer answerable is whether those officers were ever truly back there. Crilly abandoned his men. If others did as well, why do we find no historical data mentioning them at any time or point during the march. Captain Stevenson, 1st Lieutenant Plummer, 1st Lieutenant Hancock, 2d Lieutenant Stivers—where were they? Was Stevenson in command of the infantry rear guard? He was senior officer. Could only four officers, with the help of the NCOs, control a disintegrating mob? There were supposed to be twenty-one officers with seven companies of infantry, and there were only six. With 1st Lieutenant Brooks serving as adjutant, his company had no officer on the march. Was it Lynde's fault that an adequate cadre of officers was not in place?

Was every decision Lynde made incompetent, cowardly and imbecilic? One can argue against the retreat from Mesilla as being premature, or against the decision to abandon Fort Fillmore, but Lynde's actions on the road to San Augustine Springs appear completely correct, although open to changes given a different commander and a different personality.

Lynde had no control over the weather, the single and most important factor in what, up until then, had been a total disaster. One day before, or one day after, the skies might have been filled with rain, or clouds covering the landscape from horizon to horizon, lowering the heat, dimming the bright of the white sky, so that one's eyes could see again. On such a day as that the rear-guard might have done its job, even without the proper complement of officers, butchering Baylor's horsemen if they attempted to be so foolhardy as to frontally charge prepared infantry. The cavalry might have been there as well, ready as a second layer of the rear guard. On such a day as that the officers and NCOs could have had the men do anything they wanted. July 27, 1861 was not such a day.

NOTES - Chapter 13

1. Lynde to Assistant Adjutant General, August 7, 1861, M1120, Rolls 13/14.
2. *Mesilla Times*, Number 41, Mesilla, Arizona, July 27, 1861.

3. Horn & Wallace, Baylor to Washington, September 21, 1861, pp. 34-37.

4. McKee, p. 26.

5. Lynde to Assistant Adjutant General, August 7, 1861, M1120, Rolls 13/14.

6. Crilly, p. 10.

7. Horn & Wallace, Baylor to Washington, September 21, 1861, pp. 34-37.

8. McKee to Assistant Adjutant General, August 7, 1861, M1120, Rolls 13/14.

9. Horn & Wallace, Gibbs to Assistant Adjutant General, August 6, 1861, pp. 22, 23.

10. Horn & Wallace, Statement of Captain Gibbs, November 7, 1861, pp. 24-27.

11. Lynde to Assistant Adjutant General, August 7, 1861, M1120, Rolls 13/14.

12. Horn & Wallace, Baylor to Washington, September 21, 1861, pp. 34-37.

13. Horn & Wallace, Gibbs to Assistant Adjutant General, August 6, 1861, pp. 22, 23.

14. Horn & Wallace, Statement of Captain Gibbs, November 7, 1861, pp. 24-27.

15. Report of Lieutenant Richard Wilson, Adjutant 8th U. S. Infantry, date unspecified. The report was part of an appendix to the main report of the Circular-Publication Committee, The Military Service Institution, Governor's Island, N.Y. H., Nov. 10, 1889.

16. Horn & Wallace, Statement of Captain Gibbs Statement, November 7, 1861, pp. 24-27.

17. Francis Crilly, p.10.

18. Horn & Wallace, Gibbs to Assistant Adjutant General, August 6, 1861, pp. 22, 23.

19. Horn & Wallace, Baylor to Washington, September 21, 1861, pp. 34-37.

20. Horn & Wallace, Gibbs to Assistant Adjutant General, August 6, 1861, pp. 22, 23.

21. Francis Crilly, p. 10.

22. McKee, p. 27.

23. McKee to Assistant Adjutant General, August 16, 1861, M1120, Rolls 13/14.

24. Horn & Wallace, Baylor to Washington, September 21, 1861, pp. 34-37

25. Lynde to Assistant Adjutant General, Dept. of New Mexico August 7, 1861, 171120, Rolls 13/14.

14

SURRENDER AT SAN AUGUSTINE SPRINGS

What happened next is well known. Isaac Lynde chose to surrender his entire force without fighting. Before we examine the actual surrender, one questions begs an answer. Where were the 7th Infantry troops under Lynde's command physically located at the moment of surrender? According to most sources they were at a place called San Augustine Springs, or on the dirt track heading toward that place. But where exactly was that site in July 1861? There are many springs in the area, one of which still holds the modern map title to the name San Augustine Spring. The words of Lynde, Baylor, Gibbs, even McKee belie that location as being correct.

Only one place fits all descriptions. That place is now the headquarters of the Cox Ranch, just outside the boundaries of the Federal Government's White Sands Missile Range. Although the author is in doubt about some of the information concerning the history of the Cox Ranch, and especially the history of the area around the headquarters, there seems little doubt that it was here Lynde surrendered. First, there has always been an extensive series of springs in the area of the current ranch house. These springs were well known in the days of Spanish colonial administration. The springs were a stop on the salt route that ran from Paso del Norte north and linked up with routes to the east, north and west.

Although now known as the Cox/San Augustine Ranch Headquarters, in the 1850s and 1860s the area must have been called San Augustine Springs. In fact, during the 1870s a town sprang up on the site of the current ranch house. This community had a post office and a hotel, and used the name San Augustine. The post office existed there from 1876 to 1888. Water from the springs must have been sufficient in the period to support a large community, otherwise the town would not have been located at that spot.

Mr. Rob Cox and his wife Murnie, owners of the ranch, allowed the author to visit several times. The purpose was to try to locate the surrender site through finding possible reminders of the two-day sojourn the 7th Infantry and the Texans made near the springs following the surrender. The extent of the springs is hard to imagine, especially for a spot so deep in the heart of the desert as this one. The area where the water once flowed copiously has lessened in modern times, but still supports several enormous ash and oak trees that Mr. Cox believes may be three hundred to four hundred years old. This extensive grove of trees, which extends hundreds of yards from east to west, must have sheltered the travelers of one hundred fifty years ago as they might the modern visitor today. There is, however, no mention made by Lynde, Baylor, Gibbs, or any of the others of these trees. Hence, there is little proof save for the springs themselves, and their history of providing water to the thirsty among the Indian, Spaniard, Mexican, and European-American travelers, that this was the place an army laid down its arms.

Three trips produced little in the way of visible proof that Lynde and Baylor were there. A single .58 caliber Minie Ball of the period and two pieces of china which are of a type similar to that found at Fort Fillmore were located. These, along with numerous and varied spent cartridge cases from later years, including military rounds, were the extent of finds near the springs themselves. Of course the leaf packing is deep there and 1861 was a long time ago. In addition, many travelers have visited and left their mark, as did floods from the mountains and the activities of the ranching and town communities. All impacted the topography since Lynde's visit. An orchard once stood on one possible location for the surrender site.

The many rock and adobe ruins at the springs are signs of man's long history of occupation. Perhaps as early as 1800 or as late as 1865, a large adobe complex of buildings and corrals was constructed at the springs themselves, rather than up on the plateau where the town of San Augustine once stood and where the Cox ranch house stands today. A photograph from 1910 shows this structure, perhaps a mission or presidio, as well as other storage and housing facilities which have since collapsed into ruin. Only a great mound of adobe and a few standing rock walls are all that is left of a complex which some believe was standing when Lynde and Baylor visited. If these structures were there in 1861, neither Lynde or Baylor mentioned their presence. There is also the story of an early ranch house which supposedly existed at that time on the plateau where the Cox residence now stands.

Examination of the area near the old adobe structure built near the springs produced Spanish or Mexican artifacts, including a bridle rosette with a design, an 1866 1/4 Real coin from the state of Chihuahua, and the remains of a coin purse, as well as numerous square nails of the type used at Fort Fillmore and other places in New Mexico during the 1850s and 1860s, following the American occupation. The author, contrary to the story, does not believe this adobe building or the ranch house were there when Lynde came with his troops. The 1866-dated coin found at the base of one of the walls, and the type of nails used in the construction, are not conducive to a dating back to Spanish or Mexican Colonial periods. A final answer awaits future field work by experts.

The author believes the actual surrender site is not in the main San Augustine Springs area, but on the plateau just above where the Cox ranch house now stands. Given the minuscule information provided by Lynde, McKee, Baylor, and Gibbs, as well as Crilly, the most likely spot would be in the vicinity of the Cox residence. From there a route to the springs is readily available, so Captain Alfred Gibbs could water his horses without disturbing the troops on the plateau above, or knowing the exact circumstances of the coming

View of San Augustine Pass from the Cox Ranch, June 2001. The pass is in the mountainous area just above the car, a distance of almost four miles.
Courtesy: Author's collection.

surrender, which he did not. Looking west toward San Augustine Pass from the ranch house, one can visualize the situation as described in the records and can almost see the troops trudging down from those heights.

Before further examination of this theory we must return to 1861 and the situation as it developed on the wagon road from the Pass to San Augustine Springs. Isaac Lynde begins the description. "About 6 miles before reaching the Springs commences a short ascent to a pass in the Organ Mountains, and here the men and teams suffered severely with the intense heat and want of water, many men falling and unable to proceed."[1]

The distance from the crest of the modern San Augustine Pass to the Cox ranch house on the east side is about four miles. Indeed, as Major Lynde described it, about two miles from the crest on the west there is a sharp rise upward which gets steeper and where the Federal troops must have suffered greatly. It was on this rise that most of the wagon equipment, including the artillery, was abandoned, and the mules brought forward to water. This equipment never reached San Augustine Springs.

Baylor said, "Upon gaining the summit of the Pass, plain view of the road to the San Augustine Springs was presented. The road for 5 miles was lined with the fainting, famished soldiers, who threw down their arms as we passed and begged for water."[2]

The five miles Baylor mentioned must have included the steep stretch described by Lynde and a considerable portion of the trail to what is now the Cox Ranch. When standing at a point just past the summit at San Augustine Pass today one can still see what Baylor saw when he looked downward toward where the ranch house now stands. At the crest, the entire five miles he mentioned can almost be seen, east and west. Baylor could see the full extent of the spread-out Federal column, some of whom must have still been on both sides of the pass at that time. The current dirt road heading for the ranch house is not the same as it was in 1861. Mr. Cox indicated that the old road lay to the west of the modern track. Certainly the San Augustine Pass has changed greatly, what with a four-lane paved highway now present rather than a dirt track, and the roof of the pass lowered with explosives to create a smoother transition.

McKee also commented on a similar distance, "Drove after Lynde 6 miles in a buggy with two horses on a full run. He was then 5 or 6 miles in front of his whole command, with a company of Mounted Rifles under Mr. Cressey. Reported to him the Texans on our rear. He grinned in an imbecile way and said, 'Ah, indeed!' and ordered the troops back. Drove back after him."[3]

McKee appeared to be talking about the same two-mile stretch up to the crest and the four miles down to the springs as Lynde described. If so, Lynde must already have been at the San Augustine Springs when McKee made his hasty trip in his buggy from the rear of the column to the front. His description of the column is also similar to Baylor's. Both saw and passed by the same struggling mass of troops on their way up to the crest of the pass, and then down the four miles to the springs.

Captain Gibbs's descriptions are confusing, adding fuel to the mystery of the actual surrender site. Stripping away all but the basics of where he thought he was, Alfred Gibbs confirmed, "At noon on the 27th, when within 5 miles of the Springs, met Major Lynde's command, which had abandoned Fort Fillmore the night before. Rode forward and reported to Major Lynde's adjutant, Lieutenant Brooks, who told me that Major Lynde was encamped 5 miles in advance, at the Springs."[4]

Gibbs placed himself on the San Augustine Pass road about five miles from the springs. If the others were even close, Lynde, McKee, or Baylor, then Gibbs's comment puts the estimate of distance to the springs in the same ballpark as the others.

Second Lieutenant Francis Crilly, who had been shepherding the wagons hauling the artillery up the mountain is in range of the others as far as estimates of distance from the western base of San Augustine Pass to San Augustine Springs, and provides the best description. In his 1892 report to the Circular Publication Committee of the Military Service Institution, Crilly said, "The command started about one A.M., following the road along the Rio Grande to Las Cruces, and thence easterly to the Organ

Mountains, about twenty miles distant, San Augustine Springs being at the foot of the easterly slope, possibly three or four miles from the crest."[5]

Following a theoretical road from the crest of the San Augustine Pass, as Crilly describes the distance, would put a traveler right at the Cox ranch house and in the immediate area of the springs which allowed that ranch house to be built, and also later sustained a town.

Having resolved to this author's satisfaction the surrender site, it is time to turn to the surrender itself and try to understand what happened. Let us begin with the views on the surrender promulgated by Doctor McKee. His is the most vile and venom-filled tale—much longer than the rest and filled with negative descriptive adjectives—and, when all is reported, a goodly number of lies as usual. McKee, whose commentary was viewed as absolute truth when the history of the 7th Infantry Regiment in the nineteenth century was compiled at the beginning of the twentieth century, raged:

> In a short time the Confederates or Texans were seen advancing in line of battle to the number of some three hundred. Our men, numbering at least five hundred infantry and cavalry, trained, disciplined, and well drilled soldiers, were drawn up in an opposite line, forming a striking contrast to the badly-armed and irregular command of Texans.[6]

Was Dr. McKee actually there that day? It is sometimes difficult, except in isolated cases such as this, to tell when he was lying or exaggerating and when he was being truthful. Usually, the good doctor appears most truthful when he is not talking about Isaac Lynde. McKee is included in this book because his influence over historians has been paramount for over one hundred years. He influenced the way in which West Point and the 7th Infantry Regiment view Isaac Lynde to this day.

In the above paragraph a biased Dr. McKee placed five hundred ready and heavily armed Federal soldiers opposite the Texas

Cavalry at San Augustine Springs. He must have known he was lying when he wrote the words. There were not even five hundred Federal infantry in the whole command which started out from Fort Fillmore, let alone the reduced force which made its way to San Augustine Springs that boiling hot day. Unless, of course, one counts the women and children. The total number of soldiers in Lynde's com-mand, aside from estimates other people provided, has not been discussed. This omission was made deliberately. Before giving the official totals there is a need, because of the savage manner in which Major Isaac Lynde has been treated in history, to give estimates as others thought them to be.

Having given Lynde a numerical and readiness advantage at San Augustine Springs, McKee continued, "The enemy advanced to within three hundred yards of us, when Lynde raised and sent out a flag of truce, which was met and negotiations commenced with a view to surrender. They demanded an unconditional surrender, the same that Lynde had demanded of them at Mesilla."[7]

The outnumbered Confederates, according to McKee, are begged for the right to surrender by the commander of the Federal troops which then outnumbered them; their conditions—unconditional surrender.

Captain Gibbs, whose rapid race down the mountain to the springs allowed the Texans to advance to within threatening range, did not specify numbers when he made his after-action report on August 6. His words, however, do not point out the defection of the rear guard nor of any other soldiers who were then in the hands of the Texas cavalry as prisoners. He too wrote as if the entire 7th Infantry Regiment were arrayed before Baylor, flags flying, buttons highly polished, weapons ready. Gibbs wrote:

> Part of the infantry companies were already formed and men were rapidly falling into ranks. Major Lynde told me to dismount and water my men and horses. As we had been twenty-four hours without water I did so, and was ready in fifteen minutes for duty. The Texans then began to form on the plateau a quarter of a mile in our rear, and I saw Lieutenant Brooks ride out towards them. Major Lynde at this time sent

me word that I could leave for Fort Stanton, but before I could get a sack of flour and a side of bacon as rations for my men Colonel Baylor had arrived, the surrender had been agreed upon by Major Lynde himself without consulting a single officer, and I was ordered by Major Lynde not to attempt to escape. Upon being informed of the surrender, every officer in the command protested against it; but it was of no avail, and the command of seven companies of the Seventh Infantry and three companies of Rifles were voluntarily surrendered without striking a blow.[8]

At a Court of Inquiry held in November 1861, at Jefferson Barracks, Missouri, which was held not for Isaac Lynde but for Alfred Gibbs, Captain Gibbs changed his story in significant ways. He may have realized by then how bad his conduct looked, in that he had supposedly been responsible for the rear guard after the infantry collapsed and he had not fired a single shot at the enemy, nor held his position when challenged by Baylor's troops. He had also made an earlier statement that sounded very much like he had panicked in the face of the enemy (as Baylor stated) and had "at the crest of the pass galloped into camp." Making himself and his action more heroic in the Jefferson Barracks version, Gibbs reported:

> I kept deploying into line, and by rapid formations gaining ground by our superior drill, to allow the main force in camp in front to form before I reached them. I then rode rapidly to the front [toward San Augustine Springs], and reported to Major Lynde with my command that the enemy were about 2 miles in the rear and rapidly advancing. I asked him where I should take up my position. He told me that I might water my command and horses. Time, 20 hours without water. The Springs being made, while I was doing so Major Lynde sent me an order not to move. While watering, Major Lynde sent me word that I could leave for Fort Stanton if I chose. Before I could mount I received another order not to move from camp. I went towards him, distance about 100 yards, and saw him in conversation with two mounted officers, whom I did not know. The enemy at that time were in line of battle about a quarter of a mile to the rear. I heard Major Lynde say, "I agree to these terms," and I called to some of the officers to

come up. When we came up, all the officers being present, I think, Major Lynde said: "Colonel Baylor, to avoid bloodshed, I conditionally surrender this whole force to you, on condition that officers and their families shall be protected from insult and private property be respected.[9]

Captain Alfred Gibbs had plenty of opportunities to strike a blow up at the pass when acting as rear guard and did not. His race into the springs, which he now gently termed moving "rapidly to the front," a very cute choice of words, as if he were going in the direction of an enemy, merited at least a court of inquiry into why he did that maneuver, or a court-martial. Lynde had not changed his orders. In this statement Captain Gibbs's only mission was to put all the blame on Major Isaac Lynde for actions taken or not taken by others, including himself. If it is read as written, without other facts, one would have to assume that Major Lynde surrendered the entire 7th Infantry Regiment, lined up and fully arrayed for battle, weapons charged and ready. Gibbs also changed his story in another way. In this second version he and his cavalry troopers were still down the hill at the springs watering their animals when Lynde surrendered, rather than with the infantry and ready to fight.

McKee and Gibbs may have obtained their numbers from the *Mesilla Times*. A secessionist newspaper to its very core, the *Mesilla Times* invented what it couldn't expand from the basic information. Crowing loudly, the *Times* said:

> Major Lynde was camped near the San Augustine Springs and had still some four hundred [McKee said 500] men with him who formed in battle array on the appearance of the Confederate troops. Advance was made to charge on them by our troops, and they had reached within 300 yards, with eager spirits for the fray, when a flag of truce was raised by the U.S. column, desiring to know on what condition our commander would receive a surrender. The reply was, an unconditional surrender —the same terms they had endeavored to dictate to the Confederate forces. This was sought to be modified by the U.S. Commander, which request was refused further than

they could be allowed two hours to remove their women and children to a place of safety. The U.S. Commander finally agreed to an unconditional surrender.

Although the Confederate forces were advancing to the charge the number of men was concealed by clouds of dust. Captain Hardeman's company being considerably in advance of the others, the surrender was actually made to the gallant Col. Waller, with 85 men under the command of that company. In brief, during this day 11 Companies of U.S. regular troops, mounted and foot, mustering 700 effective men, surrendered to 280 Confederates, 4 pieces of cannon, arms, equipments, 220 cavalry horses, mules and wagons, and 270 head of beef cattle. The men and officers were disappointed in one thing alone—that the victory was so easily won.

Of the 11 companies which surrendered, three were of the Regiment of Mounted Riflemen, and eight companies of infantry, one or two companies of the 5th and the remainder of the 7th Regiment.

All these important movements and the great success, have been made and gained without the loss of one drop of blood on the Confederate side.[10]

It is not so much that most of this is a pack of small patriotic lies, the problem is that whoever wrote the article was obviously not on the scene and certainly received a confused account of what he wanted to hear. The *Times* provides Major Lynde with seven hundred men total, four hundred still fit for battle as the Texas forces charged down across the foothills towards the springs. Where did the *Times* get such numbers? That, we do not know.

In fact, there were about five hundred soldiers spread out along the road to San Augustine Springs, 7th Infantry and Mounted Rifles together. The source for the total and the approximate numbers will be discussed momentarily. McKee must have known the total. He used the number five hundred when he described the number of Federal soldiers lined up and ready to do their duty, flags flying, soldierly in every way, when Lynde surrendered.

The mention of the presence of 5th Infantry troops is a mystery that has been repeated over and over. McKee and Lydia Lane both

The huge ash tree at San Augustine Springs (in
background) that might be three-hundred years old.
To give some idea of the size of the tree,
the American flag stands over six feet.
Courtesy: Author's collection.

repeated the story of the presence of the phantom 5th Infantrymen, as reported in the secessionist *Mesilla Times*. It is suspected Lydia Lane took her 5th Infantry presence directly from McKee, who took his from the Rebel newspaper. The *Mesilla Times* also included an eleventh company which was not there as well. Perhaps we can charge these lapses in truth to media license. Major Gibbs was more accurate than any of the other detractors. He stated that only a "part of the infantry companies" were on line, but hinted that the numbers were well on the side of the Regulars.

With political axes to grind, careers to save, and, in some cases, a great deal of time passing, numbers are bound to be remembered differently. Indeed, Colonel Baylor, whom the *Times* reporter didn't even have at the scene of the surrender, made a different claim for numbers. He said:

> At the Springs the enemy had drawn up in line of battle some 200 or 300 strong. I ordered Major Waller to charge with Captain Hardeman's company until he reached the end of the line of straggling soldiers, then to form and cut them off from the main body. I followed, disarming the enemy, and as fast as our jaded horses would go. On reaching Captain Hardeman's company, who were formed, I saw Major Waller and Captain Hardeman riding into the enemy lines. I was in a few moments sent for by Major Lynde, who asked upon what terms I would allow him to surrender. I replied that the surrender must be unconditional. To this Major Lynde assented, asking that private property should be respected. The articles of capitulation were signed, and the order given for the enemy to stack arms.[11]

Baylor's numbers are at least a little closer to the truth, although they still appear high. The surrender document itself, which we will examine momentarily, agrees with Colonel Baylor's statement as to private property being respected. He may have mistaken two hundred or three hundred people, physical bodies, including women, children, hired teamsters, etc., for troops at that distance, and later did not correct his first impression.

We have now heard from most available sources as to the numbers of Federal troops who were at San Augustine Springs in the moments just before the surrender, save for two other individuals, young 2^d Lieutenant Francis Crilly, who was there on the scene, and Major Isaac Lynde himself. Fortunately for history, Crilly took time to count. Here is what he reported seeing after discovering the Texas cavalry to his front, as he took canteens back up the hill to the thirsting soldiers of his regiment:

> When I arrived, about half a mile from the crest of the mountain, the head of the mounted Texas force appeared. I turned back down the mountain with the horses at a run, and found about ten men of my company who had already aligned themselves with the other companies. My recollection is that there were ninety men of the regiment in line. There would have been no question of their resisting to the last man, except that back of them, huddled around the Springs, there were thirty or forty officers' and soldiers' wives and children, who would have been nearly all killed or wounded at the first volley of the Texas forces, so short was the range.[12]

This statement may be as true as any encountered so far. The situation is right, the numbers are very close to what might be expected, and Crilly had no particular ulterior motive. Second Lieutenant Crilly did not include the seventy troopers of the R.M.R. who were not on line, but watering their animals down at the springs, preparing to leave for Fort Stanton. Only some ninety infantrymen of Captain Joseph Haydn Potter's two company advance guard, plus a few others, were on line.

There is further proof that the women and children were there and in danger, and also corroboration for the number Crilly gave in his statement. Second Lieutenant Crilly gave Lynde short shrift for getting the 7th into its predicament in the first place, but he did not crucify his commanding officer through invention, as McKee, Gibbs, the *Mesilla Times,* and Lydia Lane did.

Before reporting what Lynde said about the surrender, two additional statements, both made following the great American Civil War, should be noted. The first was in a document outlining the history of the 1st Artillery Regiment as of the year 1892. In that document Major William L. Haskin described the situation during the first months of 1861, as the race to the American Civil War was only beginning. Haskin said:

> The excitement throughout the South at this time in regard to the secession of the States bid fair to lead to violent seizure of public property, and made it necessary for individual commanders to judge for themselves in many cases as to the proper course to pursue for the protection of the public property under their charge or the preservation of their commands.[13]

Haskin probably never knew of Major Isaac Lynde but he put on paper the dilemma Lynde faced. His government not yet at war (to his knowledge), what actions should Lynde have taken? One can only wonder how others might "judge for themselves in many cases as to the proper course to pursue." Baylor's South was indeed in a turmoil of excitement over secession, and had been for months. Many Southerners considered themselves at war, long before those in the North. Baylor crossed the line into improper action for a commander of troops whose government was not yet formally at war with the enemy; Baylor at that time could not have known of Bull Run or Lincoln's War Congress, et al. He was simply chasing Yankees, the breed of fellow Americans who had so often tormented the South and Texas over the condition of slavery and states rights.

A second document, written at about the same time as the one by Major Haskins, came even closer in defining the situation as Major Isaac Lynde had to view it. Lieutenant A.B. Johnson, 7th Infantry Regiment, defined exactly the situation as it was on July 27, 1861. Nevertheless, Johnson vilified Lynde in his brief history of the 7th Infantry, using Doctor McKee's book as his primary source. He didn't hesitate to use the word "cowardly" when referring to Lynde's actions at San Augustine Springs. While trying to destroy Major Lynde's reputation for the benefit of other late nineteenth century 7th Infantry officers, Johnson perhaps inadvertently described how Isaac Lynde must have seen the situation, and acted. Lieutenant Johnson said:

The Seventh Infantry, with a view to a change of stations to the States, had been ordered to concentrate at Fort Fillmore, then commanded by Major Isaac Lynde, 7th Infantry. Here all was doubt and anxiety. No authentic information of the intended policy of the government had been received, and the mail and couriers brought only the sad news of the continued secession of States, and the general inertness and doubtful course of the government.[14]

Did Johnson realize the dichotomy he had just revealed? He had accused Lynde of being a coward and then perfectly described the dilemma Lynde faced. Lynde did not possess the knowledge available to even the simplest of citizens in the East, where terrible acts were being committed in the name of Union and States Rights. On the site of San Augustine Springs that July 27, Isaac Lynde could only use what he knew. Johnson was correct. What was Lynde to do, owing to the "general inertness and doubtful course of the government?" Lynde had attacked fellow American citizens at Mesilla without a formal declaration of war. That was an act as politically charged as Baylor's invasion. How could Lynde know his career was not over the moment he attacked? Lowly Major Lynde could even have been blamed for starting the American Civil War! For all he knew, Lincoln and the Republican Party had decided to allow the South to leave peacefully, rather than fight to get them back. The only precedents Isaac Lynde had were the two independent surrenders of the 3d and 8th Infantry Regiments in Texas without a fight. General David Twiggs, Major C.C. Sibley, and Brevet-Lieutenant Colonel L.V.E. Reeve were the officers Major Lynde had to emulate, not the officers who had just fought at Bull Run a few days before.

Major Isaac Lynde's words telling of the surrender are enlightening. He came to the conclusion that there was no hope in resisting. He also gave hints of something more important, that the officers in his command had not obeyed the orders given them when the march began. The breaking of the rear guard, which he refused to believe had simply disappeared, was the final blow. He thought they had resisted, and were simply overwhelmed by the force of superior numbers. His estimates of the strength of the Texas forces show a totally different intelligence picture than was the reality. Somebody had either lied to him or his personal estimates were off the mark. In his words Lynde sounds neither imbecilic, cowardly, or traitorous.

Soon after it was reported to me that a part of the teams had given out and could not be brought up, and that large numbers of the infantry had become totally overpowered with the intense heat. At this time an express from Captain Gibbs reported that eight companies of mounted men, supported by artillery and a large force of infantry, were approaching our rear guard. I had the "Call to arms" sounded, and found that I could not bring more than 100 men of the infantry battalion on parade. Captain Gibbs, with a mounted force, now rode into camp, and stated to me that eight companies of mounted Texans (supported by a regiment of infantry, more or less) were approaching; that they had driven in or captured our rear guard and the men had given out in the rear. Three of the four mountain howitzers that we had with us were with the wagons in the rear and captured. They were guarded by one company of infantry acting as artillery. Captain Gibbs also reported that his company, men and horses, had been without water for twenty-four hours.

Under the circumstances I considered our case hopeless; that it was worse than useless to resist; that honor did not demand the sacrifice of blood after the terrible suffering that our troops had already undergone, and when that sacrifice would be totally useless. A body of mounted Texans followed Captain Gibbs to the vicinity of the camp, when a parley was held, and I surrendered my command to Lieutenant Colonel Baylor, of the C.S. Army.

The strength of my command at the time of the surrender was, Mounted Rifles, 95 rank and file and 2 officers. The infantry I have not the means of stating the exact number, but there were seven companies of the Seventh Infantry, with 8 officers, present. Since I have been at Fort Fillmore my position has been of extreme embarrassment. Surrounded by open or secret enemies, no reliable information could be obtained, and disaffection prevailing even in my own command, to what extent it was impossible to ascertain, but much increased, undoubtedly, by the conduct of officers who left their post without authority. My position has been one of great difficulty, and has ended in the misfortune of surrendering my command to the enemy. The Texan troops acted with great kindness to our men, exerting themselves in carrying water to the famishing ones in the rear; yet it was two days before the infantry could move from the camp, and then only by the assistance of their captors. The officers and men who chose to give their parole were released at Las Cruces, N.M.[15]

Later, when there was ample opportunity to do so, Captain Gibbs never once mentioned telling Major Lynde that an overwhelming Texan force of eight companies of cavalry, as well as infantry and artillery were making their way toward the springs. If he indeed gave Lynde such an incredibly false estimate, then the surrender at the springs was a foregone conclusion, and the blame might be laid at Gibbs's door. Gibbs may have given that high estimate of the forces of the enemy to justify why he abandoned his rear guard orders. When he gave his statement at Jefferson Barracks, Alfred Gibbs was quick to state that he believed Lynde had left the moment when he could abandon his rear-guard duty to his (Gibbs) own discretion.

Lynde said that he felt himself, "Surrounded by open or secret enemies, no reliable information could be obtained, and disaffection prevailing within my own command, to what extent it was impossible to ascertain, but much increased, undoubtedly, by the conduct of officers who left their post without authority." These are not empty words when uttered by a man whose orders to provide a rear guard were in every way disobeyed, and who may indeed have been provided with obvious distortions to the overall intelligence picture, the only view of the tactical situation Lynde had. McKee and McNally were open enemies. The citizens of Mesilla had proven themselves totally duplicitous. Given Lynde's distorted picture of the enemy, who could doubt that his claim of no reliable information could be substantiated, had he been given a hearing.

One other officer was abused for his actions that day at San Augustine Springs. He too was called coward, Rebel sympathizer, and traitor. That officer was 1st Lieutenant Edward J. Brooks, Major

Lynde's adjutant. Remembering back to Mesilla, Doctor McKee glossed over the wound Brooks had taken on his arm. Instead, McKee painted a picture for his readers, saying, when referring to the faces of Lynde and Brooks as they rode up, "They were the worst scared men I ever saw."

McKee's venom against Brooks came about partially because he was the adjutant, and hence Lynde's man in the 7th Infantry Regiment if there was one. Before intense research on the San Augustine Springs Incident, upon which this book is based was conducted, the words of McKee and others concerning Lynde and Brooks were taken as fact by the author. Initially, 1st Lieutenant Brooks was viewed as an individual looking out for himself only, who may indeed have turned Isaac Lynde's head in the direction of surrender, as McKee claimed. Brooks, from Michigan, resigned his commission in April, but did not leave the Regiment. He may have remained on duty because Isaac Lynde needed him. Brooks was the officer who took it upon himself to order Doctor McKee to break all his surplus medical bottles and excess equipment. When McKee told him no, not without a written order, Brooks wrote one for him and, on his own authority, ordered the destruction of the public property.

To McKee, and probably to others like Gibbs and Lydia Lane who believed McKee, Brooks was as much a traitor as Lynde. He went home to Michigan after the surrender, where he served his parole. His role in the Civil War thereafter is obscure.

Proof never stopped McKee from making libelous statements about anyone. Of 1st Lieutenant Brooks, he said, in his book:

> This man Brooks, born in and appointed from Michigan, was a secessionist and a traitor, and used his position to aid and assist the old imbecile Lynde in carrying out his infamous and cowardly schemes. As adjutant he was the confidential advisor of the commanding officer. No doubt he urged non-resistance and surrender.[16]

McKee was less ascerbic when he gave his first report on the San Augustine disaster. This was at a time too soon after the incident to make incredible and unproven accusations. He did point subtly to Brooks's complicity and agreement with the surrender. Speaking of the moments initially after Lynde's decision to surrender had been made, McKee said:

> Dr. McKee stepped in front of him and said, "Major Lynde, I protest against this surrender." The adjutant (Mr. Brooks), not minding this protest which came from the officers, at the same moment was writing the terms on his knee, looked up in the major's face and asked him what next he said.[17]

Here McKee portrayed Brooks as the loyal conspirator, doing what Lynde wanted in the face of total opposition of an outraged officer group. McKee even placed himself in Lynde's face, demanding in the name of the others that the fight continue. That outrage, if there truly was any, would have better suited Captain Joseph Haydn Potter or Captain Mathew Stevenson, than an assistant surgeon who was actually at that time still a civilian working on a contract.

Captain Alfred Gibbs gave a different view of those moments just after the surrender, saying on August 6, 1861:

> Major Lynde at this time sent me word that I could leave for Fort Stanton, but before I could get a sack of flour and a side of bacon as rations for my men Colonel Baylor had arrived, the surrender had been agreed upon by Major Lynde himself without consulting a single officer, and I was ordered by Major Lynde not to attempt to escape. Upon being informed of the surrender, every officer in the command protested against it; but it was of no avail, and the command of seven companies of the Seventh Infantry and three companies of Rifles were voluntarily surrendered without striking a blow.[18]

Not only did he *not* fight a rear-guard action as ordered, but Captain Gibbs was more than happy to leave for Fort Stanton, without fighting again. Given his words, his force of seventy to ninety cavalrymen cannot even be counted among the troops arrayed to oppose the Confederates. He was trying to make his escape. In his statement given on November 7, 1861, in the safety of Jefferson Barracks, Gibbs modified the story, making himself a grand hero in the officers's supposedly bitter reaction to Lynde's decision to surrender. He said:

> Nearly every officer protested earnestly, and even violently, against this base surrender; but Major Lynde said: "I am commander of these forces, and I take upon my shoulder the responsibility of my action in the matter." The altercation by Major Lynde's subordinates became so violent that Colonel Baylor asked who was commander of that force and responsible for their action, when Major Lynde again repeated as above. The adjutant then read aloud, by Major Lynde's order, the terms of the surrender as made by him, when I insisted that the officers and men should be allowed to select any route they might choose in leaving the country, and this was readily granted.[19]

Gibbs had Lynde saying, "I take upon my shoulder the responsibility," when what Gibbs really may have been trying to do was to get all responsibility off his own shoulders. Gibbs seemed to be placing Brooks in the camp of Lynde, and the other officers outside. Gibbs had to have known that in his heart that Brooks was the only one on the road to San Augustine Springs who did his job.

The surrender document Brooks wrote and Lynde, along with Colonel Bayor, signed, still exists. This very brief document stated the basic conditions the men agreed to. In reality, the surrender was not unconditional. Lynde won his argument for the safety of the officers' private property as well as the welfare of their wives and families. The actual wording of the document was as follows:

> The undersigned, Maj. I. Lynde, Seventh Infantry, U.S. Army, agrees to surrender his command on conditions that they receive the treatment of prisoners of war, families secure from insult, private property to be respected.
>
> Officers, after giving their parole, can elect which route they prefer in leaving the Department of New Mexico to go to any part of the United States.
>
> The enlisted men of the command will be disarmed, and given the liberty of the post of Fort Bliss until instructions can be received from General Van Dorn, C.S. Army, as to their future disposition.

Captain Joseph Haydn Potter
Courtesy: U.S. Army Military History Institute.

To all which the commanding officer, J.R. Baylor, lieutenant-colonel, C.S. Army, agrees.[20]

Fortunately, most of the enlisted men were, upon taking the oath of parole, released to go with their officers where Major Lynde intended taking them in the first place, back East. Of course, because of the surrender, they made the trip without their arms and equipment, save what they would gather as protection from the Indians. Theirs was not the fate of the young boys surrendered as part of the perfidious action which sent the 8th Infantry Regiment to Texas. Those boys spent the war years either in a prison camp in Texas or forced to serve in frontier posts without pay to protect the Texas frontier from Indian assault.[21]

The most confusing part of the surrender surrounds the totals of those actually surrendered. We know they included roughly ninety men from parts of four, not three, RMR companies, commanded in the end by Captain Alfred Gibbs. First Lieutenant Cressey, who led the combined R.M.R. force from Fort Fillmore at the start of the march, had fifty-six troopers when he started out, one having been killed at Mesilla—thirty-one from McNally's Company 'F,' and twenty-five from Cressey's Company 'B.' When Gibbs joined at San Augustine Pass he brought an additional thirty-five men from Company 'I' and Company 'G,' whom Captain Gibbs said belonged to the mail party found on the road. The actual total for the R.M.R. was three officers and ninety-one men, one officer and one enlisted man wounded. Gibbs's stated number of seventy being in his force was perhaps a lapse in memory on his part.

On August 16, 1861, Captain Joseph Haydn Potter, who then commanded the 7th Infantry Regiment in place of Major Isaac Lynde, totaled the numbers of 7th Infantry Regiment soldiers taken prisoner at San Augustine Springs on July 27, 1861. Released on parole were one major, two assistant surgeons, two captains, five first lieutenants, one second lieutenant: total commissioned, eleven. One sergeant-major, one quartermaster-sergeant, one principal musician, twenty-three sergeants, twenty-two corporals, seven musicians, 344 privates: total enlisted, 399. Aggregate, 410. In confinement as prisoners of war: one sergeant, fifteen privates: total, sixteen. Deserted to the enemy: one hospital steward, one sergeant, twenty-four privates: total, twenty-six. All included, there were 452 soldiers of the 7th Infantry who began the march to the springs.[22]

Adding the two numbers together, a total force of approximately 543 soldiers were in Lynde's command. The regiment also had forty men who were on detached service and were not there at the time, and hence were considered still available for service. Three other companies of the regiment were part of the abandonment of Forts Buchanan and Breckinridge in Arizona and were able to escape the Texans. They went on to serve the Union cause at the Battle of Valverde in February 1862.[23]

How do the actual figures compare with the estimates used in various documents after the battle?

The *Mesilla Times* referred to 700 Regulars captured, with 400 on line against Baylor's 280 at San Augustine Springs. In reality, there were 543 with 90-100 on line against Baylor. The R.M.R. could make that on line total 180-190, but Gibbs did not have them deployed for battle.[24]

Colonel Baylor also used the seven hundred figure but said there were only two hundred to three hundred on line against him at San Augustine, where he claimed less that two hundred of his own present.

Doctor McKee made no claim on the number of the Federal force when he gave his deposition on August 16, 1861, at Fort Craig. He did say there were three hundred troops in the Confederate force. In his book, written in 1886, the total number is almost right, claiming there were between five hundred and six hundred 'veterans' total in Lynde's force. The use of the latter term 'veterans' for mostly inexperienced immigrant boys was another attempt to disparage Isaac Lynde's reputation, by having Lynde seeming to have surrendered battle-hardened veterans of major warfare. McKee selected every word he used with great care and purpose—and as history attests, it worked. McKee placed all of the Federal force of over five hundred 'veterans' on line at the Springs facing Baylor, flags flying, buttons polished, muskets ready to fire.

Second Lieutenant Crilly was the only 7th Infantry officer to mildly disparage Major Lynde's actions at San Augustine, perhaps as the result of reviewing that old incident in his life through the distortions of McKee's book. Crilly mimicked McKee's words in 1890, when speaking about the surrender. He said:

> The surrender was not due to any want of skill, nerve or discipline on the part of the officers or men of the Seventh Infantry, except their commander, nor was there any time that the second in command, Captain Joseph Potter, could have arrested Major Lynde up to the time that the surrender was practically complete.[25]

Even in 1890, some of the officers were still covering their reputations at the expense of Isaac Lynde. They acted as if Major Lynde operated in his own personal vacuum, doing things entirely his own way, and against orders, Army policy, and their personal desire to do what was right.

By late afternoon, July 27, 1861, it was all over. The Confederates tried to do what they could for the Federal soldiers, allowing them a respite before marching them back to Las Cruces, where they were quickly paroled. For the soldiers in blue, the trauma was almost over. For Major Isaac Lynde, his troubles were just beginning.

After the surrender the prisoners underwent more torment, but not at the hands of their captors. They were, after all, still out in the sun and many had to be brought to water and some measure of shade. Captain Gibbs said:

> We remained where we were during the night, suffering greatly for want of water. The next day we marched to Las Cruces, on the Rio Grande, 20 miles distant. The following day [the 29th] all the public property in our charge was turned over

to the rebel forces. On the 1st of August the oath was administered to all the men and officers.[26]

Doctor McKee reported in his usual vengeful style:

> All safety and security for life left to the mercy of the enemy. Any one of the command could have been selected out for vengeance, either public or private.
>
> Was there ever such a suicidal, cowardly, pusillanimous surrender as that in all of history? Of these eleven companies, three were of the Regiment of Mounted Riflemen, of the Infantry Companies, two were of the Fifth, and the remainder of the Seventh U. S. Infantry. All surrendered to some three hundred Texas militia, without firing a shot, or losing a single man. On July 28th we were all marched back to Las Cruces, and encamped. The arms of the men were delivered up, the men paroled by their officers, and these gave their own parole ... .[27]

Once again one is tempted to ask whether Doctor McKee was really at Fort Fillmore or San Augustine Springs? One begins to wonder, considering his words. Lydia Lane, who knew nothing at all about the tactical situation, parroted Dr. McKee's statement which has echoed down through history. She was not alone. Once and for all, there were no 5th Infantry troops at San Augustine Springs. Captain Potter, in listing the total prisoners, named no 5th Infantry soldiers present. The post records tell of no 5th Infantry presence. The *Mesilla Times* started this rumor; a credulous Dr. McKee picked it up from them, followed by his later literary minions.[28]

Colonel Baylor had a few comments concerning the prisoners, one of them most patriotic. He said, "I have thought proper to release upon parole the entire command of officers and men, as I could not, with less than 300 men, guard over 600 and meet another force of 240 of the enemy that is looked for daily."[28]

In a comment a few days later Baylor added:

> I was delayed at the place of surrender for two days on account of the condition of the enemy and the want of transportation. As soon as possible I marched them to Las Cruces

and there paroled them, as I was informed that Captain Moore was en route for Fort Fillmore, from Fort Buchanan, with 250 men. I could not guard the prisoners I had and meet the coming forces. Being desirous too, to afflict the enemy in every way, I considered that it was much better for them to bear the expense of feeding the prisoners than for me to do so.[30]

The silence of two others is deafening. Neither senior captains, Joseph Haydn Potter or Mathew Rider Stevenson, ever said a word for the record that this author has been able to find. One of these officers had to have been be responsible for the rear guard. No wonder they said nothing. Perhaps it was considered noble that they did not attack Major Lynde; perhaps it is because they could not, and knew it.

NOTES - Chapter 14

1. Lynde to Assistant Adjutant General, Department of New Mexico, August 7, 1861, M1102, Rolls 13/14.

2. Horn & Wallace, Baylor to Washington, September 21, 1861, pp. 34-37.

3. Horn & Wallace, Statement of Assistant Surgeon J.C. McKee, August 16, 1861, pp. 26, 27.

4. Horn & Wallace, Statement of Captain Gibbs, November 7, 1861, pp. 24-26.

5. Crilly, p. 10.

6. McKee, p. 28.

7. Ibid.

8. Horn & Wallace, Statement of Captain Gibbs, November 7, 1861, pp. 24-27.

9. Ibid.

10. *Mesilla Times*, Issue 41, July 27, 1861.

11. Horn & Wallace, Baylor to Washington, September 21, 1861, pp. 34-37.

12. Francis Crilly, p. 10.

13. Circular Publication Committee, The Military Service Institution, Governor's Island, N.Y.H., November 10, 1889, Haskin, 1st Artillery, p. 6 of 10.

14. Circular Publication Committee, The Military Service Institution, Governor's Island, N.Y.H., November 10, 188, Johnson, 7th Regiment, p. 3.

15. Lynde to Assistant Adjutant General, August 7, 1861, M1120, Rolls 13/14.

16. McKee, p. 10.

17. Horn & Wallace, McKee to Assistant Adjutant General, August 16, 1861, pp. 26, 27.

18. Horn & Wallace, Reports of Captain Alfred Gibbs, August 6, 1861, pp. 22, 23.

19. Horn & Wallace, Statement of Captain Gibbs, November 7, 1861, pp. 24-26.

20. Horn & Wallace, Terms of Surrender, San Augustine Springs, July 27, 1861, p. 22.

21. Circular Publication Committee, The Military Service Institution, Governor's Island, N.Y.H., November 10, 1889, 8th Infantry Report, 1892.

22. Horn & Wallace, Potter to Assistant Adjutant General, August 16, 1861, p. 32.

23. Ibid.

24. *Mesilla Times*, Number 41, July 27, 1861.

25. Francis Crilly, p. 10.

26. Horn & Wallace, Statement of Captain Gibbs, November 7, 1861, pp. 24-26.

27. McKee, pp. 29, 30.

28. *Mesilla Times*, July 27, 1861, No 41.

29. Horn & Wallace, Baylor to Washington, September 21, 1861, pp. 34-37.

30. Ibid.

15

THE AFTERMATH

As early as August 25, 1861, a Confederate newspaper, the New Orleans *Sunday Delta*, had the full scoop on the situation in New Mexico as it was before Fort Fillmore was abandoned. The Rebel paper had better intelligence about what was going on in southern New Mexico than Isaac Lynde ever had. A *Sunday Delta* reporter, acting as if he were in Colonel Canby's office reading his secret mail, said:

> The confidential orders to Major Lynde from the commander of the Department of New Mexico are in substance, that the whole regular force of the department had been ordered to the States. All the Arizona forts are to be abandoned except Fort Staunton [sic], which was to be garrisoned by two companies of volunteers. The government property was to be sold, care being taken that nothing should fall into the hands of the Texans or disaffected citizens of New Mexico Territory. The garrison at Fort Fillmore was to remain long enough to cover the withdrawal of the troops from Western Arizona, when it was to be abandoned, the force to march out by way of Fort Craig and Staunton [sic], prepared to resist all attacks.[1]

Undoubtedly, as of that date, the *Sunday Delta* did not know Fort Fillmore had fallen. Still, they had better and more accurate intelligence on the truth behind the Fort Fillmore debacle than McKee, Crilly, or any of the other officers of the 7th Infantry did, or ever said they did. With the troops from Arizona ordered by Lynde to divert from the Mesilla route and head for Fort Craig, his abandonment of the post was absolutely correct, as was his taking the road to Fort Stanton, as per "the confidential orders" the New Orleans newspaper knew all about.

It should be said that Colonel Canby never commented on any such orders being given to Lynde, but no doubt would have done a song and dance if pressed. In fact, newly promoted Colonel Canby immediately jumped on the anti-Lynde bandwagon following the surrender at San Augustine Springs, just as if he had sent no order to abandon the post. Canby said on August 4, when word first reached him of the surrender:

> I have the honor to enclose a copy of a report from Major Lynde, Seventh Infantry, commanding at Fort Fillmore. This report is in all respects unsatisfactory, and subsequent rumors, not yet confirmed, give a still more unfavorable complexion to the state of affairs in the south. These rumors, although so circumstantial as to give to them an air of probability, seem incredible. If true, Major Lynde's abandonment of his position and trusts exposes the command from Arizona and the posts at Forts Stanton and Craig to great danger, if attacked by a superior force.[2]

Canby was preparing to cover his backside, even though he didn't know yet exactly what happened. Major Lynde did it, he wrote, no matter what "it" was. Soon a chorus of agreement answered him. By August 13, he was officially Colonel Canby, soon to be General Canby. By August 27, he had exonerated everybody from responsibility for the San Augustine Springs surrender save Major Isaac Lynde. General Order 31 out of Canby's office stated:

> General Order No. 31
> The Colonel commanding the department has learned with great gratification that certain reports and statements with regard to the troops included in the surrender of San Augustine Springs are unfounded and slanderous, and that, notwithstanding the difficulties in which they were involved and the

seductions with which they were assailed, they have proved themselves, with a few dishonorable exceptions, loyal and faithful soldiers of the Union.

He sympathizes with them in their misfortune, and trusts that they will bear it with patience and look forward with hope to the period when it will be removed, and San Augustine be remembered only as a watchword and an incentive to renewed exertions for the honor of their country and its flag.[3]

With the blessing of the Department commander, the infantry rear guard, and whoever their commanding officer was, were exonerated without a hearing. With the blessing of the Department commander, Captain Gibbs and the R.M.R. were absolved of their less-than-adequate performance. With the blessing of the Department commander the troops who failed to find a way up that hill were told they did their duty. Only Major Isaac Lynde didn't do his duty. Canby also said the Army would get Lynde for all the others who had done their duty bravely and honorably, save for a "few dishonorable exceptions." And the Army certainly did that duty. When the charges against Isaac Lynde were placed before President Abraham Lincoln, that honored character of American history finished Colonel Canby's whitewash job by throwing Major Lynde out of the Army without a hearing.

A statement in the West Point Register of graduates and former Cadets of the United States Military Academy reads, "Isaac Lynde. Born in Vermont. Infantry: Mexican War 1846. Surrendered his command, Ft. Fillmore NM, 27 July 61, to inferior force of insurgents: ret. 28 June 68 major."[4]

One can easily read the words coward or traitor into that statement. The fact that no other officer, not even the worst of Confederates, has so low a comment in the whole history of the Army in the nineteenth century shows to what depth the Army allowed Major Isaac Lynde's reputation to sink. Much of that degradation can be laid at the feet of the able Doctor McKee, who kept his biased version of the incident fully alive.

Lynde claimed the enemy was superior to his force in numbers when he was at Fort Fillmore, based on estimates of enemy strength he was provided by others. In those estimates were included Baylor's strength (thought to be four hundred, at least), an estimate of the Confederate militia potential in Mesilla, and an estimate that one hundred soldiers with cannon had come up from Fort Bliss. Lynde's estimates were, however, discounted completely by detractors and fellow Army officers as well, even as facts began to show otherwise. The Confederates crowed about the scam they had pulled as far as total numbers were concerned. Lynde's estimates were disallowed and his reputation shattered based on the fact that he surrendered to "an inferior force," the one absolute no-no the military seemed unable to tolerate.

In Texas, Major Sibley and Brevet-Lieutenant Colonel Reeve provided higher authorities with exactly the same exact kind of number-crunching estimates of force-on-force as Lynde did; then, feeling safe in saying the enemy had them outnumbered, promptly sur-rendered their full-strength forces. The West Point Register of Graduates carries no statement of abuse for Major Sibley or Brevet-Lieutenant Colonel Reeve, nor for any Confederates who abused their commissions by deserting, or performing service for the Confederacy while wearing the blue—as Loring, Sibley, Maury, Fauntleroy, Garland, and others may have done.

This is not intended to maltreat the reputations of Sibley and Reeve. They did what they thought was right under the circumstances, and their perceptions of enemy strength, right or wrong, were accepted without question. Isaac Lynde should have been given the benefit of a court-martial to explain his actions, if his perceptions were doubted. Lynde does not stand blameless for what happened at San Augustine Springs, but neither should he have stood alone in responsibility. It was President Lincoln's job to give orders to the Army. It was the Army's job to give Colonel Canby his orders. It was Canby's job to provide Lynde the true facts of the situation back East.

There are two stories, one true and the other a fable, that require telling before completing the narrative of the surrender at San Augustine Springs. Let us deal with the fable first.

Stories on the Internet about the Incident at San Augustine Springs, or about Fort Fillmore, usually mention that the main reason the Federal troops surrendered was that they were drunk and unable to respond to duty. They either carried whisky in their canteens or in their rifle barrels, to thoroughly hide it from the officers. This fable is believed because it is so appealing to the humorous and scandal-loving sides of our nature. Indeed, the drunken soldiers myth is probably the best known historical 'fact' about Fort Fillmore. The whole incident may have been fabricated, or the result of storytelling, a well known pastime in the nineteenth century. Major Lynde never said anything about the soldiers being drunk, nor did Captain Gibbs, Doctor McKee, Lydia Lane, Francis Crilly, Colonel Baylor, Colonel Canby, *The Mesilla Times,* or any other responsible source on or after the San Augustine surrender. Had such a tale been true, the Texans and secessionist sympathizers would have had a field day with it. It would have been the joke of the day and Southern newspapers all over the country would have reprinted the story, as they did the news of the surrender. What a blow at Union morale that would have been! Had it been true, Doctor McKee would have made the drunken soldier myth the golden nail he used to crucify Major Isaac Lynde. Such a myth was what McKee would have yearned to find true.

In his 1961 *New Mexico Historical Review* article on Isaac Lynde, A.F.H. Armstrong came to a similar conclusion about the drunken soldiers fable. He said:

> If this were true, it is understandable that Union officers omitted it from their reports. However, Baylor could have included it, but did not. The Mesilla *Times* is oddly silent if the incident really happened, considering its satirical treatment of Fort Fillmore's garrison on other occasions.
>
> The *Times* had the entire Confederate command as a source for material unflattering to the Union. If anyone at all, either from the group that pursued Lynde or from the town and valley, had known of liquor in the Union muskets and canteens, it is difficult to imagine The *Times* withholding such a morsel from a gossip-hungry countryside.[5]

Where did the drunken soldiers myth originate? Armstrong contended it was the work of a gentleman named Hank Smith, a private soldier on the Confederate side. During the 1966 excavation at Fort Fillmore, Dr. John Wilson, in his research into the background of the fort, uncovered an article in the *Las Vegas Gazette*, dated August 25, 1877, written sixteen years after the surrender at San Augustine. No author's name was provided, but the article sounds as if it were written by the editor of the paper, who was trying to raise circulation by doing a series of articles on the Confederate invasion of New Mexico during 1861 and 1862. There are enough truths mixed with the fabrications in this article to make this information probably a word-of-mouth-type tale, which was well known in the region at that time. Below is the part of the article referencing the San Augustine Springs surrender:

> Most of the Americans living in Southern New Mexico had proclaimed in favor of the South and aided and abetted Col. Bealer [sic] of the Texas Rangers, who had taken up his headquarters in that section, and Major Lyans [sic] felt quite uneasy at Fort Fillmore, below Las Cruces. One express after another reached him that the Texans, in force were ready to march upon him, and he at last concluded that "he who *don't* fight and runs away, will live to fight another day," and so ordered the troops under him to evacuate the post and march towards Fort Stanton. Our townsman, Dr. F. Knauer, who was then sutler, or post trader, of course did not want to stay there alone, so he also packed up and left, leaving most of his goods in charge of another party, who guarded it so well that our friend Knauer never saw them again. It was a sad and pitying sight to see the troops pass the Organ Mountain. For several days previous to the evacuation nearly the whole garrison had slept upon their arms. Most of the provisions on hand in the commissary were stowed away in wagons already, but several boxes of hospital brandy or commissary whisky were to be left behind and, of course, first one, then another, took a taste, then a drink, at last filled their canteens, and had to march next day, without a drop of water, over heavy sand and a long stretch of dry road, to camp at San Augustine Springs. The head of the column had arrived at their first day's destination early in the

afternoon; but hardly had the camp been laid out when horsemen were seen coming down the mountain, behind the springs. It turned out that they were Texans, in charge of Col. Bealer [sic], who came in to have a parley with Major Lyans [sic]. After representing that the main force of the Lone Star troops were 'up yonder,' ready to fight and annihilate the federal troops, should their commander refuse to turn over his sword and the arms of those under him, a council of war was held. Several of the officers of the regular army, being southerly disposed on account of their nativity, of course consented to be taken as prisoners of war, and soon thereafter Major Lyans [sic] ordered Chief Bugler Oberle to 'sound surrender.' Oberle was brought up in the army as a bugler; he loved his adopted country and the stars and stripes that had given him employment and promotion and therefore rather unsoldierly like responded: 'I never was taught that call; and even if I would know it I be G-d d - -n if I blow it.' and to evade being called upon again to "sound surrender," smashed his bugle over the wheel of the nearest wagon. 'Companies fall in' was then ordered, and this was done, 'steck [sic] arms,' was the next command given and nearly a thousand men surrendered arms, baggage and provisions to about 150 Texans. Some of the cavalry men of the 'Mounted Rifle' ran for their horse, threw on their saddle, and most of them would have made good their escape but for the cowardly action of their superiors who ordered them to stop and turn over. A few reached Fort Craig a few days after-wards, in a sad condition; their horses given out, and them-selves almost dead from hunger, thirst and fatigue. For many hours after that straggling teams and men on foot in wagons and on horseback arrived to learn of their shame. One plucky infantry man, coming down the hills a few miles from camp, setting straddled on his field piece, was met by a few rangers who ordered him to 'get off there and surrender this cannon, Major Lyans [sic] has turned over the whole outfit.' The temporary artillery man laughed at them, and thinking perhaps that his fellow stragglers would aid him in his efforts, answered, 'never shall this here piece be turned against the North as long as I have life in me and hands to defend it.' But poor fellow! He quickly fell off the field piece, riddled by bullets, to die for his country by the roadside. Major Lyans [sic] and his men were marched back to Mesilla; and then sent up to Fort Craig with only enough arms to keep guard. When the men reached Albuquerque, each carrying only a stick, the regular troops and volunteers stationed there were kept back only by almost superhuman efforts of their officers, who, either through cowardice, or treason to the government who had educated them at the nation's expense, had helped to advise a surrender. The whole force had orders to continue their march to the States, where they were kept doing garrison duty on the frontier in Michigan until relieved from patrol.[6]

How does one refute a story that is so perfectly knee-slapping believable, yet most of which is nothing but fabrication—a typical nineteenth-century yarn. The author's first impression when hearing of this story was instantaneous acceptance; this must be the single most perfect explanation for the tragedy at San Augustine Pass. The troops were drunk, having partaken of the good spirits which were going to be abandoned anyway. Putting the rest in their canteens also seemed to be a perfect next step. Remembering back to a Hollywood movie of the 1950s, *Only the Valiant*, with Gregory Peck, the incident of whiskey in soldiers' canteens was made the central theme of the movie. Soldiers are stereotyped as being enamored with every kind of alcoholic drink. We are so thoroughly indoctrinated with that stereotype that all the newspaper editor had to do was to say the words to gain instant recognition as having reported the truth. So ingrained is this belief that nothing this author or any other author writes is going to see the story buried and forgotten. As long as memory of Fort Fillmore lives, the drunken soldiers will march on up the hill to San Augustine Springs, all one thousand of them, at least according to this particular article. The writer even lied about Southern officers in Lynde's command desirous of surrender, when in fact all were Northern men and loyal to the Union.

No one will consider that there were not enough spirits on that post to fill the canteens of even a tiny fraction of the garrison, which certainly wouldn't have lasted more than a few hours of the twenty-four-hour ordeal. Most will ignore the obvious fact that none of the eyewitnesses to the tragedy, who were in a position to know the truth about drunken soldiers, ever repeated the story in open or closed chambers.

There is enough accuracy to the story to say the original narrator might have been one of the soldiers at San Augustine Pass. This author believes the person referred to as Sergeant Oberle was the originator. Sergeant Hubert H. Oberle, a twelve-year veteran, was a member of the 7th Infantry. His name, being the only name spelled correctly in the entire article, appears to point to him as being involved. The narrator, whoever he was, couldn't spell Baylor or Lynde, but he could spell Oberle. Sergeant Oberle created at least one other monumental lie arising out of the incident, and there is no reason why he couldn't have created the drunken soldier story as well. We will tell that story shortly, in which his words were proven to be of doubtful veracity.

Aside from the misspelled names for the principal characters, there are many other faults with this story. One hardly knows where to start. First, the Post Sutler at Fort Fillmore was George Hayward, an ardent Confederate, who kept his best material, including his whisky in Mesilla, where he was business partner of a Mr. McGrorty. No man named Knauer is associated with the Fort Fillmore sutler's store, though such a person may have come to Fort Fillmore with Major Lynde from Fort McLane. The hardest substance Hayward was allowed to sell would have been beer. Any whisky obtained by the soldiers was bought at grog shops off the post reservation, or in Mesilla, where it was easily obtained.

Doctor McKee was a lot of things, and he said a lot of things, but one thing is for sure, anyone seeing the slaughter of the bottles near the hospital at Fort Fillmore, viewable into the 1980s, cannot doubt McKee did what he said. He destroyed every usable bottle he could find and everything else as well if he could reach it. No libation came to the lips of thirsty soldiers via Doctor McKee's medicine bottles.

Whoever quoted Sergeant Oberle over the matter of his blowing "the surrender call" on his bugle, passed on another fable. At that point in history (1861), infantry regiments of the United States Army did not have buglers. They used drummers to sound all calls. Besides, there was no bugle call for surrender, or drum roll for that matter. It is true that in 1855 the new 9th and 10th Infantry Regiments experimented with buglers instead of drummers. It is also true that buglers began to replace drummers as the American Civil War progressed, and by the time of the Indian Wars infantry regiments had buglers. Stretching this story as far as it can be stretched, there were band instruments in the hands of 7th Infantry musicians present at San Augustine Springs. It is not known what Oberle's position was with the regiment. He may have been a member of the band. But, in no way did Major Lynde turn to him and demand he blow "surrender." It is also true that the band members were ordered to destroy their instruments. Perhaps this was the origin of the fabulous story of Oberle bending his horn.

One thousand Federal soldiers surrendering to only one hundred and fifty Confederates is simply the second biggest fabrication in the story, next to the one about spirits. Unfortunately, such ridiculous literary twaddle was handed down from source to source to source, until the lie became truth. This author does not doubt that there may have been a few of the boys who got their hands on some alcohol before, during, and after leaving for San Augustine Pass. The number was not large and these few did not impact the course of the retreat. In fact, it is equally likely that none of the soldiers obtained spirits at all. The odds in favor of procuring some would have to be very small. The odds against a mass ingestion of spirits by a large number of soldiers would be impossible to believe under the most favorable circumstance, given the situation.

Another such tale mentions putting whisky down the barrels of the rifles, then plugging them. Any soldier that could get drunk on the whisky from a rifle barrel was certainly no drinker in the first place. This fable may have come from some Texas Confederate seeing a wooden device called a tampion sticking out of the barrel of a Federal soldier's musket. Such a wooden plug is known from artifact finds at Fort Fillmore and was used to keep dust and dirt out of infantry musket barrels. Of course, some yarn teller saw it as a cork in a whisky container, and passed another fable on to the unwary and credulous, who would rather have that story than the truth.

*   *   *

The second apocryphal story to arise out of the San Augustine Springs surrender relates the tale of the saving of the 7th Infantry Regiment's honor through the destruction of the regiment's colors. That the colors were destroyed is unquestioned. Colonel Baylor was one of the first to remark on that fact: "I regret to report that the regimental colors were burned by the enemy to avoid surrendering them."[7]

In fact, unknown to Baylor, they were not burned. Before we report what did happen to the United States Stars and Stripes and the blue 7th Infantry Regimental flag, we need to point out that several individuals claimed to have destroyed them, all seeking to gather honors unto themselves for doing so. One of those individuals long credited with destroying the flags was Sergeant Hubert H. Oberle. Oberle tried to take full credit for the act, as did others, but the truth is that McKee's other traitor and secessionist sympathizer at San Augustine Springs, 1st Lieutenant Edward J. Brooks, performed the destruction, by tearing the flags into pieces and giving the pieces to the nearby ladies of the command to hide on their persons. The accurate tale as now given by the Association of the 7th Infantry Regiment is:

> In July of 1861, Texan Confederate troops invaded New Mexico, and following a disastrous retreat from Fort Fillmore, the 7th surrendered to Lt. Col. John R. Baylor. The infamous moment occurred on July 27, 1861 at St. Augustine Springs. Some three days following the surrender, former U.S. Army Colonel Albert Sidney Johnston, on his way to report to Confederate officials back East, arrived and upon finding out Baylor had captured a Federal regiment, inquired what had become of its colors. Baylor, perhaps embarrassed that he had not thought of the flags first, ordered the 7th's adjutant, Lt. Edward J. Brooks, to his office and demanded the colors. Brooks informed Baylor that the colors including the set carried in the Mexican War had been destroyed personally by him. Baylor flew into a violent rage in front of Johnston, [and] ordered Brooks arrested. After three days of close arrest, Brooks was released.[8]

Brooks was such a coward that he risked his life to destroy the colors, and to throw that fact in Baylor's face, an act which, had it been widely recognized at the time, would probably have brought him the Medal of Honor—as it did the young man who saved the 8th Infantry Regiment's colors in Texas. Colonel John Baylor was a savage man who later murdered the editor of the *Mesilla Times* in cold blood for a disparaging remark in an issue of that paper. He had an especially brutal reputation for actions he took among Indians in Texas, and threatened to take in Arizona, acts that finally led the Confederate Government to disown him for the most part. Brooks was lucky to come out alive in the face of Baylor's rage.

Kevin R. Young, writing for the Internet website *Adjutant's Call*, a site honoring the 7th Infantry Regiment, described the destruction of the regimental flags at San Augustine Springs,

> ... he [Brooks] alone made the decision to destroy the colors prior to the surrender of the command. Brooks noted that Sgt. Hubert H. Oberle (a twelve year veteran) and Principal Musician Pound assisted him (the 7th's color sergeant, Peter Molony had dropped out of the column from fatigue before reaching the Springs). Sections of the colors were cut up and given to such ladies as were nearby. The Union of one was given to the wife of Captain Matt Stevenson who wore it apron style and kept it. When Brooks was finished destroying the colors, he next wrecked the band instruments by smashing them against the wagon wheels.
>
> The 7th Infantry Regiment, the "Cottonbalers" as they style themselves, a title gained in New Orleans during the War of 1812, was re-formed in 1862, in New York, but had to win its colors back in battle. This was done during the battle of Fredericksburg, in 1862. For bravery in that battle the regiment was granted a new national and regimental flag.[9]

For years, while Oberle claimed he alone had destroyed the flags, Brooks remained silent. Something triggered the former 1st Lieutenant's wrath and led to a clarification and validation of his claim. The *Adjutant's Call* article continued:

Sgt. Oberle later claimed that he was in charge of the colors and that he was the one who destroyed them, noting that Baylor had him before a military trial for the act and threatened to hang him. While Brooks did confirm that Oberle assisted him, the adjutant noted strongly, "Permit me to say that if Sgt. Oberly [sic] or any other enlisted men or even a commissioned officer other than the commanding officer, presumed to lay hands upon the colors for any purpose whatever in my presence, I should not have hesitated to use my saber to protect them. To me they were a sacred charge to be surrendered only upon orders from my commander, and under no circumstances would I have permitted any unauthorized person to interfere with them." [10]

When the surrendered troops arrived back in Las Cruces they were in a Confederate world, no matter what the local Hispanics thought. Former Hospital Steward Charles E. Fitzwilliams was the only one to return to Fort Fillmore. He chose the Confederate side and was returned to the post to begin treating Confederate soldiers as he once had the boys in blue. One sergeant and twenty-four other soldiers took up the Rebel cause. The remaining officers, none from a Southern State, stayed loyal to the Union. Of the 7th Infantry officers only 2d Lieutenant Crilly left a written account of the battle, and that many years after the fact. The rest demurred.[11]

The women and children were obviously one of the main reasons Isaac Lynde chose not to fight. There was simply too much risk to their lives. Doctor McKee, unmarried, understood why the women were a factor, but considered them part of Lynde's overall treason. He said:

> The number of women in this command should receive the rigid scrutiny of the War Department, as five officers had their wives and children at this post. The camp women and children I will not pretend to enumerate. Yet all these were kept in the garrison to paralyze us when in presence of the enemy, seemingly prepared for the result—a surrender. Major Lynde was warned of this repeatedly, but was too weak to act. This has been one of the causes why I and others are now prisoners of war.[12]

The wounded hero of the Battle of Mesilla, 1ˢᵗ Lieutenant McNally, backed McKee up on the question of the presence of the families. One wonders what would have happened had their own families been there. Would they have sent them into the Jornada del Muerto alone? In1882, McKee was still fuming over Lynde's rein-statement in 1866. McKee noted, in a letter to the Adjutant General in Washington:

> I would respectfully call your attention and request a decision in the case of Isaac Lynde, major U.S. Army, retired, who was pre-emptorily dismissed from the service by President Abraham Lincoln, on Nov. 25ᵗʰ, 1861 for the cowardly surrender of a command of U.S. troops, to an inferior body of the enemy, at or near Fort Filmore [sic], New Mexico, on July 27, 1861.
> Major Lynde was afterwards restored by President Andrew Johnson, simply revoking the order of dismissal, as Major of the 18ᵗʰ U.S. Infantry, Nov. 27ᵗʰ, 1866.
> Under recent decisions in the cases of Fitz John Porter and Chaplain A. M. Blake, U.S.A., I claim President Johnson could not legally reinstate this officer by revoking the order of a former President, and that the only legal way was to have renominated him, have him confirmed by the United States Senate, and that he is not an officer of the U.S. Army. For these reasons I respectfully request that his name be struck from the Army register.[13]

Doctor McKee was told to forget it, the problem was far too out of date and forgotten to bother the current President about. Major Lynde died in Florida on April 10, 1886. His nemesis, Assistant Surgeon McKee, outlasted him, dying on December 11, 1897.[14]

Lydia Lane believed she was responsible for notifying Abraham Lincoln of the terrible defeat that took place at San Augustine Springs. She said:

> I was writing home on the day we heard all the news from Fort Fillmore, and when my letter reached Carlisle, Pennsylvania, a month later, Colonel Andrew Porter, Mounted Rifles, was there. He was given the contents of it, and he

telegraphed the news of Lynde's surrender to Washington, which was the first intimation they had at the War Department of what had taken place in New Mexico.[15]

NOTES - Chapter 15

1. *Sunday Delta*, New Orleans, August 25, 1861.

2. Canby to Assistant Adjutant General, August 4, 1861, M1120, Rolls 13/14.

3. Order #31, Canby to all commands, August 27, 1861, M1120, Rolls 13/14.

4. Association of Graduates, U.S.M.A., *Register of Graduates,* p. 213.

5. A.F.H. Armstrong, "The Case of Major Isaac Lynde," *New Mexico Historical Review*, Volume XXXVI, Number 1, January, 1961.

6. *Las Vegas Gazette*, Volume 5, #24 (August 25, 1877); whole number 252, p. 1 (from Wilson's papers, 1966).

7. Horn & Wallace, Baylor to Washington, September 21, 1861, pp. 34-37.

8. Internet: Http://cottonbalers/lynchburg.net/Adj_call.htm. This web site is the property of the Association of the 7th Infantry Regiment , a group that seeks to keep the history of the regiment alive, and also performs historical reenactments of events taken from the regiment's history.

9. Ibid.

10. Ibid.

11. Potter to Assistant Adjutant General, August 16, 1861, M1120, Rolls 13/14.

12. Horn & Wallace, McKee to Surgeon General, August 16, 1861, pp. 26, 27.

13. McKee, pp. 35, 36.

14. McKee, pp. 36, 37.

15. Lydia Spencer Lane, *I Married a Soldier*, pp. 112, 113.

16

ISAAC LYNDE AFTER SAN AUGUSTINE

In 1892, the United States Army set a task for each of its multifaceted parts. An officer in each branch or regiment was asked to write a brief article of twenty or so pages outlining the history of their particular organization. Lieutenant A.B. Johnson was assigned to research and complete a brief history of the 7th United States Infantry Regiment. Johnson detailed the regiment's history from its founding on July 16, 1798 to January 1891, when the regiment was stationed at Fort Logan, Colorado.

This version of history stands in Army records today to represent how the regiment viewed its performance during the entire nineteenth century. Johnson's article was composed of twelve pages, single-spaced, containing data on the movements and principal historical events in which his regiment participated. Three full pages, twenty-five percent of the total, dealt with Isaac Lynde and the debacle at San Augustine Springs. As the reader might guess, the incidents at Fort Fillmore and San Augustine were events from the past which haunted the honor of the regiment without giving a moment's thought for the terrible question—why?

Most of what Lieutenant Johnson said came straight from Doctor McKee's book, often word for word, including comments McKee took from the pages of the *Mesilla Times*. In fact, McKee is the only source quoted, and in a fashion that indicated most of Johnson's readers would be well familiar with the good doctor and his views. By 1892, McKee's view was the official view of the Incident at San Augustine Springs, with a few embellishments related to the drunken soldiers myth which Johnson dared not include, or didn't know about. This view is still prevalent today, as can be seen from the Internet sites which report on either Fort Fillmore or the surrender at San Augustine Springs.

Even the blatant lies and obvious misstatements McKee made are repeated as truth. Johnson reported, without question, McKee's view on the lack of an infantry rear guard, just as if Major Lynde had never established one. Lieutenant Johnson quoted, "The Texans pursued the troops as soon as possible, the only temporary security and intervening guard being the company of Rifles under Captain Gibbs, which was deployed as skirmishers, covering the retreat."[1]

Lynde's assignment of two infantry companies to the rear guard was ignored, if Johnson even bothered to check, for if that subject were broached someone might have to ask why this or that officer in the command failed to perform their basic military function. No one ever asked. Nor did Johnson seem to worry about the fact that, even if it were true that the R.M.R. were the only rear guard, why did they run? Why didn't they fire? Major Lynde did not have his finger on their triggers. Worst of all, Lieutenant Johnson repeated Doctor McKee's monstrous misrepresentation of the scene at San Augustine Springs, "In a short time the Texans were seen advancing in line of battle to the number of some 300, Lynde's command numbering nearly 500 well trained and disciplined troops and forming a striking contrast to the badly armed and irregular command of the Texans.[2]

As we know, there were not three hundred Texans attacking five hundred Federal soldiers, the latter finely arrayed, colors flying and ready for combat at the base of the Organ Mountain foothills—the implication being that certainly all five hundred would have fought bravely, save for the one single coward who happened to be in command. This statement is straight out of McKee's book, the very worst of his misrepresentations and lies. This literary sleight of hand stands today as the view the 7th Infantry Regiment holds towards Major Isaac Lynde. Given what happened at San Augustine, this is perhaps the only view of him the regiment could tolerate, then or now. Major Lynde did, after all, surrender his command, whatever the misadventures, betrayals, and lies. Did Johnson have any words of his own in reflection on how the Regiment should view Lynde? Yes, he did. Using McKee as a base, Lieutenant A.B. Johnson concluded:

> Was ever such a blemish and stigma attached to a regiment whose record had hitherto been full of glory wherever it had been placed? The colors of the regiment were cut from the staff, torn into pieces, and distributed to those who had fought under them in years gone by and who loved them as they loved life. To any unprejudiced mind this action on the part of Major Lynde must seem hasty and unjust towards the command, and unwarranted when it is considered that no opportunity was afforded the men to prove their courage. No matter what the ultimate consequences might have been, it certainly would have been more soldier-like and vastly more loyal to have tried to have beaten the enemy, and then, if overpowered, to have surrendered, than to have surrendered without a shot to a force inferior in numbers, discipline, in *esprit-de-corps*, and indeed vastly more poorly armed.[3]

By 1890, Lieutenant Johnson could not question any of the officers who may have commanded the rear guard whom Major Lynde believed fought bravely before succumbing to superior force. Nor could he question the commander of the cavalry rear guard.

Captain Mathew Rider Stephenson, 7th Infantry, who is the most likely candidate for command of the infantry rear guard, died in January 1863, of unknown causes.

General Alfred Gibbs, the cavalry rear guard commander, died in December 1868 of a brain tumor, while serving under George Armstong Custer in the 7th Cavalry Regiment.

Second Lieutenant George Ryan, 7th Infantry, was killed at Spottsylvania on May 8, 1864.

First Lieutenant David Porter Hancock, 7th Infantry, continued to serve in the Army until his death in 1880.

First Lieutenant Augustus Plummer, 7th Infantry, died in Texas in 1866, serving with the Army of Occupation there.

Army investigators might also have sought out and asked some of the ninety cavalry troopers who raced down the hill from the best defensive position at the crest of San Augustine Pass why they did so. Then, and only then, might his inquisitors question why Major Isaac Lynde, with women and children in his midst, failed to fire a volley to save the face of the regiment.

After a delay to recuperate, the surrendered Federal soldiers were taken to Las Cruces. Baylor did not want to be saddled with feeding a mass of paroled prisoners. On August 2, he gave the bluecoats a few old muskets for protection against the Indians and sent them north to Fort Craig. The trip over the Jornada del Muerto must have been relatively uneventful; the first of the men, belonging to the Mounted Rifles, arrived at their destination on August 6, 1861. Major Lynde traveled with this group, having given over his command to Captain Potter. The general condition of the march north was explained by Captain Gibbs of the Mounted Rifles, upon their arrival:

> We left Las Cruces on the 2nd instant and arrived here [Fort Craig] this morning. The Seventh Infantry were to leave on the 3d, and will probably be here to-morrow. I respectfully state that charges against Major Lynde, under the fifty-second and ninety-ninth Articles of War, have been preferred, and are now in the hands of Captain Potter, commanding Seventh Regiment.[4]

An apocryphal story, repeated by Lieutenant A.B. Johnson in his article *The Seventh Regiment of Infantry*, tells of Lynde's rejection by one of the remaining companies of the 7th Infantry, as well as by the Commanding Officer at Fort Craig. Like much of the rest of the San Augustine Springs surrender story it was probably a fabrication, but should be reported nonetheless. Johnson said:

> The Headquarter's, band and Companies A, B, D, E, G, I and K, left Las Cruces on the 3d of August, en route to Fort

Union, arriving at Fort Craig on the 10th. Upon their arrival there, Company F, together with the rest of the garrison, turned out and presented arms to the prisoners of war as they marched into the post. So great was the feeling toward Major Lynde, that he was not allowed to enter the garrison.[5]

Lynde was not even traveling with these troops, proving the story to be a fabrication from the outset. Isaac Lynde was not a convicted felon. There is no way Army regulations would have permitted such a perfidious act until after a court of inquiry. Of course, no hearing of any kind was ever held. This story, reported in 1892, sounds more like a scene in a Hollywood western.

In fact, Isaac Lynde made his first report to the Assistant Adjutant General of the Department of New Mexico while at Fort Craig. It is possible that he and his family, along with the soldiers, were forced to camp in tents inside or outside the fort, due to a lack of temporary quarters. Fort Craig was then, or was soon to be, one of the most crowded Army posts in all of New Mexico, with tent cities springing up everywhere around the post. Lynde was undoubtedly a social outcast by that time; with every finger pointing straight at him how could he not be. In a comment by Lydia Lane, as she and her family crossed the plains headed east, accompanied by many of the paroled soldiers, including Lynde and his family, she noted:

> I never saw men sadder nor more disheartened than the officers of the Fifth and Seventh Infantry with whom I crossed the plains in 1861. Some of them saved their ambulances when they left Fort Fillmore, so that their families were comfortable so far; but they had not been able to carry away more than a change of clothes, and were in a sorry plight. Major Lynde and his wife were with the paroled troops, but had no intercourse with the officers and their families.[6]

Aside from the fact that Lydia Lane erroneously included men of the 5th Infantry one more time, copying McKee (who copied the *Mesilla Times*), she makes a good and valid point, borne out by what may have been the true story at Fort Craig. Major Isaac Lynde and his family were pariahs, as one would expect for an officer who was to take the full blame for everything that happened at Fort Fillmore in July. He was shunned, and no doubt allowed himself to be shunned. Potter, Gibbs, Stevenson, Crilly, Plummer, Ryan, Hancock, and Stivers were walking on eggshells as well, not knowing their own status. If Lynde was not made to accept the entire blame, then much of what happened could be blamed on their own failures.

If Lynde was isolated on the plains, the same had to be true at Fort Craig. Possible proof of that isolation exists. Lynde reported having arrived on August 6 with the Mounted Rifles companies, rather than his own infantry, "I have the honor to report that I arrived at this post to-day with three companies of the regiment of Mounted Rifles on parole. I shall send my official report as soon as I can complete it, which I have not yet been able to do. The express is waiting, and I have not time to write more."[7]

The message he sent was unimportant save for telling the time of his arrival, but the hand in which the message was written tells much. The beautiful script handwriting of his former adjutant, Edward Brooks, is nowhere present. Brooks was by then reporting to Captain Joseph Potter, commanding the paroled units of the 7th Infantry, who were still out on the Jornada when Lynde sent his first message. Lynde's shaky signature was apparent on any document he wrote. Now, in this letter, the almost illegible scrawl he used is very apparent. This may have been the first letter Isaac Lynde penned in his own hand while commander of the 7th Infantry. Whatever problem was indicated by his inability to keep a steady hand in writing, it was not the result of what happened at San Augustine Springs. Every letter he wrote thereafter in his own hand tells of his isolation and has similar handwriting.

One immediate outcome of the surrender at San Augustine Springs was the abandonment of Fort Stanton, the place to which Lynde intended taking his column. No digression will be made to examine the story of Fort Stanton in depth, but it should be said that actions taken there by the commanding officer appear more worthy of censure than those of Lynde at San Augustine Springs. The commander, Brevet-Lieutenant Colonel Benjamin S. Roberts,

R.M.R., who was to display signs of equally questionable competence at the coming Battle of Valverde in February 1862, upon hearing of Lynde's defeat, simply ran away without a threat being offered. Roberts said to Canby, on August 2, 1861:

> By Corporal Hughes, of B Co., Mounted Riflemen, I have received information of the surrender of the entire command of Major Lynde (including Captain Gibbs and Lieutenant Cressey's companies of my regiment, detached from their post temporarily, to the Texans).
>
> In order to place the troops [of] this post at once at your disposal at more important points, I have this day abandoned Fort Stanton, and, conforming to your instructions, destroyed all the public stores of every kind my small means of transportation could not convey away.
>
> The two infantry companies will proceed to Albuquerque and report to the commanding officer of that post.
>
> I shall report to you in person in Santa Fe with the two companies of Mounted Riflemen.[8]

Roberts had four companies of troops, and didn't know if there was going to be a Confederate threat, or of what size. The Texans, who were not even on the road to attack Fort Stanton, received the intelligence of Roberts' abandonment with glee. Colonel Baylor reported in an August 14 letter that, "By express from Fort Stanton I learn that upon the receipt of the news that Major Lynde had surrendered, Colonel Roberts, in command of that post, fled in haste, leaving the post on fire, which was extinguished by a storm of rain. Most of the commissary and quartermaster stores were saved and a battery."[9]

Roberts fled so quickly from the phantom army that he abandoned a perfectly good military post with all its supplies and artillery to the elements. He didn't even wait to see if the fires he built did the job. Given his panicky actions at Fort Stanton and later at Valverde, where his bravery was openly questioned, what does West Point have to say about Roberts? The passage reads, in part, "Brigadier General United States Volunteers, 1862; three brevets to Major General." In other words, Roberts's panicked conduct at

Fort Stanton and Valverde were ignored. His abandonment of Fort Stanton was not mentioned. His surrender of all the public property and the mountain howitzers he left behind, which were turned against the Union and his own troops at Valverde, was not mentioned. His fleeing before an army of phantoms, let alone an inferior force, was not mentioned. His career prospered to the maximum, as his promotions indicate.

Colonel Canby, soon to be General Canby, had little to say either for or against Major Lynde. He developed a truly masterful response, perfectly suited to a coverup of his own complicity in what happened. Never once did he order Lynde to start a war with the Texans. Nor did he give Lynde the right to establish martial law, so that the secessionists in Mesilla and the vicinity could have been muzzled. He didn't order Brevet-Major Gabriel Rene Paul, when Paul commanded Fort Fillmore, to take Fort Bliss when it was still defenseless and with Federal artillery and other public property waiting there to be captured—artillery which could be used against Federal forces in southern New Mexico. He allowed Paul, without firm orders, to leave Fort Fillmore just before Major Lynde arrived, abandoning his company, 'I,' and leaving it without officers at the most critical of times, when he had said he would never do that. Canby did order Lynde to abandon Fort Fillmore as soon as he possibly could, after the companies from Forts Buchanan and Breckinridge were safe, although he did not mention this fact when he later castigated Lynde for abandoning the post. In order to cover any embarrassing questions which might arise, Canby fell back on an easy legal defense. He simply couldn't comment because Lynde's conduct was the subject of an official investigation, an investigation that was never completed, perhaps not even started. Canby's exact words were:

> I have the honor to transmit copies of two reports, the
> first from Major Lynde, Seventh Infantry, late commander of
> Fort Fillmore and the Southern District, and the second from
> Captain Gibbs, Mounted Rifles, and commander of the mounted
> force of the immediate command of Major Lynde at the time

of his surrender. These reports embody substantially all the information that has yet reached me in relation to this disaster. As Major Lynde's conduct will be made the subject of judicial investigation, I do not think it proper to express an opinion in advance of that investigation.[10]

One can be sure Canby did have an opinion. His refusal to comment appeared proper, yet added more fuel to the fire consuming Isaac Lynde's reputation.

Major Lynde, accompanied by Captain Gibbs and the men of the three paroled Mounted Rifles companies, arrived at Fort Union on August 28. Fort Union was the jumping-off point for military convoys moving east. Lynde created no correspondence on his arrival there, although Captain Gibbs did. Alfred Gibbs wrote:

> I have the honor to report my arrival at this post on yesterday with three paroled officers and the detachment of Mounted Rifles included in the surrender of the 27th ultimo. I have the honor to acknowledge the receipt of your communications of the 23rd, 24th, and 25th instant, and in reply beg to state that I herewith inclose a list of the men and officers included in the surrender, as requested by you, by name, with explanatory remarks. The number of horses and mules surrendered by me was 100 horses and 2 mules. In addition, 8 horses were stolen. The number of sets of arms and equipments corresponds with the number of men.
>
> In the order directing the paroled men of the Rifles to march to the States, dated the 25th instant, no mention is made of the disposition to be made of the four officers with them or the paroled men of Companies I and G included in the surrender, and now here under my command. I should like to be informed of this at once, and if they are to be embodied in Company F. There will then be three first sergeants with the command. How are they to be disposed of? With regard to the books, records, and property pertaining to Company I, Mounted Rifles, a part was kept in Albuquerque, to be forwarded by Captain McFerran to the ordnance officer here, a part is now sent here in daily use by the whole command, and the balance will be sent, as directed in your letter, to Santa Fe by the first opportunity. I shall be compelled, however, to retain the tents,

as the depot here is entirely stripped of them. As soon as the muster rolls are completed, Private Marius, of Company I, not paroled, will be sent to Santa Fe to report, as directed.[11]

On September 3 the Assistant Adjutant General in Santa Fe notified the commanding officer at Fort Union that Major Isaac Lynde would be accompanying the paroled soldiers as they marched east.[12] On September 7, Lynde requested all correspondence related to the Fort Fillmore surrender, no doubt in preparation for the hearing or trial that he was certain would come. He said:

> I have the honor to request to be furnished from your officer with copies of all reports received from me, during the time that I was in command at Fort Fillmore N.M. with a certificate that they were all the reports required during that time from me: also copies of all reports, letters, or other papers made by any person to the Head Quarters of the Department on the subject of the operations of the troops at Fort Fillmore between the 20th & 31 of July 1861, or in any way connected with the subject of the charges against me.[13]

On September 16, an unidentified officer of the 6th Cavalry, a Regiment only recently formed, notified Lynde that he could not provide him transportation independent of what had been provided in the amount given Captain Potter's command. Major Lynde was not even in command of the troops who would take him to Fort Leavenworth. Potter had the privilege of providing Lynde and family with accommodations on the journey, as best he could.[14]

The time of departure of the paroled column from Fort Union, which included Major Lynde and his wife, is unknown. Lydia Lane, who was accompanying the column, said only that:

> Early in the fall it was decided to send the paroled troops from Fort Union to Fort Leavenworth, Kansas; and husband, who was again ordered from Fort Craig to Fort Union, thought I, with the children and servants, had better join them, matters in New Mexico being in a very unsettled state just then, women and children were in the way, so we left for the East with the officers and families going in.[15]

The time of arrival at Fort Leavenworth is also unknown, as is the question of whether Captain Alfred Gibbs was with the party. It is known that Gibbs, immediately following his arrival at Jefferson Barracks, Missouri, requested that a court of inquiry be convened to "report upon the facts and circumstances connected with and bearing upon the surrender of Major Lynde's command at San Augustine Springs, N. Mex., July 27, 1861, more particularly as relates to my connection therewith as commanding the mounted force of that command."[16]

If he didn't know it before, Gibbs learned on arrival at Jefferson Barracks that his efforts at San Augustine Springs were the last significant action in American history of the Regiment of Mounted Riflemen. On August 3, 1861, by Act of Congress, an old tradition of the United States Army horse-mounted units was to vanish forever. The six mounted units of the Regular Army, 1st and 2d Dragoons, the R.M.R., the 1st, 2d and 3d Cavalry Regiments, were to be combined into one Cavalry Corps. All horse-mounted units would now be called 'cavalry.' The terminology of dragoons, Mounted Rifles and cavalry as separate terms was ordered dropped. The 1st Dragoon Regiment was now the 1st Cavalry Regiment; the 2d Dragoon Regiment was the 2d Cavalry Regiment; the Regiment of Mounted Rifles were now the 3rd Cavalry Regiment; the former 1st, 2d and 3d Cavalry Regiments had their designation changed to the 4th, 5th, and 6th Cavalry Regiments.

The newly designated cavalry regiments had twelve companies (A-M, minus J), instead of the former ten, consisting of one captain, one 1st Lieutenant, one 2d Lieutenant, five sergeants, eight corporals, two musicians, two farriers, one saddler, one wagoner, and seventy-two privates. That made a total of ninety-four officers and men per company. In a second important change, mounted companies were now renamed as troops, as opposed to their former designation as companies.[17]

As to the fate of Major Isaac Lynde, there was to be no hearing, court of enquiry, or court-martial provided him. Long before Lynde could find his way to Washington to plead his case his fate was decided. On November 25, 1861, President Abraham Lincoln directed that Major Isaac Lynde, formerly of the 7th

Infantry Regiment, be simply dropped from the rolls of the Army, effective immediately. This directive was issued in the form of an Order No. 102, of the year 1861. The Order stated simply:

... GENERAL ORDERS, HEADQUARTERS OF THE ARMY,
No. 102   Washington, D.C., November 25, 1861.

I. Maj. Isaac Lynde, Seventh Infantry, for abandoning his post—Fort Fillmore, N. Mex.—on the 27th of July, 1861, and subsequently surrendering his command to an inferior force of insurgents, is, by direction of the President of the United States, dropped from the rolls of the Army from this date.

By command of Major-General McClellan.[18]

The President didn't want to hear what Major Isaac Lynde had to say. Neither did Congress nor the Army. On December 4 a resolution was adopted by the House of Representatives relating to the Fort Fillmore surrender. Congress placed the final label of 'coward' on Major Isaac Lynde, this after his thirty-four years of honorable service to the nation and the Army. The Resolution stated:

Whereas, in July 1861, at Fort Fillmore, in New Mexico, Maj Isaac Lynde, U.S.A., abandoned said fort, and shortly after its abandonment surrendered a largely superior force of United States troops under his command to an inferior force of Texas troops, without firing a gun or making any resistance whatever; and whereas it is charged and believed that said surrender was the result of treason or cowardice, or both, in which surrender other officers of his command were also concerned:

Therefore *Resolved*, That the Secretary of War be requested, if not incompatible with the public interest, to report to this House what measures have been or ought to be taken to expose and punish such of the officers now on parole as were guilty of treason or cowardice in that surrender, and relieve from suspicion such as were free from blame.[19]

On December 12, 1861, in a letter from the War Department to the House of Representatives, Simon Cameron, Secretary of War, indicated that he wanted to respond to the request of

Congress to punish any and all officers responsible for what happened at Fort Fillmore and at San Augustine Springs. The Secretary said:

> In answer to the resolution of the House of Repre-sentatives of the 4th instant, asking what measures have been, or ought to be, taken to expose and punish such of the officers now on parole as were guilty of treason or cowardice in surrendering Fort Fillmore, in New Mexico, to an inferior force of Texas troops, I have the honor to enclose a report of the Adjutant-General, which, together with a copy of General Orders, No. 102, herewith, furnishes all the information in the possession of the Department.[20]

(Inclosure)

Headquarters Of The Army, Adjutant-General's Office
Washington, December 11, 1861

> Sir: I have the honor to acknowledge the reference to this office of a resolution from the honorable the House of Representatives, dated December 4, 1861, asking what measures have been taken, or ought to be taken, "to expose and punish such of the officers now on parole as were guilty of treason or cowardice in the surrender of a "force of United States troops," under Major Lynde, in New Mexico, in July, 1861, "to an inferior force of Texas troops," etc.
>
> In compliance with your instructions, I have the honor to report that Major Lynde was, by direction of the President of the United States, dropped from the rolls of the Army, November 25, 1861, for the offense alluded to in the resolution. It is believed that no other officer of the command was in any way involved in the suspicion of complicity in the offense, and the commanding officer, Major Lynde, was the only person on whom the responsibility could rest.[21]

The whitewash was complete; "no other officer of the command was in any way involved." Only one man was to be deemed responsible for everything. Major Isaac Lynde wasn't even given the courtesy of being drummed out of the army after thirty-four years service. The doors were simply closed in his face. By Abraham Lincoln's action alone, he was denied his right to a trial. The Great

Emancipator showed little mercy in this case, but then, one has to imagine the facts he was given were incredibly biased. Could Lincoln have forgotten his own ineptitude in his first months in office, when he allowed minor government departments like New Mexico to wither on the vine without adequate instructions on how to react to secession? By November 1861, with the cannons roaring to the south, Lincoln obviously had forgotten. Major Isaac Lynde, together with many former Federal officers who joined the Confederacy, was simply "dropped from the rolls of the Army."

A.F.H. Armstrong wrote in 1961 that Lynde was officially under arrest as he arrived at Jefferson Barracks, Missouri, in early December. By that time Lincoln had already thrown him out of the Army. Armstrong reports in a letter to the Honorable H.M. Rice, in Washington, D.C., that Lynde asked for a trial by his "peers" saying, "I have not served the United States for over thirty four years on the extremist frontier, to turn traitor at this late day ... ."[22] These were so many useless words in that time of turmoil. The Army, Congress, and the President had their scapegoat and Lynde's appeal was ignored.

The disgraced former Major was in Washington by December 24, where he made a personal appeal to President Lincoln to be restored to rank so that he could receive a fair hearing or trial. This appeal was also denied.[23]

In commenting on Lincoln's response, Armstrong said Lynde advanced a reason for the Mesilla attack which might have helped in such a defense. He said he made the move from Fort Fillmore to prevent an attack by the Texans on the Lane wagon train, then slowly moving up the road toward Fort Craig. Major Lynde believed his thrust against the town prevented the train from being attacked.[24]

Assaults on Lynde's reputation continued through the war years and he disappeared from the public spotlight after failing to get a fair hearing from Abraham Lincoln, Congress, and the Army. Captain Alfred Gibbs, who wanted desperately to get back into the war with an unblemished record, was the principal attacker during the war. Doctor McKee's vicious assault didn't come until much later, long after the war.

On November 27, 1866, just over five years after being, in effect, dishonorably discharged by fiat, President Andrew Johnson reinstated Lynde as a major in the 18th Infantry Regiment, and then retired him that same day. Some say it was the influence of General Ulysses S. Grant that won Lynde this decision. No hearing was held and President Johnson's action constituted a simple pardon and reinstate-ment to rank based on Lynde's long service record, rather than any changes in attitude of the government as to what happened at Fort Fillmore and San Augustine Springs.

Isaac Lynde lived until April 3, 1886, when he died at Picolata, Florida, at the age of eighty. A.F.H. Armstrong also noted a curiosity surrounding Major Lynde's death. The town of Picolata lay some twenty miles from Saint Augustine, Florida—roughly the same distance he traveled that fateful day in July 1861, when he went from Fort Fillmore to San Augustine Pass. Picolata, Florida was the site of an old Army fort in use during the Seminole Wars. Lynde's coffin made the twenty mile journey to St. Augustine before being shipped on to Baltimore for burial.[25]

Was Isaac Lynde a coward and a traitor? This author sees absolutely no sign of that. Did he trust in his fellow officers too much, demonstrating a naivete which cost him his career? Nobody can say one way or the other. At least now he has had a hearing. Is the evidence enough to raise reasonable doubt? If the author can so easily see the failure in the handling of the rear guard by unknown officers of the 7th Infantry Regiment, the failure of the Mounted Rifles to protect the front of the column, and the fact that the column at San Augustine Springs was not in any way a fighting formation due to the presence of women, children, and public property, why were these factors never considered? What about the poor estimates Isaac Lynde was given concerning such simple things as the correct distance to San Augustine Springs and the numbers of Texas troops? What the fact the New Mexico command was unsure of their being on a war footing? Would Canby providing Lynde with the ability to declare martial law and the suspension of the Writ of Habeas Corpus have saved the political situation before Baylor invaded? Canby was quick to do so after Lynde's surrender, when it was too late to do any good.

Why couldn't Lynde's peers see these simple factors and question them? Of course there was no hearing to bring them forth. Perhaps Lincoln and the Army simply needed a villain to explain away another early Civil War defeat. They were doing a lot of that in the fall of 1861. Perhaps they were protecting themselves for failing to give the command in New Mexico a complete picture of the true political and military situation in the East and in Texas. Then again, perhaps the highest authorities were simply too busy to take the time. There was an ongoing civil war, after all.

Major Isaac Lynde was a convenient scapegoat, not a coward, not a traitor. His competence or incompetence cannot be properly evaluated, given the total situation. The powers in Washington and those others who served with him at Fort Fillmore must have been glad Lynde was handy, or else they might have had to look to their own conduct.

Isaac Lynde was a man caught in a terrible dilemma. How should he have handled a situation without precedent in the history of his country? Should he fire upon his own former countrymen (the Texans) or should he not? Was there to be war or was there not? Those questions seemed impossible for Lynde to answer. The boys of the North were simply not ready to fight. Baylor's troops were. Their hatred of the North was of longstanding, and well matured by verbal conflict. They were ready to get at the Yankees. Perhaps the *Mesilla Times* said it best when speaking of Baylor's ardent and ready invaders, "The men are heroes. They might be killed one by one but only thus defeated. They are not a selection of men who have been enlisted from necessity's sake, but from patriotism and honor they are marshaled in defense of their country's rights. They are not fighting for pay but for principle."[26]

How right the *Mesilla Times* was in this statement. Patriotism and fervor defeated indecision and a lack of readiness at San Augustine Springs. Eventually, when Northern boys, so many more in number and with much better equipment and arms, were ready at last, the best of the South were killed off, one by one, until in the end the awakened giant, using the industrial power of the Northern factories, simply rolled over what was left.

NOTES - Chapter 16

1. Lieutenant A. B. Johnson's twelve page article was taken from the web site http://www.army.mil/cmh-pg/books/R&H/R&H-7IN.htm. This particular quote was taken from p. 4. Johnson's article is hereafter referred to as Johnson, with a page number following.

2. Johnson, p. 5.

3. Ibid.

4. Horn & Wallace, Gibbs to Assistant Adjutant General, August 6, 1861, pp. 22, 23.

5. Johnson, p. 5.

6. Lydia Spencer Lane, *I Married a Soldier,* pp. 119, 120.

7. Horn & Wallace, Lynde to Assistant Adjutant General, August 7, 1861, pp. 20, 21.

8. Roberts to Canby, August 2, 1861, M1120, Rolls 13/14.

9. Horn & Wallace, Baylor to Van Dorn, August 14, 1861, pp. 39, 40.

10. Canby to Assistant Adjutant General, Washington, August 11, 1861, M1120, Rolls 13/14.

11. Gibbs to Assistant Adjutant General, August 29, 1861, M1120, Rolls 13/14.

12. Anderson to Chapman, September 3, 1861, M1012, Roll 2.

13. Lynde to Assistant Adjutant General, Santa Fe, September 7, 1861, M1120, Rolls 13/14.

14. Unreadable to Lynde, September 16, 1861, M1120, Rolls 13/14.

15. Lydia Spencer Lane, *I Married a Soldier,* pp. 118, 119.

16. Horn & Wallace, Gibbs to Assistant Adjutant General, Washington, DC, November 7, 1861, pp. 24-26.

17. Gregory J. W. Urwin, *The United States Cavalry: An Illustrated History.*(London: Blandford Press, 1983), p. 112.

18. Horn & Wallace, Thomas to Secretary of War, December 11, 1861, pp. 32, 33.

19. Horn & Wallace, Ethridge to Watts, December 4, 1861, p. 33.

20. Horn & Wallace, Cameron to House of Representatives, December 12, 1861, p. 32.

21. Horn & Wallace, Thomas to Adjutant General's Department, pp. 32, 33.

22. A.F.H. Armstrong, "The Case Of Major Isaac Lynde," p. 28.

23. Ibid., p. 28.

24. Ibid.

25. Ibid.

26. *Mesilla Times*, July 27, 1861.

BIBLIOGRAPHY

Albert, Alphaeus H., *Record of American Uniform and Historical Buttons.* Boyertown, PA.: Boyertown Publishing Company, 1969.

Association of Graduates, U.S.M.A., *Register of Graduates and Former Cadets of the United States Military Academy, 1802-1979.* Chicago: R.R. Donnelley & Sons, 1979.

Bartlett, John R., *Personal Narrative of Explorations andIncidents in Texas, New Mexico, California, etc., Vol. II.* Chicago: The Rio Grande Press Inc., 1965.

Bennett, James A., *Forts & Forays: A Dragoon in New Mexico, 1850-1856.* Albuquerque: Univ. of New Mexico Press, 1948.

Bloom, Lansing B., "Hugh Stevenson And The Brazito Grant," *New Mexico Historical Review,* Vol. 17, No. 3, 1942, p. 279.

Bowen, Ezra, editor, et al, *The Soldiers.* Alexandria, VA: Time-Life Books, 1975.

Browne, J. Ross., *Adventures in the Apache Country.* New York, 1869.

Cleaveland, Agnes Morley. *Satan's Paradise.* Boston: Houghton-Mifflin Co., 1952.

Conkling, Roscoe P. & Margaret B., *The Butterfield Overland Mail 1857-1869, Volume II.* Glendale, CA: The Arthur H. Clark Company, 1947.

Crimmons, M.L., "Fort Fillmore," *New Mexico Historical Review,* Vol. 6, No. 4, 1931, p. 327ff.

Faulk, Odie B., *Crimson Desert—Indian Wars of the American Southwest.* New York: Oxford University Press, 1974.

Garber, Paul Neff, *The Gadsden Treaty.* University of Pennsylvania Press, 1924.

Giese, Dale F., *Forts of New Mexico.* Silver City: Dale F. Giese, 1991.

Goetzmann, William H., *Army Exploration in the American West 1803-1863.* Lincoln and London: University of Nebraska Press, 1979.

Griggs, George, *History of the Mesilla Valley.* Mesilla: New Mexico, 1930.

Hart, Herbert, *Old Forts of the Southwest.* Seattle: Superior Publishing Co., 1964.

Heitman, Francis B., *Historical Register and Dictionary of the United States Army, from Its Organization, September 29, 1789, to March 2, 1903.* Washington: Genealogical Publishing Co., Inc., 1994.

Kupke, William A., *The Indian and the Thunderwagon: A History of the Mountain Howitzer.* Silver City, New Mexico: privately printed, 1991.

Lane, Lydia Spencer, *I Married A Soldier.* Albuquerque: Horn & Wallace, 1964.

Larson, Robert W., *New Mexico's Quest for Statehood.* Albuquerque: The University of New Mexico Press, 1968.

Leach, Colonel James B., *Report on the El Paso and Fort Yuma Wagon Road. Pacific Wagon Roads.* (U.S. Senate Documents, 35th Congress, Session II, Vol. 1, 125pp., with map, February 1859.)

McKee, James Cooper, *Narrative of the Surrender of a Command of U.S. Forces at Fort Fillmore, New Mexico in July, A.D. 1861.* Houston: Stagecoach Press, 1960.

Miller, Darlis A., *The California Column in New Mexico.* Albuquerque: University of New Mexico Press, 1982.

Moorhead, Max L., *New Mexico's Royal Road: Trade and Travel on the Chihuahua Trail*. Norman: University of Oklahoma Press, 1958.

Pierce, T.M., *New Mexico Place Names: A Geographical Dictionary.* Albuquerque: University of New Mexico, 1965.

Price, Paxton P., *Pioneers of the Mesilla Valley.* Las Cruces, NM: Yucca Tree Press, 1995.

Richardson, James D., *A Compilation of the Messages and Papers of the Presidents, Vol VI.* New York: Bureau of National Literature, Inc., 1897.

_____, *A Compilation of the Messages and Papers of the Presidents, Vol. VII.* New York: Bureau of National Literature, Inc., 1897.

Roberts, Calvin A. & Susan, *A History of New Mexico.* Albuquerque: University of New Mexico Press, 1986.

Sweeney, Edwin R., *Cochise.* Norman and London: University of Oklahoma Press, 1991.

Taylor, John, *Bloody Valverde—A Civil War Battle on the Rio Grande, February 21, 1862.* Albuquerque: University of New Mexico Press, 1995.

Terrell, John Upton, *Apache Chronicles.* New York: World Publishing, Times Mirror, 1971.

Thrapp, Dan L., *Encyclopedia of Frontier Biography. 3 vols.* Lincoln & London: University of Nebraska Press in association with Arthur H. Clark Co., Spokane, Washington, 1988.

Twitchell, Ralph Emerson, *The History of the Military of New Mexico from 1846 to 1851.* Chicago: The Rio Grande Press Inc., 1963.

Urwin, Gregory J.W., *The United States Cavalry: An Illustrated History.* London: Blandford Press, 1983.

Warner, Ezra J., *Generals in Blue: Lives of the Union Army Commanders,* Baton Rouge: Louisiana State University Press, 1964.

Wellman, Paul I., *Death in the Desert: The Fifty Years War for the Great Southwest.* New York: The McMillan Co., 1939.

Williams, Jerry L., et al, ed., *New Mexico in Maps.* Albuquerque: University of New Mexico Press, 1979.

Winther, Oscar O., *The Transportation Frontier.* New York: Holt, Rinehart and Winston, 1964.

INDEX

Alden, Asst. Surg. Charles Henry
106, 207, 227; history 193-195;
on march 286, 287; *photo* 194
Anderson, Capt-Maj. 36, 174, 177,
180, 182
Apache Agency 25
Apache Pass 25, 90, 92, 93, 95, 98,
100, 104
Apache Tejo (Teju) 5, 6, 25, 32
Apache Tejo Spring, Lynde new
post 20, 21
Army to leave New Mexico 159ff

Backus, LCol. Electus 55, 57
Bailey, J.C. 106
Baker, Lawrence 148
Barnes, Mr. 285
Bascom, 2L. George Nicholas 99,
100, 108, 116-117, 133, 166;
chase & chastise 90-91
Bascom Affair/Incident 90ff; marks
beginning of Indian Wars 93-94
Baylor, LCol. John 1, 79, 201;
chases Lynde 281ff; description
of surrender 317; estimate of
Lynde's forces 301; history
219; marches north 209ff; on
total surrendered 330-331, 336;
surprise foiled 315; welcomed
in Mesilla 220ff; *photo* 214
Bean, Samuel 98
Blake, Captain 71
Bliss, Lt. Z.R. 71, 74ff
Bliss, Fort Bliss, Fort 4, 5, 12, 13,
15, 22, 31, 36-37, 42, 55, 66-67,
70, 72, 77, 79, 81, 96, 109, 122;
reinforced by Southerners 196-
197; to Dept. of Texas ramifica-
tions 13ff
Bomford, J.V. 293
Bomfors, Colonel 70
Bonneville, Colonel 55
Bowman, Capt. Andrew 55, 60, 61
Brazos Island 51
Brazos Santiago 47, 51, 80
Breckinridge, Fort 4, 5, 12, 107,
108, 114, 129
Brennan, Pvt. John, deserter 23-24
Brocchus, Perry E. 195

Brooks, 1L. Edward J. 91, 92;
arrives at Ft. Fillmore 128-129;
on march 272, 303; orders
supplies destroyed 243; saves
7th colors 343ff; vilified by
McKee 322-323; wounded
241, 245, 247; writes surrender
document 325
Brown, Fort 42, 51, 52, 80, 81;
surrender 55
Buchanan, Fort 4, 5, 9, 11, 12, 18,
20, 28, 86, 90, 93, 101, 103, 107ff,
114, 117, 118, 128; abandoned
178-179, 209; problems 125ff
Buchanan, Pres., final message
26-27
Buckley, William 99, 100
Buell, Major 36
Burro Canyon, wagon train
attacked 86
Butler, Fort 136
Butterfield Overland Mail Company
20, 33, 42, 91, 96, 99-100, 101,
104, 106, 113, 116, 129, 136;
Trail 93

Callaghan, Sergeant, wounded/died
245, 266
Cameron, Simon 195
Camp 80, AZ 9
Camp 38 11
Canby, Col. E.R.S. 26, 43, 91-92,
105, 108, 128, 137, 140, 147,
150, 250; arrives in New Mexico
85ff; follows Special Order 134
159ff; history 157; lack of support for Lynde 334ff, 356; Navajo
Campaign 111; orders wagon
train north 210-211; promotions
139, 157; replaces Loring 139;
takes command 152ff; wishes
to retake Ft. Bliss 166-167
Cantonment Burgwin 12
Carpenter, Capt. D.S. 53, 104;
first to face Texans 49; surrenders 50-51
Catlett Express 22
cavalry, lack of 37
Chaboncito, Chief 32, 98, 104
Chadbourne, Fort 42, 53; surrender 53

Chandler, Brev-LCol. David T. 53
Chapin, 1L. 134
Chapman, William 178
Chiricahua Apaches 3, 90ff
Cochise 20, 93, 95, 116, 136, 140, 166, 195; meets Lt. Bascom 90-91; returns to raiding 148
Clark, Fort 42, 45, 46, 67, 72, 73, 79, 81
Colorado, Camp 42; evacuated 52
Conrad, Fort, *see* Ft. Craig
Cooke, 2L. John Rogers 100
Cook's Peak 149, 195
Cook's Springs 103, 204
Cooper, Adj. Gen. Samuel Mason 17, 27, 29, 34, 36, 46, 71
Cooper, Camp 42, 49, 50, 53, 104
Coopwood, Captain 240
Cottonwoods 205ff
Covey, Dr. E.N. 96
Cox/San Augustine Ranch 305ff; probable surrender site 307ff; *photo* 308
Cox, Rob 306; Murnie 306
Craig, Fort 12, 25, 66, 87, 94, 96, 104, 121; escorts mail 136-137
Crawford, Pvt. Robert 141
Cressey, 2L. Edmund Potter 168, 170, 197-198, 202, 206, 207, 218-219, 240, 247, 261, 286, 310, 327; about march 272; Battle of Mesilla 234, 235; familiar with San Augustine Pass 276; in march 269
Crilly, 2L. Francis 127, 133, 147, 195, 207, 268, 289, 293, 295, 297, 354; assigned to artillery 245ff; criticizes Lynde 329; description of surrender 310, 318; on march 284, 287, 302; report on abandoning Ft. Fillmore 266-267; report on Texans 299-300; *photo* 296
Crimmons, M.S. 17
Crittenden, Brev-LCol. George Bibb 23, 92, 94, 110ff, 119, 121, 135-136, 148
Crosby, ___ 155

Dalrymple, W.C. 49-51
Davis, Fort 42, 43, 70, 72, 77, 79, 81

Defiance, Fort 5, 12, 24, 31, 105-106
desertion 150
Devine, Thomas J. 48
'disunion flag' 150-151
Dog Canyon 119, 121, 122
Doña Ana, pop. 22
Donaldson, Maj. James L. 125, 151, 152
Donohue, Pvt. 92
Dragoon Springs 99-100
dragoons 37, 116; become cavalry 42
Duncan, Captain 178

'Eastern Arizona' census 22
8th Infantry Reg. 13, 15, 28, 43, 48, 56ff, 62, 68, 100, 105, 108; abandons artillery 82; Co. E 37, 52, 65ff, 89, 96; Co. I 52; Co. K 91; colors saved 77-78; headquarters 5; paroled 82; prisoners of war 13; sent into Texas 14; surrender 69ff; recruits 11; transferred 91-92
El Paso, secessionists 37
Elias, Chief 32, 36
Elliott, Capt. Washington 94
Ewell, Capt. Richard Stoddard 137

Farber, Pvt., wounded 245
Fashion (steamer) 60, 91
Fauntleroy, Col. Thomas Turner 13, 23, 33, 34, 36, 47, 65, 86, 91-92, 105, 106, 109, 117, 121, 150, 152, 156, 336 com. Dept. of NM 5, 6; leaves 15; petitioned by Mesilla 98-99; pulls troops north 37; replaced 118; resigned 27
Fauntleroy, Fort 85, 105-106
5th Cavalry Reg. 42
5th Infantry Reg. 18, 105, 106; Co. K 92; mistakenly identified as being at San Augustine Pass 317; ordered to leave NM 159; recruits 11
.54 Mini-ball 232
.58 rifle/musket 231, 233, 306; *photo* 233
Fillmore, Fort 5, 12, 22ff, 31, 36-37, 43, 47, 51, 55, 69, 79, 89,

110, 121, 130; abandoned 161ff, 242ff, 255ff, 265ff; cemetery 247; Confederate threat 137ff; indefensible 201; officers at 133; rebel stronghold 148, 150; strength 202ff; cemetery, *photo* 246; fort, *painting* 30

Fillmore, Pres. Millard, speech 187-188

1st Dragoon Reg. 3, 15, 42; becomes 1st Cavalry 11; recruits 11

1st Infantry Reg. 42, 49, 53, 56ff, 68; Co. G 54; Co. H 53; Co. I 54; paroled 82

Fitzwilliams, Charles E. 243, 345

Floyd, UT, Camp 9, 21

Floyd, Fort, *see also* Fts. McLane & Webster, 19, 21, 22, 25, 26, 27, 32, 33, 86, 96, 100; renamed McLane 87

Floyd, Sec. of War John 27, 35, 36; believed in secession 15; defects 87

Ford, Colonel 80

Francisco, Chief 95

Frank, 2L. Royal Thaxter 37, 65ff, 89, 98

Frazier, George 147

Freedley, Lt-Capt. Henry 69, 71

Gadsden Purchase 3

Garland, Col. John 41

Garland, Capt. Robert R. 145ff, 156, 158, 176, 183, 200, 207, 336; deserts Ft. Fillmore 197

Garland, Fort 105

General Order 31 334

Gibbs, Capt. Alfred 24, 321-322, 327, 329, 354, 356-357; absolved 335; arrives at Ft. Craig 209; arrives at San Augustine Springs 187ff; at Jefferson Barracks 289ff, 313-314, 324-325, 358; ordered to Ft. Fillmore 203; ordered to return to Ft. Craig 244-245, 248, 259; death 351; description of surrender 310, 312-313; meets Lt. Lane 263-264; on surrender 324; report on column 268; report on Texans 297ff; RMR collapsed 298ff *photo* 288

Goss, Pvt. Wounded 245

Grant, Mr. (contractor) 162

Green Lake, TX 56, 58, 68

Greene, 1L. James B. 60

Griffin, Fort 42

guns used at Ft. Fillmore 231ff

Hancock, 1L. David Porter 189, 207, 354; death 351; history 189ff; on march 303

Hanover Cooper Mines, pop. 22

Hardeman, Capt. 239, 292, 298, 315

Hart, Judge 155

Hart's Mill 168, 181

Hartz, Capt. Edward L. 78

Haskin, Maj. William L. 318-319

Hatch's Ranch 105, 136

Hayward, Ellen 98

Hayward, George A. 98, 147, 204, 341

Herbert, Colonel 225

Hesse, Cpl. John C., saves 8th Inf. colors 77-78; Medal of Honor 78

Hill, Capt. B.H. 51, 52

'hog ranches' 21

Holloway, Capt. E.B. 91

Horace (ship) 57

horse-mounted formations 11-12

Houston, Gov. Sam 44-45, 48

Houston, Fort Sam 41

howitzer 247, 269; at Mesilla 229, 233, 235; *photo* 230

Hughes, Corporal 355

Indianola, TX 68, 69; Confederate trap 56, 58, 60

Indians in Lynde's area of control 19-20

infantry, ineffective against Apaches 37; replaced by volunteers 161, 167, 171

Inge, Fort 42, 79, 80, 81

Irwin, Dr. B.J.D., leads rescue 93, 116

Ives, Camp 42

Jackson, 2L. 136

Johnson Lt. A.B., description of Lynde 319-320, 349ff, 352

Jones, Capt. J.M. 205

Jones, Lt W.G. 71; funds confiscated by Texans 66
Jornada del Muerto 4, 94, 109, 262
José, Chief 32

Kelley, Robert 98, 164-165; seditious comments 25-26
Kendrick, Indian Agent 111
Kirk, William D., steals wagon train 113, 117, 172
Knauer, Dr. F. 338, 341

La Cueva, Pass of 287
Labadi, Mr. L. 164-165
Labardine, Mr. 198
Lancaster, Fort 42, 79
'Land Pirates,' see Pinos Altos, miners
Lane, Lydia Spencer 87ff, 117, 134, 148, 150, 155, 207, 210, 241; about Lynde 164-165; error in dating 168; in charge of Ft. Fillmore 121ff; life at Ft. Fillmore 97-98, 131-132; notifies Pres. Lincoln 346-347; on personal goods 271; on trail to Ft. Craig 261-262; to Ft. Fillmore 94
Lane, 1L. William B. 87ff, 85-97, 99ff, 103, 110, 112, 119, 121, 126, 133, 137-138, 146, 168, 193, 206, 207; cannot pay troops 129, 149-150; commands Ft. Fillmore 104-105; leads wagon train north 209ff, 259; McKee's 'Fighting man' 208; meets Gibbs on trail 263-264; oath of allegiance 206, 209
Lane, Pvt., killed 245, 247
Las Cruces, pop. 22, 25
Lavaca, TX 60
Lay, Col. George W. 35, 44
Lazelle, 1L. Henry 69
Leavenworth, Fort 82
Lee, Robert E. 15, 42
Lincoln, Pres. Abraham, calls for volunteers 57; elected 22; election signal for secession 13; refuses Lynde a hearing 2, 359ff
Longstreet, Maj. James 27, 121, 150
Lord, 1L. 100, 109
Loring, Col. William Wing 27, 118ff, 123, 129-130, 135, 136,

146ff, 169, 336; Confederate sympathies 130-131, 176-177, 179-180, 199-200; keeps Southern Dist. 154; leaves 15; resigns 139
Lucas, George 98
Lucas, James 106
Luckett, P.N. 48, 55
Lynde, Maj. Isaac 92, 110; abandons Ft. Fillmore 248ff, abandons Ft. McLane 118-189; aftermath 333ff; approached by Apaches for peace 98; arrives at Ft. Fillmore 103ff, 187ff; at Apache Tejo 23; Battle of Mesilla 225ff; career 17-19; charges quartermaster negligence 151-152; condition at Fts. McLane & Buchanan 134-135; description of surrender 321ff; enemies 322; escape route 287ff; faith in Garland 200-201; families in march 270ff; given all blame 7, 294ff; given carte blanche 101; given confusing orders 171-172, 174; handwriting 20; lack of hearing 6, 359ff; learns of Baylor advance 215-216; learns of possible Texan invasion 161ff; leaves New Mexico 352ff; march to Ft. Fillmore 195ff; no knowledge of declared war 182ff; on Gibbs' arrival 290; on march to San Augustine Springs 281ff, 302; on total surrendered 327ff, 335-336; order of retreat column 267ff; ordered to establish Express riders 135; ordered to establish post 17, 20; ordered to fight and punish Apaches 95, 118; ordered to stop building at Ft. McLane 113; preservation of public property 114ff; rank 86; receives orders from Canby 163-164; Reeve's example 69ff; report on Battle of Mesilla 250-251; signs surrender document 325-327; stricken from Army rolls 2, 359ff; surrenders 305ff; West Point Register 335; *photo* 16; route of march, *map* 260

Lynde, Mrs. Isaac (Margaret Wight), *photo*   16

Maclin, Major   80
Magoffin, Colonel   155, 181
mail   147; difficulty   33, 87-89, 94; Overland route   33; Southern route   33
Mangas Coloradas   5, 19, 32, 95, 104, 195
Marmaduke, 2L. John Sappington   23-24, 27, 32, 146, 148, 176; first secessionist defection   24
Martin Scott, Fort   42
Mason, Fort   42
Massachusetts, Fort   31
Masten, Thomas   98
Matagorda Bay, TX   82
Maury, Brev-Capt., 1L. Dabney   23, 27, 52, 85, 100, 105, 106, 109, 121, 129, 134, 135, 156, 158, 168, 336; resigns   139, 150, 152
Maverick, S.A.   48
McCallister's Company of Inf.   79
McCulloch, Col. H.E.   52ff, 82
McGowan, Judge Ned, 'Arizona Terr.' delegate   25
McGrorty, William   98, 204
McIntosh, Fort   42, 55, 58, 79
McKavitt, Fort   42
McKee, Dr. James Cooper   1ff, 24, 106, 147, 150, 210; arrives Ft. Fillmore   105; attacks Brooks   324; Battle of Mesilla   226ff, 237-238; Baylor crossing river   222-223; Baylor arrival at Mesilla   216-217; description of surrender   310ff; facts wrong   170-171; hatred of Lynde   1ff, 208, 345ff; in march   270; on surrender   330; on total surrendered   328; on women and children   249; ordered to destroy supplies   243; praises Lane   206ff; reports Texans coming   286; supports Gibbs   301
McLane, Capt. George   87; death   23-24
McLane, Fort, *see also* Fts. Floyd & Webster,   5, 37, 98, 103, 105, 107, 108, 113, 117, 130; ordered abandoned   162; problems

141ff: 7th arrives   131, 134
McLane's Peak   24
McLaws, Capt. Lafayette   24, 27, 92, 146, 158, 179; resigns   184
McNally, 2-1L. Charles Hely   168, 170, 183, 197, 202, 232, 234, 327; Battle of Mesilla   234-235; wounded   240, 245
Medal of Honor   78-79
Mescalero Apaches   3, 4, 19
Mesilla, Battle of   225ff; casualties   238ff, 245;   Lynde's report   250-251
Mesilla, La   3, 4, 22, 23;   post office   147; residents petition Fauntleroy   98-99; secessionists   37, 116, 150, 163ff; welcomes Baylor   220ff
Miles, LCol. Dixon Stansbury   1, 37; commands 3rd Inf.   3; establishes Ft. Fillmore cemetery   247
military correspondence, style   10n
Mills, Anson   98
Mills, W.W.   150, 198, 202
Mimbres Apaches   19, 25
Mischler, Brev-2L. Lyman   133
Mogollon Apaches   24
Monkey Springs   140
morale   149-150
Morris, Capt. Robert M.   136, 177
Morris, LCol. Gouveneur, concern for personal property   54; surrenders   53-54
Morrison, LCol. Pitcairn   18, 20, 86, 90, 107ff, 117, 125, 135, 158; commands 7th Inf.   5, 9ff; requests leave   28
Myer, Maj. Albert J.   92, 106
Myers, Pvt., wounded   245
Mystic (*ship*)   57, 61

Navajo Campaign   1, 24, 128
Navajos   37
New Mexico Militia   177, 197, 201-202; 2nd Reg.   177-178
Nichols, E.B.   51, 52
9th Military Dept.   31

oath of allegiance   177, 206, 209
Oberle, Sgt. Hubert H., claims to save 7th Inf. colors   344-345; origin of alcohol myth   341ff

officers leaving for Confederacy
121ff
Oury, James 98
Overland Mail, *see* Butterfield

Paul, Brev-Maj. Gabriel Rene 23,
86, 102, 119, 140, 146ff, 153,
161, 171, 180, 183, 356; history
132-133; leaves 176; letter
from Canby 164-165
Peck, Lieutenant 71
Peters, Asst. Surgeon 71
Phantom Hill, Fort 42
Pinal Indians 90
Pino, Col. M.E. 177, 196
Pinon, Chief 32, 98, 104
Pinos Altos, miners 4, 114, 117,
137, 220; population 33;
secessionists 37
Plummer, Capt. Augustus H. 122,
126-127, 133, 139, 147, 195,
207, 247, 352; death 351; on
march 303; prisoner of war 127
Point Brazos Santiago 41-42
Point of Rocks 263, 264
Potter, Capt. Joseph Haydn 205,
220, 221, 226, 242, 245, 273, 278,
294, 318, 324, 327, 331, 354;
history 191-192; receives command from Lynde 352; takes
Lynde east 358; *photo* 326
Powderhorn 60-61
prisoners of war 13, 59ff, 70, 82,
127
protocol, Army 14

Quitman, Fort 42, 43, 55, 67, 70,
72, 77, 79, 81, 123

Reeve, Brev-LCol. L.V.D. 66, 251;
claimed inferior strength 75ff;
paroled 82; surrender 69, 320,
336; surrender important to
Lynde 69ff
Regiment of Mounted Rifles (RMR),
become cavalry 12, 42; Co. A
87ff, 119, 123, 137, 145, 184, 202,
209; Co. A horses stolen 154,
156, 168ff, 180-181; Co. B 218,
236, 247, 327, 355; Co. B in
march 269ff; Co. F 157, 168,
197, 202, 236, 245, 327; Co. F
in march 269ff; desertions 147;
recruits 11; officer's button,
illus. 12
Rencher, Governor 171
Rhett, Maj. Thomas Reimke 27,
121, 129, 150, 183 disappears
with money 55, 123
Rich, Lt. L.L. 106
Richmond Convention 57
Rico, D. Pablo, captures Kirk 128
Ringgold, Fort 42
Roberts, Brev-LCol. Benjamin S.
354ff; abandons Ft. Stanton
111, 177, 355
Ryan, 1L. George 207, 225, 354;
history 190; death 208, 351

San Antonio-El Paso road 42
San Augustine Ranch, *see* Cox Ranch
San Augustine Springs 54;
location 256ff, 305ff; *photo* 316
San Lucas Spring, TX 69ff, 74
San Pedro Station 148
San Simon Station 136
Santa Fe Trail 10
Santa Lucia Springs 19, 25
Santa Rita Copper Mines 4, 17, 20;
miners 36; pop. 22; seces-
sionists 37
Santo Tomás 3, 22, 205, 215-216,
218ff, 221, 226
Scott, Col. H.L., charters steamer 47
Scott, Gen. Winfield 5, 13, 29, 34ff,
44, 48, 226; does not foresee his
actions 15
Secession Convention, Texas 48
secession, officers who opt for
27ff; forces in Mesilla 25ff
2nd Cavalry Reg. 11, 42, 52, 56;
Co. D 53; Co. H 53
2nd Dragoon Reg. 3, 42; becomes
2nd Cavalry Reg 11
Selden, Capt. Henry 24
Selden, Fort 24
7th Infantry Reg. 1, 3, 43, 48, 85ff,
90, 92, 95, 100; arrives at Ft.
Fillmore 199ff; arrives in NM
Terr. 4ff; arrives at Ft. McLane
134; band 11, 131, 188, 199;
Co. A 119, 134, 141, 190; Co.

A, arrives at Ft. Fillmore 195;
Co. B 10, 11, 21, 32, 191, 273;
Co. B, arrives at Ft. Fillmore 195;
Co. C 10, 11, 146; Co. C, considered lucky 10; Co. D 10,
119, 183, 184; Co. D, arrives at
Ft. Fillmore 128, 145; Co. E
134, 188ff, 199; Co. E, arrives at
Ft. Fillmore 195; Co. F 183;
Co. G 10, 11, 21, 23, 191-192,
245, 327; Co. G, arrives at Ft.
Fillmore 195; Co. H 10-11;
Co. H., considered lucky 10;
Co. I 119, 145, 153, 176, 183,
184, 199, 245, 268, 273, 284, 327;
arrives at Ft. Fillmore 132; Co.
K 10, 11, 119, 122, 126, 139,
145, 183, 184, 245, 247; colors
saved 270, 343ff; loses first
officer to secession 24; ordered
to Ft. Fillmore 119; ordered to
Ft. McLane 107; ordered to leave
NM 159-160; recruits 11; sent
to Fts. Buchanan & Breckinridge
5; sent to Washington Terr. 12;
surrendered 7; insignia, photo
126; officer's button, photo 12
Seward, Augustus Henry 150
Sherwood, Pvt., killed 245, 247
Sibley, Maj. C.C. 55, 58ff, 68, 69,
70, 251, 320, 336
Sibley, Brev-Maj. Henry Hopkins
24, 27, 121, 148, 155-156, 158,
199-200
Silver City 5, 10
6th Infantry Reg. 70
.69 smoothbore muskets 231, 232;
photo 233
Smith, Gen. J.M. 45
Smith, Maj. J.R. 19
Smith, Capt. E. Kirby 52
Soledad Canyon road 201, 258,
259, 285, 287
Southern Convention 25
Special Order No. 10 45, 46
Special Order No. 22 46
Special Order No. 85 162
Special Order No. 134 159ff
Sprague, Brev-Maj., Capt. P.T. 65, 67
St. Vrain, Colonel 196
stagecoach express 22

Stanton, Captain, buried at Ft.
Fillmore 248
Stanton, Fort 4, 12, 20, 110, 121;
prepares for invasion 165-166
Stapleton, Robert H. 177
Star of the West (ship) 57ff, 68
Steck, Dr. Michael 19, 20, 32,
198, 199, 262; distributes gifts
to Apaches 25
Steen, Maj. Enoch 104
Steen's Peak, see Stein's Peak
Stein's Peak 99
Stevenson, Capt. Mathew Rider
32, 207, 225, 242, 273, 278, 324,
331, 354; history 191; death
351; on march 287, 303
Stith, 1L. Donald C. 91, 92;
prisoner of war 203-204;
southern sympathies 172
Stivers, 1L. Charles Bryant 207,
354; history 193; oath of allegiance 206, 209; on march 303
Stockton, Camp/Fort 42, 79
Sumner, Brev-Col. Edwin Vose
31, 42
surrender fables, alcohol 337ff;
7th Inf. colors 343ff; 'surrender
bugle call' 341-342
surrenders, based on estimates of
strength 251-252

Taliaferro & Grant 137
Teel, Captain 215, 239
Teel's Company of Artillery 79
10th Inf. 126; Co. A 105
'Territory of Arizona' 34, 99;
government 31
Texas, evacuation of Union troops
47ff, 57
Texas Confederates 6
Texas Conv., seizure of funds 55
Texas General Order No. 8 79-80
Texas invasion of NM 213ff
Texas Mounted Rifles, 2nd 79, 80,
209, 284
Texas secession 14, 29ff, 44ff, 48
Texas State Militia 58
3rd Cavalry Reg. 12, 42
3rd Infantry Reg. 29, 37, 42, 53,
55ff, 68; headquarters 4;
ordered to Texas 3; paroled 82

Thomas, Gen. Lorenzo   34, 47, 48, 66, 67, 91, 111, 123
Thompson Ranch, raided   166
Tortugas Pueblo   279
treason   13, 17
Twiggs, Gen. David E.   29, 34, 35, 43-44, 61, 66, 68, 70; awarded Sword of Honor   29; cast adrift 36; commander Dept. of Texas 17; leaves   17; orders Morris to leave post   53; provides Lynde precedent   31; surrenders   45-46, 48ff, 320

Union, Fort   11, 12, 31, 94, 121
Urbana (ship)   57, 60
US Regular Army, strength   117-118
Utah Campaign   85, 128

Vaila, Capt. Miguel, arrests Rico   128
Valverde, Battle of   354; Mesa   24
Van Dorn, Col. Earl   58, 59, 70, 71, 74ff, 77, 80ff, 155, 325
Van Horn, Lieutenant   71
Verde, Camp   42, 45
Victorio   32, 98, 104
volunteers, *see also* NM Volunteers 174ff, 195, 198
vouchers, not accepted   134

Waite, Col. Carlos A.   44ff, 48, 53, 55ff, 66ff; interior strength   75; surrenders   58
Wallace, Mr.   91, 93
Waller, Maj. H.B.   51, 55, 215, 225, 285, 298, 301, 315
Ward, Felix, captured   90
Ward, John   90
Watts, Judge John S., organizes volunteers   174
Webster, Fort Daniel, *see also* Ft. Floyd,   5, 21, 24, 31, 53; name change denied   23
Wheeler, 1L. Joseph   94-95, 111, 127; denied leave   105
Whipple, Capt. William   60, 61
Whiting, Brev-Maj. David P.   126, 140, 146, 153, 176
Wilcox, Capt. Cadmus   139, 140, 146, 148, 153, 158, 176

Wilson, Col. Henry   19
Wilson, Sgt. Maj. Joseph K   78
Wingate, Captain   92
Wood, Camp   42, 79, 81